D1562776

MULTINATIONALS IN A NEW ERA

THE ACADEMY OF INTERNATIONAL BUSINESS

Published in association with the UK Chapter of the Academy of International Business

Titles already published in the series:

Multinationals in a New Era

International Strategy and Management

Edited by

James H. Taggart

Maureen Berry

and

Michael McDermott

palgrave

First published 2001 by
PALGRAVE
Houndmills, Basingstoke, Hampshire RG21 6XS and
175 Fifth Avenue, New York, N.Y. 10010
Companies and representatives throughout the world

PALGRAVE is the new global academic imprint of
St. Martin's Press LLC Scholarly and Reference Division and
Palgrave Publishers Ltd (formerly Macmillan Press Ltd).

ISBN 0–333–96389–X

This book is printed on paper suitable for recycling and made from fully managed and sustained forest sources.

A catalogue record for this book is available from the British Library.

Library of Congress Cataloging-in-Publication Data

Multinationals in a new era : international strategy and management / edited by James H. Taggart, Maureen Berry, and Michael McDermott.
        p. cm.—(Academy of International Business series)
        Papers from the 27th Annual Conference of the UK Chapter of the Academy of International Business hosted by the University of Strathclyde in 2000?
        Includes bibliographical references and index.
        ISBN 0–333–96389–X (cloth)
        1. International business enterprises—Management—Congresses.
    2. Globalization—Economic aspects—Congresses. I. Taggart, J. H. (James H.), 1943– II. Berry, Maureen. III. McDermott, Michael C. IV. Academy of International Business. UK Chapter. Conference (27th : 2000? : University of Strathclyde) V. Academy of International Business series (New York, N.Y.)

HD62.4 .M844 2001
658'.049—dc21   2001027363

10   9   8   7   6   5   4   3   2   1
10   09   08   07   06   05   04   03   02   01

Printed and bound in Great Britain by
Antony Rowe Ltd, Chippenham, Wiltshire

Contents

List of Tables

List of Figures

Preface

I have great pleasure in introducing Volume 8 of the Palgrave series produced in conjunction with The Academy of International Business (UK Chapter). I am grateful for the enthusiastic and tireless contributions of this year's conference editors, Maureen Berry and Michael McDermott of Strathclyde, and for the participation and support of Zelah Pengilley at Palgrave.

The 27th Annual Conference of AIB, from which the chapters in this book are drawn, was organised by the Strathclyde International Business Unit at the University of Strathclyde. This is the third time our colleagues at SIBU have arranged our conference, the previous occasions being in 1983 and 1990. As then, this year's occasion was hosted and chaired by Stephen Young and Neil Hood, and we are grateful to them for the excellent facilities and arrangements. Perhaps the highlight of our time in Glasgow was Willie McCallum's rendition of 'Flower of Scotland' on the great Highland bagpipe at the conference dinner in the magnificent Barony Church. Willie is on the staff at Strathclyde and in recent years has won an astonishing number of piping gold medals and championships. Steve and Neil welcomed us to Strathclyde (our second successive conference in Scotland) with a Gaelic greeting: 'Ceud mile failte'. May I declare in return: 'Alba gu bràth'.

As well as Steve and Neil, we must also thank all those at Strathclyde who helped to organise such a great event. Perhaps a special mention might be made of the PhD students who stewarded the conference, whose smiles made us feel so welcome at all times, and whose good humour helped to get over a few minor crises. They are Karl Alorbi, Luis Bernardino, Dev Boojihawon, Rasha Mostafa, Prathap Oburai and Penelope Quah.

By the time this book is published, we will have visited Manchester Metropolitan University for the 28th Annual Conference, and we will be preparing for the 29th at the University of Central Lancashire. Chì mi leibh an sin.

University of Glasgow   JAMES H. TAGGART

Notes on the Contributors

Jim Bell is Professor of International Business Entrepreneurship at Magee College, University of Ulster. He has published widely in the international business field and is currently researching the activities of small firms in the globalising economy.

Maureen Berry is Senior Lecturer in the Marketing Department at the University of Strathclyde and a member of the Strathclyde International Business Unit.

Peter Brown is Lecturer in International Business at the University of Otago in New Zealand. His research focuses on the internationalisation of small firms.

Peter J. Buckley is Professor of International Business and Director of the Centre for International Business, University of Leeds (CIBUL). He has published 18 books in English and one in German. He was elected a Fellow of the Academy of International Business in 1985 for 'outstanding achievements in international business'.

Francisco B. Castro is Lecturer in International Economics at Faculdade de Economicia do Porto (University of Portugal) and researcher at CIBUL, University of Leeds.

Paul Edwards is Professor of Industrial Relations and a member of the Industrial Relations Research Unit, Warwick Business School, University of Warwick.

Paul N. Gooderham is Professor of International Management at the Norwegian School of Economics and Business Administration. His most recent publications include articles in *Administrative Science Quarterly, Management International Review* and *Employee Relations*.

Kevin I.N. Ibeh is Lecturer in the Department of Marketing at the University of Strathclyde. He has also taught and researched marketing at the University of Uyo and Abia State University, both in Nigeria. His research interests include export entrepreneurship and small firm internationalisation, emerging markets and development marketing.

Jeffrey E. Johnson is Lecturer in International Business at the University of Strathclyde. He received an MBA in international business at the University of Colorado and is currently completing a PhD in international business at Strathclyde. His current research focuses on success factors for small high technology international start-ups in the United Kingdom and United States.

Jürgen Kai-Uwe Brock joined the Department of Marketing (University of Strathclyde) in October 1997 as a full-time doctoral researcher. His research interests include strategic management and strategic marketing, the marketing of technology, diffusion of innovations, channel marketing and management, as well as international business management and marketing.

Reijo Luostarinen is Professor in International Business, Director of International Business Studies, Director of Center for International Business Research, former Vice Rector, Helsinki School of Economics and Business Administration, Finland. His teaching and research interests focus on firms' internationalisation and globalisation processes and strategies. More recently, he has conducted research on so-called 'born' global companies. He has published a number of books and articles in the field.

Julia Manea is completing doctoral research on subsidiaries of multinational corporations in the Department of Economics at the University of Reading.

Rebecca Marschan-Piekkari is a Lecturer at the University of Bath. Her teaching and research centre on foreign subsidiary management in large and geographically dispersed multinational corporations. She has a particular interest in communication and language issues in inter-subsidiary relationships, and the use of qualitative methods in international business research. She has published a number of journal papers in this area.

Michael McDermott is Senior Lecturer in the Marketing Department at the University of Strathclyde and a member of the Strathclyde International Business Unit.

Dennis Nickson is a Senior Lecturer at the Scottish Hotel School, University of Strathclyde, Glasgow. His teaching, research and publications focus on globalisation of the tourism and hospitality industry and international and domestic human resource management. He has published a number of articles on these subjects.

Robert Pearce is Reader in the Department of Economics at the University of Reading. His research interests include the international management of technology, and the strategy and management of MNC subsidiaries. He has published widely in both fields.

Leonor Sopas has been a researcher at the Catholic University of Portugal for the last ten years. She is now completing her PhD on Portuguese exporting firms.

James H. Taggart is Professor of International Business Strategy at the University of Glasgow. He is Chairman of the UK Chapter of the Academy of International Business and series editor for the AIB/Palgrave volumes.

Ana Teresa Tavares is a Lecturer at the University of Porto (Portugal), also linked to the University of Reading through research. Her main research interests focus on modelling the impact of economic integration on multinationals' subsidiaries and other aspects related to subsidiary strategy and evolution, in particular linked to inward investment policies and host country/region impact.

Svein Ulset is an Associate Professor at the Norwegian School of Economics and Business Administration. He has a particular interest in economic organisations, strategy and telecom economics. His work has been published in the *Journal of Economic Behaviour and Organisations*.

Chris Warhurst is Senior Lecturer in Human Resource Management at the University of Strathclyde, Glasgow. His teaching, research and publication focus on work, management and labour issues in the international economy. He has authored and co-authored a number of books and journal papers in this area.

Martyn Wright is Lecturer in Industrial Relations and Organizational Behaviour and a member of the Industrial Relations Research Unit, Warwick Business School, University of Warwick.

Mo Yamin is Senior Lecturer in International Business at the Manchester School of Management, UMIST.

Hideki Yoshihara is Professor at the Research Institute for Economics and Business, Kobe University. His research focuses on the strategy and management of international Japanese companies. He has authored or co-authored 17 books in this field, as well as a large number of journal papers in both Japanese and English.

Antonella Zucchella is Professor of International Management in Insubria University in Varese. She also teaches International Financial Management in the University of Pavia. She has published 30 articles and four books on management and finance. Her recent publications are focused on SMEs internationalisation.

1 Introduction: Companies and Countries, Changes and Choices

James H. Taggart

This book, the eighth volume of the Palgrave series, is based on some of the best papers delivered at the 27th Annual Conference of the Academy of International Business (UK Chapter) which was hosted by the University of Strathclyde. The emergent theme of the conference, as in the previous year at the University of Stirling, was globalisation in all its aspects. The antipathetic cultural dimension of globalisation was underlined at the opening of the conference by Tom Brewer, editor of the *Journal of International Business Studies*. He quoted the US Ambassador to France in these words: 'The anti-Americanism today encompasses not only a specific policy ... but a feeling that globalisation has an American face on it and is a danger to the European and French view of society. There is the sense that America is such an extraordinary power that it can crush everything in its way.'

Perhaps the ambassador has become overly sensitive to anti-American criticism during his sojourn in Paris, but there is no doubt that he is expressing a concern that many Europeans experience from time to time. In the practice of international business, it is not easy to assess the impact of such a sentiment. Whether real or imagined, it changes the approach to transactions by minimising the feeling that American and European commercial interests have much in common. In fact, cultural sensitivity about the US can lead to the feeling that what is bad for 'them' may well be good for 'us'.

This theme of globalisation/Americanisation is developed extensively in Chapter 15 by Dennis Nickson and Chris Warhurst. Using the international hotel sector as a basis of evaluation, they find that American firms dominate with their products and practices. Indeed, American practices, ideas and techniques have substantially penetrated non-American hotel firms. Though their study is as yet at the exploratory stage, Nickson and Warhurst do not demonstrate the anxiety shown by the US Ambassador to France, but suggest that American standards are becoming identified with acceptable global standards.

KEYNOTE ADDRESS

Alan Rugman, Thames Water Fellow in Strategic Management at Templeton College, University of Oxford, gave the keynote address to the conference. Working from his own research base of 20 multinational corporations (MNCs) (eleven from the EU, three from Asia, six from North America), he observed that the internationalisation process generally consisted of consolidating in the respective triad base, then moving into other triad markets. Rugman's basic hypothesis is that both globalisation and global strategy are myths rather than useful or real concepts.

Entry into a rival triad market is effectively a game theory move for most MNCs. It is based on careful analysis of market and business environment factors. With respect to Bartlett and Ghoshal's (1989) integration/responsiveness (IR) framework, there are four generic strategies for MNCs (Rugman, 2000):

- in the high *I*–low *R* quadrant, firms follow a pure integration strategy;
- high *I*–high *R* gives the transnational solution of a balance of integration and national responsiveness strategies;
- low *I*–high *R* yields a pure national responsiveness strategy;
- low *I*–low *R* leads to an unsatisfactory set of strategies with few or no benefits of either integration or national responsiveness.

On the basis of Rugman's analysis, the high *I*–low *R* firms in his group of MNCs include Ikea, Nokia, Ericsson, Thames Water, Matsushita, Fuji Xerox, Xerox, HSBC and Enron. High *I*–high *R* MNCs include Benetton, Tate and Lyle, Procter and Gamble, Hewlett Packard, 3M and Nortel. Low *I*–high *R* companies include Unilever, Kingfisher, Rhône Poulenc, P&O and Philips. There are no low *I*–low *R* firms in Rugman's sample, perhaps suggesting the selection of 'successful' MNCs for the research.

Note that MNCs that follow the pure national responsiveness strategy (low *I*–high *R*) are all European, four of the six North American firms follow transnational strategies (high *I*–high *R*), all three Japanese firms are in the pure integration (high *I*–low *R*) category. Perhaps this indicates some cultural contribution to the selection of international strategy, but Rugman made no reference to this.

Rugman concluded from his analysis of these 20 MNCs that in no case could successful performance be identified with globalisation drivers. Rather, strategy effectiveness seemed more closely linked with regional/triad inputs and skills. Unilever, for example, draws its national responsiveness from its regional operations, while its main competitor in world markets, Procter and Gamble, does so on the basis of a top management team that is spread around the triad. Nokia and Ericsson, by contrast, are highly integrated MNCs, domestic champions that enter other triad markets despite strong national regulations that characterise the mobile phone sector.

KEYNOTE DEBATE

The response to Alan Rugman's contribution was led by Chris Warhurst of the University of Strathclyde. He outlined the popular currency of the term 'globalisation', noting that is embedded in popular discourse as a key factor of international business, it is widely (if mistakenly) used in the media, it is a point of reference for many contributions in the business press, it is included in the title of many recent management textbooks and it appears to be at the heart of many initiatives of governments and economic development agencies. The popular use of 'globalisation' is reminiscent of the Queen of Hearts: 'When I use a word, it means exactly what I want it to mean.' It is used as a point of reference in describing a quickly changing environment, as a way of looking at the world, as an explanatory framework for step changes and paradigm shifts in the world of international business.

While it is used as an alternative term for international economy and the triad concept, globalisation either exists as a process accompanied by the countervailing process and with an emergent point of arrival or it does not exist and its apparent manifestations are little more than misconstructions of known concepts and developments. Kenichi Ohmae is a strong advocate of globalisation whereby business can circumvent the obstructions of meddling bureaucrats in individual states and supranational bodies. He believes the global economy should be governed by market forces alone, which can only be achieved by extensive decoupling of politics from the global economy.

The search for meaning may be eased by considering globalisation as the state of increasing interdependence of national economies and business structures. In this scenario, internationalised firms (especially, but not solely) acquire resources in 'global' resource markets and sell output in 'global' demand markets. Events in the most developed countries have implications for others and, as this effect works down the scale of 'development', so the extent of 'globalisation' can be said to increase. This has led, in turn, to the emergence of 'global governance', whereby international institutions attempt to manage relationships and solve problems within the so-called 'global economy'. Consequently, we might consider global firms as those that work within the interdependent (global) economies and that are subject to global governance, whether actively or passively. When this line of thinking is pushed to the extreme, it leads to the assumption that 'global problems' are in some way susceptible to 'global solutions'.

On a less esoteric level, many would settle for a four-dimensional synthesis of the relationship of MNCs and globalisation (Harrison *et al.*, 2000):

- Worldwide convergence of consumer tastes and preferences and other demand patterns has made the production and marketing of standard products and services much easier and less costly.
- The ease with which the firm's ownership advantages can be spread globally has increased appreciably following recent trends in the liberalisation of trade and investment worldwide.
- Enormous advances in transport and communication technologies have made it easier for parent companies to exercise effective control over their subsidiaries and affiliates operating globally.

- The development of strategies based on global profit potential by the world's major MNCs has intensified the search for global markets and resource acquisition.

CHANGES AND CHOICES

For the first time in this series of international business books, we are highlighting a contribution based on what was judged the best paper of the conference. This is written by Peter Brown (Otago) and Jim Bell (Magee, Ulster) and appears in Chapter 2. It is an investigation into the impact of close spatial concentration on the internationalisation processes of small firms. Throughout the 1990s, small firm internationalisation has increasingly attracted the attention of policy makers and academic researchers. Policy focus, in particular, in many countries, is starting to converge on ways of supporting groups or networks of firms, rather than individual companies. Researchers have long recognised the production-based benefits that accrue to small firms from such cluster membership, and many suggest that this contributes to improved international competitiveness. There are fewer research findings about the linkage between cluster membership and the marketing-derived benefits of internationalisation. This chapter attempts to close the gap by reporting findings of a recent New Zealand study of the electronics cluster based in Christchurch. Marketing-derived benefits due to cluster membership seem to be significant, and produce measurable internationalisation benefits in intra-cluster referrals, new product development and discovery. The authors conclude that policy makers should encourage cluster members to exploit colocational advantages more vigorously and proactively.

PART ONE: INTERNATIONALISATION OF SMALL
AND MEDIUM-SIZED ENTERPRISES

There are five chapters in this part, though Brown and Bell's contribution is also within this broad heading. Chapter 3 is provided by Leonor Sopas (Catholic University of Portugal) and again uses the concept of clusters as a research platform. The empirical results presented here derive from a number of case studies of start-up exporters of plastic moulds in Marinha Grande, Portugal. Preliminary indications are that cluster membership not only benefits members in the start-up process, but also indicates why and how start-ups manage to be 'born' exporters. Apparently, living and working in a concentrated locational environment fosters frequent, long lasting and overlapping relationships: professional, business, kin-based, friendship and neighbourliness. These play an important role in detecting opportunities, lowering perceived risk and aiding access to necessary start-up resources. In addition, outward-oriented clusters attract foreign buyers and encourage the emergence of local specialised institutions that support the internationalisation process. This interplay of factors increases the likelihood that overseas actors become included in the personal networks of such entrepreneurs. Thus export opportunities are more easily identified, perceived risk is lowered further, and access to resources is incrementally facilitated.

Antonella Zucchella (Insubria, Italy) contributes Chapter 4 based on research with Italian SMEs. She sees this type of firm as a convincing interpreter of internationalisation processes that approach foreign markets in a variety of ways. This throws some doubt on the traditional theories that view SME internationalisation as a framework of homogeneous behaviours and growth paths. New paradigms must consider a variety of strategic and organisational approaches, as well as a multiplicity of international growth paths. Zucchella asks the perceptive question whether the concept of size itself has to be revisited in the light of the parallel destructuring of large corporations and the innovative market seizing and growing organisational complexity of small firms. As a partial answer, her research findings suggest that neither size nor age is correlated to the export performance of firms in her sample. Internationalisation of small firms leads to a segmentation strategy irrespective of customer location, thus allowing a more rapid penetration of world markets.

Jeffrey Johnson (Strathclyde) also addresses the question of 'born' international firms in Chapter 5. Increasing incidence of start-ups that are distinctly international in nature at or near inception do not easily fit into traditional models of the internationalisation process. The accepted view is that start-ups focus initially on domestic markets, then gradually internationalise. This chapter examines the paradigm through two case studies, from the UK and US, focusing on the early internationalisation drivers and activities of the international start-ups. Changes in industry structure and entrepreneurial mind sets emerge as the primary focus for paradigm shift. Though the author is careful to identify the limitations of his case study methodology, his research suggests strongly that we must revisit the characteristics and early internationalisation drivers of 'born' international firms.

Kevin Ibeh (also Strathclyde) contributes Chapter 6, an exploratory study of internationalising firms in Nigeria. He examines their behaviour from three major theoretical perspectives (incremental, network, resource-based) via a study involving in-depth interviews with 78 such firms. His findings suggest the importance of psychic distance and network concepts, with particular regard to market selection patterns. Resource-based considerations, however, seem to give better explanation of overall internationalisation behaviour. In Ibeh's view, this presents a suitable platform for integrating incremental and network explanations (complementary, he claims) into a holistic theory of small firm internationalisation. Accordingly, policy makers should regard the resource position of firms as a basis for articulating and targeting support programmes for SME internationalisation. These are bold claims, and we look forward to further developments from Kevin as well as, perhaps, comparative studies across countries.

Chapter 7 is the third in the book from Strathclyde, and it is written by Jürgen Brock. He focuses on the market space concept – an infrastructure of global information and communication that is location-insensitive – as a driver of internationalisation. He identifies some advantages of market space: reduction in interaction costs, overcoming information barriers and development of new interaction capabilities. Using survey evidence from 112 technology-based SMEs in Germany, he explores the impact of market space in a number of ways. There appears to be a twofold market space impact on SME internationalisation. First, it can reduce barriers due to cost and information; second, it can increase the opportunity horizon of firms. Ultimately, this even influences foreign market selection by SMEs by providing appropriate information and contacts.

PART TWO: MANAGING THE MULTINATIONAL

Appropriately, Part Two begins with a critical review of Bartlett and Ghoshal's 'New Organisational Model', written by Paul Gooderham and Svein Ulset of the Norwegian School of Economics and Business Administration. Bartlett and Ghoshal (1989) propose that transnational companies represent a radical new organisational form, distinctly different from the M-form. Gooderham and Ulset are not convinced by this claim, and particularly question the emphasis put on normative control compared to other mechanisms of corporate governance. They revisit ABB (used previously by Bartlett and Ghoshal) to illustrate that a complex, multi-level network of specialised management roles and relationships can achieve the necessary degree of lateral coordination. A number of organisational aspects are examined in detail: status of the front line unit, business/geography matrix, role of middle management, role of top management, organisational psychology. Gooderham and Ulset demonstrate a quite different perspective, and argue that most of the observations of Bartlett and Ghoshal's 'new' model can also be explained by a modern transaction cost interpretation of the M-form. To some, this may resemble mere revisionism, but it really underlines the nature of scientific research where new theories are obliged to go beyond existing interpretations if they are to survive and develop.

Chapter 9 is a further development of work on MNCs in Central and Eastern European transition economies by Julia Manea and Robert Pearce (Reading). It analyses the position of technology at the interface of potentially mutually supportive dynamic processes in a transition environment. Transition economies need to go through the sequence of industrial restructuring followed by sustained and orderly growth. This relies more on technological progress and skill generation, and seeks a basis in dynamic or created comparative advantage. MNCs' contributions must extend into the phase of sustained and orderly growth, and their own evolutionary processes at subsidiary level may facilitate this. From another perspective, an MNC may contribute positively to transition by sustaining a dynamic balance between market seeking, efficiency seeking and knowledge seeking. This chapter provides survey evidence on MNCs' motivations and sources of subsidiaries' technology in transition economies, and discusses in detail the contribution subsidiaries can make in these situations.

Martyn Wright and Paul Edwards (Warwick) review transfer of best practice within MNCs in Chapter 10. Their contribution is based on a case comparison of a Canadian aluminium MNC and a European oil major. In the first case, best practice is transferred through direct personal interaction between senior managers, whereas new communications technology (e-mail networks and Intranets) is the favoured method in the second. The people-based mode proves a more efficient means of disseminating best practice than the IT mode, since the information provided is commonly more salient, structured, and permits greater opportunity for feedback. The authors note that, while the two MNCs share many characteristics, they are different in three notable ways. They have different cultures, they differ substantially in size, and the different organisational structures produce quite different patterns of everyday communication. These differences are clearly connected with diffusion methods for best practice, and point to some important future research tasks.

Chapter 11 is from Hideki Yoshihara (Kobe); it deals with Japanese management style and the use of Japanese language in managing foreign operations. The strategy of internationalised Japanese firms has changed drastically over the last fifty years. Originally exporters, they made the strategic move into foreign production after the sharp appreciation of the Japanese yen started in 1985. Foreign R&D facilities followed more recently. However, changes in management practices have been subtler. Global operations are managed by Japanese nationals and in the Japanese language. Japanese language also plays a significant role in international communication on important matters. Japanese expatriates manage foreign subsidiaries. While the Japanese management style is suitable in the home market, Yoshihara argues that in foreign operations it is costly and depresses initiatives of local capable staff. While changes in management style are desirable and would yield substantial benefits, this area is much more culture-bound than international business strategy.

PART THREE: IMPLEMENTING INTERNATIONAL STRATEGY

Mo Yamin (UMIST) makes a radical assessment of advantage of multinationality in Chapter 12. He indicates that operational flexibility is currently seen as a potential source of MNC advantage, but that this requires much centralisation of decision making at headquarters. Yamin argues the alternative hypothesis, that what he calls 'organisational isolation' at subsidiary level enhances the potential for entrepreneurial action and promotes a differentiated set of competencies within the MNC. This, he says, is an important source of MNC advantage as it counteracts strategic inertia at headquarters and improves the firm's adaptive capabilities. Consequently, the author puts forward two tentative hypotheses. First, compared to sub-units of a national firm, MNC subsidiaries will display a greater degree of entrepreneurial orientation. Second, they also have a greater ability to undertake innovation successfully. Multinationality, Yamin concludes, evens out the odds between exploitative and exploratory aspects of firm activities.

Chapter 13 is contributed by Reijo Luostarinen (Helsinki) and Rebecca Marschan-Piekkari (Bath); it proposes a new conceptual framework for the strategic evolution of MNC subsidiaries. There is, of course, much previous work in this field, but the bulk of it has been cross-sectional in nature. In what will probably be a long-running research project, the authors will have access to a very extensive Finnish longitudinal database, that will allow them to track subsidiary roles and responsibilities over time. They regard subsidiary evolution as being linked specifically to changes in value from the perspective of headquarters. Here, they classify the forces behind strategic evolution of subsidiaries into parent- and subsidiary-based drivers. They also seek to explain evolutionary paths in a specific host country with regional and global implications. The conceptual framework presented here builds on the literatures of internationalisation, strategic management and subsidiary management. Testing the framework will be the authors' next task.

Ana Teresa Tavares (Reading) reports on a survey of MNC manufacturing subsidiaries in Ireland in Chapter 14. She suggests that the Irish case is unique in the European context. As a host country, Ireland is probably the most proactive EU member in the use of industrial policy instruments to attract foreign direct investment. It epitomises the small open economy that relies on belonging to a free trade environment. EU membership is a decisive factor in boosting Ireland's attractiveness, especially for US investors with a pan-European strategy. This chapter discusses operational aspects of foreign subsidiaries in Ireland, including an evaluation of strategic evolution. Tavares concludes that rationalised operations are currently the most important but that higher value-added product mandate subsidiaries are increasing their relative importance in the Irish context. Other strategy-related dimensions are also discussed including market scope, product scope, value-added scope, and headquarters' motivations for investing in Ireland.

The subject matter of Chapter 15 by Dennis Nickson and Chris Warhurst (Strathclyde) was discussed briefly above in relation to the keynote debate at the conference. In their view, there is a very close link between Americanisation and globalisation, and their survey of 80 managers in three multinational hotel companies supports their hypothesis. They identify the abiding influence of the 'American model' of hotel internationalisation in terms of both the 'hardware' (for example, rooms and operating systems) and 'software' (for example, utilisation of human resources, style of service delivery). As is fitting with exploratory research in a complex area, the authors end by posing two further questions. First, will convergence of strategies, forms and practices in this industry still be dominated by the 'American model'? Second, is the American dominance they find in the hotel sector replicated in other service industries and, indeed, in manufacturing?

Chapter 16 describes results from a survey of foreign direct investment (FDI) in Portugal carried out by Peter Buckley and Francisco Castro (Leeds). They do a thorough statistical analysis on responses from 238 manufacturing and commercial subsidiaries, taking care to lead us through the complexities with a number of tables and figures. Stability emerges as the most consensual determinant of FDI, but the evidence suggests it may be more a necessary precondition. There is clear evidence of a dichotomy between efficiency-seeking and market-seeking FDI in Portugal. The former is essentially associated with producers of textiles, clothing, and footwear, and manufacturers of machinery and equipment. In the remaining industries, FDI is essentially market-seeking. Efficiency seeking is associated with Germany and other north European members of the EU. Spanish firms are more strongly oriented towards the local market. Geographical and cultural proximity are critical determinants for Spanish and Brazilian firms, and to a somewhat lesser extent for firms from France and Italy. Market-seeking investors seem to choose Portugal regardless of relative conditions. Generally, only efficiency-seeking firms consider other locations before investing in Portugal, most commonly from Spain and Eastern Europe.

IN CONCLUSION

The purpose of this book, as with all others in the series, is to bring together an integrated set of research conceptualisations and results. We believe that this volume contains some of the most interesting international business output of the last twelve months. Inevitably, many of the findings here will be overtaken by new research, but that is the nature of our business. The purpose of putting forward new ideas, theories and models must always be to encourage academic colleagues to critique, rethink and do better. It will be some time yet before the final word is written on international business theory.

In the seven volumes of this series published previously, some themes emerge continually. The internationalisation process (coupled with entry strategies) constitutes a major topic. There have been many contributions about the emergence of Central and East European countries as players in world markets. There have been a number of chapters that discussed aspects of globalisation, though, according to Alan Rugman (above), this may be a misplaced focus! Subsidiary strategy is always a popular theme, and the number of researchers involved is constantly expanding. The fifth recurring theme has been alliances and other cooperative ventures, though it does not appear in the current volume.

We are pleased that a new major theme has been introduced here to the Palgrave series: internationalisation of small and medium size enterprises. The 'best paper' by Peter Brown and Jim Bell also contributed to this theme. To a large extent, future volumes can only represent the best of what is presented at AIB conferences, but we would hope to feature alternative major themes in the future. These might include international technology management, impact of national culture, exporting, and organisational issues. All of these have featured in the past as individual chapters, but there is an opportunity to make more of these themes.

As always, we are in the hands of academic colleagues, but we hope to continue with the AIB purpose of providing a forum for ideas, research, professional contact and discussion of matters of common interest in international business.

2 Industrial Clusters and Small Firm Internationalisation (Best paper)

Peter Brown and Jim Bell

INTRODUCTION

Trends towards the globalisation of finance, communication, technology and markets have resulted in unprecedented business competition, especially for small firms (Knight and Cavusgil, 1996). Firms are constantly reminded that this globalisation of economic and business activity will result in competition that occurs increasingly between networks of firms (Thorelli, 1986; Axelsson and Easton, 1992; Welch *et al.*, 1997). Morgan and Hunt (1994) have suggested that to be an effective competitor in the global economy will require one to be a trusted cooperator in some network. Firms are beginning to pay closer attention to their own connections with one another, to recognise the common problems they face and to look for relationships and alliances which provide collective solutions and enable their competitive advantage to be maintained. Moreover, in an increasingly globalised market, where production technology is widely diffused, they must seek out ways of differentiating themselves and their products to establish or maintain a *marketing* competitive advantage.

As globalisation has increased, interest in regional clusters of firms has also heightened. Porter (1990), Enright (1998), Storper (1992) and Humphrey and Schmitz (1996) all discuss the phenomenon of regional clusters in the context of home-base competitive advantage in an international market. Where general network strategies once formed the basis of government programmes designed to address issues of growth and internationalisation, there has been a growing interest in *localised* networks, where many firms within a particular sector are 'clustered' in a distinct geographical region. Firms within these clusters apparently derive support and competitive advantage through highly localised inter-firm relationships, place-specific history, economic factors, values and culture. Clusters are, more and more, seen as the driving forces of international trade (Putnam, 1993; Ffowcs-Williams, 1997). Clusters are also credited with providing the environment for developing leading-edge technology and the acquisition and use of information and innovation (Swann and Prevezer, 1996; Baptista, 1996). This environment is created through cooperation and competition between firms within the cluster (Porter, 1990; Pouder and St. John, 1996).

The significance of these developments for small firms is twofold. Firstly, small firms must recognise and respond to an increasingly competitive global market place. They can no longer focus on a purely domestic market and, whether they want to or not, they must become internationally competitive to survive. This issue is particularly important if such firms are located in small, open economies that have a limited domestic market (for example, New Zealand, which has fewer than 4 million inhabitants and where 98 per cent of firms have fewer than 50 employees). Secondly, while small size may be an advantage because of their 'flexibility' to quickly adjust to changing market conditions and consumer preferences, an atomised, individual approach is no longer appropriate (McNaughton and Bell, 1999). Small firms wishing to compete internationally must do so from a position of strength within a network or cluster of other like firms. Inter-firm relationships and management style will need to be different for them to benefit from geographical clustering.

While there is general agreement that clusters provide production benefits to firms (Marshall, 1910; Krugman, 1991; Putnam, 1993; Storper and Salais, 1997; Baptista, 1998), limited research exists to indicate the degree of impact clustering has on marketing activity in a domestic or international context. To date, most enquiry has focused on supply-side initiatives which concentrate on production innovation, but the process of actually bringing that production to the market has largely been ignored (Humphrey and Schmitz, 1996). The increasingly competitive demands of the global market place, coupled with the ability for firms to mitigate many input-cost disadvantages through global sourcing, makes innovation and marketing an ever more crucial part of a firm's international competitive advantage.

In consequence, the primary objective of the research outlined in this chapter is to evaluate the impact of geographic colocation – clustering – on the marketing activities of individual firms within the electronics cluster in Christchurch, New Zealand. Given that New Zealand has a relatively small domestic market for the goods and services these firms provide, much of the marketing activity undertaken is, of necessity, in the international arena. The core research questions were whether membership of the cluster had an impact on the marketing activity and performance of individual firms and in what specific areas this influence was most significant. As the literature also suggests that cluster externalities can be characterised as either *active* or *passive*, depending on how they arise, the research also sought to identify the relative importance of active and passive marketing externalities.

SYNTHESIS OF THE LITERATURE

The Benefits of Clusters: Positive Externalities

The implications of being embedded within a cluster of economic activity flow from the externalities (or benefits) associated with colocation. These traditionally

Table 2.1   Cluster externalities

Production driven externalities	*Market driven externalities*
Technological spill-overs	Intermediate outputs/local demand
Specialised labour pool	Chance of discovery
Intermediate inputs	Credibility and reputation
	Informational spill-overs
	Active joint marketing activity

include information spill-overs, access to labour pools and more efficient sourcing of inputs (Marshall, 1910; Krugman, 1991) as well as social and cultural norms of behaviour within the cluster (Putnam, 1993; Storper and Salais, 1997). Considerable research has been undertaken on the impact of clusters on firm innovation (Feldman, 1994; Pouder and St. John, 1996), competitive advantage (Porter, 1990, 1998) and organisation (Williamson, 1985; Scott, 1998).

However, much of the focus of the extant literature is on *production* externalities and less on the implications for marketing activities of individual firms within a cluster. Few serious attempts have been made to bridge the gap between production-related firm benefits from colocation and the prospect that there are parallel benefits and advantages to be derived from *market-related* externalities simply by locating near other similar firms in an industrial cluster. Drawing from several different streams of literature (retail, organisation buying behaviour, industrial buyer–seller, international, NPD and network) it is possible to identify market-related externalities associated with colocation that may impact on individual firms and their ability to internationalise (See Table 2.1). While the desire for firms to locate near other firms to take advantage of strong local demand, and the opportunity it provides to garner trust, is well covered in the cluster literature (Marshall, 1910; Krugman, 1991; Harrison, 1991; Baptista, 1998) its focus is on domestic production rather than international supply. However, concepts like *discovery, credibility, market information spill-overs* and *joint marketing activity* within a cluster context have direct bearing on a firm's attempts to internationalise.

Location within a cluster is a powerful externality for industrial firms. Visiting buyers can see many vendors in a single trip. They may also perceive a lower buying risk because the location provides alternative suppliers allowing them to switch to or source from multiple suppliers (Porter, 1998a). This concept of *discovery* corresponds directly to the literature on search costs and organisational buying behaviour as well as aspects of internationalisation. Partner information search often involves uncertainty (Reid, 1984) and random methods such as trolling the informal social networks of existing suppliers (Simon, 1974), conducting searches within pre-established vendor locations (Liang, 1995) or simply following others into currently fashionable regions (Levinthal and March, 1981). The often *ad hoc* approach to searching for and selecting future trading partners suggests that locating a firm within an established and recognised cluster (with existing international networks) may put the firm directly in the search path of others and help develop new markets for that firm.

Consequent to the discovery externality is the idea that being found within a cluster of firms known for their particular expertise in a manufacturing or production sector enhances the *credibility* of individual firms. A cluster frequently enhances the reputation of a location in a particular field, making it more likely that customers will turn to a supplier or producer based there (Porter, 1998a). Some products may be evaluated more positively because of where they come from and the reputation of that location, especially in the absence of other informational cues (Niss, 1996). This may have significant implications for firms that come from locations with strong images abroad. Using the international profile of a region as a positioning tool may prove to be an effective strategy for firms in international marketing. The possibility of an informational externality that relates to marketing activity also exists within a cluster. A new entrant who sees an established firm trading successfully at a particular location will be drawn to locate in the same area because of apparent market strength that exists around that location (Prevezer, 1997). Similarly, there are many instances where infrastructural support for a cluster takes the form of providing information about market trends, competitor activity at home and abroad, prices and availability of products, opportunities and technological developments (Humphrey and Schmitz, 1996).

While the externalities discussed above indicate that there are passive or unconscious marketing benefits derived from cluster membership simply by locating together, there are other, more active or conscious marketing externalities that also accrue. These *active* marketing externalities require some motivation on the part of clustered companies to actually make something happen. For example, locating near similar firms creates the opportunity to consciously pursue joint action either between individual firms or between groups of firms joining together as business associations or producer consortia. This can lead to action in terms of joint trade fair participation, joint marketing delegations to clients, trade missions, inter-cluster firm referrals and shared market information gathering and sharing.

The Disadvantages of Clusters: Negative Externalities

Up to a certain point, the attractions of locating in a cluster may be compelling, but the benefits can, eventually, be outweighed by negative conditions (Baptista, 1998). Traditionally, the main concern regarding clusters is the impact of congestion and increased competition on firm costs (rents, labour and inputs) and subsequent performance (Swann, 1998). But there are also negative externalities that relate to labour, innovation and the effective operation of network relationships within the cluster (see Table 2.2).

Both congestion and increased competition can have an impact on labour (Forester, 1980) as demand for certain skills exceeds supply and results in higher

Table 2.2   Negative externalities

Market related	Production related
Congestion	Congestion
Increased output competition	Increased input competition
Loss of informational advantage	Increased labour costs
Groupthink	Increased real estate costs
	Loss of technological advantage
	Groupthink

labour costs for firms. There is also a risk of losing an innovative or technological lead to other firms within a cluster. Also a cluster could become locked in to what they have done well up to the present and ignore market trends or new developments occurring outside the cluster's information sphere (Saxenian, 1994; Porter, 1998a). Porter (1998) describes this situation as 'groupthink' and cites it as a possible reason for the decline of a cluster. The social capital literature suggests strong ties between existing members of a cluster may be used to exclude newcomers or outsiders, reinforce poor management practices and limit the extent to which firms have the resources or inclination to search out new suppliers or customers, import new technologies or enter new markets (Portes and Landolt, 1996). Increased competition, or competitive intensity, on the demand side may lead to reduced sales, prices, profits, market share and growth, at least in the short term and especially in a static market (Brown, 1989; Jaworski and Kohli, 1990; Swann, 1998; Slater and Narver, 1994).

Active and Passive Externalities

Past discussion of cluster externalities has centred on *describing* the types of externalities that arise from geographical colocation (Hoover, 1937; Scitovsky, 1963; Enright, 1998). It is also possible for these externalities to be categorised in terms of *how* they arise. Most occur as a result of firms locating together, without any conscious effort on the part of individual firms. In fact, this has been part of the definition of externalities: that they occur outside the firm and provide benefits that have not been directly sought (Marshall, 1910; Krugman, 1991; Scott, 1998). In contrast to these *passive* externalities, there are externalities that arise directly through firm action. These can only occur because of firms within the cluster working together in networks to progress an opportunity or situation. Table 2.3 categorises cluster externalities in terms of production or marketing orientation and the degree of activity required by firms to derive benefit from them.

The traditional externalities of skilled labour pools, technological spill-over and specialised inputs, plus several of the marketing externalities listed above, can be described as passive externalities. Examples of *active* externalities are the marketing externalities relating to market information and joint action. These active externalities result from the existence of familiarity and trust developed

Table 2.3   Active and passive cluster externalities

	Market driven externalities	Production driven externalities
Passive	Output multipliers Localised demand Increased market share Chance of discovery Credibility Informational spill-overs	Specialised labour force Technological spill-overs Input multipliers Informational spill-overs Infrastructural support
Active	Active joint marketing activity – trade fair participation – delegations to clients – trade missions – firm referrals – information gathering/sharing Infrastructural support	Joint research and development

through experiencing passive externalities like input–output multipliers and the social networks that evolve around growing clusters.

The concept of active or passive externalities may also be linked to the stage of development of clusters with the implication that the type of externalities might influence the dynamism or development of that cluster. Understanding the nature of these externalities may be particularly important in the context of public policy in support of cluster development.

RESEARCH APPROACH

The present research adopted a case study approach utilising in-depth interviews to collect data. The sample population of 27 firms was drawn from a directory of electronics and software businesses, listing all firms actively engaged in the Christchurch electronics cluster. This register was provided by the Canterbury Development Corporation (CDC) and had been compiled by them in 1997, and updated in 1998, for use in cluster stimulation activity. This list was supplemented by information from the University of Canterbury and, in two instances, by information from one of the cluster's member firms on new, start-up firms not registered by the CDC. The 27 firms identified represent the *entire* population of electronics firms in Christchurch at the time the research was undertaken. Interviews were conducted with representatives from 23 of the 27 firms with four firm representatives unable to be interviewed on either of the two research visits to Christchurch. In addition, a number of interviews were conducted with expert witnesses and key informants in the CDC, Canterbury Employers Chamber of Commerce and Trade New Zealand.

The interview subject in all firms approached was the owner/proprietor or chief executive officer of the firm. The advantage of this was twofold. In nearly all cases these individuals had established the company and were able to provide first-hand information and knowledge on the reasons why the firm had been established in Christchurch. Secondly, as key decision makers, they were and are still involved in all aspects of the business. Consequently they had first-hand knowledge of the firm's strategies and administrative activities within the cluster's business environment (Uzzi, 1997).

Each respondent was contacted by telephone and the purpose of the research was introduced. In all cases, a positive response was elicited and an interview time was scheduled within a discrete period of nine days between 1 July and 9 July 1999. The interviews were open-ended, lasting between one and a half and two hours. The interview schedule was moderately directed and the interview items were based on four categories – demographic profile of the firm, location decision of the firm, interaction with other firms and cluster benefits to the firm. As part of this process, respondents were asked to rate the usefulness of cluster membership for access to externality benefits on a scale of 1 to 5, where 1 was *extremely useful* and 5 was *not at all useful*. These data were analysed, to explore differences in response between smaller firms within the cluster (those with annual sales of less than NZ$10 million and larger firms with sales of NZ$10–100 million (see Table 2.4, NZ$ = US$0.50).

The use of a predominantly qualitative case study approach enabled the gathering of comprehensive, systematic and in-depth information (Patton, 1990). This facilitated the comparison of the impact of clustering on different firms based upon the 'thick description' developed from each case (Hirschman, 1986). It was also advantageous because it generated rich data for theorising and conducting detailed analysis of the dynamics of inter-firm ties within this particular cluster (Uzzi, 1997).

FINDINGS

The Christchurch electronics cluster has been identified as a high-technology cluster by the New Zealand government and has been the target and symbol of government policy towards cluster development. The cluster consists of 27 firms of varying size and experience. Its genesis was in the telecommunications industry, dating from the late-1940s, and it remains largely centred on that industry with the addition of several firms active in automotive and medical electronics manufacturing.

Table 2.4 summarises the profile of the cluster. As can be seen, almost 35 per cent of firms are very small, with fewer than ten employees. Over 50 per cent have annual sales of less than NZ$10 million (US$5 million). Just over 20 per cent have more than 100 employees and sales greater than NZ$30 million (US$15million). For over half the cluster firms, exports account for at least 50 per cent of total sales and seven of the firms exported virtually all their production (90 per cent + of sales). Typically, cluster firms with very small export ratios provide support services to other firms within the cluster and elsewhere in New Zealand.

Table 2.4   Cluster characteristics summary

Firm	Year est.	Ownership	Size	Staff (FTE)	Product	Sales NZ$	Export (Per cent)
A	1995	Private NZ	Small	3	Design/Manu.	250 000	40
B	1978	Private NZ	Medium	32	Design/Manu.	10 m	90
C	1991	Private NZ	Small	8	Encryption	2 m (est)	100
D	1948	Private NZ	Medium	30	Moldings	5 m	70
E	1984	Private NZ	Medium	35	Hard. peripherals	35 m	2
F	1974	Foreign	Large	300	Motor Controls	50 m (est)	99
G	1989	Private NZ	Medium	30	Contract manu.	6 m	5
H	1939	Private NZ	Medium	100	Metal fab.	16 m	50
I	1974	Private NZ	Medium	80	Cables	20 m (est)	50
J	1990	Private NZ	Small	14	Design	1.5 m	5
K	1974	Private NZ	Medium	32	Ind. Measurement	5 m	20
L	1992	Private NZ	Small	5	Automotive	650 000	33
M	1993	Private NZ	Small	5	Telecomm.	1.5 m	100
N	1996	Private NZ	Small	1	Marketing	500 000	10
O	1984	Private NZ	Small	4	Design	500 000	0
P	1988	Private NZ	Medium	55	Medical	18 m	95
Q	1985	Private NZ	Medium	14	Design	2 m	5
R	1996	Private US	Small	7	Design	500 000	50
S	1964	Private NZ	Medium	35	PLC Controls	3 m	66
T	1985	Foreign	Large	400	Power DC	90 m	95
U	1968	Private NZ	Large	1 000	Telecomm	100 m	90
V	1997	Private NZ	Small	2	Measuring	>50 000 (Start-up)	0
W	1991	Foreign	Large	180	GPS Systems	80 m (est)	99
Total: 23				2 372		447 m	

Note:
NZ$ = US$ 0.50.

Traditional Externalities

While the primary focus of the research was to explore marketing externalities, the findings support the literature in respect to the importance of traditional colocation benefits within the Christchurch electronics cluster (see Table 2.5).

The usefulness factor for *access to labour pool* was heightened by the fact that there was strong competition within the cluster for skilled workers. Larger firms indicated that access to engineering graduates from the University of Canterbury was an important external benefit of their location. Smaller firms also benefited from sourcing trained staff from larger firms, although this led to some hostility and accusations of 'poaching' by the later. Several larger firms had formed an informal network with local government support agencies and the university to identify and address issues relating to availability of skilled staff.

Table 2.5   Usefulness of cluster for traditional externality benefits

Traditional externalities	Mean smaller firms[1] n=13	Mean larger firms[2] n=8	Overall mean n=21	Std.dev.
Access to labour pool	2.50	2.00	2.39	0.94
Access to new technology	2.67	3.00	2.74	0.96
Buying intermediate inputs	3.67	1.80	3.26	1.18
Selling intermediate outputs	3.22	4.40	3.48	1.44

Notes:
Scale: 1 = 'extremely useful' and 5 = 'not at all useful'.
[1] Annual sales of less than NZ$10 million.
[2] Annual sales of more than NZ$10 million.

In the area of *technology spill-over*, a dichotomy between larger and smaller firms was apparent. Smaller firms described location within the cluster as being in an 'atmosphere of innovation' where it was possible to hear about innovations in other firms on an informal, unstructured basis. Larger firms, with proprietary technological knowledge, were less likely to view the cluster as positively for technology spill-over, and sought to protect themselves from any spill-over at all. Several of the larger firms suggested that, while there was evidence of good relationships between firms, these were on a social or low-technology level and never involved the exchange (formal or informal) of proprietary knowledge. Even firms engaged in sub-contracting were concerned about the prospect of their processes being expropriated by large customers. Several firms that operated in a hard network structure within the cluster agreed there was considerable exchange of information and technology spill-over between network firms which they had not consciously been aware of. This had aided understanding and cooperation and had sparked innovation within the group.

A dichotomy also existed between cluster firms in the area of *intermediate inputs–outputs*. There was a significant difference in response to the usefulness of cluster location for this externality between firms depending on size, industry sector and technology level. Respondents from smaller firms, who were active in non-electronic manufacturing, and operated with a lower level of technology, found location within the cluster to be useful for selling intermediate goods. Respondents from larger firms, operating in the electronics manufacturing sector of the cluster and utilising a higher degree of technology, found the cluster more useful for sourcing intermediate goods.

Marketing Externalities

The research revealed that cluster membership had a significant impact on marketing externalities for firms, particularly in respect to exporting and international activity. Table 2.6 summarises the degree of usefulness (in rank order) firms believed their cluster location provided in relation to marketing externalities. Firms believed location within the cluster was useful for *active* marketing externalities like *intra-cluster customer referrals* and *new product development* (which may relate to *access to technology*). There was less consistency on the other marketing externalities explored. However, further analysis of these externalities revealed that the size or type of firm had considerable impact on the perception of the cluster's usefulness in providing benefit from marketing externalities. In particular, smaller firms generally had more positive perceptions across all the items measured, even where the externality was not rated particularly highly.

Intra-cluster Referrals
Many of the firm respondents interviewed believed their location within the cluster had been a factor in giving or receiving domestic and international customer referrals within the cluster. As Table 2.6 shows, intra-cluster referrals were amongst the most useful aspects of cluster location noted by all firms. Many respondents said they regularly referred customers to other firms within the cluster if they were unable to assist the customer directly.

The size and type of firm clearly influenced the perception of usefulness of intra-firm referrals in the cluster. Firms that were smaller, less heavily involved in export activity and who utilised lower levels of technology were more likely to have benefited from an intra-cluster referral, while firms that were cluster drivers, utilising

Table 2.6   Usefulness of cluster for marketing externality benefits

Marketing externalities	Mean smaller firms[1] n=14	Mean larger firms[2] n=9	Overall mean n=23	Std. dev.
Intra-cluster referrals to other firms	2.44	3.20	2.61	1.20
Intra-cluster referrals to your firm	2.44	3.60	2.69	1.29
Innovation – new product development	2.56	3.00	2.65	0.88
Market information	3.00	4.00	3.22	1.17
Finding new customers	3.11	4.40	3.39	1.34
Discovery – new customers finding you	3.44	4.00	3.57	1.04
Credibility/enhanced reputation	3.39	4.20	3.57	1.20
Joint market information search	3.33	4.60	3.61	1.53
Greater local demand	3.56	4.40	3.74	1.05
Joint trade fair participation	3.78	4.20	3.87	1.25
Joint marketing delegations to clients	3.61	5.00	3.91	1.47
Joint trade missions to new markets	4.11	5.00	4.30	1.11

Notes:
Scale: 1 = 'extremely useful' and 5 = 'not at all useful'.
[1] Annual sales of less than NZ$10 million.
[2] Annual sales of more than NZ$10 million.

leading edge technology, with high export sales, were less likely to have benefited from a referral. This suggests that larger, leading edge firms are more independent or have already developed contacts and have less need for referrals from others. Smaller firms with less developed contacts appeared to rely on these intra-cluster referrals to widen their customer base and initiate international activity.

All firms who referred customers stated they only referred to firms they knew and trusted personally, and usually the firms had a long-term relationship prior to any referrals taking place. Location within the cluster was clearly seen as a prerequisite for this kind of relationship development.

International New Product Development
Information derived from the interviews indicated considerable new product development (NPD) occurred as a result of location within the cluster, especially amongst leading edge firms. Respondents from Firms C, L and T noted their existence depended on developing new products either in tandem with the university, or with their former parent company. While many of the smaller, second-tier firms did not acknowledge that NPD resulted from cluster location, several did concede that they were working closely with lead firms as well as external contacts to develop new products cooperatively. Larger firms were more likely to claim NPD was a result of international market demand or relationships outside the cluster. A typical response from the chief executive (CEO) of Firm F was 'relationships with customers are important for innovation, not relationships with other cluster members'.

While information from interviews was inconclusive, information derived from analysis of responses to the measurement scale of cluster benefits was not. This analysis showed that all firm respondents rated their location within the cluster as useful for new product development. Unlike other externalities, there was no significant difference between firms based on their age, size, sales, export status or level of technology, although the mean score for younger, smaller and less international firms indicated a slightly greater perceived benefit.

Market Information
Within the Christchurch electronics cluster there was a clear distinction between small, new firms and their older, more experienced counterparts in perceptions of information benefits accruing from location. This was particularly significant for small firms with lower sales and less export experience. These respondents consistently expressed more positive attitudes towards interaction with other firms and the benefits of colocation, indicating that they often passed information to other firms and enjoyed a reciprocal experience. They also felt that, by locating near larger firms and by working with them, there was a benefit to them in terms of identifying international market trends and conditions. Several small, new firms had found international customers through a previous association with a parent firm.

Respondents from firms that were active in marketing networks fully supported the concept of location within the cluster providing access to market information.

In all cases this had been a motivating factor in the establishment of a marketing network. In one case, the sharing of information between firms had been part of the initial teething problems of the network with one firm keeping information to itself, while trying to expropriate other firms' knowledge for its own benefit. However, respondents from larger, more international firms were less inclined to acknowledge a market information benefit of cluster location. The CEO of Firm F commented that 'New Zealand's style of business works against sharing any kind of information – including market information.' This reflected the views of respondents from most of the larger firms.

The clear dichotomy between small and large firms became even more evident when their export experience was considered. Firms with less export experience were significantly more likely to consider their location within the cluster had been useful for finding new customers and obtaining market information. This suggests that firms that have worked through the difficulties of developing an export operation and who derive a substantial part of their sales from exports, feel confident in their own ability to source market information and new customers. They are also more likely to have well-developed international networks which provide more specific and relevant information than local networks within the cluster. Firms new to exporting must rely more on informal local networks for information gathering because they have yet to develop their own international networks and competencies.

Several small firm respondents (from Firms A, L, M and O) commented that they believed there was a gap in the Christchurch cluster for the provision of relevant market information, which could be disseminated to all cluster members. They believed this was a role for TradeNZ to perform, but felt it either 'did not have the skills required or was driven by commercial motives' (general manager, Firm L) which directed it to act for fee-paying clients and to keep information confidential to those clients.

Discovery and Credibility

While some respondents disputed the value of the cluster for discovery or credibility, several firm respondents clearly indicated that international customers had discovered them in Christchurch through contact with other firms in the cluster. This was certainly the case for design firms and contract manufacturers who acknowledged that they had secured export contracts with new customers because of their proximity or relationship with another firm in the cluster. The managing director (MD) of Firm G described a situation where an international customer visiting an existing supplier in Christchurch met representatives of Firm G who were in the factory at the same time. They were introduced and identified the opportunity to establish a working relationship. Another company (Firm H) was approached by an international contact who had seen evidence of its production quality at another firm's factory in Christchurch, for whom it sub-contracted. This led to a direct approach by the contact and the development of a trading relationship. The new customer had actually seen components that were being rejected for unsatisfactory quality and had later told the firm 'I thought if that was the quality of your rejects then the stuff that got approved must be bloody good.' These examples suggest that while an international search for electronics manufacturers may not lead directly to Christchurch, once contact is established it is possible for other firms within the cluster to benefit from discovery. Analysis of firm responses clearly showed that while most firms did not rate discovery highly, firms new to exporting and with a lower level of technology perceived their location within the cluster to be of benefit for discovery.

Similarly, respondents from larger, more export-oriented firms consistently stated their ability to secure customers and sell products was not a result of locational credibility. It was a result of 'our own credibility, not anybody else's' (MD, Firm U). These respondents stressed their firms had worked hard to find international contacts and their business credibility had developed over time. For some of these firms, location in Christchurch was actually a marketing disadvantage as the 'perception of Christchurch as a cluster is strong within New Zealand but the rest of the world wouldn't have a clue' (MD, Firm E).

Respondents from firms that were less export focused, including design firms O and Q, stated that their location in Christchurch provided a degree of credibility with new customers but this was on a national, not international basis. The general thrust of responses was that active exporters believed that location had little to do with any credibility they might have in international market. This was more likely to be based on their trading history, performance and customer focus over time. Those firms that did perceive some credibility enhancement from locating within the cluster were more likely to have a domestic focus or fewer international contacts and were not technology leaders.

Joint Marketing Activities

A wide disparity in cooperative marketing activity was discovered during this research. At one end of the spectrum was an almost total lack of cooperative activity between firms and a low rating of the cluster's usefulness for achieving cooperation in certain areas of joint international marketing activity. Conversely, there was a greater degree of cooperation, amongst particular firms, who appeared to benefit from these *active* marketing externalities. Firms that were involved in marketing networks within the cluster were positive about the existence of joint marketing externalities, such as joint market research and joint approaches to potential customers, even though there were occasional problems with network partners. Nearly all these firms believed their location within the cluster and the opportunity to observe and work with other firms had enabled some joint marketing actions (like inter-firm referrals) to arise from the association. They had experienced real successes from jointly identifying key overseas markets and customers and then securing business for the group.

A number of smaller firms noted that no *direct* benefit had derived from locating near large, leading technology firms and that these firms were uncooperative in efforts to establish joint marketing activities. The MD of Firm S summed up the general feeling of smaller firms when he said, 'I suppose they provide an environment where the rest of us get some kind of marketing spin-off, even if they don't work with us directly.'

Respondents in larger firms believed they were able to develop new markets effectively on their own, while smaller ones felt they were more successful working in some kind of network. Those firms not already involved in network activity believed the cluster was beneficial in helping them identify potential marketing partners either through referrals or informal market information spill-over.

Inter-firm Relationships and Stage of Cluster Development
While many firms acknowledged the existence of informal network ties within the cluster, they often had not distinguished personal networks from a business network of focused and strategic intent. Whether deliberate or not, there was too much emphasis on informal ties and not enough on formal ties. Firms that had moved to initiate cluster networks had successfully built on historical informal ties and trust to become more dynamic players within the cluster. However, underdeveloped inter-firm relationships appear to be a barrier to the growth of the Christchurch cluster, with the transfer of market information and technological innovation being limited by the absence of these networks. There are resource problems and a reluctance to relinquish autonomy to achieve the benefits of collaboration within cluster networks. Frequently, there is suspicion of other firms, government agencies and research institutions. There is also a need to prevent internal firm conflict from derailing cluster development.

Another issue concerns the impact of *active* externalities (and in particular, marketing externalities) on the dynamic development of clusters. Humphrey and Schmitz (1996) state that dynamic clusters are driven by the needs of customers or marketing issues. What this research has shown is that cluster development can be perceived as a continuum defined by the degree of inter-firm relationships and type of externalities that exist within the cluster. The development of active externalities and consequent increase in cluster dynamism is determined by inter-firm network relationships. The stronger these network relationships are, the more benefit is derived from the active externalities. Coupled with this classification is the acknowledgement that specialist network management skills are required to achieve strong inter-firm relationships. Such skills are not commonly found in smaller firms.

The Christchurch electronics cluster can be placed on this continuum at the level of increasing inter-firm relationships and network activity where firms are benefiting from *passive* externalities and are beginning to benefit from active marketing externalities. It cannot be described as dynamic at this stage, but the preconditions exist for this to occur. The identification of the cluster's stage of development has implications for what might be done to encourage it to develop to a more dynamic stage where firms are actively attracted to it because of cluster externalities rather than just passively emerging out of their home location. These implications, for firms and policy makers, are discussed in the following section.

DISCUSSION

The research findings provide strong evidence that marketing externalities exist within the Christchurch electronics cluster, and that these externalities play a significant role in the international development of firms, especially smaller ones. Colocation in the cluster creates an environment where firms can derive benefit from traditional passive externalities such as access to labour pool, technology spill-over and availability of intermediate inputs–outputs. It also provides an environment where firms can develop knowledge about – and trust between – each other, providing a foundation for active marketing externalities to be pursued.

There was a clear distinction between large and small firms in the amount of importance and value placed on cluster membership and benefits that arose from that membership. Smaller firms perceived cluster membership as being a key factor in their efforts to internationalise. They believed the benefits of location near other internationally focused firms, large or small, positively impacted on technology transfer, innovation and NPD, inter-firm referrals and export market information flows. It also provided potential for discovery by new customers, and the opportunity to collaborate to enter new overseas markets. Although inter-firm referrals were most highly rated by firms, perhaps the most important benefits relate to innovation and NPD. However, the net effect of all these benefits is to expand exporting opportunities and improve international competitiveness.

Smaller firms who provide support services or sub-contract to other cluster members also derive benefits. In most cases, they stand to gain additional sales and indirect exports from any improvement in the international performance of cluster partners. However, some have actually obtained overseas enquiries and orders as a direct result of these inter-firm relationships. In all cases, smaller firms with fewer international connections were more likely to utilise networks within the cluster to help develop and enter export markets.

Larger firms, while acknowledging some of the benefits of cluster membership, were more likely to see their international success as a function of individual perseverance and hard work. They were also more likely to emphasise the importance of external networks in their internationalisation. Nevertheless, their ability to source high-quality components, obtain support services, sub-contract manufacture or assembly and avail themselves of specialist design expertise from other firms within the cluster cannot be underestimated as sources of international competitive advantage. Local sources of supply undoubtedly contribute to lower costs, smaller inventories and shorter lead times in design, manufacturing and delivery. Moreover, there is clear evidence that some of these firms do collaborate very effectively with other cluster members in joint product and market development activities.

These findings have significant implications for public policy in the area of cluster development. Firstly, it is important that the many soft network relationships between cluster firms are developed and extended into hard networks where firms actively translate their knowledge and trust of each other into joint production and marketing efforts. Much of the New Zealand focus on cluster development has revolved around management up-skilling in areas like financial, operations and marketing management. However, the concept of management skill has been restricted to aspects of individual firm management. With the importance of inter-firm relationships being underlined by this research, policy makers must consider training programmes for firm management within a cluster that focus on networking and communication skills within the cluster, and the benefits of cooperation in marketing and collaborative new product development.

Secondly, the identification of international market opportunities for these networks must be a priority to encourage cooperative activity. A specific recommendation is for TradeNZ and/or the Canterbury Development Corporation to provide a network broker service, experienced in the electronics industry, to lever soft, informal network ties into stronger marketing networks, and to investigate market opportunities for the cluster.

Thirdly, it is clear that, although many of the CEOs of larger firms within the cluster do not see a particular need to collaborate with smaller firms in joint marketing activities, they can still be very influential in the development of the cluster in two important respects: first as role models, given that the owner/managers of smaller firms are likely to seek to emulated their international business strategies; second as advocates, in ensuring that the support needs of the cluster are clearly articulated to – and acted upon by – policy makers.

Finally, there is good evidence from the research that the University of Canterbury provides valuable support to cluster firms in terms of R&D and in providing suitably trained graduates. However, not all of the firms appear to utilise, or even fully recognise, the value of this resource and opportunities undoubtedly exist for greater interaction and collaboration. Moreover, it may be argued that there is an expanded role for academic institutions in the locality, which is greater than providing the technical skill base required by firms within the cluster. It also goes further than collaborating with cluster firms on NPD projects. Where these institutions can and should become much more active is in assisting cluster firms to commercialise their offerings internationally.

There are two limitations of this research that should be noted. The first is that a case study approach, involving a relatively small number of firms, reduces the generalisability of the findings to other clusters. However, because of the unique nature of clusters and their formation, such a methodology is considered appropriate The findings are deemed to present a comprehensive and accurate inquiry into the Christchurch electronics sector and provide pertinent policy implications for support measures for the sector. Second, as the research has been limited to one cluster, the findings reflect its specific characteristics and those of the dominant industrial sector therein. A future direction may be to test and verify these findings in other industry sectors and locations, both in New Zealand and elsewhere.

Notwithstanding these limitations, this research has identified certain marketing externalities associated with colocation and investigated the impact of these externalities on firms within the cluster. In doing so, it has identified a distinction between types of cluster externalities and suggested that this active/passive distinction may usefully inform attempts to categorise the characteristics of a dynamic cluster.

A quantifiable insight into how clusters affect a firm's marketing activity and how marketing activity affects cluster growth could be achieved by measuring the number and strength of relations between cluster firms, and the frequency of inter-firm interaction. Research on the extent of identification with group goals, the number and strength of personal relations among individuals in different firms, and the frequency of informal, non-business personal interaction among firms would complement this approach.

Part One

Internationalisation of Small and Medium-sized Enterprises

3 'Born' Exporting in Regional Clusters: Preliminary Empirical Evidence

Leonor Sopas[1]

INTRODUCTION

Only in the last decade did International Business research start to address a long-ignored issue: why a growing number of firms are international from the moment of birth or in the very first years of activity (Ray, 1989; McDougall *et al.*, 1994; McDougall and Oviatt, 1996; Oviatt and McDougall, 1997; Westhead *et al.*, 1998; Burgel and Murray, 1998). In the case of international new ventures[2] (INV) from small countries the major research question is how early internationalisation is possible rather than why. Even the less sophisticated mode of entry into foreign markets, exports, usually requires a minimal knowledge of foreign languages and external trade techniques. Also exporting firms will generally be in a disadvantageous position in relation to local competitors that benefit from better information about buyers' tastes and preferences and potentially enjoy higher credibility near local customers. These are likely to be especially important advantages when products sold are customised, technically complex, and require frequent contacts between the buyer and the supplier.

Another emerging issue in international business research has to do with the role of location (namely location within regional clusters) in internationalisation strategies (Dunning, 1997; Oviatt and MacDougall, 1997; Enright, 1998; Anderson, 1999). Therefore this chapter focuses on INV located within a cluster, that is, on 'interdependent' INVs.[3] As far as internationalisation modes of entry are concerned, exports and exporting new ventures (ENVs) are analysed. More specifically research is based on case studies of companies located in the plastic moulds cluster of Marinha Grande, Portugal.

While collecting information about this cluster a series of short articles about member firms of Cefamol – Portuguese Association for the Mould Industry – published in its quarterly magazine *O Molde* between 1988 and 1999 were gathered (Cefamol, 1988–99). Geographic concentration around the area of Marinha Grande, a pattern of start-up through spin–offs, strong and early export orientation and the supporting role of relations with customers (including several large MNCs from different industries and countries), suppliers and peers seem to be common features of these 37 reports. A series of question on the role of location within clusters in early export strategies emerged from a thorough review and analysis of these reports. How do mould makers from Marinha Grande manage to start exporting so early after foundation? How does location within a cluster influence early exports? What is the role played by customers, suppliers and other firms in the process? How does location within a cluster influence relations with other local firms and relations with customer firms located outside the cluster?

This chapter presents the preliminary results from an on-going research project and is organised as follows. In the first section a short review of the existing literature on INVs is presented. Since 'interdependent' ENVs introduce the concept of location into the research on international entrepreneurship, a brief survey of cluster theory and its potential contribution to the explanation of INVs is also made. The main goal of this summary of literature is to guide the design of the research project (Eisenhardt, 1989; Yin, 1994). Therefore, the research design and the method of information collection and analysis are presented in the methodological section that follows. After a short introduction of the basic characteristics of mould production, preliminary findings are disclosed. In the concluding section implications of major findings are discussed and questions for future research are identified.

LITERATURE REVIEW

Borrowing from concepts of entrepreneurship and strategic management literature to explain INVs, McDougall *et al.* (1994) argue that the founders of INV have unique competencies that enable them to detect opportunities for operating in foreign markets. Networks, knowledge and background, namely international experience, are referred to as key competencies of these entrepreneurs. In addition, these entrepreneurs tend to choose hybrid forms of governance in order to preserve scarce resources. Internationalisation from the inception is further justified as a way to avoid 'path dependence' on domestic competencies. Placing the focus of their research on the competencies of the entrepreneur, Oviatt and McDougall (1997), tend to play down other potential explanatory factors of the process of INVs. For example, location, industry and value chain linkages receive no more than a brief reference as potential explanatory variables in the case of 'interdependent' INVs. Even there it is simply suggested that location in geographic clusters or networks results in economies and internationalisation for all participants. Moreover the mechanisms through which this happens are not demonstrated and empirical research on different types of INVs is called for (Oviatt and McDougall, 1997, p. 93).

Organisational and sociological research into entrepreneurship has been arguing that a detailed explanation of entrepreneurship should start by recognizing that it is 'embedded' in the social context and that entrepreneurs obtain information, resources and social support through social relationships (Granovetter, 1985; Aldrich and Zimmer, 1986; Starr and MacMillan, 1990; Smilor, 1997; Baker, 1999). Empirical research has revealed that entrepreneurship is related to relationships external to the working place and to the previous working career of the entrepreneur. In the specific case of spin-offs it is shown that during their previous working experience entrepreneurs have not only acquired practical knowledge about the product and the business but have also established personal relations with specialised suppliers, potential customers, other producers, specialised institutions, skilful employees and even potential partners (Lipparini and Sobrero, 1998, p. 204; Saxenian, 1990, 1994). These former business connections contribute to the development of reputation, foster mutual understanding and trust, and enhance early sharing of information (about opportunities, the locus and quality of resources) and inter-firm co-operation (Dubini and Aldrich, 1991; Lipparini and Sobrero, 1998). Other researchers applying network theory concepts have investigated specific aspects of network structure, such as a size, reachability, density and diversity, that benefit entrepreneurial activity and success (Aldrich and Zimmer, 1986; Burt, 1992; Nohria, 1992; Baker, 1994; Smilor, 1997). Aspects of geographic location and their impact on networks have continued to be largely neglected.

Cluster theory attempts to address this gap. A cluster was recently defined as 'a form of network that occurs within a geographic location, in which the proximity of firms and institutions ensures certain forms of commonality and increases the frequency and impact of interactions' (Porter, 1998; p. 226). Combining concepts from both network and competition theories, recent theoretical developments view entrepreneurs and firms located within clusters as 'embedded' in networks of personal and inter-firm relationships in which 'strong ties' and 'weak ties' coexist (Granovetter, 1973; Granovetter, 1985; Porter, 1998). Hence the mechanisms through which the social structure of networks within regional clusters produces benefits for a particular firm have just started to be explored. Porter argued that clusters contribute to stimulating new business formation. Entrepreneurs within clusters benefit not only from better information about opportunities but also from lower barriers to entry. Furthermore, the presence of other successful firms/entrepreneurs contributes to lowering the perceived risk of entry and stimulates other start-ups through imitation (Porter, 1998).

Clusters influence business opportunities through a variety of forms. First of all, knowledge spill-overs are likely to materialise in spin-offs. Also persons working and living in a limited geographic space tend to be involved in a dense web of personal relations, fostering trust, which enable rich information flows. As a result, gaps in products, services or supplies are more likely to be identified quickly. Furthermore, clusters constitute a significant local market for firms supplying specialised inputs or related goods and services. Finally, by comprising a significant number of successful firms in a particular field, clusters attract new entrants, both domestic and foreign (ibid.). As far as resources are concerned, besides the traditional external economies underlined by Marshall (1920/1890, p. 221), the emergence of specialised institutions within clusters reduces the need for specialised investments. Local financial institutions familiar with the cluster may require a lower risk premium on capital (Porter, 1998).

Empirical research focusing on the potential impact of location within clusters on the internationalisation process of firms is still scarce and INVs are not at all mentioned (Porter, 1990; Porter, 1998; Enright, 1998, Porter and Solvell, 1998; Andersen, 1999).

This review of the literature has enabled the identification of potentially important analytical dimensions of the entrepreneurship process. The specific contributions of different relations to motives behind start-up and to the process of opportunity recognition, risk evaluation and resource gathering should be examined. The influence of location within a cluster on the composition (actors, content of ties) and structure of the personal network of an entrepreneur constitutes another dimension of analysis. As a consequence, research questions presented above may be rephrased as follows. What are the mechanisms through which location within a cluster influences the network of personal relations of local entrepreneurs? What are the main consequences for the entrepreneur's personal network? How does the network of personal relations of the entrepreneur contribute to – identification of opportunities in foreign markets soon after start-up, finding the resources necessary to be able to sell in foreign markets or managing the risk normally associated with selling in foreign markets? These questions suggest a hypothetical causal chain that runs from location within clusters to start-up exporting passing through the network of relations of the entrepreneur. Nevertheless, the mechanisms of the causal chain remain largely unknown and will be the focus of this research project.

RESEARCH DESIGN AND METHOD

Like almost all the other empirical research on INVs and clusters our study is based on case studies, in this case of exporting companies located in the plastic moulds cluster of Marinha Grande,[4] Portugal. Case study methodology was chosen since it has been considered the adequate strategy for research on process, that is, when 'how' and 'why' questions are being asked (Yin, 1994) or when little is known about a phenomenon (Eisenhardt, 1989). As regards the operational definition of international new ventures, a firm qualifies as an INV if it has a significant percentage of sales coming from foreign countries (export intensity) within the first six years of activity (Oviatt and McDougall, 1997, pp. 91–2).

Identifying and Selecting the Cases

Since research focuses on plastic mould exporters located in Marinha Grande, both mould makers and mould traders are included in the population. The unit of analysis is the 'embedded' firm, that is, the firm within the cluster (Grabher, 1993;

Granovetter, 1985). The unit of observation is the 'embedded' entrepreneur, that is, the entrepreneur within his personal network of relations.

As a complete list of mould exporters is not available, cases were identified through the list of members of Cefamol, which includes the great majority of mould exporters. This on-line database comprised 60 mould-making firms and ten mould-trading firms located in Marinha Grande at the beginning of 1999. All these firms were contacted and asked whether at least one of the founding partners was still active and how significant were direct exports as a percentage of total sales within the first six years of activity. Twelve firms were excluded since information about the start-up process was no longer available. Because most firms were no longer able to quantify their export orientation during their early years of activity, the identification of foreign customers within the six-year period was finally taken as an indicator of early involvement in foreign markets. The research project is still under way but up to the present 25 manufacturing and eight trading firms have agreed to participate in the research. The relatively large number of case studies with a moderate level of detail aims at uncovering the relationships between location within a cluster and early exports.

Data collection: Instruments and Protocols

Data were collected through semi-structured interviews of at least one of the founders of the venture who was still involved in the management of the company, complemented by archival data (company financial reports, internal memoranda and articles in newspapers and magazines). Interviews of founders of 33 firms were conducted by the same researcher and took place in the two different periods – first in February/March and then in June/July 1999. An interview protocol was prepared to this effect. First entrepreneurs were asked to make a brief description of the start-up process. This was followed by more focused questions on the reasons for start-up, the process of identification of the business opportunity and access to the necessary resources and competencies. Relations among partners and between partners and other actors they considered relevant for start-up were carefully explored.

All but three interviews were recorded on tape and later used as the main basis for the interview report organised according to the above-mentioned protocol. Written notes were the basis for the report of the other three interviews. The case studies' database is composed of tapes, interview reports and the archival data collected (Yin, 1994).

Method for Data Analysis

Within case analysis followed by cross-case analysis based on tabulation of the evidence available for each case was used (Eisenhardt, 1989; Miles and Huberman, 1994; Langley, 1999). Analysis of trading and manufacturing firms was done separately in order to enable inter-group comparison. Within-case analysis was based on the interview reports. In each case the process of export start-up was analysed carefully, emphasising the major factors that intervened. Patterns were investigated and a short summary was produced. Cross-case analysis began with the organisation of evidence along the following dimensions: opportunity identification, main reasons for start-up, resource gathering process. This was followed by comparison between cases along each dimension aimed at detecting similarities and differences. The importance of different types of personal relationships was explored with regard to both start-up and the beginning of direct exports.

MOULD MAKING: A RELATION-INTENSIVE ACTIVITY

Neither consumer nor equipment goods, moulds are essential tools for the operation of injection machines. Every product incorporating plastic – a car, a washing machine, a container, a doll – requires one, if not several, moulds. In fact, each different plastic part requires one mould in order to be produced. As a consequence, moulds are customised, made-to-order products. Also the customers for moulds belong to different industries. Futhermore, moulds are in general unique products. Each mould can be used to inject millions of identical plastic components or products. Often, even after the product is off the market, its moulds are still capable of injecting many more plastic parts. Moulds are also technologically complex. Mould making involves the knowledge of many different technologies, from mechanics to electronics, including materials technologies, optics and information technologies, just to mention a few. These characteristics explain why quality is such an important feature of moulds and also why these are relatively expensive goods that take a long time to manufacture. Nowadays delivery time is on average 12 weeks. Customisation and technological complexity require frequent and wide-band information exchange between the mould maker (MM) or the mould trader (MT) and each customer. Even though communication is likely to be more intensive at the beginning of the process, it varies throughout the process from daily to once a week or every two weeks and it may continue after delivery. Therefore one can say that moulding is a relation-intensive activity.

Established payment conditions – a third after the preliminary design is approved, a third when first samples are sent and a third before the mould shipment – also contribute to the creation of a bond between both parts of the transaction. Buyer and seller have to trust each other. The customer has to do so because he makes an advance payment and relies on the supplier(s) to deliver the mould(s) on time and according to specifications; even if just one mould fails, it may well compromise the introduction of the product in the market according to schedule. For his part, the mould seller has to believe the customer will pay the remaining two-thirds of the price, since it is not easy to find an alternative client for such a highly customised product. It is understandable, then, that both customers and suppliers value stable and long-lasting business relations. Moreover, through repeated transactions MM learn the technical procedures and specifications of buyers and become familiar with their equipment (where moulds work). Technical staffs from both sides of the transaction meet, learn to communicate and to work together when necessary. This contributes to a reduction of misunderstandings and to ease communication and problem solving, resulting in improved quality and quicker delivery time.

A final note is due regarding the different average size of MM and mould buyers. Owing to limited economies of scale, MM tend to be small and oriented towards manufacturing, employing few designers and with only one or two persons in charge of the commercial department. Customers for moulds include different types of firms, including multinational companies (MNC), with or without injection facilities, and trading firms. Both of these generally have several people in charge of procurement. Communication between the buyer and the seller takes place essentially through persons in charge of the purchasing and the marketing departments, respectively. These are the ones most likely to develop a personal relation overlapping the business tie. Sometimes engineers involved in the conception of the product and designers of the mould are also involved. Manufacturing workers are far from the border of the firm and, hence, are only likely to meet employees of local contractors.

ANALYSIS OF PRELIMINARY FINDINGS

Eight mould traders (MT) and 25 mould makers (MM) that have up to the present agreed to participate in this research constitute a diversified group of firms with regard to age, number of partners, current size and export intensity (Tables 3.A.1 and 3.A.2). Their stories reveal multiple ways through which location within a cluster influences personal and interorganisational networks of relations of entrepreneurs and how these contribute to new business formation and especially to early internationalisation.

Opportunity Detection: Local Market versus Foreign Markets

The majority of MMs interviewed started producing moulds for a variety of local customers. Since around 90 per cent of Portuguese mould production is normally exported this means many firms were working as subcontractors (ISTA, 1980–98). Local MTs were the most popular type among MMs' first customers and other local MMs (sometimes including former employers) followed. Local procurement offices of MNCs like Hasbro or Matchbox were also frequent among the group of first customers, while local injection-moulding companies (IMs) were almost residual. Finally, it is worth noting that seven MMs mentioned foreign customers among their very first clients. All MMs interviewed acknowledged having some prior relation with their first customers. Except in the case of one firm whose first customers were identified through a common friend, in all the other cases there was a direct tie with the buyer and this relation was established during the former working experience of at least one of the partners of the venture.

As far as the beginning of the export process is concerned, all MMs confirmed having exported within the six years deadline, including sales to local purchasing offices of MNCs (five MMs) and to local traders (two MMs) but only when technical details were discussed directly with foreign customers. First exports resulted from previous direct ties with foreign customers (the great majority of cases) or from relationships established through a third party or simply benefit from location within the cluster. All direct relations were developed during the former working experience of partners. Emigration contributed to firm internationalisation both in the case of two MMs whose relations with foreign customers were established during the time the main partner was an emigrant and in the case in which exports went to an IM owned by a Portuguese emigrant in Latin America (previously an employee of an MM's Portuguese customer). Typical examples of foreign customers that came through third party contacts are the ones that once bought moulds through trading firms but either by their own initiative or by answering a contact of MMs managed to establish direct trading relations.

Additionally, two MMs mentioned the reference from common friends, suppliers, or other customers as the main link between them and their first foreign customers. Location within a cluster facilitated random contacts since the geographic concentration of specialised firms attracted customers. Four MMs acknowledged having been found by their first foreign customers while these were visiting Marinha Grande. The first contact happened just by pure chance (while driving around the area the customer happened to pass by several MMs and decided to visit some firms) or because buyers and sellers accidentally met in local IMs where moulds from several MMs were being tested side by side. Even if the MM was not present at the site of the test, it was not difficult for the customer to find out his name and address.

Also local institutions, in cooperation with national ones, periodically planned a series of initiatives aimed at promoting Portuguese mould exporters both in Marinha Grande and abroad. Some examples are the organisation of trade missions and the presence of Portuguese mould exporters in the main international fairs, the preparation of export catalogues and the publication of the directory of Portuguese MMs and MTs. All of these schemes facilitated the establishment and development of relations with foreign customers. It is important to recognise, however, that some (though few) MMs took active steps to enter foreign markets. These firms sometimes benefit from the support of local and national specialised institutions. Moreover, the fact that other local firms were already exporting provided role models for new entrants. Self-organised visits to customers previously identified through mailing lists were among the most frequently mentioned actions. Finally, the small number of hotels in Marinha Grande further facilitated the contact with foreign customers while these were visiting the area.

As regards MTs, all firms started up selling to foreign customers. In all but two cases at least one of the partners of the MT had a previous direct or indirect

relation with customers that once more could be traced back to the former working experience of the entrepreneur. One of the exceptions is partially explained
since it corresponds to a MT founded by MMs with the specific aim of sharing
the costs associated with the enlargement of their portfolio of customers. The
other case corresponded to a MT whose partners have very limited previous experience in the mould making business; actually only one of them supplied design
services to some local MMs and to a few foreign customers. Both started exporting through trade fairs, direct mailing and telephone calls followed by personal
visits to selected customers.

New Customers

As regards new customers, MMs and MTs alike used a variety of means to establish contact, including classical marketing strategies. Still the majority of firms
stress the importance of customers' reference as the best way to get new, reliable
and faithful customers in this process. When customers appear through recommendation, each party to the transaction has some information about the other.
Being present at international fairs was considered useful by almost all firms
questioned but even here a reference from customers that were present played a
decisive role in securing orders. New customers also appeared through the job
mobility of customers' procurement staff. The latter often contacted the mould
suppliers they were used to working with even though this did not necessarily
mean they interrupted relations with usual suppliers of their new employer.
Likewise, some customers were lost because personal relations with customer's
staff were broken. Personal relations with MTs were also considered as potential
sources of new customers. The importance of relations in the moulding business
suggests that the more direct customers a MM has, the more requests for quota-
tions it is likely to receive.[5] Hence getting the first direct customers seems to be
the main difficulty. Nevertheless, self-organised trips to foreign markets scored
highly as an effective means of finding new customers. Still other firms hired
administrative staff speaking foreign languages, collected official lists of potential customers, sent mailings followed by telephone contacts and invited customers to visit the firm. Finally, reference should be made to the case of
Tecmolde, since some of its first new customers came through the foreign partner. This underlines the benefits of jointly analysing external trade and foreign
direct investment.

Reasons for Start-up

As regards MMs, the experience of founding partners in mould making was the
most often mentioned reason for start-up. Within-case analysis was followed by
cross-case comparison in order to look for patterns. It revealed that the majority
of partners interviewed attributed start-up to several reasons, the most frequent
combinations being 'own skills and competencies' coupled with one of the three

following reasons: achieving personal goals/improving living conditions, exploring a surplus in demand or solving a somehow unsatisfactory professional situation (Table 3.A.1). The fact that other colleagues had already succeeded as entrepreneurs provided an additional incentive to start-up. Demand was generally taken for granted since most entrepreneurs stated that, as long as someone was locally recognised as a skilful mould-making worker, this person could be sure to receive orders. Besides, while working for other local MMs employees easily became aware of demand for moulds and of one another's competencies. Sooner or later groups of workers started to talk about the possibilities and advantages of starting their own firm and after some time spin-offs were likely to occur.

With three exceptions MTs identified the existence of a surplus in the external demand for moulds coupled with the local capacity to make, but not necessarily to export, moulds as an opportunity to start up a trading firm. Two exceptions correspond to MTs founded by MMs that stated as main goals (a) to split the costs of entry into foreign markets and (b) to achieve a size to be able to quote large orders from multinational customers (several moulds to be delivered at the same date) or to negotiate with official procurement offices of central planning economies. The final exception is explained by the very particular historical context that followed the 'April Revolution', when orders from foreign customers were cancelled and local MM were in a difficult situation. Two workers of a MM spotted the opportunity to use their personal credibility with foreign customers to export moulds produced in Portugal or Spain.

Resources

Besides opportunity (and incentive) entrepreneurs need resources to start up a venture. In the case of trading firms financial resources did not seem to be a problem since a rented room with some basic furniture and equipment was enough. As a result, main financial sources were derived from individual and family resources, in some cases supplemented by personal credit and by the up-front payment of customers. Some MTs benefited from the resources of partner firms. Personal credit and individual resources were also the most important means of financing for the majority of MMs. Nevertheless, these firms required more significant investments, especially in specialised machinery,[6] which justified the use of more diversified sources of finance. Equipment rental is not common owing to the rapid pace of technological change, but equipment suppliers supported start-ups by granting special payment conditions or credit schemes or even by guaranteeing bank loans. MMs generally asked for this type of support from suppliers they already knew from their experience in the mould business. Customers also helped both through cash advances and by confirming orders with local banks. Finally, the need to pool personal and family savings to finance the venture was one of the reasons for the high number of partners found in many MMs. In one case even former employers became partners of the spin-off.

As regards human resources, partners constituted the main work force, sometimes complemented by some apprentices and ex-colleagues. This guaranteed the quality of the work and labour flexibility, avoiding the need to pay high wages. And, while family-owned MM were mainly able to provide specialised services or components, MMs founded by several partners with complementary specialisations were able to start producing whole moulds. MTs naturally considered personal ties with other local MMs of key importance. These relations provided first-hand information about who could do what and how well, contributing to the identification of the most appropriate subcontractor(s) for each order received, simultaneously guaranteeing access to the firms and reducing coordination problems when several subcontractors were involved in the production of the mould.

As for the kind of competencies more specifically required to export – such as the knowledge of foreign languages and external trade techniques – these could be obtained either through the partners' former experience in sales, through specialised employees that were hired, or though learning by doing. Location within a cluster helped in a variety of ways. First MMs could start selling to local MTs and experienced MMs, which then took care of exports. Second, foreign customers were attracted to the cluster, making contacts easier. In addition, proximity enabled firms to split marketing costs and to learn from other firms. Finally, geographic concentration of firms induced the establishment of specialised institutions (namely training centres) and focused the attention of public policy makers assisting the external promotion of the cluster.

Risk Evaluation

The higher uncertainty associated with entering into foreign markets is pointed to as a powerful obstacle in the internationalisation process (Johanson and Vahlne, 1977). MMs face a relatively higher risk than MTs when selling in foreign markets. Both receive one-third of final price as a cash advance, but costs incurred are quite different. Hence it came as no surprise that interviewees underlined former relations with customers as contributing to reduce the perceived risk of entry in foreign markets. Furthermore, the presence of local suppliers and institutions in the cluster lowered the level of initial investment necessary for start-up and, along with other local firms (like MTs), provided privileged information about foreign customers' credibility, contributing to reduce the perceived risk of entry. Finally, the simple presence of other exporting MMs created through spin-offs reduced the perceptible risk.

**The Impact of Location within the Cluster on the
Personal Network of the Entrepreneur**

The role played by location within the plastic mould cluster of Marinha Grande is explored further through the analysis of the personal network of relations of the entrepreneurs. Most MMs studied were either founded by fellow workers

(16 firms) or were family-owned (eight firms). The only exception relates to a firm founded by an individual partner and an industrial group involved in the plastic and injection molding business. The high number of founding partners in several MMs founded by workers is one of their most striking characteristics: 12 firms had more than four partners and seven firms had even eight or more partners. As regards family-owned MMs all except one firm (founded by four brothers) had two partners, most frequently a couple. MTs were founded by a relatively small number of partners and can also be organised in two groups. Half of the cases studied are independent MTs that were founded by two individual partners with no connection to MMs at the date of founding. Dependent MTs have among their partners one or more MMs. The latter cases indicated the existence of cooperation among MMs, at least regarding sales.

As in several other regional clusters (Saxenian, 1990, 1991; Enright 1998), spin-offs were the dominant form of business creation, hence the large majority of partners had previously worked for at least one but often several other local MMs and in some cases for a rather extended period of time; major exceptions correspond to wives in firms owned by couples and two partners with a background in administration and finance in two different MTs.

A background in the moulding business did not mean that all of the partners from one firm worked in the same MM or that all of them knew each other previously to start up. Even though seven MMs are spin-offs from one single firm, in seven other cases a core group of partners came from one firm and other partners either came from different firms or were connected to at least one of the core partners by some kind of relation (kinship, friendship, neighbourhood, business, former acquaintances during school or military service). Also many of the firms interviewed have partners who once worked in one of the oldest mould makers of Marinha Grande and among more recently founded firms there were already spin-offs from some of the older firms included in this study. Once more the fact that partners from two different firms had once worked in the same firm did not imply they were contemporaneous. Nevertheless, certain older firms have the habit of organising events (like dinners) open to all present and ex-employees. This, coupled with the high rate of job mobility within the Marinha Grande cluster and with the fact that most employees and entrepreneurs have always lived and worked in the region, increases the probability that two people working within the cluster have either met or have common acquaintances. As a result, the local personal networks of entrepreneurs located inside a cluster tend to be large (number of people each focal actor has a direct relationship with), dense and thick (business and working relations overlapping social ones).

Working experience of MM's partners was mostly in manufacturing and in the case of firms with a large number of partners each one seemed to master a specific manufacturing operation. Partners with design or marketing experience were less commonplace: only seven MM included designers among partners and six firms partners with commercial experience. MT's entrepreneurs presented a more diversified set of competencies since almost all of them included partners with a direct experience in manufacturing along with other partner(s) with experience in design and/or sales. The only exception was a dependent MT founded by MMs. Different functional experiences of partners contribute to explain why the personal networks of business relations of MM's entrepreneurs were mainly rich of links to other local actors: employees of mould making firms they had worked in, workers of local suppliers of services or materials, workers of main local contractors (MTs and MMs) of former employers. Only a few partners from MMs included in their personal business network a significant number of relations with foreign customers. Naturally, personal networks of partners from all independent MTs and some dependent ones were simultaneously rich in relations with local firms, namely MMs, and final customers. These were mostly foreign ones since the majority of moulds produced in Portugal were exported every year.

CONCLUSIONS AND ISSUES FOR FUTURE RESEARCH

The cases of export new ventures located in Marinha Grande reveal the impact of location on personal networks of relations of entrepreneurs and, hence, on early internationalisation of start-ups. It appeared from the analysis made above that entrepreneurs located within a cluster were likely to have large, dense and thick local networks of relations. In addition several, but not all, entrepreneurs presented personal networks that were rich in ties with actors located in foreign markets and this seemed to be partly related to functions performed in past jobs, to the cluster's area of specialisation and its degree of openness.[7] Moreover, location within a cluster facilitated the establishment of relations with outside actors, namely with foreign customers either when these were visiting the cluster or abroad. Entrepreneurs with personal networks that combined ties with local and foreign actors obtained information about opportunities in foreign markets, could generally access the necessary resources and attributed a lower risk to entry into foreign markets (precisely because barriers to entry are lower and other local firms are used as role models). As a consequence, early internationalisation was facilitated.

As regards local relations, entrepreneurs located within Marinha Grande benefited from dense networks similar to those found in ethnic groups or immigrant communities (Aldrich and Zimmer, 1986). This resulted from the positive effects of proximity on the frequency of (often unplanned) face-to-face contacts, on the overlapping of business and other kinds of ties and on the average number of years of relationships. Spin-offs were frequent and during their working career entrepreneurs enlarged their local networks of relations. Since these entrepreneurs were also living in Marinha Grande, kinship, neighbourhood and other kinds of ties overlapped. As a result, even if two people living in Marinha Grande did not know each other personally, they most probably had common acquaintances that acted as brokers. Densely connected networks facilitated entrepreneurship by guaranteeing the access to a variety of local buyers (MTs and MMs) and resources necessary for the new venture (Aldrich and Zimmer, 1986). The existence of previous relations (and, hence, trust) with buyers was of key importance for start-ups owing to the relation-intensive characteristic of the mould-making business as mentioned above. Also relations among partners facilitated the start-up of integrated MMs. Within clusters support was provided both at the informal level by friends and relatives of entrepreneurs and through local specialised institutions and suppliers.

The impact of location within a cluster on the number and depth of international ties within the entrepreneur's personal network of relations has just begun to be demonstrated. First, success and critical mass naturally attracted foreign customers, suppliers and competitors. These foreign firms came for different reasons. The large number of foreign suppliers' representatives located in Marinha Grande were attracted by the significant potential local market. More recently a few foreign competitors acquired local MMs to benefit from innovation and productivity benefits commonly associated with clusters. Foreign customers have been attracted for quite a long time by the existence of a large number of competitive suppliers. Secondly, outward-oriented clusters (like Marinha Grande) include a substantial number of international competitive firms able to sell their products in foreign markets and even to invest abroad. In the mould-making business those persons in charge of sales and (to a lesser extent) engineering met foreign customers frequently and repeatedly. Meanwhile, workers in manufacturing dealt mainly with other workers from the same department, with workers performing up stream and down stream activities, as well as with employees of main contractors (MTs and MMs). Also the more export-oriented the firm, the more personal networks of its sales persons were likely to include links with foreign customers' procurement staff.

Thirdly, clusters often included specialised institutions supporting internationalisation either on their own or in liaison with national institutions. More and more clusters are drawing the attention of national policy makers. In the case of Marinha Grande, Cefamol and ICEP have been jointly supporting internationalisation efforts at the level of the firm and also at the level of the cluster. Finally, some MMs took active steps to establish their first contacts with foreign customers in outside markets. But even these proactive firms recognized themselves as having benefited from role models present in the cluster and from some minimal institutional support. To sum up, several factors contribute to increasing international contacts in personal networks: (a) location in an outward-oriented cluster; (b) a main area of specialisation which is relations-intensive (plastic moulds, for example); (c) the entrepreneurs having previously performed boundary-spanning activities; (d) outward-oriented firms operating in the cluster.

This does not mean that all new ventures within an outward-oriented cluster will be born international. Location within a cluster does not automatically lead to internationalisation. The fine division of labour characteristic of most clusters favours the emergence of specialised new ventures aiming primarily at supplying other local firms. Only those firms selling moulds are likely to get the full benefit from international contacts and, thus, to internationalise earlier.

This study has potential implications for entrepreneurs, policy makers and existing theories. Entrepreneurs located within a cluster may well take advantage of a clear understanding of their networks of personal relations and from an active management of these relations. As was shown above, when formulating internationalisation strategies entrepreneurs frequently exploited their network of personal relations to gain access to opportunities in foreign markets at a lower cost, simultaneously limiting the risk generally involved in international transactions. Public support for internationalisation and cooperation may be more effective if it takes into account the specificities of networks of relations operating within and across clusters. For example, evidence presented above pointed out that inward foreign direct investment appears to facilitate the export development process of a firm. This may suggests the need for an effective articulation between foreign investment and external trade policies. Incentives to cooperation at the local level should be aware of the benefits associated with a certain degree of diversity and redundant ties within networks of relations. This study also intends to be a contribution to filling the gap in empirical research on the role of location within clusters and the internationalisation process. By bringing together concepts from international business, cluster and network theories, it aims at a better understanding of the process of INVs.

There are several aspects that still need further investigation. The relationship between local and international ties is far from being fully understood. If there are cases in which the link between a MM and a foreign customer was established through a reference from a local firm, in other cases a long-lasting relation between a MM and a local MT made the former unavailable to accept direct orders from certain foreign customers or, alternatively, reduced business with local traders. Trade-offs between local and international relations need to be examined. Another issue that has still to be investigated corresponds to the consequence of clusters both for the balance of 'strong' and 'weak' ties within the personal networks of relations and for the diversity of networks (Granovetter, 1973; Burt, 1992). A regional cluster is expected to raise the salience of group boundaries and identity, thus contributing to the emergence of strong ties (Aldrich and Zimmer, 1986). Nevertheless, the net effect of strong ties on entrepreneurship may be difficult to predict. On the one hand, strong ties carry with them a history of past dealings in or out of a business setting that can form a basis for trust. On the other hand, strong ties are less effective than weak ties as regards access to business information and to potential customers (ibid.). Weak ties corresponding to non-redundant contacts may constitute key sources of information about persons and firms located outside the cluster. An obvious example in the case of Marinha Grande is the relation between some entrepreneurs and firms with highly export-oriented local trading firms that are regarded as an important and constant source of new customers. The fact that MTs are considered customers and/or competitors by different local MMs is something that has to be further investigated. Finally, the role of local specialised institutions deserves a more detailed study. How do these institutions contribute to international and local relations? How can they improve this contribution?

Notes

1. I thank Alberto Castro and Gianni Lorenzoni for suggestions. Financial support from 'Sub-Programa Ciência e Tecnologia do 2º Quadro Comunitário de Apoio' is acknowledged.
2. Defined by McDougall and Oviatt (1994) as 'a business organization that, from inception seeks to derive significant competitive advantage from the use of resources and the sale of outputs in multiple countries'.
3. Defined by (Oviatt and McDougall, 1997: 93) as 'entrepreneurial start-ups ... located in subnational geographic clusters or networks'; two other types of INVs were named 'dependent' and 'independent'.
4. The Marinha Grande area corresponds to the place where moulds for plastic injection were first produced in Portugal in 1946. It is still the location of at least half of all Portuguese mould makers. The plastic mould cluster of Marinha Grande was identified within the project Building the Competitive Advantage of Portugal coordinated by M. Porter (Monitor Company, 1994). Barbosa de Melo (1995) identified a Marshallian industrial district in the area of Marinha Grande.
5. A Portuguese MT had a customer in the US whose employee in charge of acquisitions had a brother who owned a mould injection firm in the UK. Through reference of the former, the latter became the first European customer of the MT and has recommended the MT to several other customers in the UK.
6. A recently established firm estimated the minimal initial investment in the equipment necessary to make a mould to be between 150 000 and 200 000 Euros. Other firms confirmed these values.
7. External trade flows and foreign direct investment stocks eventually complemented by immigration and emigration movements measure the degree of openness of the cluster.

Appendix

Table 3A.1   Main reasons for start-up

Mould-makers	Founded	Partners	Main reasons for start-up
Somema	1958	5 I	demand for moulds + experience in Mm
Irmãos Gomes	1966	4 I	experience in Mm
Molde Matos	1968	2 I	experience in Mm
Novateca	1968	8 I	experience in Mm + profitability of Mm/ new entrants
Geco	1969/75	1 C	experience in Mm + employer in the UK placed order
Planimolde	1978	9 I	experience in Mm + succession problems in previous job
Inpomoldes	1979	3 I	experience in Mm + aim at a better future
Famplac	1980	10 I	experience in Mm + aim at better future/others 'made it'
M. Catarino	1981	2 I	experience in Mm + local demand/MT
Rosagui	1982	1 C	experience in Mm + ambition
Famolde	1984	4 I	experience in Mm + wish to have own firm
Plafam	1984	9 I	experience in Mm + aim at a better future
Socimoplás	1984	7 I	experience in Mm
Virmolde	1984	8 I	experience in Mm + ambition/will to own something

Table 3A.1 (*Continued*)

Mould-makers	Founded	Partners	Main reasons for start-up
Efemoldes	1985	7 I	experience in Mm + aim at a better future + demand
Celmex	1986	5 I	experience in Mm
Socém	1986	5 I	own views of business (different from former employer)
I.T.M.	1987	8 I	experience in Mm
Moldegama	1987	11 I	experience in Mm + demand surplus
Ribermolde	1987	1 C	former employer had shut down
LN Moldes	1988	1 C	partner had experience in Mm + will to win/ambition
UPM	1988	2 I	experience in Mm + acquisition of former employer
RAPIDTOOL	1993	1 C	partner had experience in Mm + his trading firm closed
MGM	1996	1 I + F	partner had experience in Mm + invitation to start-up
Fozmoldes	1996	2 I	experience in Mm + will to work for themselves
Mould-traders			
Tecmolde	1968	2 I	foreign customer of ex-employer hired Mr.S. to supervise acquisitions and then referred Mr S. to other foreign customers, encouraging establishment of MT
SETSA	1975	2 I	demand for moulds made in Portugal crashed after April Revolution; partners quitted jobs and leverage on contacts with foreign customers to secure orders
Mouldexport	1983	4 F	four MM joined efforts to achieve the size necessary to negotiate with procurement units of ex-USSR
Europlaste	1985	F + 3 I	an American agent of a firm in Marinha Grande had excess demand + direct subcontracting by the MM was considered difficult so MT was established with agent.
Cemo	1986	3 F + 1 I	three MM wanted to develop the commercial function + split the cost of entry into foreign markets + achieve the size necessary to answer large orders.
Deltamolde	1987	2 I	former jobs did not fulfil the ambitions of partners + complementary skills: Mm/drawing and finance
Helomoldes	1991	F	commercial department of a local MM that had excess demand and decided to improve subcontracting
F.R.CAD	1994	2 I	former foreign customer of drawing started to place orders for moulds and the firm developed into a MT

Notes:
I = individuals; C = couple; F = firms; Mm = mould making.

Table 3A.2   Size and export intensity in 1998

	Workers	Exports per cent
Mould-makers		
Somema	75	100
Irmãos Gomes	26	80
Molde Matos	100	90
Novateca	38	65
Geco	250*	100
Planimolde	75	95
Inpomoldes	58	100
Famplac	50	90
M. Catarino	30	80
Rosagui	10	98
Famolde	60	100
Plafam	30	70
Socimoplás	37	60
Virmolde	24	100
Efemoldes	35	75
Celmex	25	100
Socém	35	93
I.T.M.	40	70
Moldegama	58	95
Ribermolde	35	95
LN Moldes	50	95
UPM	35	90
RAPIDTOOL	17	100
MGM	42	90
Fozmoldes	11	n.a.
Mould-traders	*Workers*	*Exports(%)*
Tecmolde	36	100
SETSA	50	95
Mouldexport	7	100
Europlaste	10	95
Cemo	3	100
Deltamolde	12	100
Helomoldes	6	100
F.R.CAD	4	100

Notes:
* group of firms.

Source: *www.cefamol.pt/directorio* and author.

4 The Internationalisation of SMEs: Alternative Hypotheses and Empirical Survey

Antonella Zucchella

INTRODUCTION

This study aims at investigating the existence of alternative approaches to the internationalisation of SMEs, in the perspective of the small firm as an important and not a marginal player in world markets. Traditionally, the international growth of SMEs has been depicted in literature as a gradual and sequential process, conditioned in its extension and intensity by organisational (management, expertise, and so on) and financial (capital rationing due to small size) constraints. The predominance of exports in SMEs as a means of internationalisation and their preference for 'near' markets are demonstrated by national statistics on foreign trade, that seem to confirm the above-mentioned perspective. But the available statistics on foreign trade do not evidence the existence of different strategic groupings in relation to the intensity of internationalisation, as measured by the export/sales ratio, and in relation to its width, as measured by number of countries reached by the various strategic groupings.

For these reasons an empirical survey on a sample of Italian firms has been conducted in order to provide an answer to two basic questions. First, is export performance correlated to the size or the age of the firm; that is, do export intensity and width follow the sequential path predicted by theory? Second, is it possible to identify and describe alternative approaches to small firms' internationalisation?

LITERATURE REVIEW

The literature on internationalisation processes of firms has frequently been based on the observation of large firms' behaviour, while SMEs have been depicted as an "evolving" species, destined either to fail or to follow the growth path and international behaviour of large firms. In the recent decades the largest firms began a push toward internationalisation that affected both sales and production, as well as the purchase of products, materials, semi-finished goods, services and capital.

In a context of world markets still separated by important natural barriers (the nature of demand, distribution systems and so on) and artificial ones (duties, quotas, technical regulations) the model of the multinational firm has relied on diversity and market lag (also in temporal terms) by creating commercial and productive branches in the various countries (Bartlett and Ghoshal, 1989; Buckley and Casson, 1976; Dunning, 1993a; Hood and Young, 1979; Prahalad and Doz, 1987; Rugman and Verbecke, 1998; Vernon, 1991) and through policies of product adaptation to local specificities (Cateora, 1993; Jain, 1989; Martenson, 1987; Porter, 1986; Walters, 1986; Whitelock, 1987; Whitelock and Pimblett, 1997). At the same time the multinational has fully exploited the possibility of centralising those activities that had already taken on a global structure, such as finance (Lessard, 1986).

Beginning in the second half of the 1980s, a growing number of sectors has seen the gradual dismantling of many natural and artificial barriers, along with a substantial elimination of the market lag (Levitt, 1983; Dunning, 1993b), which has given the large firms the chance to extend the global organisational approach to a large range of functions (Bartlett and Ghoshal, 1989; Ohmae, 1989; Porter, 1986).

For their part, small firms have continued to show in the 1990s a strong attitude to be present and competitive in foreign markets, with an approach primarily based on exports. This internationalisation process has often been defined as "asymmetrical", since along with a strong international commitment for the commercial function there exists a "domestic" organisation of the remaining activities (Depperu, 1993). This "asymmetrical" view has often led to the belief that such an international strategy is incomplete; asymmetry implicitly holds that, owing to the presence of financial and managerial–organisational constraints (Moini, 1997), the choices of the smaller firms have been sub-optimal with respect to the one best way represented by the model of the large firm.

The international literature has often taken this view, based on the idea that the small exporting firm represents the first step toward more intensive forms of internationalisation, which in turn accompany a parallel growth in the size of the firm, from non-equity agreements to joint ventures and direct foreign investment (Bilkey and Tesar, 1977; Cavusgil, 1980; Cavusgil *et al.*, 1979; Cavusgil *et al.*, 1987; Czinkota and Tesar, 1982; Miesenbock, 1988; Johanson and Vahlne, 1977).

The hypothesis underlying this conventional view of internationalisation is that of the classical growth paradigm, which sees the small firm as a transitory model of corporate organisation, by nature destined to grow or to be unsuccessful. The continental-European literature, Italian in particular, has advanced a view of the small firm as an interpreter of the economic space *alternative* to the large firm, capable of continuing over time in its original structure by exploiting in the best possible way the advantages it has with regard to strategic and organisational flexibility and entrepreneurial commitment (Golinelli, 1992; Grandinetti and Rullani, 1992; Mele, 1986; Pepe, 1984; Usai, 1981; Velo, 1997). Also international literature has devoted growing attention to this topic, evidencing the capability of small firms to produce original approaches, that boosted their international competitiveness, as the case of industrial districts suggests (Porter, 1990; Casson, 1997).

In this framework, some studies have been devoted to the emerging case of niche firms that – even though small in size – appeared to be leaders in their market segment on a global scale (Bonaccorsi, 1992; Calof, 1994; Gomes-Casseres, 1997; Kohn, 1997; Malaksedh and Nahavandi, 1985; Simon, 1996). These firms represent a challenge to evolutionary theories on small firms' international growth, as this chapter tries to demonstrate.

THE INTERNATIONALISATION OF SMEs:
RESEARCH HYPOTHESES

For a number of SMEs it is likely that a sort of evolutionary approach to world markets has been explicitly or implicitly adopted. Such firms have started from sales concentrated in the domestic market and only later on they have progressively exploited the opportunities of foreign markets. The geographic range of these firms is limited to "near" markets, in order to reduce barriers to entry and transaction costs both of technical (transport costs, different regulations) and cultural nature.

Other firms seem to have adopted a completely different approach: their geographic range is wide, their export/sales ratio is very high, but this is not the result of a gradual growth and of a long history started from the domestic business. In these firms the global push started together with their business idea and the domestic market plays a minor role for their competitive positioning.

On the basis of these considerations it is possible to hold that there are two main strategies explaining the behaviour of smaller firms: (a) *the proximity approach*, which leads the firm to expand into the nearest markets from a cultural-geographical point of view, with a gradual and sequential process of international learning; (b) *the global approach*, which leads the firm to segment horizontally the world market, seen as a single entity, aiming at a restricted group of clients, wherever they may be located, with a supply of homogeneous products/services (global niche strategy) and adopting a serial-type internationalisation process.

In the first instance the firm selects markets on the basis of the so-called 'psychic distance' (Johansson and Vahlne, 1977), favouring the better-known contexts (Liesch and Knight, 1999), as these are culturally closer and thus entail only limited local adaptations of the product. This strategic option is coherent with an exporting strategy, which sees the organisational hub of the firm remaining in the home country (Brooks and Rosson, 1987; Reid, 1982). In the past this organisational hub tended to coincide with the productive one. Today in many productions the need to control labour costs leads to the growing spread of production delocalisation. Regarding product distribution, collaboration agreements with local partners allow for a more effective learning of the specific aspects of foreign markets, making it possible to adapt the product to different situations, even though, as we have already mentioned, this adaptation process is somewhat limited due to the choice of the proximity model.

It is thus possible to develop a new model of the *small international firm, as the organising hub of international supply and selling processes*, by means of its own units (production plants, sales networks) and alliance systems with other firms. To the extent there exists a learning process regarding cooperation experiences among the firms, exploiting strategic alliances can ensure a flexible and effective road to the goal of a presence in a growing number of markets which are increasingly more 'distant'. In the global approach the firm completely overcomes the psychic distance problem and the difficulty of dealing with the diversity of foreign markets through an alternative and original view of the world market. This represents an *alternative approach* since, rather than proceeding by clusters of 'similar' countries, from which the market segment to be reached is then determined, this view carries out a horizontal segmentation of the world market and seeks to satisfy a specific need that arises in all different parts of the world (Takeuchi and Porter, 1986). It is an *original approach*, since it leads to a highly creative process for determining the group of potential customers, which are not pre-constructed segments from which to choose but groups originating from the firms' product/service choice (creative segmentation). The uniqueness of a firm's supply is coherent with the decision to export from the firms home country, with very limited, if any, forms of production delocalisation, since the exclusive know-how behind the product leads to a coincidence between the organisational and productive hubs of the firm. In fact, uniqueness is often the result of business competencies and creativity joined together with 'territorial competencies' (specialized workforce, services). If we consider the case of many small Italian firms that have a world leadership in their niches, we discover that their competitive positioning is the result both of firm-specific and of local system-specific factors (firm embeddedness).

Moreover, the uniqueness of supply shifts the competitive strategy onto nonprice elements, making it inopportune to decide to produce in low labour-cost countries as well as in outlet markets in order to reduce transport costs. Finally, creativity in the vision of world markets and uniqueness of supply lead to creating a favourable competitive environment for the firm, especially the small one, since at the same time there is: (a) a strong reduction in the degree of complexity of international markets, in the sense of knowledge and control of the segment created; (b) a strong reduction in the degree of complexity in the competitive environment, in the sense of determining a context dominated by non-price logic and highly circumscribed as well in terms of the number of actual and potential competitors, where a small firm can aspire to a market leadership role; and (c) a strong reduction in the degree of organisational complexity, since, by means of a centralised organisational structure, the firm operates on a global scale.[1]

The global niche firm represents a strategic model that makes us rethink the idea of company size, as well as go beyond a 'conventional' view of the small firm and its path towards international growth. The emergence of this new topic of study sees in recent years a gradual convergence of interests and views between the continental European and Anglo-Saxon literature, just as in the

1980s when there was a similar convergence on the topics of inter-firm cooperation, networks and local systems of small firms.[2]

In the global model the reinterpretation of the world context as a creative space and advantageous to the small firm does not imply, however, the existence of a stable niche protected from competition. The dynamism of markets, the transversality of new technologies and the recently acquired ability of large firms to respond with a flexible strategy and to penetrate the market at the niche level (also by acquiring small firms) has created a continual challenge for small enterprises.

RESEARCH DESIGN

National and regional statistics on foreign trade provide a general view of exports either by industry or by destination. Such figures have a number of important limitations:

- the perspective by destination evidences the relevant weight of the nearest and biggest markets, but does not permit to identify beyond the still dominant group of firms adopting the proximity approach, the emergence of alternative strategic behaviours, like the global approach;
- the perspective by industry does not make it possible to evidence the important reality of niche firms, since they couple a focus on a restricted group of customers with a highly specialised product offer, so that it is difficult to include them in some of the traditional industry classifications;
- the perspective by trade flows does not provide any information about international partnerships and the various forms of cooperation among firms; this gap is not filled either by statistics on FDI. Because of this potentially wide and unknown 'grey' area, it is impossible to quantify the diffusion of inter-firms agreements to approach foreign markets, that represent the basis for an innovative interpretation of the two strategic approaches mentioned before, and appears to be particularly promising as a possible evolution of the proximity approach.

The present research aims at filling these gaps, demonstrating the existence both of the proximity and of the global approach in SMEs, and quantifying the diffusion of inter-firm agreements to approach foreign markets.

The research design is structured in three stages. First there is an empirical survey on a sample of Italian SMEs, in order to test the working hypotheses described using a general data set, representative of the variety of small firms. For this reason 200 Italian SMEs have been sampled[3] and a correlation analysis among exports, sales and number of employees (measures of size) and age has been carried out. Only quantitative data have been processed (sales, number of employees, age, percentage of exports to sales), extracted from the Italian Chambers of Commerce data base. Correlation analysis aims at verifying the validity of the traditional belief that size and age of the firm influence (that is, are statistically correlated to) export performance. If no correlation is found this means that alternative hypotheses regarding the degree of internationalisation of SMEs can be formulated, according to the two main approaches previously presented.

The second stage of the research aims at identifying more accurately the product/market strategy of exporting SMEs, in order to understand the features of the alternative strategic models identified. This analysis concerned a business context, that of the province of Varese, where small and medium-sized firms predominate; significant here is the degree of international openness, understood as the share of sales revenue represented by exports.

This second statistical survey uses a sample of small enterprises belonging to a uniform territorial and industrial context, in order to bring out possible alternative approaches to the international strategy of small firms, thereby minimising the 'interferences' resulting from the differences in the industrial and territorial environments. The need to focus on province-based analysis is confirmed by some international studies (Brooks and Rosson, 1982). The sample is represented by 153 small- and medium-sized industrial firms located in the province of Varese, extracted from the data base of exporting firms of the local Association of Small and Medium Sized Enterprises (API). The sample reflects the local distribution of manufacturing SMEs; the firms are distributed by size as follows: small enterprises (up to 49 employees, according to EU parameters) make up 89 per cent of the total, while medium sized ones (from 50 to 249 employees) the remaining 11 per cent. In terms of sectors, mechanical firms represent 60 per cent of the total, plastic and rubber 19 per cent, clothing-textile firms 9 per cent, while the remaining enterprises are distributed over various manufacturing sectors. In this second stage the methodology is based on the distribution of questionnaires to the firms in order to collect data, both quantitative (export, sales, employees, age) and qualitative (products, competitors, competitive positioning, product positioning, marketing mix adopted, foreign markets served) on the export activity of firms. This analysis is aimed at defining more accurately the existence and features of alternative strategic groupings as far as export strategy is concerned.

The third stage comprises semi-structured interviews for deep niche firms, providing an insight on competitive forces and business policies for such enterprises. Deep niche firms are characterised by a small scale, very high export/sales ratios and a very wide range of countries reached. The interviews have made it possible to outline their product/market segment strategy, that is the key variable explaining their global commitment.

RESEARCH FINDINGS

Table 4.1 refers to the first test, regarding 200 Italian SMEs, and shows the correlation matrix obtained. According to this correlation analysis, export performance does not depend on the size of the firm, expressed either by revenues or by number of employees, and it does not seem to be influenced by the age of firms, thus denying the 'experience effect' on international growth. In fact, the level of

Table 4.1 Matrix of correlation between exports
and size–age parameters (200 Italian firms)

	Exports
Exports	100%
Revenues	10.944%
No. of employees	16.411%
Age	3.094%

Table 4.2 Matrix of correlation between exports and
sales revenue (153 firms in the province of Varese)

	Exports
Exports	100%
Revenues	20.499%
Age	7.526%

correlation between exports and age is the lowest (3.094 per cent), but also the correlation figures between exports and size measures (revenues and employees) appear low (10.944 per cent and 16.411 per cent, respectively) and cannot qualify the existence of variables capable of influencing each other significantly.

In conclusion, the *export commitment does not respond to size constraints*: smallest firms are not necessarily confined to local markets owing to lack of financial and managerial resources or to lack of expertise.

Such figures should not lead to the search of an alternative model, which is capable of explaining SMEs' internationalisation. The traditional evolutionary model may keep on working for a number of small firms, but for others alternative approaches have to be found. According to the above described working hypothesis, the analysis of the product/market policy of the firm may constitute a good perspective in order to identify 'strategic clusters' of SMEs according to their international behaviour.

The second survey carried out on the province of Varese confirms also, for this local sample of 153 exporting SMEs, that size and age are not correlated to their degree of internationalisation (Table 4.2).

In fact, the sample includes very small firms that export nearly all their sales revenue and larger firms (even though below 250 employees) which look almost exclusively to the home market. This preliminary check by means of correlation analysis has enabled us to confirm the guiding working hypothesis, which states that it is the choice between the two models of reference that determines the degree of international opening and not the size of the enterprise.

What then is the variable that explains why and how much firms export? The result of questionnaires analysis reveals the product as the key element; or better, the combination of product/market segment served. In fact, according to the

Table 4.3   The degree of internationalisation of the 153 enterprises surveyed (by groupings of export to sales ratios)

Exports/sales revenue	% of enterprises
0–10%	31.1
10–20	14.2
20–50	7.4
60–80	10.8
80–90	5.4
90–100	5.5

figures showed in Table 4.3, firms that have the highest export/sales ratios are typically global niche firms, while the others seem to have adopted the proximity approach.

The Global Niche Firm

The presence of tiny and small firms with a considerable exporting vocation (in some cases almost encompassing the whole of sales revenue) is explained by the type of production, which reveals itself to be the key vehicle for internationalisation.

In particular, the most internationalised enterprises undertake niche activities; that is, they produce a single product (or only a few products) aimed at a restricted segment of customers. These are firms influenced by the natural limits of domestic demand that are looking for foreign outlets; often, however, it is the highly specialised product itself that attracts foreign customers, giving rise to the creative segmentation described above. Niche production shows a high price–quality ratio: together with the high product specialisation and an often high technological and innovative content there is the careful attention to cost control.

The study conducted through questionnaires clearly shows that product quality and differentiation must combine with a competitive price in order to support the competition from international markets, which is intense even at the niche level with a reduced number of direct competitors. These observations have been further examined and confirmed for enterprises with very high sales revenue from abroad, above 80 per cent. The latter, while not large in number (11 per cent of the total, according to Table 4.3), represent the benchmark for the other firms that have made international growth their dominant strategy.[4] For this reason these enterprises have undergone a further examination by means of interviews, in order to grasp, in addition to quantitative data, the strategic direction of the firm.

These enterprises have not gradually broadened their international experience. In fact, it is surprising to note that nearly two-thirds of these firms have directed almost all of their sales at foreign markets from the beginning of their activity. This statistic confirms the hypothesis that niche firms adopt a serial and not a sequential/gradual approach to foreign markets.

Emblematic here is the fact that these firms do not mention among the reasons for their internationalisation the excessive competition on the home market: often for niche productions the competition is restricted to a reduced number of firms at the world level. More than 60 per cent of those interviewed measure themselves against competitors from the main industrialised countries, proving the fact that competition in niches is not from developing countries but involves a limited number of firms usually spread throughout developed countries.

We can assume that the strong international bent thus depends, not only on the restricted market niche served, but also on the need to respond in a timely and effective way to a numerically restricted competition which is nevertheless well-tested in terms of quality and technology.

A deeper comprehension of the global strategy approach – as outlined earlier in this section – requires understanding the product characteristics of these firms, and above all whether they undergo local adaptations in reaching the various markets. Of these 'strong exporters', 93 per cent do not introduce any modification in the product for foreign markets: we are thus witnessing a true global product, maintaining the same features in the various countries, and confirming the previously-formulated hypothesis regarding the global model.

The Proximity Approach

The figures showing the geographic range of activity of SMEs help us in determining the importance of the proximity approach in SMEs. The adoption of such an approach is demonstrated by the high number of firms with a limited exporting activity (Table 4.3). For these firms the domestic market still represents the core, and questionnaires reveal that their exports are primarily addressed to low-distance countries, both in geographic and psychic terms. Their segmentation of international markets aims at isolating an homogeneous group of countries (macro-segmentation) to be reached minimising product adaptation, transport costs and cultural distance.

The proximity approach – in its consequences for the geographic range of activity of the firm – is demonstrated by the prevalence of European markets in the exporting strategy. The European Union is a target export market for 80 per cent of the firms interviewed, independent of company size. This certainly depends on the geographical proximity to Italy, but above all on a certain cultural homogeneity that makes the needs and expectations of consumers similar, thus allowing the firms to avoid or limit the product adaptations needed for exporting activity.

The growing economic, monetary and regulatory integration will soon turn the European Union into a home market. Within this area we can identify two positions that stand out: France (destination country for 58 per cent of enterprises exporting to Europe) and Germany (49 per cent), which constitute for these firms the so-called 'core Europe'. Outside the EU, 32 per cent of firms concentrate on other West European countries, among them Malta, Norway and Switzerland.

Eastern Europe represents the centre of interest for 13 per cent of the enterprises as well as a pool of consumers for the near future, thanks to the gradual movement of some countries towards the EU. The most intensive commercial ties are in Hungary, the Czech Republic and Poland.

On the whole, Europe in its wider sense represents the main exporting area for the enterprises. The changes under way in the EU market, with the shift to the single currency and the prospects for the growing participation of the other European countries as well in the economic and monetary union, are thus destined to have strong repercussions on the enterprises studied.

The analysis of the geographic range of action reveals that the most diffuse strategic model is the proximity one, which leads firms to choose contexts characterised by a short psychic distance, often coinciding with markets that are geographically close. The advanced process of European integration results in the proximity approach tending to translate in the medium term into the home market approach, which is destined to reach a continental scale (Lannon, 1988; Vandermerve, 1989).

Outside Europe, North America (19 per cent) stands out among the present outlet areas coming out of the survey. This statistic should make us think, because – if we add it to the statistics regarding exports to European countries – it indicates a greater interest of these firms in developed markets than in developing ones. The North American market, the US in particular (which accounts for three-quarters of exports from these firms to North America), represents a commercial area which is rich in opportunities. This is due to its size, wealth and the considerable growth it has undergone in recent years, compared with repeated market crises in the developing markets. Nevertheless it is a difficult market to penetrate because of the existence not only of some artificial trade barriers (duties, quotas, technical regulations) but also of important natural barriers represented by the distribution system, the sophistication of demand, and in general the complexity of the market itself.

The distribution of exports by market shows less importance and similar weight for the Far East (11 per cent), the Middle East and Latin America (both with a 10 per cent share) and Africa (9 per cent).

In conclusion, small and medium-sized enterprises do not choose their target markets on the basis of their own size. The choice is once again dependent on the product/market segment strategy. The common feature of different international policies is represented by the need of avoiding excessive adaptations of the product to the different markets: this may be done either by means of the global niche approach or by means of the proximity one.

The internationalisation of the SME: Solitary Exporter or Network Builder?

The high degree of competition among enterprises, due to the growing globalisation and integration of markets, means that firms of any size must deal with competitors from all countries. The greater complexity that firms have to deal with makes it necessary to adopt an international approach that goes beyond simple exporting.

Agreements with foreign firms or direct investments in other market makes for more effective and deeply-rooted penetration, which aims not only at reducing the production or marketing costs of the product but also at a better understanding of the market the firm intends to enter with its products. Even where alliances or direct investment produce an increase in costs with respect to traditional exports, these could be more than compensated for by middle-term advantages in the form of higher shares of sales revenue from foreign markets and better control of international competitive pressures.

The positioning in niche markets leads many small firms not to seek forms of internationalisation which are different from simple exporting activity, since the latter turns out to be the best choice with respect to the firm's product/market strategy, and not necessarily for reasons connected with a lack of resources and capabilities. Nevertheless, we can hypothesise forms of cooperation and direct investment for niche firms, at least in terms of product distribution, in order to increase the chances of penetrating the world's main markets and of dealing better with the competition at the international level.

The case is different for the other firms: these seem to have more need for more intense forms of internationalisation of the value chain. It thus seemed appropriate to examine the sample in terms of forms of internationalisation, among which cooperation agreements, joint ventures and direct foreign investment in particular (See Table 4.4).

To better understand the significance of the data obtained we must distinguish between the non-equity forms of internationalisation and the equity forms. The former, which include cooperation agreements and contractual joint ventures, allow two or more firms of different nationalities to pursue common objectives and to take advantage of synergies, thanks to a flexible and moderately binding relationship. The sample revealed that 12.6 per cent of the cases involved an absolutely balanced division between commercial and production agreements. This percentage is rather low, even if in line with that emerging from studies carried out at the national level.

From this further study we deduced that 63 per cent of the commercial cooperation agreements involve foreign agents, distributors or trading companies,

Table 4.4 Beyond exports: equity and non-equity international agreements and FDI in 153 SMEs

Non-equity agreements (NEA)	12.6%
commercial NEA	6.1%
productive NEA	6.5%
Equity agreements (joint ventures)	3.1%
FDI	3.1%

25 per cent exclusive retailers, and the remaining part channels to which the foreign partner has access. Among the main reasons that have moved firms to stipulate an international agreement there is above all (75 per cent of the cases) the desire to overcome difficulties in the distribution of products in foreign countries. In the remaining cases, the determining factor is the chance to exploit the expertise of the partner in the markets analysed, which underscores the critical importance of the choice of partner.

We found several reasons for production agreements, which consist in delegating the carrying out of one or more phases of the manufacturing process: the reduction of manufacturing costs through collaboration with firms in countries with low labour costs, the widening of the firm's range of suppliers through production complementarity with the partner, and the exploitation of know-how not possessed by the firm and which is difficult to imitate.

Turning now to equity forms of internationalisation, business joint ventures are engaged in by 3.15 per cent of the sample; the same percentage was found for direct foreign investments. These figures reveal that for the absolute majority of SMEs going international is still largely a sole venture and that cooperative and networks arrangements are not so widespread, particularly in their equity forms.

As for the level of exports and the geographic range of activity, a further analysis by means of interviews has revealed that in the world of SMEs, there is a cluster of firms that is following a gradual step-by-step approach to international growth, while other firms – even with a global range of activity – do not utilise such forms of internationalisation simply because they are not coherent with the strategic option of the firms, and not due to financial or managerial constraints. Finally, other firms make FDI without previous experience of cooperative agreements or joint ventures.

CONCLUSIONS

The analysis of the internationalisation strategies of small enterprises allows us to understand the great diversities that are emerging within a world that until now has been treated in a substantially homogeneous way.

The study of the relationship between small enterprises and international markets requires today a more complex approach than those commonly adopted, in the light of a strong segmentation within the world of SMEs, apparently linked to the product/market option. The research conducted is not necessarily exhaustive of all the possible approaches and strategic options adopted by SMEs. The findings of this study refer to a sample of Italian firms that do not necessarily reflect all the possible approaches to the international growth of SMEs. It is important to point out that in the Italian environment small-scale firms are particularly rooted and they have frequently produced original phenomena, as the experience of industrial districts suggests.

The main objective of this research has been that of demonstrating that confining the internationalisation of SMEs in one given model does not reflect the actual differentiation in small firms' strategic behaviour. Moreover, the idea was to demonstrate that SMEs are not necessarily minor players in international markets, owing to the ability demonstrated by a number of small firms to reinvent their market space and positioning, becoming market leaders in tiny global niches. Other firms, and they still remain the majority, have contrasted the complexity of international markets with the traditional proximity approach.

In this scenario small niche enterprises have been able to anticipate a strategic model that is effective and coherent with the geographical expansion and the growing complexity of international markets. By concentrating resources on a limited product-market combination and developing exclusive competencies, these enterprises have projected themselves onto a global scene through the supply of a given product/service to a restricted segment of the international market. These enterprises have shown that they have overcome a country-by-country approach that leads the firm to gradually move towards foreign markets, starting from markets which are closer and more similar and then gradually widening their range of activity. Their international strategy leads to a segmental approach no matter where the customer is located, and permits a rapid and contemporaneous penetration of world markets in relation to the group of clients chosen. Within the segment, the small firm can be one of the market leaders: firm size and market share are no longer necessarily correlated variables when the competition moves from mass markets to niche markets.

This strategic model poses questions both to managers and to academics. For managers and entrepreneurs, the global approach is an example of effective and innovative international strategy, but – at the same time – it may involve some shortcomings. The most important of these concerns the technological and market risk inherent to the choice of the niche strategy. For academics, the niche firm raises the problem of a different perspective for two core questions in economic analysis: the concept of size of the enterprise and the concept of industry.

In fact, *a similar strategic choice revolutionises both the concept of sector – which in fact tends to break up into a myriad of niches – and that of the size of the enterprise, which from an absolute and objective parameter becomes relative and subjective*, thereby creating new challenges for economic analysis. The latter problem is also raised by approaches which are alternative to that of the niche strategy.

In fact, alongside the model of the solitary international niche enterprise, that of the small firm engaged in international relations will come to the fore, even though the research revealed that this strategy is not so widespread as yet. This model gives such enterprises the advantage of the large enterprise in terms of critical assets and the global reach of the value chain, while preserving the identity and attributes of the small firm. The agreements between firms regard not only the production of some simple components, but more and more involve advanced outsourcing processes, through which the firm obtains the essential know-how for a global competitive advantage.

It is interesting to note that even the large firms, particularly from the 1980s, began processes of deverticalisation and decentralisation inside their organisations, and created networks of alliances with other firms in order to gain the organisational and strategic flexibility of the small firm and to focus internal resources and competences on core activities (Buckley and Casson, 1998).

From the two cases of international strategy mentioned above emerges, in short, the capacity of the small firm to become 'large', by preserving its strategic–organisational flexibility and customer orientation, to which corresponds a sort of rush by the large firm to become 'small', flexible and customer-oriented.

The creation of the European market and a growing global interdependence have not led to the assertion of the traditional model of the large firm as the one best way to internationalisation. On the contrary, the spread of the horizon of reference has led the small firm to have a better understanding of its limits, but also to choose from a number of alternative options the one which best suits the characteristics and potential of the firm.

Notes

1. The centralised hub concept (Bartlett and Ghoshal, 1992) has been proposed as the organisational model of the global enterprise, and typically considered for the large firm. In the case of the small firm , the recurring centralisation of the main functions, beginning with production, has instead often been indicated as an obstacle to achieving an international presence.
2. See, for example, Porter (1990) and Casson (1997) on Italian districts and their small enterprises, and the authors cited at the end of the literature review, that wrote about niche firms.
3. The concept of SMEs adopted is that of the European Union, primarily based on the number of employees (up to 49 for small firms and from 50 to 249 for medium ones).
4. In the second research, data were collected through questionnaires, followed by interviews to those firms that demonstrated the highest internationalisation standards. Note that these enterprises, which make up 11 per cent of the total, qualify as niche firms, but do not exhaust this category of firm, since in firms with a medium to high level of export revenues we can find more than a few cases of niche strategy. We decided to isolate the former group (11 per cent) in order to conduct interviews with firms that demonstrated the clearest and most advanced implementation of the global approach.

5 International Start-ups, a Paradigm Shift for the 21st Century: Two Illustrative Cases Spanning the Atlantic

Jeffrey E. Johnson

INTRODUCTION

Traditional models depict the small firm internationalisation process as being incremental in nature, whereby the firm commences with a domestic business orientation and gradually internationalises either as experiential and market knowledge accumulates (Johanson and Wiedersheim-Paul, 1975; Johanson and Vahlne, 1977) or through a series of distinct stages (Bilkey and Tesar, 1977; Cavusgil, 1980; Reid, 1981; Czinkota, 1982). However, a myriad of empirical studies focusing on the operational dimension of these internationalisation process models has found little or no support for their underlying incremental internationalisation principle (for example, Turnbull, 1987; Sullivan and Bauerschmidt, 1990; Bell, 1995; Petersen and Pedersen, 1997). Moreover, both the OECD (1997) and a host of researchers (Litvak, 1990; McDougall *et al.*, 1994; Knight and Cavusgil, 1996; Madsen and Servais, 1997; Oviatt and McDougall, 1997) have recently noted the increased commonality of new ventures that are distinctly international in nature at or near inception, thereby deviating from established internationalisation process models. As furtherance to this research, this study provides a two-country illustration of these international start-ups as well as mail survey findings and posits that they represent a paradigm shift away from traditional start-ups with initial domestic focus to 21st century start-ups with founding international outlook, orientation and activity.

While traditional start-ups generally originate as domestic firms and gradually evolve into multinational enterprises, contemporary start-ups increasingly begin as international firms. The primary differentiating characteristic is the age of the firm when it becomes international. International start-ups commence with an international business strategy, manifested by the early sourcing and employment of their resources as well as the sale of their products and services in multiple strategic markets worldwide, with the intent of gaining competitive advantage (Oviatt and McDougall, 1994). Oviatt and McDougall distinguish between the terms 'international start-up' and 'global start-up', which are often erroneously utilised synonymously, by defining global start-ups as the most extreme type of international start-up, characterised by the extensive co-ordination of many value chain activities (Porter, 1985) across numerous geographically dispersed countries. Porter describes the value chain as the primary organisational activities of inbound logistics, operations, outbound logistics, marketing and sales and service, and the secondary organisational activities of human resource management, technology development and procurement.

While a precise and universally accepted set of definitional criteria for a firm to be classed as an international start-up does not exist, this paper proposes the following definition and criteria, which are influenced largely by the work of Oviatt and McDougall. *An international start-up is a new venture that exhibits an innate propensity to engage in a meaningful level of international business activity at or near inception, with the intent of achieving strategic competitive advantage.* The determination of definitional fit is gauged in this study by the analysis of a variety of indicators and measures. First, the founder(s) of the firm must have had an international vision (that is, international outlook and aspirations) for the company at or within one year of inception, so as to evidence its founding international intent. Second, the firm must demonstrate its commitment to international activity by conducting business in at least four foreign countries, including evidence of geographic dispersion measured by at least one country in a different continent than the home country, within five years of founding. Third, international sales must represent a minimum of 20 per cent of total firm revenue over the first five years of the company's international activity, indicating substantive international business intensity. And finally, although not a direct definitional criterion, evidence of foreign value chain activity (for example foreign-based sales or service offices) indicating early globalisation efforts is reviewed and regarded as indicative of a higher degree of internationalisation.

SYNTHESIS OF THE LITERATURE

A brief overview of the literature encompassing traditional small firm internationalisation process models, which represent the theoretical base to this study, as well as empirical challenges to the models was provided in the opening paragraph of this chapter. Additionally, the work of several researchers noting the common early internationalisation of contemporary new ventures was highlighted. This section provides a succinct profile of international start-ups and a review of key literature examining the driving forces for their marked early internationalisation.

International start-ups are often small, high-technology, niche-type firms that rely on alternative governance structures, strategic alliances and business and social networks to overcome their commonly inherent resource deficiencies. Their survival, growth and profitability has been found to be attributable in part to the international vision of the founders, the international commitment of top management, having internationally experienced and culturally aware managers, having strong international business networks, continuous innovation, and competing in niche markets worldwide with products that are unique, innovative and of high quality (Johnson, 1999).

A key method of providing an explanation for the emergence of international start-ups is to analyse the driving forces for their salient early internationalisation. A review of literature provides empirical evidence of some of the factors that account for their founding international orientation and activity. McDougall and Oviatt's (1991) case studies of four United States international start-ups found the following six factors or needs to be driving the creation of international start-ups: to obtain resources at a lower cost, to obtain foreign financing, to achieve economies of scale, to pre-empt competitors worldwide, to establish a worldwide technological standard and to preclude domestic inertia. Coviello and Munro's (1995) in-depth case studies of four New Zealand entrepreneurial computer software firms found that their early internationalisation was driven by the highly competitive nature of their international industry, short product life cycles, the size of the domestic market and the influence of the firms' network partners. Bloodgood *et al.*'s (1996) quantitative study of 61 US new high-potential ventures found that the early internationalisation of these firms was driven by either industry conditions which required an international presence in order to be competitive or to capitalise on an unique set of firm resources. Finally, Madsen and Servais's (1997) review of existing literature on international start-ups concluded that their creation and emergence is driven by new market conditions (for example, increased specialisation leading to international niche markets), technological advances in production, transportation and communication and enhanced capabilities of entrepreneurs stemming from prior international experience.

RESEARCH METHODOLOGY

The primary research objective of this study was to identify factors influencing the early internationalisation of small high technology international start-ups in order to provide an explanation for the recent emergence of international start-ups and facilitate an examination of the implications for traditional start-up paradigms. 'Small' was defined in this study as having fewer than 100 employees at the time of initial international activity, while a firm was deemed to be 'high technology' by virtue of its industry/sector, which in this study included computer software, computer hardware and electronics firms, coupled with evidence of ongoing R&D activity. Both qualitative and quantitative methods were utilised. The first phase of the research involved 12 in-depth exploratory interviews with early-internationalising small high technology firms. Six of these firms were located in the United Kingdom and six in the United States. The basic selection parameters for the interviewed firms were for a founder of an existing computer software, computer hardware or electronics company founded between 1981 and 1994, with evidence of international sales, to be available to meet for 60–90 minutes. The intent of the selection process was to include likely international start-ups in the sample.

The following section presents brief case studies of two such firms, one from each country, so as to provide an exemplary profile of this emerging class of new ventures. The names of the firms in the chapter are both disguised, since the researcher promised anonymity in order to encourage an open dialogue and be provided with sensitive company data. Each case study provides an overview of the company's background and current business operation, describes its early international activity and outlines the driving forces for its early internationalisation. This is followed by findings from a mail survey aimed at UK and US firms meeting the same selection criteria described in the previous paragraph for the interview phase.

FINDINGS

Case Studies

Brit-Tech Limited
Background and current profile. 'Brit-Tech' is a Glasgow area computer software firm providing management solutions to the telecommunications industry. More specifically, the company develops complex software systems designed to enhance the management of broadband telecommunications networks. Brit-Tech was founded in 1992 by three individuals, who all presently remain with the company, with extensive technical and management backgrounds in the computer and telecommunications industries. They transformed their fledgling company into a world leader of network management system solutions over a period of only a few years. The company's technical expertise and marketing skills are perhaps best exemplified by its software being utilised by well-known telecommunications companies worldwide, such as AT&T, Bell Atlantic, MCI, British Telecom, Deutsche Telecom and Swisscom. Brit-Tech is both ISO9001 and ISO9000–3 (TickIT) certified.

Although Brit-Tech currently has an annual turnover of approximately £8 million, it remains marginally unprofitable; 80 per cent of its revenue is obtained from the licensing of its software, while the other 20 per cent is generated from consulting services. The company's focus on international business is clearly manifested by nearly 100 per cent of its revenue being derived from international sales and consulting since its inception. The company employs 104 people throughout its Glasgow area headquarters and five offices in the Unite States. The US offices perform sales, service and support functions and are located in Boston, Denver, San Jose, Columbus and Raleigh. All of the company's overseas staff is American. Brit-Tech maintains a high level of R&D intensity, as evidenced by 65 per cent of its employees and 60 per cent of its revenue being allocated to R&D activities.

Early internationalisation activity. Brit-Tech engaged exclusively in international business activity from the outset. All of the company's direct customers are located in the United States, where it licenses its software on an OEM basis. Indirectly, through its US customers, it has conducted consulting services in an additional six countries. These countries are Sweden, Italy, Spain, Switzerland, Germany and its home nation, the United Kingdom. Brit-Tech transacted business in each of these nations in the first five years of its existence.

Brit-Tech established five sales, service and support offices in the United States between 1997 and 1998. The company's chief executive officer (CEO)/co-founder, who was interviewed for this study, indicated that customer circumstances led to the opening of these offices. The decision to set up the offices was based on the perceived needs to establish a presence in key United States markets in order to enhance sales efforts and to physically locate near important customers so as to facilitate the delivery of high calibre service. The company's foreign offices are part of a firm-wide coordinated strategy with shared information and open discussion, achieved in part by computer groupware communications.

Brit-Tech can definitively be classified as an international start-up, based on the definitional criteria stipulated in the Introduction section. Its founders had a profound international vision for the company from the beginning. As previously indicated, virtually all of the company's revenue has been attributable to international sales and consulting services since its inception. In its first five years the company has conducted business in six foreign countries across two continents. Moreover, the company has demonstrated early globalisation intent by the establishment of foreign value chain activity (that is foreign-based sales, service and support functions). Based on these attributes, its industry/sector coupled with a high degree of R&D intensity and having fewer than 100 employees during its first five years of existence, Brit-Tech can clearly be labelled a small high-technology international start-up.

Early internationalisation drivers. The origin of the founders' distinctive international vision for Brit-Tech can be traced back to their previous work experience in the United States. They not only gained industry knowledge from this experience, but valuable business contacts and customer knowledge as well. This accumulated industry and market knowledge ultimately led to the United States being selected as Brit-Tech's initial target market. Three additional reasons for the selection of the United States as the company's initial target market were given. First, it represented a large and key market for the company's industry. Second, its common language and culture greatly eased the international business process, particularly in light of the company's lack of experience. And third, the founders recognised that the worldwide relationships and global sales presence of their prospective US customers could subsequently lead to unparalleled opportunities for the young company.

Aside from country-specific explanations, the interviewee identified several industry factors as having played an integral role in the firm's early internationalisation. The founders believed that the global and competitive nature of the company's industry necessitated an international strategy from the beginning in order to survive and prosper. Furthermore, very short product life cycles likewise necessitated an international strategy in order to achieve profitability. The interviewee stated that industry characteristics led the founders to conclude that the company must 'address the global market from day one', and hence transformed Brit-Tech into a distinctly international company.

Ameri-Tech Corporation
Background and current profile. 'Ameri-Tech' is a Boston area computer software firm providing database marketing software and consulting services designed to assist businesses in maximising the value of their customer relationships. The software and consulting services enable businesses to identify customer segments with the highest profit potential and subsequently optimise the value of these segments by planning a highly targeted direct-marketing campaign. Ameri-Tech was formed in late 1994 by a single founder who transformed his marketing consulting firm into a marketing software solutions company. The new company began selling licenses for its proprietary software in 1996 and has since experienced rapid expansion and growth through a series of strategic alliances and partnerships. These alliance partners, who include prominent computer firms such as IBM, NCR and Compaq, resell Ameri-Tech's software, resulting in its products being utilised by companies worldwide. Its impressive customer list crosses numerous industries and includes Federal Express, Staples, Bank of America, NatWest, Sky TV and Dutch Railways. Furthermore, its software has been the recipient of numerous awards and has received wide-spread recognition.

Although the company is very young, it has achieved noteworthy sales growth and currently has an annual turnover of approximately $25 million. However, the company is presently unprofitable, with a current annual net loss of nearly $1 million; 60 per cent of Ameri-Tech's revenue is derived from software licensing, while the remaining 40 per cent stems from consulting services; 20–25 per cent of this revenue is currently attributable to international sales. The company employs 70 people and maintains offices in London, Sydney and Denver in addition to its headquarters in Boston, with 35 per cent of its employees and 22 per cent of its revenue being dedicated to R&D. Ameri-Tech became a publicly traded company in 1998.

Early internationalisation activity. Ameri-Tech sold its first international license, which was implemented across three European countries, in 1997, the year following its commercial product release. Over the next two years, 1997–9, the company's international business rapidly expanded, as evidenced by its sales in 20 foreign countries spanning several continents. These country markets included: Australia, Singapore, Hong Kong, Japan, Taiwan, India, Argentina, Chile, Canada and most of Western Europe. The selection criteria for these markets were primarily based on market potential, ease of delivery and language (that is, English speaking markets first). The company's rapid international sales growth is further illustrated by

5 per cent of its total 1997 revenue being attributed to international sales, 20 per cent of 1998's revenue and 29 per cent forecast for 1999. Ameri-Tech's goal is to expand its international business to a level equating to 40 per cent of total firm revenue.

In support of its expanding international business the company invested in two sales, service and support offices abroad. In 1997 it opened an office in London, with a staff of 20. Then in 1998 it opened a seven-person office in Sydney. Ameri-Tech's chief operating officer (COO), who was interviewed for this study, stated that these offices provided both a springboard and a presence into their regions. In addition, the company's largest European competitor was located in the UK and it felt compelled to have a presence in the competitor's home ground. The interviewee indicated that these foreign sales offices are very much part of a coordinated strategy throughout the firm and are computer linked to benefit the entire organisation. Two additional sales, service and support offices are scheduled to open in late 1999, one in Germany and the other in Japan.

Ameri-Tech can clearly be classified as an international start-up, based on the criteria previously set forth in this chapter. The founder of the company had international aspirations for the firm from the beginning, which was manifested very early in its existence. In its first five years the company conducted business in 20 foreign countries spanning several continents in addition to investing in two foreign sales, service and support offices. The company's commitment to internationalisation is further demonstrated by its early and rapid international sales growth and its planned opening of two additional foreign sales offices in 1999, which is within the first five years of its existence. Based on this data, its industry/sector coupled with a high degree of R&D intensity and having only 70 employees, Ameri-Tech can accurately be classed as a small high technology international start-up.

Early internationalisation drivers. While the founder of Ameri-Tech had clear international aspirations for his new company from the outset, international sales were not pursued until 1997. During the first two and one-half years of the company's existence the founder focused on preparing his software products for commercial release and introducing them to the large US domestic market while developing the company's worldwide product launch. The founder recognised the necessity of hiring an experienced specialist in international marketing in order to achieve his international objectives and hired such an individual in June 1997. The specialist was made executive vice president, worldwide sales and service, and later promoted to chief operating officer. His background included extensive international business experience in the software industry, where his accomplishments included expanding his previous employer's international business to 45 per cent of total revenue across 40 countries, as well as the formulation of a global strategic alliance with IBM. This new executive was largely responsible for the sale of the company's first international licence one-month after being retained and its subsequent transformation into an international company.

The interviewee contends that several factors led to the company being international very early in its existence. The primary driver was the international vision of the founder. The founder had a genuine appreciation for the opportunities offered by expansion into international markets and planned to pursue these markets once the initial products were introduced into the domestic market and an experienced international marketing executive could be recruited. Furthermore, the founder strongly desired to be a market leader in his industry, which he believed required a strong international presence. He believed that being a market leader necessitated the ability to be the first to enter markets worldwide and consequently developed Ameri-Tech into an international company.

Mail Survey Results

A total of 600 questionnaires were sent to randomly selected computer software, computer hardware and electronics firms in each country meeting the parameters previously delineated. A total of 102 usable responses were received from the United Kingdom (19.25 per cent adjusted response rate) and 89 from the United States (18.09 per cent adjusted response rate).[1] Of the 102 UK respondents, 49 met the previously delineated definitional criteria to be classed as international start-ups (48.04 per cent), while 47 of the US respondents met the criteria (52.81 per cent). Whereas the primary focus of the survey was to determine the significance of numerous factors to the early success of international start-ups, data pertaining to the driving forces for the firms' early internationalisation was collected and measured. The drivers analysed in the survey were drawn from prior empirical study findings as well as the current study's interview findings. The respondents were asked to rate the importance of 25 factors to the firms' initial involvement in international activity, utilising a Likert scale ranging from 1 (low) to 7 (high).

The five most important factors leading to the early internationalisation of the UK and US international start-ups in the study are listed in Table 5.1. The five most important early internationalisation drivers for the UK firms were (ranked in order): the international vision of the founder(s), having a large proportion of prospective customers that were foreign, the desire to be an international market leader, the international and competitive nature of the company's industry, and the international business experience of the founder(s).[2] The five most important early internationalisation drivers for the US firms were (ranked in order): the international vision of the founder(s), the identification of a specific international opportunity, the desire to be an international market leader, the opportunity to supplement domestic sales, and the possession of international contacts and sales leads.[3] These key early internationalisation driver findings support those of the two cases studies illustrated above.

DISCUSSION AND CONCLUSIONS

Numerous parallels are readily discernible between the early internationalisation process of Brit-Tech and that of Ameri-Tech. First, the founders of each firm had

Table 5.1   Important early internationalisation driving forces

Early internationalisation driving forces	United Kingdom Ranking and mean rating*	United States Ranking and mean rating*
International vision of the Founder(s)	1 6.21	1 5.67
Large proportion of prospective customers were foreign	2 5.79	
Desire to be an international market leader	3 5.72	3 5.17
International and competitive nature of the firm's industry	4 5.71	
Founders' international experience	5 5.68	
Identification of a specific international opportunity		2 5.20
Opportunity to supplement domestic sales		4 5.17
Possession of international contacts and sales leads		5 5.04

Note:
* 7-point scale; 1 = low, 7 = high.

clear international visions and agendas for their companies from the beginning. While Brit-Tech's strategy mandated an exclusive international orientation from the outset, Ameri-Tech's called for an initial domestic product introduction while preparing for its impending international product release. Second, both firms transacted their first international sale very early in their existence. Brit-Tech sold its products abroad during its first year of business, while Ameri-Tech's first international transaction was achieved in its third year, which was only one year following its initial domestic product release. Third, both firms conducted business in numerous countries spanning at least two continents in their first five years of existence. Brit-Tech sold its products and services in six foreign countries across two continents and Ameri-Tech twenty foreign countries crossing five continents, all within five years of founding. Interestingly, Ameri-Tech achieved this noteworthy international expansion in a period of only two years. And fourth, both firms had a high level of international sales relative to total firm turnover over their first five years of international business activity. Brit-Tech's international sales accounted for nearly 100 per cent of its total revenue, while Ameri-Tech's equated to well over 20 per cent of total firm sales in its first two years of international activity alone.

In addition to the noted internationalisation process parallelisms of Brit-Tech and Ameri-Tech, the firms exhibited similar early globalisation activity as well. Each firm invested in foreign value chain activity in its first five years of existence. Brit-Tech set up five sales, service and support offices in the United States, while Ameri-Tech likewise established sales, service and support offices in the

United Kingdom and Australia, with a further two offices scheduled to open in Germany and Japan within the first five year window. Furthermore, each office represented part of a coordinated firm-wide strategy for both companies, which included a high degree of intercommunications and shared learning experiences.

Other key distinguishing characteristics emerge when analysing the case studies of these two international start-ups. The founders of both firms had profound international visions for their companies from the beginning, which as described above was largely responsible for their marked early internationalisation. The firms commenced with explicit international strategies, which prescribed the identification and targeting of multiple key country markets for their product/ industry from the start. Moreover, while both firms employed strategic alliances in order to preserve scarce resources, they allocated their limited resources to the establishment of sales, service and support offices in leading industry markets world-wide in order to facilitate successful market penetration.

As indicated in the Introduction, numerous researchers have noted the recent emergence of new ventures that are distinctly international in nature at or near inception. Brit-Tech and Ameri-Tech, both formed in the 1990s, are among the firms in this emerging class of start-ups. A key to providing an explanation for the emergence of international start-ups is to analyse the drivers for their marked early internationalisation. The principal factors that drove Brit-Tech and Ameri-Tech to be distinctly international at or near inception include the international vision of the founders, the international experience of the founders and top management team, the perceived necessity of rapidly entering key industry markets worldwide, the international and competitive nature of their industries and the desire to be an international market leader.

Holistic analysis of the case study and mail survey findings suggests that international start-ups increasingly commence with an international strategy due to changes in founder and industry characteristics. The international vision of many contemporary founders coupled with their prior international experience, possession of international contacts and sales leads, identification of specific international opportunities and desire to both supplement domestic sales and be an international market leader has driven them to form companies that have international agendas and objectives from the outset. Furthermore, changes in the structure of numerous industries have led to competitive environments that are intrinsically international, subsequently resulting in a high proportion of firms' prospective customers being located worldwide, which in turn necessitates an international strategy from the beginning in order to compete.

In summary, the advent of the global economy and its ensuing impact on entrepreneurial orientation and industry competitive environment has led to the emergence of start-ups that are distinctly international in nature at or near inception, thereby deviating from traditional internationalisation models. This evolution represents a paradigm shift away from traditional start-ups with initial domestic focus and gradual internationalisation to that of 21st century start-ups with founding international outlook, orientation and activity.

The study's findings have important implications not only for existing academic theories, but also for top management teams of current and prospective start-ups, policy makers and future research projects. Traditional internationalisation process models need to be revisited in light of contemporary empirical evidence indicating accelerated firm internationalisation. Top management of current and prospective start-ups should be informed about factors influencing early internationalisation so as to facilitate the development of appropriate international strategy. Policy makers should be cognisant of factors influencing the emergence of international start-ups in order to develop policies and programs designed to promote early international business activity and subsequently advance economic development. Finally, recognising the exploratory nature of this research, this study should serve as a foundation for future research projects to further validate the emergence of international start-ups and enhance academic knowledge of the factors influencing their early internationalisation.

Several limitations are inherent with this research. First, the small scale of the study necessitates prudence as to the generalisation of the findings. The study's findings provide a point estimate of the population mean and should be analysed in conjunction with extant literature. Second, the study primarily focused on two illustrative case studies and did not expound on the methodological details of the mail survey and its subsequent findings. This will be provided in a forthcoming paper. And third, the construction of the mail survey's sampling frame led to a bias towards the inclusion of international start-ups. Therefore, the frequency of international start-ups relative to the sample size is largely over-represented.

Notes

1. The 600 UK firms and 600 US firms originally sent questionnaires were reduced to 530 UK firms and 492 US firms for response rate calculation purposes after adjusting the number for undeliverable surveys (for example, companies that ceased business, moved away without a forwarding address or experienced ownership changes) and companies that responded indicating that they were not suitable for the study (for example, not an international or high technology company).
2. The five least important early internationalisation drivers for the UK firms in the study were (in descending order): the influence of the company's business partners (2.82), short product life cycles necessitated international sales (2.49), advice and assistance from governmental agencies (2.26), the avoidance of intense or direct domestic competition (2.18) and the need to obtain foreign financing (1.39).
3. The five least important early internationalisation drivers for the US firms in the study were (in descending order): a small domestic market (1.91), advice and assistance from governmental agencies (1.78), short product life cycles necessitated international sales (1.78), the avoidance of intense or direct domestic competition (1.64) and the need to obtain foreign financing (1.24).

6 On the Resource-based, Integrative View of Small Firm Internationalisation: an Exploratory Study of Nigerian Firms

Kevin I.N. Ibeh

INTRODUCTION

The past three decades of research into SME internationalisation have yielded a number of frameworks that sought to illuminate and explain the process through which small firms internationalise. These include the 'stage of development' approach, the network perspective and the business strategy/contingency/ resource-based frameworks. Judging by its pervasiveness and the amount of academic debate that it has generated, the stage of development approach would appear to be the most dominant. This may be about to change, however, as consensus appears to have emerged among academic researchers and policy makers that SMEs negotiate varying paths to internationalisation (Madsen and Servais, 1997; Bell and Young, 1998; Coviello and McAuley, 1999).

Decades of extensive and successful critiquing have, indeed, forced the 'stage' theory to yield its traditional hegemony to a more inclusive, integrative view of SME internationalisation. This perspective, evident in recent works by Bell and Young (1998) and Coviello and McAuley (1999), presents extant frameworks as complementary rather than competing explanations. The incremental internationalisation model is, thus, appropriately viewed as one of the ways to internationalise; across a spectrum that comprises network-driven (Coviello and Munro, 1997) – including accelerated internationalisation (McDougall *et al.*, 1994) – and strategy/resource-based internationalisation (Young *et al.*, 1998).

This chapter examines the initial internationalisation behaviour of a sample of Nigerian firms in the light of the above-mentioned explanatory frameworks. It should be noted that the term 'internationalisation' is used in a limited sense in this chapter since none of the surveyed firms has developed beyond the exporting mode. Organised in five sections, the chapter starts with an overview of SME internationalisation theories. This is followed, in section two, by an outline of research methodology. Section three is devoted to the analysis of obtained data, subsequently discussed in section four. The chapter ends with a section on conclusions and policy implications.

SME INTERNATIONALISATION THEORIES

There is no gainsaying the importance of the contribution made by the Uppsala internationalisation model to the understanding of SME internationalisation. This model, which grew out of Johanson and Wiedersheim-Paul's (1975) Swedish research, posits that firms adopt an incremental, evolutionary approach to foreign markets, gradually deepening their commitment and investment as they gain in market knowledge and experience[1] (Johanson and Vahlne, 1977, 1990). Firms are also said to initially target neighbouring, psychically close countries, and subsequently enter foreign markets with successively larger psychic distance.

Although these 'intuitively appealing' propositions (Sullivan and Bauerschmidt, 1990, p. 29) have found support in several studies conducted mainly in mature industries, serious doubts have consistently been raised regarding their conceptual (Bell and Young, 1998) and methodological (Andersen, 1993) foundations. Indeed, many studies involving firms with small domestic markets, service firms, high-technology firms, entrepreneurial firms, subcontractors, and international new ventures have reported evidence that counter the incremental model (see, for example, Turnbull, 1987; Young *et al.*, 1989; Bell, 1995). The psychic distance concept has also been increasingly questioned in the face of vast improvements in global communications and transportation infrastructures, and the resulting increasing market convergence (Stottinger and Schlegelmilch, 1998). The remarks by Bell and Young (1998, p. 15) that the incremental internationalisation models 'merely identify the internationalisation patterns of certain firms – but not of others – and ... they fail to adequately explain the processes involved' would appear to reflect the consensus position on the topic.

In their attempts to improve on the scope of the explanation offered by the 'stages' theory, researchers looked to the field of industrial marketing where the *network/interaction/relationship* concepts had been found useful in explaining the internationalisation process. The result was an integration of network perspectives into the incremental model, thus: internationalisation proceeds through an interplay between increasing commitment to, and evolving knowledge about foreign markets, gained mainly from interactions with market actors (Johanson and Mattsson, 1988).

It was also argued that successful entry into new foreign markets depended more on a firm's relationships with its current markets, both domestic and international, than on the chosen market and its cultural characteristics. Later remarks by Johanson and Vahlne (1992) that many firms enter new foreign markets almost blindly, propelled by social exchange processes, interactions, and networks apparently endorsed this expanded view of the internationalisation concept. Evidence, indeed, abound in the service industry (Lindqvist, 1988; Hellman,

1996) and the computer software sector (Bell, 1995; Coviello and Munro, 1997) of internationalisation driven by various inter-firm (customers or clients, suppliers) relationships, including importing (Welch and Luostarinen, 1993).

The review, so far, has covered the stages theory and network perspectives, both of which present useful, albeit partial, explanations of SME internationalisation. Recent research would appear to have advanced the search for a more holistic theory. Drawing on the resource-based perspective of the firm (Wernerfelt, 1984), Young *et al.* (1998) present a view of internationalisation in which major decisions (on country market choice, market servicing mode, product-market strategies) are based on total consideration of all available resources and capabilities of the firm, as well as environmental (including competitive) realities. Such resources may be internal to the firm (for example, appropriately oriented top management, specific product or financial advantages, organisational learning or market knowledge), but can also be externally leveraged (for example, through network relationships). Firms, according to these authors, 'will have a different mix of resources/competencies and resource/competence gaps, and their strategic responses to these allow for the possibility of different paths to growth and internationalisation' (Young *et al.*, 1998, p. 17). One implication is that while a new firm having some unique competency may initiate international activity by acquiring existing businesses in psychically distant markets, a more established firm may be unable to do so. The latter may be constrained by certain resource gaps or competitive realities to stagnate at a given market servicing mode or even regress to a more limited form of international involvement (see Wheeler *et al.*, 1996).

The resource-based theory of internationalisation is, arguably, a more grounded restatement of the business strategy and contingency frameworks. It is consistent with the views of Reid (1983) – a key proponent of the contingency view of internationalisation – that exporting results from a choice among competing strategies that are guided by the nature of the market opportunity, *firm resources*, and *managerial philosophy* (this researcher's emphasis). It agrees also with the business strategy explanation that internationalisation decisions are made in the context of the firm's overall strategic development, guided by an analysis of relevant *internal and external environmental* factors (Young, 1987; Young *et al.*, 1989): managerial resources, for example, are internal while network-related benefits are external.

METHODOLOGY

The specific questions addressed in this chapter are the extent to which internationalised Nigerian firms (a) behave in the manner suggested by the incremental model, that is, deepen their foreign market involvement as they gain more market experience, or enter psychically close foreign markets; (b) are driven by relationships formed with domestic or foreign network partners, and (c) differ from their non-internationalised counterparts with regard to competitive competencies and capabilities.

Primary data for this study were collected late in the summer of 1996, using questionnaire survey and depth interview methods – methodological pluralism, as advocated for behaviour-oriented studies by Kamath *et al.* (1987). The study population was defined as comprising Nigerian-based firms which met a range of criteria: (a) they manufacture/export textiles and wearing apparel, footwear and leather, food and beverages, plastics and furniture; (b) they are listed in the most recent editions of either the Nigerian Exporters directory or Nigerian Industrial directory; (c) they are located in one of three major Nigerian industrial cities, Lagos, Kano and Aba; and (d) they have a minimum annual turnover of five million naira (about US$0.07 m), and at least 50 employees. The product areas specified above fall within the category of labour-intensive, light manufactured goods, which previous developing country-based exporting studies (Dominguez and Sequeira, 1993; Katsikeas and Morgan, 1994) and relevant Nigerian agencies (Manufacturers Association of Nigeria, 1994; Nigerian Export Promotion Council, 1995) consider suitable platforms for export development.

The total number of firms which met the above, pre-specified criteria was 226. Given this modest population size, the decision was taken to approach all the identified firms, with structured and properly pilot-tested questionnaires. The drop and pick technique (Yavas, 1987) was adopted to minimise the envisaged impact of Nigeria's poor and unreliable infrastructure (postal and telephone systems) on the response rate. This method involved an average of four visits to each of the identified firms: there were 188 of them eventually; 38 were not found owing to reasons including wrong address, relocation and business failures. The process was facilitated by three experienced field supervisors and nine well-trained field assistants. A total of 112 questionnaires were returned, 78 of which were useable; this produced an overall response rate of 52.4 per cent, and a useable response rate of 41.2 per cent.

The key informant technique was employed in eliciting responses from the sampled firms. The questionnaire respondents eventually comprised 23 chief executive officers (CEOs), 14 general managers, 30 marketing/sales managers and 11 export managers. In view of the limitations of the key informant technique (Philips, 1981), second responses were collected from some five randomly selected firms. Further analysis of these five pairs of responses through paired sample *t*-tests validated this key informant approach. The later stage of primary research involved the selection of a quota sub-sample of sixteen firms for in-depth interviews. The actual number of firms interviewed, however, was nine (four CEOs and five marketing managers), as the cooperation of the other interview targets could not be secured before the end of the field visit.

ANALYSIS AND FINDINGS

The findings presented below are based on aggregate analysis of data from 78 completed questionnaires (34 exporting and 44 non-exporting firms) and nine

Table 6.1   Profile of responding firms

	Textiles n = 30	Plastics n = 29	Others n = 19	Overall n = 78
	Percentages			
Age of firm (years)				
Less than 5	16.6	18.2	15.8	16.6
Less than 10	36.6	45.8	50.0	42.2
Less than 20	49.9	73.4	73.7	64.0
More than 20	50.0	27.6	26.3	35.9
Size of firm				
(No. of employees)				
Less than 100	20.0	37.8	36.7	30.8
Less than 500	70.0	48.8	94.7	87.2
More than 500	30.0	—	5.3	12.8
Turnover p.a				
Less than N10 m	36.7	41.3	36.7	37.2
Less than N50 m	56.7	75.9	68.4	66.7
Less than N100 m	70.0	89.7	94.7	84.6
More than N100 m	30.0	10.3	5.3	16.4
Exporting status				
Exporters	50.0	37.9	42.1	43.6
Non-exporters	50.0	62.1	57.9	56.4

in-depth interviews (three exporting and six non-exporting firms) – see Table 6.1, below, for a profile of the responding firms. To maintain the anonymity of the nine interviewed companies, each is assigned one of the first nine letters of the alphabet, A to I. Letters A to C refer to three exporting interviewees, while letters D to I refer to six non-exporting firms. Findings on the focal issues of this chapter are now presented.

Internationalisation as an Incremental Process

The evidence from the sampled Nigerian firms on the issue of incremental internationalisation appears mixed. For clearer analysis of the findings, the two planks of the stage theory are presented separately, thus: (a) foreign market experience and extent of involvement and (b) the psychic distance concept.

Organisational Learning/Market Knowledge and Export Involvement
To explore the influence of size/experience-related factors on the foreign market servicing modes used by internationalised Nigerian firms, respondents were asked to indicate their number of years of exporting involvement and the channel(s) through which they serve the foreign market(s). Table 6.2 presents the relevant descriptive statistics, including *cross-tabulation* results. It can be seen that only 17 per cent reported having sales subsidiaries abroad, and these comprise mainly

Table 6.2   Extent of foreign market involvement by export experience

No. of years in exporting	Market servicing mode used				Total
	Indirect exports*	Foreign agents	Foreign distributors	Sales staff abroad	
	(Percentages; n = 30)				
5 years and less	26	13	7	7	52
6 to 10 years	20	13	0	7	27
11 to 20 years	17	4	3	0	12
21 years and above	7	0	7	3	9
Total**	70	30	17	17	

Notes:

* defined as Nigerian-based intermediaries including export houses, export trading companies, multinational customers and other exporters.

** the total percentage exceeds 100 owing to double counting. This was inevitable because some firms use more than one channel.

firms at the lower end of exporting experience, that is, five years and less and six to ten years. Evidence does not, indeed, suggest that firms with greater exporting experience employ more committed market servicing modes than their less experienced counterparts. What can be observed, however, is that an overwhelming majority of the sampled international firms adopt limited foreign market servicing modes: 70 per cent use indirect export channels, with 47 per cent using foreign agents and distributors.

These aggregate findings are largely reinforced by insights from the exporting firms interviewed. The managing director of Company A reported on her firm's reliance on 'merchandisers and representatives', which organise the company's participation in fashion shows in different US cities. Another interviewee, Company C's marketing manager, also indicated their dependence on foreign distributors. According to this source, the firm had been exporting plastics for only two years, and had, thus far, done so through distributors from Ghana who visit and buy from their factory. Only the Company B source reported having export sales staff abroad. As the chief executive remarked, 'We have a depot in Benin Republic. We shift goods to our men and they sell.'

While this widespread recourse to limited commitment modes and the relatively low international market experience of the sampled firms lend some support to the stage of development explanation, the lack of consistency in internationalisation behaviour observed among firms of comparable size and market experience raises doubt about its generalisability. As can be seen from the *one-way analysis of variance (ANOVA) tests* in Table 6.3, the exporting and non-exporting parts of the sample do not appear to differ significantly in size, whether defined by firms' age, employment or annual sales. This is worth noting because firm size and age[2]

Table 6.3   Firm size/age and exporting status

Size variables	Exporters (n=34)	Non-exporters (n=44)	K-W Anova*
		*(Recoded mean values**)*	
Firms' age	1.54	1.43	0.44
Firms' sales (1995)	1.61	1.40	0.12
Number of employees	1.86	1.76	0.36

Notes:
* significant at alpha = 0.05 or greater.
** For the purposes of the one-way ANOVA tests, each of the size variables was recoded on a dichotomous scale, 1 or 2. This eliminates empty cells, which would have arisen from the relative small size of the present study's sample. It also reduces possible distortions arising from firms not being sufficiently different.

have sometimes been viewed as surrogate measures of organisational learning and experience.

Further illustration can be drawn from the depth interview sub-sample, specifically from two fair-sized firms[3] with vastly different internationalisation behaviour. The first, Company B, employs over 500 staff and was actually set up in the mid-1950s, as an importing organisation. It meets the logic of the incremental model that this firm's internationalisation must have been facilitated by the organisational learning and market experience, which it had accumulated over the years in the domestic market. It may be added that its 'enormous trading (importing) experience and (Nigeria-wide) distribution network' satisfy the other planks of the Uppsala model, inward internationalisation and extraregional expansion, as training ground and intermediate stages in the gradual, but inexorable progression toward internationalisation.

That this 'stage of development' explanation is not always applicable is exemplified by the case of the other fair-sized company, referred to as Company D. This apparently well established and experienced company has 1295 employees and an extensive (Nigeria-wide) distribution network. It, however, has neither internationalised nor appeared likely to do so. Similar illustrative evidence was obtained in respect of comparably sized smaller firms which demonstrated remarkably different initial internationalisation behaviour: Company A is of comparable size with Companies E, F, G, H and I, none of which had demonstrated half its commitment and innovativeness in developing exporting.

The foregoing bears out earlier cited remarks about the selective relevance of the stage theory. It also agrees with the emerging consensus among international new venture and network scholars (McDougall *et al.*, 1994; Coviello and Munro, 1997) on the limited usefulness of organisational size and age (experience) as predictors of internationalisation behaviour.

Psychic Distance

To explore whether the foreign market selection patterns of Nigerian firms reflect the psychic distance concept, respondents were asked to indicate their first export markets and their current major markets. Aggregate analysis suggests that Nigerian international firms behave in a way indicated by the psychic distance concept. As can be seen from Table 6.4 below, the West African region (including Benin Republic, Ghana and Togo) serves as the first export destination and first current major market for 57 per cent of the respondents. Though Cameroon is, geographically speaking, not in West Africa, it shares borders with Nigeria, and was cited as the first export market by 12 per cent of the respondents. When this is added to another 12 per cent represented by two other African countries, the total proportion of respondents who reported African markets as their first export market came to 81 per cent. The UK at 12 per cent was the most cited non-African market, followed by the USA (6 per cent) and Hong Kong (3 per cent).

There is little doubt that these findings generally support the psychic distance concept. It is intuitively plausible (Sullivan and Bauerschmidt, 1990), for example, that while 57 per cent and 75 per cent of the responding Nigerian firms

Table 6.4 Foreign Market Selection Patterns

First export market	per cent; n = 34
1 Other West Africa*	21
2 Benin Republic*	18
3 Ghana*	15
4 Cameroon**	12
4 United Kingdom	12
6 Tanzania**	9
7 Togo*	6
7 United States of America	6
9 Malawi**	3
9 Hong Kong	3
Current major markets	
Ghana*	15
Benin Republic*	13
Other West Africa*	8
United Kingdom	7
Cameroon**	6
Côte d'Ivoire*	6
Togo*	6
Tanzania**	5
Malawi**	5
Zambia**	4
United States of America	4

Notes:
 * refers to West African countries;
** indicates other African countries.

reported West Africa and Africa respectively as their current major market, none reported having exported to the Middle East/Mediterranean zone. To be sure, the non-African markets cited are those with considerably low psychic distance: the UK and USA are both countries with strong historical ties with Nigeria, and are home to millions of people who trace their ethnic origin to Nigeria.

Internationalisation as a Network-influenced Process

To explore the relative influence of network relationships on the initial internationalisation behaviour of Nigerian firms, respondents were asked to rate the quality of their firms' relationships with middlemen, in both domestic and foreign markets, on a five point scale, where one represents 'considerable weakness' and five, 'considerable strength'. The responding decision makers were also asked to indicate whether or not they communicate regularly with contacts abroad. Table 6.5, presents the results of one-way ANOVA tests, which suggest significant differences between the sampled exporters and non-exporters with respect to relationships with domestic and foreign intermediaries. Exporting firms tend to rate their relationships with middlemen, in the domestic and foreign markets, higher than do their non-exporting counterparts. Aggregate results also indicate that decision makers from exporting firms, relative to their non-exporting counterparts, have a greater tendency to maintain contacts abroad – personal contact network,[4] according to Carson *et al.* (1995).

The above finding is further illustrated by remarks made by the exporters within the depth interview sub sample. The CEO of Company B reported that the company had 'extensive distributor network running through a few West Coast (African) countries'. Company A's managing director also reported having very useful business associates who market her company's designs and ensure her presence in appropriate exhibitions – sometimes by getting her sponsors. This source identified other value-adding roles performed by her channel partners as including product improvement suggestions and logistics support, such as taking delivery of goods air-freighted from the company's Nigerian base for onward distribution to merchandisers in the USA. The MD's regular visits to the USA market, it emerged, greatly facilitated the company's relationship with its USA-based partners – corroborating the several reports in the literature on the importance of export market visits (Styles and Ambler, 1994). As of the time of this study, another of the exporting interviewees, Company C's marketing manager was anticipating some business from his market exploration visits to Ghana.

This Nigerian study adds to the growing body of evidence on the importance of networking and channel relationships in the internationalisation process. The limited extent of the surveyed firms' outward internationalisation activity apparently restricts the scope of the evidence obtained (for example, the lack of data on such dimensions as customer-, competitor- and supplier-driven internationalisation), but the greater tendency to network among the internationalised Nigerian firms and their decision makers is instructive.

Internationalisation as a Resource-based Process

Data on the resource profiles of sampled firms were generated through a number of questions. Respondents were asked to rate their firms on a five-point scale (where one means 'considerable weakness', and five 'considerable strength'), with respect to a list of 16 competitive factors. These decision makers were further asked to respond to some dichotomous questions on specific demographic variables. Table 6.5 presents the results of the one-way ANOVA tests, which suggest some significant differences between the firms that export and those that do not, with respect to some key competencies. It can be seen that the former firms scored significantly higher than the latter regarding such competitive factors as developing new markets, channel (network) relationships, adoption of innovation and technology, and export information search. They also appear to have performed better with respect to decision makers' previous business experience and international orientation.

The foregoing would appear to reflect the observed differences in resource profile between two of the three interviewed exporting firms (Companies A and B) on the one hand and the six non-exporting interviewees (Companies D–I) on the other. Some of the capabilities of Companies A and B have already been highlighted in the earlier sections. It is considered necessary, however, to reiterate these and other competencies which set the two firms apart from their non-exporting

Table 6.5 Firms' characteristics and competencies by exporting status

	Exporting	Non-exporting	Significance
	(mean scores)		
*Competitive competencies**	*(n=34)*	*(n=29)*	*K-W Anova*
Developing new markets	3.68	3.00	0.01**
Middlemen network in Nigeria	3.55	2.70	0.01**
Middlemen network abroad	2.71	2.44	0.00**
Innovation	3.76	2.98	0.00**
Technology	3.38	2.77	0.02**
Export information search	2.15	1.43	0.00**
*Decision maker characteristics*** (%)*	*n=34*	*n=44*	
Was in family business	44.1	20.5	0.02**
Was running own business	23.5	6.8	0.04**
Maintained regular contacts abroad	55.9	25.0	0.00**

Notes:
  * Measured on a 5-point scale, where 1 equals 'considerable weakness' and 5 'considerable strength'.
 ** Significant at alpha 0.05 or greater; only the significant variables are shown.
*** Measured on a nominal scale, where 1 means possession of the attribute, and 0 the reverse.

counterparts, that is, enabled them to overcome the disincentives to internationalise that emanate from their operating (developing country) environment.

Company B started exporting in 1992, driven largely by the Harvard-trained CEO's resolve to take the business further than his founder-father. According to this CEO, the company's business had grown over a 40-year period 'through horizontal integration, with a strong emphasis on product research and market development'. He also indicated that the company had 'extensive distributor network running through a few West Coast (African) countries'. As of the time of this interview (1996), the company was already exporting to four West African countries, and had seen its export-sales ratio rise from 2–3 per cent in 1992 to 8 per cent in 1995. The company's good financial base can be implied from the CEO's remark that they 'provide credit facilities' to their customers.

Company A exports regularly to the United States, a market which it had nurtured over the previous six years through visits and participation in fashion shows and exhibitions, as well as quality relationships with USA-based representatives and merchandisers. The initial motivation for exporting, according to the company's MD, was to show, at an international stage, their excellence in African designs – which is understandable given this firm's leading status in the Nigerian fashion market. The MD, whose exhibitions earned her an induction into the 'Atlanta Alumni Hall of Fame in 1992', revealed plans to visit Europe in the summer of 1998 for market exploration purposes.

When the above two resource profiles are contrasted with insights from the non-exporting companies (D, E, F, G, H, I), the disparity would become obvious. Companies E and F, for example, appear to lack products of sufficiently good quality. The marketing manager of Company E, indeed, conceded that their upholstery products could not meet the stringent standards expected in the more profitable international markets. The resource situation in Company G seems even weaker. As of the time of the interview, the textiles manufacturing firm had only recently resumed operations after a 12-month closure, which the marketing manager attributed to lack of production materials.

More fundamentally, all these firms appear to lack the one defining resource whose influence on firm internationalisation has enjoyed consistent support in previous studies, namely the support of internationally oriented management (Miesenbock, 1988; Aaby and Slater, 1989; McDougall and Oviatt, 1997; Young *et al.*, 1998). To illustrate, Company E had a sole owner whom, it emerged, was not keen on exporting. Company H had a continuing contract for the supply of military uniforms, which apparently leaves it no room for any serious exporting consideration. Company D, on the other hand, claimed an assured domestic market, the satisfaction of which remains the height of its aspiration. The Marketing manager, indeed, wondered why they should get involved in 'risky export business' when they had not yet satisfied the domestic market.

The above evidence on the internationalisation behaviour of Nigerian firms adds to the limited empirical literature on the resource-based view of firm internationalisation. The simple summary appears to be that SMEs, which possess, or can access, relevant resources have a greater tendency to exhibit positive internationalisation behaviour than those lacking requisite resources.

DISCUSSIONS

The preceding part of this chapter has assessed the extent to which each of the major theoretical frameworks explains the initial internationalisation behaviour of the sampled Nigerian firms. The findings emerging from these analyses are now discussed with a view to drawing relevant conclusions.

This researcher prefers to start with the psychic distance concept, possibly the clearest of the issues raised in this chapter. There is hardly any doubt that this concept explains the foreign market selection pattern of the Nigerian firms studied. It should be noted, however, that this additional empirical support for the psychic distance concept does not detract from the equally founded concerns raised about its relevance to high-technology, service, and highly 'resourced' (including 'networked') firms, particularly those from small countries (Bell and Young, 1998). This is because this present study used an essentially low technology firms' sample, a generic grouping from which much of the earlier empirical support for the Uppsala model had come.

It is clearly plausible to see how Nigerian manufacturers of low differentiated consumer items, with only very recent national history of outward internationalisation, would enter exporting through markets which they consider familiar. It would appear, also, that these firms view these export markets as extensions of their domestic market, since they sell to customers who basically share similar demand (Linder, 1961). It should be noted that even, when these firms export to the UK and the USA, their main targets are the Nigerian and African people resident in these countries.

This last observation has some resonance with the network view of internationalisation. Although the psychic distance concept explains the occurrence of the UK and US markets among the major export markets, it does not rule out the equally compelling network explanation. Simply stated, those markets are the targets of Nigerian exporters because of the several existing links – ethnic, familial, friendship – between them and the exporting firms' decision makers. As indicated earlier, both the UK and USA have significant populations of 'ethnic Nigerians'. It would appear that this substantial concentration, in foreign markets, of naturally created networks proved too good an opportunity for entrepreneurial Nigerian exporters to miss.

Indeed, supportive findings on the importance of international ethnic ties or contact networks are proliferating. Crick and Chaudhry (1995) have recently explained the choice of East Africa as first export destination for many British-Asian exporters, as arising from the ethnic links which the latter have with East Africa. An earlier study by Jackson (1981) had found similar evidence in respect of Israeli exports to Britain. Zafarullah *et al.*'s (1998) Pakistani study equally reported on the catalytic impact of ethnic (cultural) ties in the internationalisation of their SME sample. These add to a growing body of findings on entrepreneurial networks and relationships, some of which are nationally or ethnically based.

Available evidence appears to preclude any definite conclusions, either in favour or against the Uppsala incremental model. To recapitulate, the finding that firms of comparable size and market experience exhibited remarkably different internationalisation behaviour reflects one of the major criticisms of the 'stages' theory i.e. its selective applicability or relevance. Similar conclusions can be implied from Madsen and Servais (1997) three-tier classification[5] of international firms into traditional exporters, late starters, and born globals; and Coviello and Munro's (1997) finding of evidence of internationalisation stages, network-driven as well as accelerated internationalisation among the New Zealand firms surveyed.

Observations such as the above provide the *raison d'être* for the holistic approach to internationalisation recently propagated by Bell and Young (1998) and Coviello and McAuley (1999). This emerging consensus clearly favours the broadening of the small firm internationalisation theory (beyond the 'narrow' stage of development perspective) to encapsulate other relevant perspectives.

One such useful perspective is the resource-based view of SME internationalisation: firms differ with respect to resource bundles or position, which differences account for their respective, even conflicting, paths to growth, internationalisation included. It is arguable that this approach presents a suitable platform for integrating the competing theories of SME internationalisation. In this integrative framework, the key drivers of extant internationalisation theories – increasing organisational learning and market knowledge (incremental model) and external relationship benefits (network perspective) – are seen as different manifestations of firms' resources, some internal, others coming from outside.

It is gratifying that this holistic framework explains the differing internationalisation behaviour exhibited by the Nigerian firms discussed in this chapter. The internationalised companies, A and B, appear to possess the key resources/competencies (internationally-oriented decision makers; strong management support; quality products; organisational learning and market experience; good financial base; and, in the case of Company A, good network relationships). The domestic ones (D to I), on the other hand, show obvious resource gaps in such key areas as top management support and decision makers' international orientation.

CONCLUSIONS, POLICY AND RESEARCH IMPLICATIONS

This present study suggests that firms' competencies and capabilities are critical determinants of internationalisation behaviour. The specific resources which are likely to be important include decision maker(s)' international orientation and experience, product quality and technology, networking/relationships, finance (including access to credit facilities) and foreign market information. It should be

	Less-resourced	Better-resourced
Domesic	**[I]** *Introduce change agents *Provide access to relevant technologies *Provide training/information support *Encourage networking	**[II]** *Help to redress competency gap *Provide specially±tailored training and support *Ease access export development resources *Initiate mentoring relationship
International	**[III]** *Seek positive reinforcement *Improve access to credit and relevant technologies *Deploy liaison officer/problem solver *Provide links to useful networks, e.g local export club membership	**[IV]** *Encourage continuous improvements *Encourage better structure/practices *Facilitate participation in network structures *Mitigate operational problems policy, infrastructure and market access

Figure 6.1   Targeting internationalisation support by resource base

noted that this list is neither exhaustive nor obligatory. Indeed, SMEs need not possess all these specified resources in order to internationalise or perform well in the international market. What is rather more crucial is the skill and vision with which they are guided by their decision makers toward deploying internal capabilities, while leveraging external resources in areas of slack.

The key thrust of internationalisation support policies, therefore, should be on improving and strengthening firms' resource position. This is even more critical for SMEs operating in difficult (developing country) environments. To ensure effective deployment of relevant support measures (Seringhaus, 1987; Crick and Czinkota, 1995), it is suggested that SMEs be targeted by resource profile, thus: (I) less-resourced domestic firms, (II) better-resourced domestic firms (III) less-resourced international firms, and (IV) better-resourced international firms (see Figure 6.1). The resource profile (including the orientation of key decision makers) of SMEs in quadrant I could benefit from provision of access to relevant new technologies and practices, seminars and workshops, and sponsorship to trade fairs. It may also be helpful to introduce appropriately qualified managers on part or full-time basis, provide links to foreign customers, as well as encourage networking.

For SMEs in quadrant II, the key may lie in understanding the specific competency gap that is hindering internationalisation. This may be the absence of managerial vision or lack of access to international market information, or any other factor. But the weak spot, whatever it is, would have to be addressed in order to enable such firms internationalise. Potentially useful support measures may comprise specifically tailored training programmes, initiating mentoring relationships, providing foreign market reports and contacts.

Although firms in quadrant III have already internationalised, their resource base needs to be strengthened in order to enhance their foreign market prospects. Such firms may have started exporting accidentally through the receipt of unsolicited foreign orders or related external–reactive stimuli. It is, thus, suggested that they be supported with easier access to relevant technologies, credit facilities, training programmes as well as assistance in employing suitable decision makers. Provision of links to useful networks may also be helpful.

The policy thrust for quadrant IV firms should be in shoring up their key competencies and renewing the international vision of their top management. Such firms should be encouraged to continually improve their competitiveness through appropriate innovations in products, processes, organisations, markets, and technology (OECD, 1997), as well as mutually beneficial relationships with other market partners – intermediaries, suppliers, financiers, government officials (domestic and foreign), and other stakeholders.

Further research is obviously needed on the key themes of this chapter. Given the relative recency of the use of the resource-based view in explaining firm internationalisation behaviour, greater scholarly effort is required at both conceptual and empirical levels to further illuminate this perspective. Researchers, indeed, have a challenge to improve the clarity and rigour with which firms' resource profile is measured in the internationalisation context, as well as delineate necessary ground rules for quality resource-based internationalisation research. This, clearly, can only be achieved through more active engagement with the research-based approach as a veritable tool for understanding firm internationalisation, particularly small firm internationalisation.

It remains to acknowledge the *limitations* that underlie this study. For one thing, the general reluctance of the surveyed firms to divulge hard export data limits the confidence with which the outward international market activity of Nigerian firms can be estimated, a situation worsened by the high level of unrecorded cross-border trade in Nigerian manufactured products. It is worth noting, also, that an overwhelming majority of the firms studied are, like most developing countries firms, small: 85 per cent had less than 100 million *naira* (about US$1.2 m) annual turnover when the study was undertaken.

Notes

1. The 'stages of development' tradition has spawned many behavioural models. The actual number of 'stages' differs, according to models, but, as observed by Andersen (1993, p. 212), this 'reflects semantic differences rather than real differences concerning the nature of the internationalisation process'. A recent (integrative) review article by Leonidou and Katsikeas (1996), which covered eleven of these empirical export development models, identified three generic stages, namely pre-export stage, the initial export stage and the advanced export stage.

2. It is worth noting that only a minimum size (Withey, 1980), not a maximum size, was specified for the study population. This was intended to allow for the generation of as many insights as possible into the outward internationalisation activities of qualifying Nigerian firms, be they fairly large (over 500 employees / N100 m annual sales revenue) or small. It emerged, however, that 87.5 per cent of firms in the sample were, like most developing countries firms, small–medium-sized, that is, with fewer than 500 employees / N100 m annual sales (US$1.2 m). The classification of the remaining 12.5 per cent of the firms as large-sized owes more to the above 500 employee profile than to any remarkable annual sales figure.

3. The additional use of firms' age as a constituent measure of organisation's size is based on the assumption that younger firms are more likely to be small, while older firms have a greater likelihood of being large. This researcher recognises that this is not always the case, hence the use of two other measures of firms' size: employees number and sales revenue.

4. The criticality of international orientation and decision makers' contact networks is widely acknowledged both in the 'more traditional' export literature (for example, Simmonds and Smith, 1968) and in the emerging literature on international entrepreneurship, networks and resource-based internationalisation.

5. 'Traditional exporters' describes firms whose internationalisation pattern reflects the stage approach; 'late starters' refers to those that have only domestic sales for many years, but suddenly leapfrog some stages and invest in a distant foreign market; 'born globals' accelerate through the process.

7 Market Space and the New Mechanism of Internationalisation: Some Preliminary Insights

Jürgen Kai-Uwe Brock

INTRODUCTION

Firms are consumers, producers, managers and distributors of information (Egelhoff, 1991; Casson, 1996), and information use is an essential element of organisational operations in order to reduce uncertainty and ambiguity about its external environment and its internal operations (Daft and Lengel, 1986). Consequently, it is not surprising that at the core of internationalisation process theory is lack of knowledge and subsequently uncertainty about markets abroad, due to a lack of location-sensitive foreign market information (Johanson and Vahlne, 1977, 1990). The internationalisation process is in essence seen as a costly experiential learning process of information and knowledge accumulation in order to gradually reduce uncertainties about markets abroad.

Recent developments in location-insensitive, less costly information and communication technology (ICT) infrastructures could therefore significantly alter the nature and process of internationalisation and international organisational operations by impacting this core process.

In order to discuss and assess this potential new mechanism of the internationalisation process of the firm critically, this chapter is organised as follows. The following section briefly reviews the internationalisation theory of the firm. Thereafter, the internationalisation theory of the firm will be related to the emergence of the location-insensitive and global information and communication infrastructure, the 'market space' (Rayport and Sviokla, 1994). The discussion of its possible impacts on the internationalisation process of firms will mainly draw on ICT theories. Preliminary quantitative findings, based on a survey of small technology-based firms (STBFs) involved in market space-based activities, are reported subsequently. A brief discussion of the findings, their limitations and concluding remarks close the paper.

INTERNATIONALISATION THEORY OF THE FIRM

The timely fashion of internationalisation and its underlying forces are the focus of internationalisation process theories. Despite criticism (see for example: Andersen, 1993; Casson, 1993; Clark *et al.*, 1997; Hadjikhani, 1997; Bell *et al.*, 1998), its most dominant theory is still the Uppsala Internationalisation Model (UIM) (see for example Andersen, 1993; Leonidou and Katsikeas, 1996). Incorporating these criticisms and expanding the model in this review is however beyond the scope of this paper. The focus here is rather on a new possible expansion that was not previously proposed in the literature. The following sub-sections briefly review its assumptions and the suggested process forces. The postulated organisational manifestations of this process – the psychic distance-sensitive establishment chain – are not further discussed here due to space limitations. Suffice it to say that the author shares Buckley's view that its rigid outcome typology can now be considered outdated (Buckley, 1996) and that a falsification of its postulated surface manifestations is not necessarily the same as a falsification of the reasoning behind its suggested process forces (Madsen and Servais, 1997).

Assumptions

The UIM assumes that a firm first develops in its domestic market and then gradually develops its operations abroad. It is based on the assumption that firms are growth-seeking and risk-minimising organisations (Johanson and Vahlne, 1977).

At the core of the internationalisation process is lack of knowledge and subsequently uncertainty about markets abroad, due to lack of location-sensitive and costly foreign market information (ibid.). The accumulation of experiential knowledge about foreign markets is assumed to be the main source and key driver in the gradual internationalisation process (Johanson and Vahlne, 1990), as it reduces uncertainty and the related perceived risk, by providing the firm with information about a foreign market.

The Process

The underlying basic mechanisms of the internationalisation process are determined by an interaction of the current experience, knowledge and commitment of the firm with its current activities and commitment decisions (Johanson and Vahlne, 1977). These commitment decisions are influenced by the firm's opportunity horizon, as well as, by economic and uncertainty effects. Assuming that decisions regarding international market opportunities are dependent on and formed by a firm's experience, means of addressing market opportunities are searched for within the environment the firm is interacting with. This environment constitutes the firm's opportunity horizon.

In 1990, Johanson and Vahlne theoretically extended their original process model. They incorporated findings originally developed in the area of industrial marketing, reporting on the important influence of a firm's network on its operations in general and on its internationalisation process in particular (see for example Johanson and Mattson, 1988; Blankenburg and Johanson, 1992). This extension can be seen as a specification of the nature of the opportunity horizon in the change aspects of the original model.

Analysed this way, the internationalisation emphasis is more on a firm's external relationships and its impact on the firm, rather than merely focusing on internal aspects. This approach views the interaction with other firms as providing a firm with the capabilities to perform its activities (Ford *et al.*, 1986). Thus its external network becomes a crucial resource and a valuable asset in its own right, in addition to its internal resources and assets.

In summary, the traditional UIM proposes that growth-seeking and risk-minimising firms gradually increase their international operations as their domestically accumulated internal resource-base expands, their external resource-base (the firm's business network) expands and their information and consequently knowledge about foreign markets increases.

Recent developments in ICT, most prominently the emergence of a global and universally accessible market space (Rayport and Sviokla, 1994), challenge some of the key assumptions of this traditional model. Besides introducing a new mode of internationalisation (Brock, 2000), this market space has the potential to reduce or even eliminate the information and resource-related barriers in the internationalisation process of the firm. Within this new international business context, one author even argues that this market space 'presents a fundamentally different environment ... and new paradigms will have to be developed to take account of internationalization processes in an electronic age' (Hamill, 1997).

The following section will address these issues. First, it will briefly explain what is meant by 'market space'; and second, it will address the market space's potential of reducing resource and information related barriers. The section will close with some suggestions on how these factors might impact the internationalisation process of firm. These will in turn be empirically assessed in the final section of this chapter.

INTERNATIONALISATION OF THE FIRM: POSSIBLE
MARKET SPACE EXTENSIONS

Whereas the market place represents the physical world of resources, the market space represents the virtual world of digitised information (Rayport and Sviokla, 1994). The Internet-based worldwide web is probably its most prominent incarnation. The distinction between the market place and the market space is important, because both worlds represent unique characteristics, albeit being interconnected, which usually means that companies have to operate in both 'worlds' (see Figure 7.1).

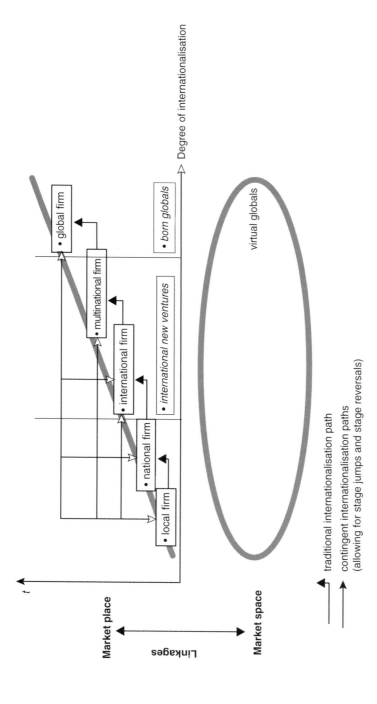

Figure 7.1 Internationlisation: market place versus market space

Source: Adapted from Brock (2000), with the permission of Pearson Education.

Market Place and Market Space Linkages and the Internationalisation Process of Firms

As noted above, the internationalisation process of the firm is strongly influenced by resource and information-related factors. Both factors can be influenced by the market space.

Reduction in Interaction Costs
Using the market space can save costs, because communication on market space reduces interaction costs (Butler *et al.*, 1997; OECD, 1998). Interaction costs refer to the costs involved in searching (data gathering), coordinating and monitoring, as opposed to costs involved in non-interactive tasks like data processing and production (Butler *et al.*, 1997). Is also relates to marketing activities, considered to be cheaper compared to traditional marketing channels (Angelides, 1997). In addition, due to market space's digital nature, transformation costs, the costs of transforming information from one medium to another, are reduced (Rice and Bair, 1984; Culnan and Markus, 1987). Written communication on the Internet is also faster compared to analogue forms of written communication (Butler *et al.*, 1997), thereby reducing potential opportunity costs associated with 'information float' (Hammer and Mangurian, 1987). Additionally, 'shadow functions' – non-productive microactivities in the communication process like redialling a busy telephone number – are reduced (Rice and Bair, 1984; Culnan and Markus, 1987) because various activities involved in the communication process on the market space can be automated. Due to its global nature and the time delay between sending and receiving messages (for example e-mail), market space-based services decrease interaction costs further by reducing spatial constraints and the importance for temporal availability (Culnan and Markus, 1987). Finally, due to the market space's technical openness, firms no longer need to set up their own network or search for feasible trading partners before they can participate in and benefit from electronic networks.

This overall reduction in interaction costs is important, because interaction costs account for a significant percentage of all costs faced by firms (Rice and Bair, 1984; Butler *et al.*, 1997) and the economy as a whole (Rice and Bair, 1984; Wallis and North, 1986; Butler *et al.*, 1997). This reduction is particularly important in the context of the internationalisation of the firm, because organisational growth, which is often viewed as the background to the internationalisation of the firm (see above), is inseparably coupled with the collection of additional, interaction cost sensitive information (Egelhoff, 1991).

Overcoming Information Barriers
Providing global access to information and potential business partners is the second and probably most influential factor of the market space on the internationalisation of the firm. This is in addition to the reduced costs of acquiring and distributing information as discussed above.

International awareness. Still little is known about the specific internal processes of information processing and its role in the internationalisation of the firm (Liesch and Knight, 1999). However, it was noted early on that firms located near international 'information centres' are exposed to more external internationalisation stimuli (Olson and Wiedersheim-Paul, 1978). While these authors referred to a firm's location in the market place – they suggest for example a location near a border to be rich in such stimuli – it can be argued that stimuli exposure taking place on the market space can have similar effects. Hamill (1997) for example argues that the active participation on the global market space can potentially reduce attitudinal barriers by increasing a firm's exposure to international stimuli, thereby increasing its international awareness.

Experiential versus objective knowledge. Besides the passive awareness dimension, firms can also utilise the market space actively to improve their information and subsequently knowledge about international markets. However, it is important to reconsider the postulated importance of experiential versus objective knowledge in the internationalisation process of firms, because the market space cannot supply firms with market place-based experiential knowledge.

Numerous empirical studies have not found support for the postulated importance of experiential, market specific knowledge (see, for example, Millington and Bayliss, 1990; Clark *et al.*, 1997; Hadjikhani, 1997; Bell *et al.*, 1998). General industry knowledge and objective knowledge derived from systematic market investigations were at least of similar importance. The globalisation of markets further reduce the overall importance of market specific, experiential knowledge, thereby facilitating simultaneous market entry strategies exploiting economies of scale (Casson, 1993).

Therefore, the market space can indeed be of importance in the internationalisation process of market space-active firms. However, its potential usefulness in reducing knowledge-based barriers depends on the perceived 'international wiredness' at the industry and business peer level (see next section and Figure 7.2).

Networking on market space. According to the expanded UIM, external links or networks are another important source of information and knowledge generation in the internationalisation of the firm. Taking the distinction between market place and market space into consideration, the market space thus opens up a new sphere of network influence (see Figure 7.2).

Although the literature on international industry networks does not explicitly consider the potentially different effects of whether these networks are initiated and maintained in market place or market space (or both), a review of the ICT literature suggests additional factors. These factors need to be considered, because firms often rely on informal and personal relationships as sources of information (Leonidou and Katsikeas, 1999). According to traditional media choice theory, this is a type of relationship whose formation is hampered when taking place on market space.

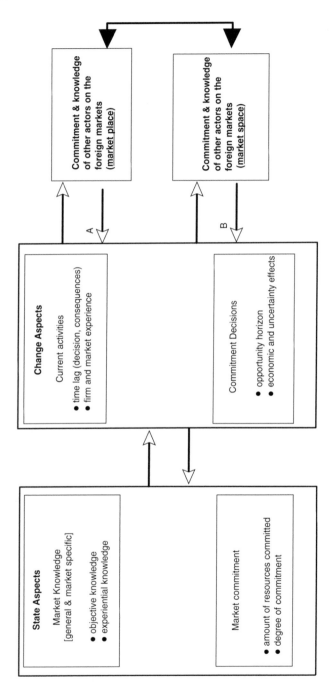

Figure 7.2 The expanded internationalisation process model

Networking on market space and media richness theory. Media richness theory (Daft and Lengel, 1986) suggests that an individual determines his or her choice of media by rationally assessing the requirements of a communication task and selecting an appropriate medium matching these requirements (Fulk *et al.*, 1990). This theory categorises media along a continuum of information richness, which depends on the medium's ability for immediate feedback, the number of carried cues, its language variety and its level of personalisation. The higher the perceived need for information richness in a communication situation, the higher the postulated likelihood of communication partners conducting their information exchange in a face-to-face manner, the richest mode of information exchange.

In contrast to face-to-face communication, mediated communication – like interacting on the market space – ranks lower on the proposed continuum. It follows that the reduction in channel capacity makes interaction on the market space more difficult compared to non-mediated market place interactions. Based on rational media choice theory, the market space thus offers only a limited possibility for interaction and thus its role in network-influenced internationalisation is comparatively low compared to market place-based networking opportunities like trade fairs and personal visits abroad.

Networking on market space and social media theories. Mixed empirical findings regarding the predictive validity of the rational media choice theories (see for example, Fulk *et al.*, 1990; Markus, 1994; Ngwenyama and Lee, 1997) have led to the development of social influence models of communication technology use (Contractor and Eisenberg, 1990; Fulk *et al.*, 1990; Ngwenyama and Lee, 1997; Carlson and Zmud, 1999). Social influences are particularly important for new media like the market space, because standardised ways of communication have not yet fully developed (Markus, 1994) and a critical mass of user (Markus, 1987) becomes important with regards to its usefulness. In the international context of this chapter, the perceived degree of 'international peer wiredness' and the perceived degree of 'international industry wiredness' thus become important factors for the potential usefulness and influence of market space-based networks on the internationalisation of the firm (see Figure 7.2).

Social media choice theories all regard information richness in communications not as attributable to the channel capacity of the medium alone, but as emerging from the interaction between people and contexts (Ngwenyama and Lee, 1997). Media perceptions are not fixed but they vary across people, organisations, situations, tasks and the users' experience with the medium. Communication richness is therefore an outcome of social behaviour (Markus, 1994), not an outcome of the nominal media richness of the communication channel alone (Carlson and Zmud, 1999). Hence informal, interpersonal interactions can take place over mediated communication channels, as user experience with the medium and the communication partners increase. An empirically supported phenomenon that has been termed the 'channel expansion effect' (Carlson and Zmud, 1999).

96 Market Space and Internationalisation

Consequently, market space-based networking and subsequent impacts on the internationalisation process are theoretically possible, depending on the degree of perceived international wiredness, on the firm's experience with the medium and depending on the accumulated experience with its interaction partners. But in contrast to the location-sensitive market place (von Hayek, 1945) implicit in the UIM, market space-based experience is location independent.

New Interaction Capabilities on Market Space
The above discussion compared interaction taking place on the market space with interaction taking place in the market place. Such a comparison has been criticised on the grounds that new media offers capabilities and functions that traditional media lack (Culnan and Markus, 1987; Contractor and Eisenberg, 1990). Therefore it is fruitful to consider these effects and how they might impact the internationalisation of the firm.

Of major relevance here is the observation among communication researchers that participation in 'communication spaces' (Culnan and Markus, 1987), like the ones offered by the market space, can increase the range and diversity of strong and weak interorganisational ties (Contractor and Eisenberg, 1990). It is argued that especially the range and diversity of an organisation's weak ties are important, because they are more likely to provide an organisation with information different from that received via its network of close business contacts due to its 'bridging function' to other spheres of information (Granovetter, 1973). Weak network ties can in essence de-encapsulate an organisation from its immediate operational environment of strong network ties, thereby increasing the important opportunity horizon of firms stated above. Increased utilisation of the market space for international business and the subsequent increase in the opportunity horizon of a firm could therefore influence the direction of internationalisation (the foreign markets selected). A potential impact in addition to the cost and information related factors discussed above.

Table 7.1 summarises the discussed observations regarding the potential impacts of the market space on the internationalisation process of firm, including some of the empirical results presented in the next section.

MARKET SPACE-INFLUENCED INTERNATIONALISATION: PRELIMINARY EMPIRICAL INSIGHTS

To the present day no empirical investigation has systematically tried to assess the potential impacts of the market space on the internationalisation of firms. The few studies that do exist (see, for example, Bennett, 1997) are either limited in scope (e.g. case study-based or export-focused), lack a strong theoretical background (e.g. rather descriptive without references to relevant ICT theories) or are weak in their construct operationalisation and assessment (e.g. use of binary measures). This section will present some of the preliminary findings of a survey-based investigation by the researcher.

Table 7.1 Internationalisation factors, potential market space impacts and empirical findings

Internationalisation factors	Potential effects	Finding
● Costs	– reduction in interaction costs	RQ2a supported (only experience with web sites significant)
● International awareness	– increase in international awareness	RQ2b not supported
● Lack of international contacts	– increase in the range of international interorganisational ties (market space networking)	RQ2c supported (only level of use significant)
● Lack of information/lack of knowledge	– global information provision reduces information-related barriers	RQ2d not supported (supported for the total sample)
● Lack of resources	– reduction in resource-related barriers due to reduced interaction costs	RQ2e not supported
● Foreign market selection	– market space increases the opportunity horizon of firms and subsequently its impact on market selections	RQ2f supported (see Table 7.2)

Methodology and Tested Research Questions

In order to empirically assess potential market space impacts on the internationalisation of the firm, a survey was conducted in Germany in the federal state of Northrhine-Westphalia. Selecting small technology-based firms (STBFs) located in science parks, the survey achieved a net response rate of 40%, with 112 participating firms. The organisational characteristics of the sample are shown in Figure 7.3. This population was purposely selected because (a) STBFs are known to have a strong international orientation early on (see, for example, Knight and Cavusgil, 1996), (b) STBFs' managers are known to be early adopters of new technology (Brock, 2000) and (c) science parks provide infrastructure support for STBFs. All these factors together are crucial for an impact study, since the diffusion of market space technology among small firms in general is still comparatively low (Brock, 2000). STBFs in science parks constitute a population rich in internationally active and market space active firms, thus allowing for an assessment of potential market place–market space linkages.

Based on the discussion above, the following research questions were developed and tested:

1. Is the level of market space use influenced by the perceived international industry and peer wiredness? (RQ1)

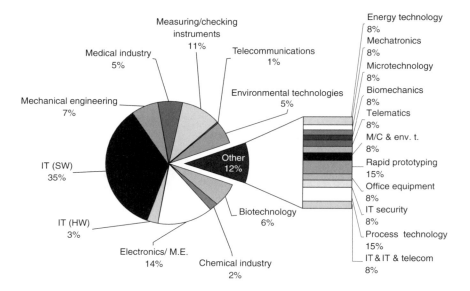

Figure 7.3   Characteristics of the sample

2. Does market space use for international business:
   (a) decrease a firm's average cost of conducting international business? (RQ2a)
   (b) increase a firm's international awareness? (RQ2b)
   (c) increase a firm's number of international business contacts? (RQ2c)
   (d) reduce information-related internationalisation barriers? (RQ2d)
   (e) reduce resource-related internationalisation barriers? (RQ2e)
   (f) influence the selection of foreign markets? (RQ2f)

In order to test the research questions posed above, a measure was developed to scale the level of market space use drawing on diffusion of innovation theory (Rogers, 1995) and exploratory interviews with market space-active firms. The measure, routinised level of market space use for international business, exhibited a good reliability ($\alpha = 0.82$) and trait validity (based on a factor analytic investigation) taking its exploratory stage into consideration. Following the behavioural model of ICT use (Seddon, 1997) and the literature review, this measure and two experience related measures (experience with using the Internet and experience with a corporate website) were subsequently used to assess their influence on the internationalisation of firms. In order to assess research question number 1, a wiredness scale was developed by asking the STBFs how they perceive the level of relevant international business information on the market space and how they perceive the level of market space use among their international business partners. A factor analytic investigation revealed the two expected sub-dimensions international industry and peer wiredness. Both sub-dimensions exhibited good levels of reliability ($\alpha = 0.89$ for industry wiredness and $\alpha = 0.75$ for peer wiredness).

It should be noted that the results presented below are based on a sub-sample of the original survey (50 STBFs). Only firms with market space experience prior to their first international activities were considered. It is assumed that the market space influence is therefore more formative and might reveal more interesting insights for subsequent studies.

Determinants of Market Space Use for International Business

A regression analysis gave strong support for the notion that the usefulness of the market space for international business depends on the perceived wiredness (RQ1). Levels of use were significantly influenced by the perceived international peer and industry wiredness (adj. R^2 0.70; F-value 102.59; p-value 0.0000). Particularly peer wiredness is a strong determinant (Beta 0.60; t-value 8.634; p-value 0.0000), nearly twice as influential as industry wiredness (Beta 0.34; t-value 4.933; p-value 0.0000).

Market Space Impacts

A regression analysis gave support for some of the suggested impact dimensions in research question 2. A perceived reduction in the average costs of conducting international business activities (RQ2a) found positive support. It increased significantly with increases in a firm's website experience (adj. R^2 0.15; F-value 3.04; p-value 0.043; Beta 0.54; t-value 2.72; p-value 0.0102). But a significant increase in international awareness due to increases in market space use could not be found (RQ2b). Assessing RQ2c showed that firms using the market space

Table 7.2 Overview of the market space's perceived impact on foreign market selections

Variable	Mean	Std. dev.	Meaning (Likert scale 1–7)	Regression results (experience & level of use impact)
IMPIPULA	3.74	2.24	impact of Internet information search on selection of foreign markets	adj. R^2 0.177; F-value 5.39; p-value 0.0085 Beta 0.47; t-value 3.27; p-value 0.0023 (only level of use significant)
IMPIPULP	3.83	2.17	impact of Internet information receipt on selection of foreign markets	adj. R^2 0.355; F-value 12.28; p-value 0.0001 Beta 0.62; t-value 4.87; p-value 0.0000 (only level of use significant)
IMPUINQ	3.74	2.12	impact of Internet-based unsolicited inquiries on selection of foreign markets	adj. R^2 0.22; F-value 6.62; p-value 0.0034 Beta 0.48; t-value 3.59; p-value 0.0016 (only level of use significant)

extensively experienced a significant increases in the number of market space-based international business contacts (adj. R^2 0.32; F-value 10.62; p-value 0.0002; Beta 0.51; t-value 3.89; p-value 0.00004). Despite this overall increase in business contacts, perceived information barriers (RQ2d) did not exhibit a significant reduction for high levels of market space use (although they did for the total sample: adj. R^2 0.039; F-value 5.171; p-value 0.025; Beta -0.22; t-value -2.274; p-value 0.025). Additionally, despite the market space's ability to reduce costs (see RQ2a), resource related barriers (as measured by a scale previously used by Preece *et al.*, 1998) were not reduced either (RQ2e). The actual selection of foreign markets entered was significantly influenced by market space-based factors as use increases (RQ2f; see table 7.2). Overall, the average perceived market space impact increased with levels of use ($r = 0.85$, p-value 0.000) and the importance of market space-related factors compared to market place-related factors also increased with use ($r = 0.53$, p-value 0.000).

DISCUSSION AND CONCLUDING REMARKS

The reported empirical findings give preliminary support to the notion that using the market space can play an influential role in the internationalisation of firms, although not all the potential impact dimensions found support.

It was shown that utilising the market space for international business helped the sampled STBFs to reduce costs, to reduce the lack of information and to increase their range of international business contacts. Ultimately, even influencing their foreign market selection by providing information and contacts. Effects that depended mainly on organisational levels of use. Levels, which were influenced by the perceived usefulness of this new medium (the perceived degree of international wiredness at the industry and business peer level).

Hence, the market space impact on the internationalisation process of firms is mainly twofold. First, it can reduce cost and information related internationalisation barriers and second, it can increase the opportunity horizon of firms. Both of which are key influential process forces according to the UIM. Thus, the assumption of the UIM that firms first develop purely domestically, due more or less to their locational isolation from international business aspects, no longer holds. The location-insensitive market space enables even the smallest firm to act as a 'global scanner' for business opportunities. An activity that was previously confined to MNEs (Vernon, 1979).

Taking the increasing importance of international business due to a more integrated global economy for small firms in general into consideration (Brock, 2000), this finding is of importance for managers in small firms. Depending on their industry specifics (the degree of wiredness), the market space can constitute an important support tool in small firm internationalisation. Manager should be aware of that. And, more importantly, managers should learn that simple adoption is not enough. This study has shown that experience and particularly levels of use mattered. These organisational levels of use, although not further explored here, are not achieved instantaneously. They require the development of internal managerial ICT skills. Skills that are quite different from the traditional managerial skills needed in international business. Managers should remember that it is not the technology per se, but their firms' internal managerial skills in putting this new technology to an effective use that makes the difference (Brock, 2000).

From a theoretical and research perspective the empirical investigation showed that considering ICT research is a fruitful complimentary theoretical base for assessing and explaining the role of the market space on the international operations of firms. Particularly social media choice theories found empirical support. The perceived wiredness strongly influenced market space use levels and market space-based networking did not only take place, but it also impacted the selection of foreign markets.

The most important implication for the UdIM is that the sphere of network influence needs to be expanded to account for the ICT-enabled market space. The findings clearly showed that market space-based business contacts and networks also play an influential role in the internationalisation of firms.

However, the reported findings have to be interpreted with some caution. First, the statistical analysis is at an early stage and potential moderating and mediating influences are not yet assessed. Second, the population of STBFs was purposely selected due to their tendency for early internationalisation and high levels of ICT use compared to other firms (see above). This obviously constitutes a 'pro-innovation bias' (Rogers, 1995) and generalisations to other firms are therefore limited. The specific nature of the population might also explain the non-significant findings regarding an impact on the international orientation of firms. The sampled STBFs might simply be too internationally oriented anyway. Third, the statistical power of the test is relatively low due to the sample size. This could imply that potentially significant impact dimensions were not detected if small effect sizes exist. Fourth, it might still be relatively early to assess the market space's impact on the internationalisation of firms. It was only since the birth of the worldwideweb and the browser software 'Mosaic' in 1993 that using the market space slowly started to make business sense. Thus, it can be expected that the overall market space influence will increase in the future, as its global diffusion levels continue to increase. Therefore it is hoped that this paper encourages additional researchers to also embark on the new research agenda, 'Market Space and International Business', in order to validate or falsify the early, preliminary findings of this study.

Part Two

Managing the Multinational

8 Is the Governance of Transnationals Really 'Beyond the M-form'? A Critical Review of Bartlett and Ghoshal's 'New Organisational Model'

Paul N. Gooderham and Svein Ulset

INTRODUCTION

In a series of articles and books published over the last 13 years, Bartlett and Ghoshal have described and analysed the evolution of multinational companies with a particular focus on the functioning of the so-called transnationals such as ABB, General Electric, 3M, Toyota and Canon. Their approach has been heavily managerial in the sense that 'the model was developed by analysing the operations of a firm from the perspective and in the language of the managers who live within the system' (Bartlett and Ghoshal, 1993: 117). In their view, managers of transnationals tend to lead their company more by influencing cultural, social and psychological processes than by influencing strategy, structure and system. They contend that their roles have evolved so radically as to make them significantly different from those typically found in M-form organizations (Chandler, 1962, 1986; Williamson 1971, 1986, 1981). In their view the classic responsibilities of M-form leadership comprise the formulation of corporate strategy, the design of formal structure and the implementation of systems of control. In the last decade, in the context of the transnational, Bartlett and Ghoshal contend that each of these has been respectively replaced by three distinctively new responsibilities. The first involves an emphasis on shaping institutional purpose in such a way that employees can identify with it and commit to it. The second is the development of organisational processes that both capture individual initiative and create supporting relationships. The third is a focus on the individual as the primary unit of analysis in the leadership task. In short leaders of transnationals are 'molders of people' (Bartlett and Ghoshal, 1993: 40).

Even if one accepts this leadership role as the defining characteristic of the transnationals this does not by itself imply that transnationals have moved 'beyond the M-form'. For this to be the case the new leadership role must also to a significant degree have replaced the traditional management role associated with the M-form enterprise. This is an enterprise in which there is a separation of operating from strategic decision-making and in which the requisite internal control apparatus is operative. In terms of the M-form optimum divisionalisation involves:

(1) the identification of separable economic activities within the firm; (2) according quasi-autonomous standing (usually of a profit centre nature) to each; (3) monitoring the efficiency performance of each division; (4) awarding incentives; (5) allocating cash flows to high-yield uses; and (6) performing strategic planning (diversification, acquisition, divestiture, and related activities) in other respects. (Williamson, 1986: 68)

The adjective 'optimum' is used comparatively to indicate that the M-form possesses advantages over the unitary or holding forms of organisations. The question is then whether the management practice of ABB and similar transnationals really constitute a break with the above.

Bartlett and Ghoshal relate that their research gradually led them to the conclusion that what they were witnessing represented 'nothing less than the unfolding of the most profound change in management in a lifetime' (Ghoshal and Bartlett, 1997: ix). As a result they started to develop an alternative managerial theory of the firm. At the core of this theory is a model comprising three fundamental processes: entrepreneurship, integration and renewal. The management of these processes are the domains of front-line managers, middle level managers and top-level managers respectively (Bartlett and Ghoshal, 1993, 1995; Ghoshal and Bartlett, 1997).

The purpose of this chapter is to question both the usefulness of the managerial approach and Bartlett and Ghoshal's interpretation of the transnationals, as exemplified by ABB, as representing a radically new form, distinctly different from the M-form. We will argue that their managerial approach has not only blinded them to many of the essential conditions of the management of multinational enterprises, but also to the essential features of the M-form and the differences and similarities between this and their 'New Form'. In particular we will argue that the management roles and relationships characterising the New Form may be easily subsumed under the M-form and that consequently the Bartlett and Ghoshal process model reflects the efficient workings of the modern M-form rather than any distinctly different New Form.

After discussing the main features of the M-form we turn to the new model thesis and the associated evolutionary hypothesis 'that many worldwide industries have been transformed in the 1980s ... toward a transnational form' (Bartlett and Ghoshal, 1995:475). Thereafter, Bartlett and Ghoshal's evidence for the emergence of a new organisational form will be presented and evaluated. Finally, we will focus on the issues of conflict and opportunism that arguably represent the transnational's Achilles heel. In our view, while normative control may provide valuable assistance, it can never take on the leading role in promoting the type of strategic direction and coordinated behavior needed among geographically dispersed units of large multinationals.

THE MODERN M-FORM

Since Chandler published his highly influential monograph, 'Strategy and Structure' (1962), the multidivisional organisational structure – the so-called M-form – has generally been recognised as the structural form of choice for large global corporations aiming at product and market diversity. In short the M-form is distinguished by the delegation of operating responsibility from corporate level to the operating division level and even further down to smaller business units. This leaves the corporate office to focus on mainly strategic tasks, the chief of which is to stake out the strategic direction of the corporation, monitor the performance of its divisions, and to allocate resources between operating divisions and business units. By practicing hierarchical decomposition, that is, by drawing horizontal and vertical boundaries around these in a way that maximised intra-unit (intra-division) and minimised inter-unit (inter-division) dependencies, total costs of communication were minimised. To further assist management in carrying out their strategic and operating responsibilities a range of information systems and expert staffs were also included. Along with various committees, task forces and liaison devices were deployed to promote lateral coordination between divisions or business units (Lawrence and Lorch, 1967; Galbraith, 1973, 1977; Mintzberg, 1979, 1983).

Although these may regarded as the main features of the modern M-form, considerable variations have been detected within this structure. These concern the size of the corporate office, the use of internal governance mechanisms (such as operating budgets, strategic plans and performance reports) and the vertical delegation of strategic tasks (Goold and Campbell, 1987; Chandler, 1994). Whereas the corporate office may content itself with the simplest form of financial control when divisions are non-interdependent (that is, conglomerate or unrelated diversified companies), substantial strategic planning on the corporate level will be needed when underlying divisions are highly interdependent sharing the use of non-tradable common assets (related diversified companies). In the former case, the corporate office mainly takes on the role of an internal capital market, while in the latter case, the capital allocation role is combined with the role of defining and controlling strategic direction and priorities.

Breaking ranks with the received wisdom of the M-form, Bartlett and Ghoshal (1993) claim that a new organisational model, significantly different from the M-form organisation that has dominated corporate structures over the preceding five decades, is emerging. They argue that the genesis of this new form can be understood best in the context of a gradual evolution in the strategic role foreign operations play in MNCs. They divide this evolution into four stages of strategic mentality, the international, the multinational, the global and finally, an emerging mentality, the transnational. It is within the context of the transnational mentality, as epitomised by ABB, that Bartlett and Ghoshal claim to have uncovered a new organisational form every bit as distinctive as the M-form.

THE FOUR STAGES OF INTERNATIONALISATION

Bartlett and Ghoshal concede that their evolutionary four-part schema is 'over-generalized', 'somewhat arbitrary' and that there is 'no inevitability in either the direction or the end point of this evolving strategic mentality in worldwide companies' (Bartlett and Ghoshal, 1995: 14). However, their contention is that it nevertheless captures significant changes to the objectives of MNCs. They argue that the earliest motivations that drove companies to invest abroad were the need to secure key supplies of raw materials, to acquire new markets to achieve additional sales and to access low-cost factors of production such as cheap labour or lower-cost capital. At this initial, international, stage foreign operations were regarded as organisational appendages or as distant outposts to the domestic business and treated in an opportunistic rather than a strategic manner.

With increases to the efficient scale of production, escalating R&D costs and shortening product life cycles, internationalisation became essential in many sectors thus bringing about a change in strategic mentality. More attention was focused on international activities so that products, strategies and management practices were increasingly adapted to local environments.

While this multinational mentality results in highly responsive marketing approaches to the various national markets the many local adaptations involved cause some loss of production efficiency. By way of response the global strategic mentality viewed product standardisation, as opposed to nationally differentiated product variants, as perfectly viable. Thus the world became the unit of analysis and was served by centrally coordinated, highly efficient plants, often located at the corporate centre. Global companies – many of them Japanese – enjoyed great success exploiting scale economies throughout the 1970s and 1980s.

However, during the 1990s, Bartlett and Ghoshal argue that global companies have had to contend with increasing restrictions imposed by host governments, consumers' rejection of homogenised global products and volatile currency exchange rates. At the same time developments in computer-aided design and production technologies have made the concept of flexible, small batch, local production a viable alternative. Bartlett and Ghoshal (1995) conclude that while some products and processes must still be developed centrally for worldwide use, equally others must be created locally in each environment to meet purely local demands. As a consequence MNCs must increasingly use their access to multiple centers of technologies and familiarity with diverse customer preferences in different countries to create innovations that are transnational in character.

The management challenge has therefore, according to Bartlett and Ghoshal, become one of creating social structures that can produce global efficiency, national responsiveness, and worldwide learning simultaneously. To accomplish this, a more complex governance structure than the M-form is called for. Using ABB as the primary illustration of their new form. Bartlett and Ghoshal argue that the necessary degree of lateral coordination may be achieved by developing a complex, multilevel network of specialized management roles and relationships. Let us now examine their depiction of ABB.

THE CASE OF ABB

Percy Barnevik (ABB's former CEO) regularly referred to ABB as being simultaneously 'local and global, big and small, radically decentralised with central reporting and control'. For Bartlett and Ghoshal this is 'almost a perfect description of the transnational' (Bartlett and Ghoshal, 1995: 788). However, for Bartlett and Ghoshal not only is ABB a transnational but an example of how successful transnationals are destined to be. They point to that between 1988 and 1995 ABB not only succeeded in growing its revenues from $17 billion to $34 billion in 1995 but also in assuming industry leadership by stealing market share from such formidable competitors as GE, Hitachi, and Siemens (Ghoshal and Bartlett, 1997). In other words it represents the transnational *par excellence*. Bartlett and Ghoshal acknowledge that at the broadest level ABB resembles the classic M-form, in that at its corporate centre is a 13-man executive team that closely monitors developments in its highly decentralised activities around the world on the basis of a formalised system of monthly performance data. However, they insist that closer analysis reveals a number of radical differences each of which we will now briefly review.

The Status of the Front-line Unit

ABB is organised around a much greater degree of decentralisation of assets and responsibilities than is the case with the classic M-form, so that crucially the locus of entrepreneurship lies not at the corporate center but with the operating unit. Indeed front-line managers have a 'mandate to build their businesses as if they owned them' (Ghoshal and Bartlett, 1997: 248). Thus, in Bartlett and Ghoshal's view, the basic building block of ABB is not its 65 business areas (the equivalent of Chandler's divisions) but its local operating units. Together these encompass a network of 1300 separate companies, each a legal entity with its own balance sheet and profit and loss statement, with an average of 200 employees per company (Bartlett and Ghoshal, 1995).

   In this 'multi-domestic organization', as Barnevik refers to it, Barlett and Ghoshal (1993, 1995) observe that it is explicit corporate policy to allow managers to inherit results over the years through changes in their company's equity. Each unit is permitted to retain one third of its net profits giving front-line management substantial financial independence. Another significant indication of the status of these units is that rather than concentrating R&D in centralised corporate laboratories as in the M-form, within ABB more than 90 per cent of its R&D budget is invested in centres of excellence in front-line companies.

The Business/Geography Matrix

In the integrated network of ABB any local unit can be upgraded to take on a central task if and when the global strategy requires it, while equally resources and capabilities of many different units can be at any time pooled either at headquarters or subsidiary level. Significantly, ABB's operating companies are not functionally complete units, but rather dependent on being able to use one another's resources, including R&D expertise, to achieve their own goals. But rather than simply subsuming them under divisions, as in the M-form, or letting them stand entirely on their own feet as in the holding company model, at ABB these units are linked both to their global business area organisation and to their national managements. Thus ABB is deploying a business/geography matrix with dual reporting channels.

The Role of Middle Management

Unlike the eight or nine layers of middle management typical of the M-form, at ABB there is only one intermediate level between the corporate executive committee and the managers of the 1300 front line companies. Moreover, the role of middle management is not to secure vertical integration, as in the M-form, but to facilitate the realisation of the key strategic task of horizontal integration between units, not least in respect to knowledge. That is each business area head has a worldwide charter both as a business strategist and global optimiser. 'He decides which factories are going to make what products, what export markets each factory will serve, how the factories should pool their expertise and research funds for the benefit of the business worldwide' (Bartlett and Ghoshal, 1995: 853). Bartlett and Ghoshal characterise this role as one of being a coach developing and supporting the front-line initiatives.

The Role of Top Management

Having radically decentralised the resources and entrepreneurial responsibility to the front-line, top management focuses 'much more on driving the entrepreneurial process by developing a broad set of objectives and by establishing stretched performance standards that the front-line initiatives must meet' (Bartlett and Ghoshal, 1993: 29). The clearly articulated objectives ensure that front-line initiatives are aligned with ABB's overall strategic priorities, while the performance standards are used as signalling devices. Thus, instead of the remote top management of the M-form, at ABB top management will, when ABB's PC-based ABACUS 'fine-grained' reporting system indicates a problem, actually involve itself directly in front-line activities. However, Ghoshal and Bartlett

(1997: 189) insist the objective of this involvement is first and foremost 'to help rather than interfere'.

A New Organisational Psychology

While each of the above have their role to play at ABB, Bartlett and Ghoshal emphasise that structural fit is no longer of critical importance. In short, they argue that because of the complexity and volatility of environmental demands MNCs must go beyond structure and develop other fundamental types of organisational capabilities in order to achieve the necessary cross-border economies of scale. By this they do not mean additions to the basic structure in the form of micro-s tructural tools. Task forces and committees that grant responsibility to non-line managers and that enable top management to continually adjust the basic structure have a role to play. However, they are simply not capable of eliminating the opportunistic we/they attitudes economic theories (for example, Williamson, 1975) indicate will beset organisations separated by time, distance and national background.

Instead Bartlett and Ghoshal single out the creation of a common organisational psychology as the most critical aspect to ABB's success. Indeed they argue that it is the distinguishing feature of the transnational. The essence of such a psychology is one of a shared understanding of and respect for the company's mission and objectives combined with non-parochial, collaborative attitudes. It is a central tenet of Bartlett and Ghoshal's New Model that such a common psychology is 'often a much more powerful tool than formal structure and systems in coordinating diverse activities' (Bartlett and Ghoshal, 1995: 483). Bartlett and Ghoshal are intensely conscious that such a concept involves a much more 'positive view of human nature' (1993: 44) than that associated with economic management theories which they label as 'pathological' (ibid.). However, it is Bartlett and Ghoshal's firmly held belief that companies can promote non-opportunistic and collaborative individual characteristics to a substantial degree. This can be done by in two complementary ways. First, attention should be paid to selecting and promoting those individuals whose personal characteristics predispose them toward the desired norms of behavior. Second, consistent effort should be made at creating an internal context which encourages people to act in the way they would as a member of 'a functional family or a disciplined sporting team' (ibid., p. 45).

Table 8.1 summarises similarities and differences between the M-form and the organisation and management practice of ABB.

As the table indicates, the most significant differences between the M-form and Bartlett and Ghoshal's depiction of ABB are the level of interdependencies deliberately designed into the organisation and the reliance on social normative control as superior control mechanism. A key issue is then how achievable such social normative control (common organisational psychology) actually is, particularly if it is to function as the linchpin of the transnational organisation. Indeed in the final analysis moving beyond the M-form reveals itself to be dependent on whether 'a more positive view of human nature' is viable. If it is found not

Table 8.1   M-form and ABB compared

	M-form (Chandler, Williamson)	ABB (Bartlett and Ghoshal)
Main structure	Divisionalised structure	Divisionalised matrix
Strategic decision making	Centralised, conditioned by level of inter-division dependency Separated from operating decision making	Less centralised Less separated from operating decision making
Inter-unit relations	Interdependency minimised by hierarchical decomposition, coordinated by formal mechanisms	Interdependency actively pursued through inter-unit specialisation, coordinated by formal and informal mechanisms
Status of operating unit	Quasi-autonomous profit centre	Less quasi-autonomous profit centre
Superior control mechanism	Hierarchical control, exercised both vertically and horizontally	Social normative control, exercised through a complex matrix of management roles and relationships

to be achievable then it casts serious doubts on whether there really is a new organisation form beyond the M-form.

SUBSUMING THE TRANSNATIONAL UNDER THE M-FORM

Our response to the issue of the achievability of a common organisational psychology can be divided into three parts. First, we are obliged to scrutinise the validity of Bartlett and Ghoshal's empirical evidence. Second, we must ask whether both vertical and lateral coordination visible in ABB owes more to the conceptualisation of the modern M-form as a governance structure than it does to organisational psychology. Last, but by no means least, we must examine whether ABB's management roles and relationships can be more easily explained by applying the standard logic of transaction cost economics (TCE) than by resorting to organisation psychology.

The Validity of the Empirical Evidence

As we have observed, of critical importance to Bartlett and Ghoshal's new organisational form thesis is their claim that ABB has achieved normative integration. Birkinshaw *et al.* (1998: 228) have pointed out that this is substantially undocumented and that, moreover, in their experience, 'Normative integration is very hard to assess at a subsidiary level (Ghoshal polled head office managers) in part because it is a corporate-wide concept'. That is, the most central pillar to their thesis is based on anecdotal evidence provided, for the most part, by head office managers. This is particularly critical given the stream of research into cultural values by, for example, Hofstede (1980). This indicates that 'assumptions about what objectives should be achieved in people management, how people should be trained and valued, what motivates them and how they should relate to colleagues and supervisors, vary from culture to culture' (Brewster and Hegewisch, 1994: 2). One should therefore have expected a substantial empirical effort by Bartlett and Ghoshal to underpin their claim that homogenous norms prevail across ABB's international subsidiaries. The lack of such an effort clearly undermines the credibility of their thesis and legitimises our scepticism. Thus we are left with the impression that normative integration in this case may reflect more what managers want to achieve rather than what they actually have achieved.

Vertical Coordination

Despite Bartlett and Ghoshal's emphasis on the normative leadership by top-level managers their description of ABB actually provides substantial support for the importance of the M-form-style hierarchical governance. For example decisions about diversification, acquisition and reorganisation made by top level managers, decisions about technology development, the allocation of export markets, the selection of key personnel and the location of production plants made by middle level managers are all critically supported by the ABACUS system. This is a highly centralised system that feeds performance control data to ABB's top-level managers. Thus all units, regardless of whether they sell to customers or produce for internal customers, are subjected to the same budgeting and monitoring systems. Indeed, this kind of centralisation of strategic activities supported by a corporate wide performance control system, combined with the radical decentralisation of operating and entrepreneurial activities, is in full accordance with the M-form hypothesis. That is the entrepreneurial process, carried out by the front-line managers, is efficiently restricted by current strategy and established lines of business. In fact, Bartlett and Ghoshal's crucial distinction between entrepreneurial and renewal processes corresponds perfectly with the basic distinction between high-frequency operating activities and low-frequency strategic activities, underlying the M-form (Simon, 1962; Williamson, 1986). Consequently, what Bartlett and Ghoshal view as a new form cannot, on the basis of the evidence they themselves provide, be distinguished from the traditional M-form.

Lateral Coordination

The explicit strategy by ABB's top-management of focusing on related diversification as the company expanded across national borders created the need for extensive lateral coordination across the same corporate and national borders. In ABB, just as in other divisionalised companies, lateral coordination is taken care of by a dedicated cadre of middle level managers supported by an increasing number of liaison devices (committees, task forces and integrators) as complexity and interdependency between operating business units increases. In the most complex cases, such as ABB, it is common practice that relations between highly interdependent units are governed under a matrix structure where business units and profit centres are under the double leadership of business area and country managers. Decisions involving common interests are to be accepted by both business area manager and country manager. However, almost invariably, one of the matrix dimensions has priority over the other, and in ABB this is the business dimension, rather than the regional or national dimension. This has become even more apparent after ABB's recent reorganisation.

ABB's matrix system is only one way in which discipline and integration is achieved. In addition there are a number of other significant governance mechanisms, none of which can be subsumed under the concept of normative control, whose origins can best be understood in terms of a TCE perspective.

A TCE Perspective

It may be noted that TCE has already been successfully applied to explain why the earlier U-form was out-competed by the M-form and how the latter enabled and facilitated the subsequent development of the conglomerate company and the multinational enterprise (Williamson, 1981; Teece, 1977, 1980, 1983, 1986). We will argue that TCE can account for the evolvement of multinational enterprises, from the international to the multidomestic, the global and finally the transnational form. Additionally, we will argue that TCE strongly suggests that the basic internal structures and processes of these multinationals, not least the most complex of them all, the so-called transnational company, will be those of the M-form.

Under the TCE approach normative control assumes a more conditional role, depending on the attribute of the transactions in question and their underlying productive assets. According to TCE normative control should only be used in the case of transactions where performance and behavior cannot be measured and evaluated, and where not only market contracting, but also hierarchical governance is likely to fail for the same reason (Ouchi, 1980). Thus according to TCE while normative control is a relevant governance mechanism it is definitively less important for large diversified MNCs than mechanisms such as direct supervision, performance monitoring and performance-based incentives.

Such mechanisms are unequivocally in place at ABB, also at the individual level. Thus Barham and Heimer (1998: 267) conclude that: 'ABB's compensation system is designed to reward performance'. By way of support they quote Percy Barnevik, who states categorically that he believes strongly 'in differentiation of base pay based on responsibility and performance', and a line manager who says that: 'ABB rewards success ... We don't tolerate failure. We can't afford to have a profit centre leader who is not profitable. So it is ruthless. If you are successful, you are rewarded.' Barham and Heimer note that ABB's bonus scheme, in particular, rewards performance against budget targets. Additionally, they emphasise that

ABB is wary of opportunistic behavior. In order to curtail any such behavior on the part of managers, bonuses are agreed during the annual budget process. Not defining bonus formulas beforehand means that managers cannot try to bias budget targets in order to secure higher bonuses.

These mechanisms are, however, not confined to the individual level. The degree to which ABB's local profit centres are expected to share both their financial surplus, locally developed technology and best practice with the rest of the enterprise also illustrates ABB's non-normative managerial approach to the challenge of coordinating the specialised and interdependent units of the transnational. To promote such a sharing, ABB clearly recognise that simply attempting to persuade or socialise local managers into thinking and acting the way top management wants them to will not suffice. Normative mechanisms have to be supplemented with other governance mechanisms such as an enterprise wide performance control system, an advanced information system, and a motivating compensation system. Thus the 'performance league tables' which rank all front-line units according to measures that reflect ABB's strategic priorities are supplemented by systems that reward front-line managers for sharing behavior, and which sanction those who do not.

The point is not that normative control by top management is not featured at ABB but that it is no more than one of many control mechanisms ABB has in place. Moreover, there is no reason to expect this particular mechanism to be especially influential. For this to be the case it would have to be shown that the other control mechanisms are seriously handicapped in overseeing the necessary transactions. Furthermore, since ABB is primarily an industrial enterprise, and not a missionary organisation, recruitment and promotion based on loyalty and devotion to a corporate vision and behavioral style will, in the long run, invariably be of secondary importance. This applies despite the emphasis that leaders may like to ascribe to their visionary power.

From a TCE perspective the use of a common performance control system, such as ABACUS, supplemented by direct supervision and reporting, are more suitable in developing, standardising and transferring superior technology and best practices than socialisation and normative control. The challenge as such is to counterbalance hierarchical control so that the autonomy of profit centres will not decline and with it the associated highly prized entrepreneurial drive. The solution lies, however, not in increasing normative integration, although this may reduce the need for frequent monitoring, but rather the balancing of opposing forces through the promotion of both competition and cooperation.

CONCLUSIONS

In their enthusiasm over the ability of transnational companies to manage innovation and growth through entrepreneurship, integration and renewal, Bartlett and Ghoshal almost totally ignore the fact that top management is invariably about more than just communicating a stretching ambition, corporate objectives and shared beliefs. The primary responsibility of top management of private enterprises is basically to allocate resources to high-yield uses developed by their operating divisions and business units. To the degree they fail, share prices will fall, the company may be raided, its board of directors replaced, management removed, and the company restructured or integrated into a more profitable enterprise. In the work of Bartlett and Ghoshal the sanctions and rewards managers have at their disposal are assigned a secondary status.

Although economic theories of the firm tend to ascribe less importance to normative control than does Bartlett and Ghoshal's managerial approach, we accept that it does have a role to play in economic organisation theory. Arguably, normative control, if successfully implemented, may reduce the need for frequent monitoring for the purpose of preventing dysfunctional local goal pursuit. However, it will be of much less value for the purpose of computing local performance differentials and for the development, standardisation and dissemination of superior technology and best practice. Moreover, as emphasised above, achieving enterprise-wide normative control is both extremely difficult and costly. Consequently, large-scale investment in normative control can only be justified in cases where other governance mechanisms are seriously handicapped. These are instances where both output and effort are invisible, or the causal relation between effort and output are basically unknown. Clearly these attributes simply cannot be the most typical characteristics of operating companies and profit centres of most multinational enterprises. All in all, it is hardly the unifying force of a common culture or psychology that has provided ABB with profitability and growth, but rather the ongoing tension and stimulating trade-off between competition and cooperation, and between market and hierarchy, especially on the business units and profit centre level.

Clearly, the economic theory of the firm needs a more detailed description of the inner working of corporate enterprises, for which the works of Bartlett and Ghoshal may prove helpful. However, the negative assumptions concerning human agency is also part of human and organisational life as we know it, and cannot be eliminated without also destroying the theory that has so successfully explained organisational structure and safeguarding mechanisms in the 1990s. Although the behavioral assumptions in TCE may prove highly offensive both to managers and management theorists, TCE clearly acknowledges the limits within which management operates as well as the sheer size and diversity of multinational companies.

In a number of respects the major strength of the Bartlett and Ghoshal managerial approach, that is the detailed outlines of transnational management, is also its major weakness. The structure of interrelated tasks and roles summarised in the 3×3 matrix of management levels (front-line, middle and top management) and business processes (entrepreneurial, integrating and renewal processes) is extremely complex. It is definitely more helpful in illustrating the enormous complexity in transnational management, than in clarifying the theory of transnational organisation and management. In the Bartlett and Ghoshal model, the risk of dissolving the multinational company through excessive decentralisation is avoided in two ways. First by middle management's efforts in linking and transferring knowledge across business units and second by the critical efforts by top management of providing corporate purpose and motivating stretch among business units (local companies). These, however, are normal functions for exploiting synergies in most M-form enterprises, especially among closely related business units belonging to the same division or core segment.

FUTURE CHALLENGES

From a research point of view there are two major challenges that need to be addressed. The first concerns theory development and involves the development of management theory that is able to cope with both the assumptions concerning human behavior contained in TCE, with its focus on opportunism and the monitoring of behavior, and the assumptions underlying normative control theory. In short there is a need for a model that synthesises these two sets of assumptions and which specifies the conditions under which the one set will be more relevant than the other set. A second challenge involves research methodology. Studies of management practice in MNCs are needed which are less corporate-centre oriented in their data gathering approach than that of Bartlett and Ghoshal. Instead data should be collected not only at head office level but also at subsidiary level. Moreover, data should be assembled at various employee levels within MNCs. The field of MNC studies is not well served by uncorroborated data.

From a practitioner perspective our chapter touches on a concern that goes to the heart of human resource management in a multinational setting and to which Bartlett and Ghoshal are apparently oblivious. It concerns the use of normative or collaborative mechanisms of control and TCE or calculative mechanisms of control. The evidence from previous research indicates that, although these mechanisms may be used in tandem their respective use varies markedly across national settings (Gooderham *et al.*, 1998, 1999). In other words future research should specifically aim at helping managers assess the appropriateness of applying these mechanisms not only according to attributes of international transactions and their underlying productive assets, but also according to national setting.

9 Multinational Strategies and Sustainable Industrial Transformation in CEE Transition Economies: the Role of Technology

Julia Manea and Robert Pearce

INTRODUCTION

The material presented in this chapter closely reflects the two dominant concerns of the wider research project from which it derives. The first of these broad concerns is to analyse the content and policy implications of the dynamic interface between the evolutionary processes within MNEs and the industrial transformation and developmental needs of particular Central and Eastern European (CEE) transition economies.[1] The second is then to understand the key position of technology within both of these processes, and therefore to elaborate its vital influence in determining the effectiveness and implications of their potentially mutually supportive evolution.

From the point of view of the CEE transition economies we argue that the key issue is to analyse the possibility of MNEs providing a *sustained* contribution to host-countries progress through two phases of change. The first of these is the process of industrial transformation itself. The industrial sectors inherited from the centrally-planned era are likely to be inefficient and unbalanced, so that the priority is to move towards a logical, competitive and balanced set of industries that have been upgraded around genuine sources of comparative advantage.

Thus the inherited industrial structure that needs to be addressed in first phase restructuring is likely to include some industries that have no true or sustainable basis for competitiveness, which emerged and survived as the result of bargaining and negotiation within political and bureaucratic (and not effectively economic) structures. The corollary of this is that the industrial sector will have left seriously underdeveloped (again owing to malign and distorting elements of bargaining processes) other industries that would have reflected genuine sources of competitiveness. Finally, many of the industries that do exist (rightly or wrongly according to the structural balance criteria of the two previous points), at the entry to phase one, will have been ineffectually developed in terms of realising their potential efficiency. This could reflect a generalised lack of competitive pressures and fear of risk taking in the earlier institutional environment.

Much of the early discussion of MNEs' potential contribution to CEE economies' industrial transition saw this predominantly in terms of 'gap filling'. Thus new 'inward investments' by MNEs into transition economies were expected to bring *flows* of capital, technology, managerial practices, entrepreneurship and international market access. These flows would then initiate the operationalisation of the immediate sources of *static* comparative advantage available in CEE countries. This, by activation of competitive forces, will then help to secure the emergence of the more appropriate and balanced industrial sector that is needed.

Once the rebalancing of the industrial sector has been achieved then its more sustained evolution needs to be addressed in second phase progress. With the successful securing of internationally competitive status, normal processes of industrial growth and development become a routine but crucial priority. In the main this means the continuous upgrading of competitiveness within those industries that have now asserted their position. Technology is likely to be at the core of this, whether in the form of R&D inputs, the tacit knowledge of personnel, or upgraded skill levels reflecting education and training. It is then crucial to acknowledge that MNEs that have participated (in the ways suggested above) in the securing of phase one need to be coopted as part of this second phase, technology-based, solution; otherwise they may easily manifest a very precise problem.

As the transition economies move away from the processes of restructuring and into the pursuit of sustainable development, the emphasis turns from activating underutilised sources of *static* comparative advantage towards the deepening and enhancement of inputs in the form of the generation of *created/dynamic* comparative advantage. From the point of view of MNEs this means crucial changes away from these conditions that attracted their initial entry. Local inputs become higher quality and more distinctive, but also more expensive. If MNEs cannot, or are not willing to, change the basis of their operations they will exit these economies. Such footloose behaviour is a real possibility if, as is very often the case, the local factors that attracted initial entry were standardised/homogeneous inputs. These would have no distinctive characteristics, that might embed the operation locally, and so are likely to be equally readily available in other rival economies.

But the nature of the contemporary MNE as a dynamic differentiated network can provide the basis for the detection of a more positive potential. This allows for the co-option of these firms' CEE operations as a key developmental force in securing the orderly progress of local economies into their sustainable phase two progress. The competitive mechanisms within MNEs now provide an openness to subsidiaries in particular countries upgrading their operations, in ways that reflect and respond to emerging capabilities in these countries. This is expected to contribute, in a logical and coherent way, to the extension of the knowledge capacity and product range of the group (Taggart, 1999; Birkinshaw and Hood, 1998c). Thus there can be a mutually supportive dynamic technology-based interface between the developmental needs of MNE groups and the deepening of knowledge, skill and science potentials of individual countries.

From the point of view of MNEs these evolutionary potentials can be manifest (at the subsidiary level) in three motivations or imperatives (Behrman, 1984; Dunning, 1993) that underpin the analysis of this chapter and the wider research programme.[2] The first of these, *market seeking* (MS), represents the extension of an MNE's production and distribution activity into a new country or region. This has the primary motive of securing an effective development of the local market for the most successful of the group's existing products (which may have been previously supplied through trade, but where a more active commitment is now desired). The objective is to be actively locally responsive in terms of adapting products/processes to local circumstances and generally securing early-mover experience of conditions in these new market spaces. This may mean that some intuitive creative dynamism emerges from the, at least low-level and informal, localised learning processes involved. The key attracting factor for MS is the current status and, especially in CEE countries, the growth potential of local markets.

In the second motivation, *efficiency seeking* (ES), MNEs relocate the *production* of established goods to, in our case, CEE economies. This seeks to improve the cost efficiency of supply, with the goods then being (mainly) exported back to the markets (Western Europe in particular) where they have an established high level of demand which is, however, perceived as needing to be actively defended. Whilst MS complements existing production capacity (and thereby secures market extension), ES substitutes for parts of it (in supply of existing markets). This probably makes such ES-oriented supply expansion much more contentious (than MS) intra-group, especially where existing Western European subsidiaries are more mature and therefore more adept in terms of intra-group politics and bargaining.

In its pure form ES behaviour provides no natural impulsion towards any dynamic generation of individualised local creative capabilities. Firstly, there is no scope for product adaptation, since the motivation is to supply mature goods to markets where their characteristics are already well accepted. Secondly, the immediate ability of the local economy to attract this role derives from the supply of standardised cost-effective inputs. Thirdly, the cost-driven core of ES behaviour provides no room for knowledge-generating overhead expenditures that in no way relate to support of the short-term supply role.

The third imperative, *knowledge seeking* (KS), does then reflect the acknowledgement in the contemporary MNE of a need to use dispersed facilities (subsidiaries and/or scientific laboratories or research collaborations) to support the longer-term regenerative dimensions of strategic competitiveness (Pearce, 1999a; Papanastassiou and Pearce, 1999). Thus at its broader level KS means the pursuit by MNEs of new technological capabilities, scientific capacity (research facilities) and creative expertise (for example, dimensions of tacit knowledge) from particular host countries, in order to extend the overall competences (product range and core technology) of the group. As investigated here, in the context of early MNE involvement with the transition economies, KS is treated as manifest in localised product development. In the survey reported this is specified in two forms.

Firstly, KS1 involves developing products in a particular CEE subsidiary to focus on the market of that host country and other CEE markets. Thus KS1 represents a logical extension and deepening of the MS role, and might emerge as a way of building on, and formalising the value of, those locally-responsive learning processes that we suggest may emerge within MS. In turn KS2 involves developing products in a particular CEE subsidiary to target the MNE's long-established market areas outside the CEE. Intuitively, by analogy, this represents an extension and deepening of the ES role. However, we suggest two rather different routes through which KS2 activity may emerge.

Firstly, KS2 may indeed derive from ES subsidiaries using their familiarity with intra-group supply networks and political/bargaining processes in order to claim permission to extend their capabilities to encompass product development activity aiming at the group's wider markets. To do this they will probably need to have perceived some quite distinctive potential that is based on local knowledge or research capacity, and which can plausibly be advocated as ultimately likely to extend the group's product range in logical and valuable ways.

Secondly, KS2 may emerge through a widening of the markets made available to successful KS1 product development. Thus goods that have asserted their originality in CEE markets (with no officially mandated aim of supplying other markets of the MNE) may be subsequently perceived as revealing new characteristics that are in fact quite radical and high-potential extensions of the group product range. Permission may then be granted to initiate supply to markets outside CEE.

Whatever their origins KS2 products are likely to be quite distinctive extensions of MNE product range, and thus are not likely to challenge the immediate supply interests of extant Western European subsidiaries. This may, therefore, be politically (intra-group) a quite viable means of generating dynamic potentials into CEE operations. In fact it may be that, given the right host-country support (in terms of commitment to technology, science, education, training) KS2 may be the more viable (compared to ES) means of inserting CEE supply capabilities into the MNE group's wider market areas.

Certainly KS2 is likely to be the most valuable imperative from the point of view of host CEE countries: firstly, because it operationalises a wider range of higher value-added local inputs, secondly, because it addresses dynamic processes that are compatible with sustained growth and resource upgrading in the local economy, and identifies the potential of the most valuable and challenging areas of the MNE's markets and functional competences. In this way KS2 gives the CEE operations a distinctive status within the core, technology-related, evolutionary procedures of the MNE group.

In the next section we review the positioning of the investment motivations in MNEs' CEE operations, using evidence from two questions in the survey. The first of these assesses the current relative prominence of the four motivations, whilst the second evaluates anticipated changes in their future status.

As already indicated, we argue that at the core of the ability of subsidiaries in CEE economies to upgrade their activity, in ways that are symbiotic with host-country transformation and development, is the scope that is made available to them, in the modern MNE, to reconfigure the technological bases of their operations. In essence they seek to go through a creative transition (Papanastassiou and Pearce, 1994, 1999) in which dependence on mature and standardised technologies of their MNE is replaced by locally generated knowledge and capabilities. These then provide them with strongly individualised competences that can underpin a claim to a distinctive position in the group's wider programmes for competitive regeneration.

Thus MNEs are expected to have initiated their CEE operations through the MS and/or ES modes of operation, and will be likely to have secured their effective entry around the use of those strong and familiar group technologies that are already embodied in the successful products through which the subsidiaries establish their bridgehead in these unfamiliar markets and production environments. At this stage the new subsidiaries' motivations relate to the extension of the effectiveness with which their MNEs utilise their already proven sources of competitiveness, either through widening of market scope (MS) or enhanced productive efficiency (ES). However, strategic competitiveness in MNEs requires continual upgrading of technological capabilities, with innovation persistently revitalising the product range and provoking reconfiguration of production networks. If CEE subsidiaries remain submissively dependent on the inheritance of new products and technologies that have been derived elsewhere in the group, the possibility emerges that their capabilities (reflecting the local resource base, which should itself be changing due to the process of development) will move out of line with those now required. If this occurs their survival within these (MS or ES) modes of operation is systematically compromised.

The alternative, enshrined here in the KS motivations, is for CEE subsidiaries to pursue participation within the knowledge-related evolutionary processes of their MNE groups. Securing this route of escape from undue dependence on established MNE technology involves the co-option by subsidiaries of various types of local knowledge and scientific capability in order to generate those unique competences that can be exercised through creative interdependence with wider programmes (Pearce, 1999b). This defines the process of creative transition as one where the status of the subsidiary derives less from its responsiveness to the local market or the cost competitiveness of standardised local inputs (both activated mainly around established group technology), and instead increasingly reflects its ability to assert an individualised position that builds on distinct local technology and tacit knowledge. Overall subsidiaries seek to generate a flexibility and diversity in their technological base that can embed them into the developmental processes of both their MNE group and their host countries.

It is suggested here that the potential exists for MNE subsidiaries in CEE economies to move towards an effective KS motivation with unusual alacrity. The normal expectation is that processes of routine and orderly development in most countries (what we term phase two for the transition economies) will involve reinvestment in science, education and training, which can then be supported and activated by the KS needs of MNEs. In CEE this can be manifest in MNEs' establishment of in-house R&D laboratories (staffed by well-trained local scientists whose capacities may reflect distinctive elements of the local technological heritage) or through collaboration with local University laboratories (where, again, MNEs may benefit from accessing elements of a unique technological tradition). Though policies supporting this research- and education-based dimension are clearly desirable in CEE economies it may be that they can often build on a certain scope for 'short-cuts' that may be especially amenable to activation by MNEs.

This relates to the view (Manea and Pearce, 1997, 1998, 1999) that under the previous communist regimes there had been a strong commitment to pure scientific research, and to the generation of certain industrial skills. However, due to the lack of a commercial incentive structure and risk aversion, this had not become adequately reflected in product innovation or competitive production. As just noted, the persistence of elements of this research output in the local CEE scientific community may provide a particular short-cut potential to those R&D activities (in-house laboratory or collaborative research) that would be a normal element of KS activity. Another facet of these possibilities is that those technologies that did emerge in CEE enterprises under central planning had not been developed to their full capacity, so that their adoption by MNEs may provide a basis for a more complete realisation of their potential. In a similar fashion skills (tacit knowledge) of local engineers may help to individualise the competences of MNE subsidiaries, and thereby enhance their own value in the process. The preceding discussion is summarised in Table 9.1.

To investigate the technological bases of MNEs' CEE activities respondents to the survey were asked to evaluate the relevance to their operations in the region of seven sources of technology. These reflect both the intra-group and host-country possibilities outlined above. The replies are summarised in section three. To obtain some indication of how these technology sources relate to the investment motivations, and evolutionary possibilities, regression tests were run. These are reported in section four.

The survey involved a questionnaire that was sent to the global or regional HQs of 408 leading manufacturing and resource-based MNEs.[3] Replies were received from 50 of these, of which 28 had manufacturing operations in CEE economies and 11 more had subsidiaries there which carried out other significant parts of the value-added chain (marketing, distribution, resource exploration, strategic planning offices).[4] The respondents reported on in this chapter covered all those with manufacturing operations and a selection of the group with other significant value-adding activities in CEE economies (which felt they were operationalising technology in a meaningful way through their local activities).[5]

MNEs' MOTIVATIONS FOR CEE INVESTMENTS

Respondents to the survey were requested to evaluate the relative importance in their current CEE operations of each of the four motivations introduced in the

124

Table 9.1 Potential benefits to MNEs and CEE host countries of particular subsidiary roles

Subsidiary motivation	Benefit to MNE	Benefit to CEE host economy
MS	Secures the competitive entry of established goods into a new market area	Provides local consumers with new goods in a manner that helps with the marketisation of the emerging economy
ES	Improves the cost efficiency of supply of existing goods, and thereby sharpens their competitiveness in established markets (e.g. Western Europe)	Secures the improved activation of sources of static comparative advantage and, therefore, helps to move the economy towards competitiveness in international markets
KS1	Generates a distinctive and sustainable basis for competitiveness in an important and differentiated emerging market area	Helps with the effective generation of sources of dynamic (or created) comparative advantage. Helps deepen the marketisation of the local economy by generating goods that are fully responsive to consumer needs. Increases the embeddedness of MNEs' operations in the local economy
KS2	Secures access to a set of new and differentiated creative inputs, and activates them to extend worldwide product scope and global competitiveness	Provides a very strong stimulus to the generation and application of localised sources of dynamic comparative advantage, through the provision of complementary creative attributes and access to the challenges of international market growth and needs. Embeds the development of MNEs' local operations in the dynamic competitive evolution of these companies' overall scope

previous section. The replies are summarised, in terms of average response (AR), in Table 9.2.

In this question the MS imperative was defined as 'to help our MNE group to effectively extend the supply of its established products into the host-country and other CEE markets'. This was rated as a 'main' role by 88.2 per cent of respondents, with 8.8 per cent more considering that it occupied a 'secondary' status. This makes it, as Table 9.2 confirms, the overwhelmingly dominant motivation in early MNE activity in CEE economies.

Success in such broadly defined MS behaviour clearly provides immediate benefits to both MNEs and individual transition economies. For MNEs it does extend the effective market scope of the existing product range and also expands their learning environment, in the sense of providing insider experience of a new customer base and supply conditions. Though the assumption of pure MS is that the latter circumstances would only provoke response in the form of securing better supply of the local market, we have already indicated wider potentials for such

Table 9.2 Evaluation of the motivations of MNEs' subsidiaries in CEE economies

	Motivation (average response)*			
	MS	ES	KS1	KS2
By industry				
Chemicals	2.71	1.57	1.71	1.57
Electronics	3.00	2.00	1.89	1.67
Mechanical engineering	2.67	2.33	1.33	1.17
Motor vehicles	3.00	2.00	1.33	1.33
Petroleum	3.00	1.50	2.00	1.50
Miscellaneous	2.86	1.71	1.14	1.00
By home region				
Asia	3.00	2.67	1.67	1.67
North America	2.93	1.73	1.53	1.40
Western Europe	2.75	1.88	1.56	1.31
Total	2.85	1.88	1.56	1.38

Notes:
Investment motivations: MS – to help our MNE group to effectively extend the supply of its established products into the host country and other CEE markets; ES – to help improve the competitiveness of our MNE group in supplying existing products to our already established markets; KS1 – to use specific local creative assets (e.g. local market knowledge, original local technology) available to the subsidiary to develop new products for the host country and other CEE markets; KS2 – to use important creative assets and talents available to the subsidiary to help develop new products for wider markets (e.g. Western Europe) of the MNE group.
* Respondents were asked to grade each strategic position as (i) the subsidiaries' main objective, (ii) a secondary objective of the subsidiaries, (iii) not a part of the subsidiaries' objective. The average response was calculated by allocating 'main' the value of 3, 'secondary' the value of 2 and 'not' the value of 1.

localised learning in more sustained evolutionary processes. From the point of view of CEE host countries MS entry of MNEs may save foreign exchange and generate jobs, as well as provide a crucial stimulus to the process of marketisation through the introduction of competitive new products and challenging marketing and distribution practices.

Nevertheless, despite its direct tactical benefits, the innate introversion of pure MS activity would be likely to prove alien to the strategic orientation and needs of both MNEs and host-country economies. For the MNEs MS treats the CEE region as a separate newly emergent market space that needs to be addressed, in the short term, through different aims and priorities. However, this isolated pursuit of localised success may not generate the types of subsidiary-level attributes or ambitions that would then allow them to emerge into distinctive positions within the wider competitive evolution of their MNE groups. Explicitly, the priorities and competitive situation of MS operations may not secure efficiency in the production of existing goods (relative to the capability of other parts of the group) or encourage the systematic inculcation of locally derived sources of creative dynamism. In a similar fashion the dominance of demand-side characteristics and potentials in attracting MS operations may compromise the precise activation of those local supply side capabilities that represent the core potential of effective and internationally-competitive phase one industrial restructuring.

It may be, however, that despite its pervasiveness in early MNE activity in the CEE transition economies the MS imperative will not preclude the emergence of behaviour patterns that can differentiate subsidiary capabilities and move them towards a more symbiotic involvement with their group's wider competitive needs. We can point to two plausible impulsions towards strategic diversity within MS-originated operations. The first has already been alluded to in the form of the broadening of the locally responsive learning processes of MS into a more complete KS1 type of product development.

The second evolutionary possibility reflects the coverage by the broad MS motivation (in the definition offered) of both the host-country national market of a subsidiary and the rest of the CEE region. In fact other evidence in the survey (Manea and Pearce, 2000a, 2000b) indicates that direct supply of the host country is clearly the stronger element in MS, but that export to the rest of the CEE is usually also quite significant (indeed, it is often the most important export market for MNEs' operations in CEE countries). Thus it seems that an initial aim of much MS entry to the transition economies has indeed been to explore, through direct experience, the potentials (both in terms of market needs and supply capabilities) of separate CEE countries. It would then be likely that the normal priorities of MNE competitiveness, while still mainly driven by the MS development of the broad CEE region, would generate a gradual process of subsidiary rationalisation. In this rationalisation process individual subsidiaries may increasingly specialise in the supply of select goods to the wider CEE region, with diminishing emphasis on host-country national markets. Thus ES priorities may become more relevant, within what remains a strongly MS-driven development of competitiveness in the region, and this may incorporate more effectively those local inputs that activate phase one transformation.

The most decisive contribution of MNEs' CEE activities to the securing of phase one industrial restructuring is, however, expected to derive from a more precise and immediate emphasis on the aim of ES. Here local inputs are activated into MNEs' standardised production processes in a way that achieves international competitiveness by securing cost-effective entry into these companies' most important established market areas. Thus the ES motivation was defined for respondents evaluation as 'to help improve the competitiveness of our MNE group in supplying existing products to our already established markets'. This was rated as a main objective of the CEE operations of 23.5 per cent of respondents and as a secondary one by 41.2 per cent more. It does seem, therefore, that the pervasiveness of a strong MS interest in the development of the transition economies as a significant new market space has not precluded the emergence of a willingness and ability to also activate competitive local supply potentials as a complementary objective.

The ability of MNEs to prolong their contribution to CEE evolution into these countries' sustained phase two development depends on the capacity of their subsidiaries to reconfigure their motivations in order to encompass (rather than be alienated by) those changes in host-country inputs that are an innate part of such progress. The national sources of growth are expected to move from the provision of more extensive opportunities for the use of standardised physical inputs towards the systematic upgrading of capabilities. This will take the form of enhanced skills and the emergence of distinctive local technologies. A repositioning of the technological status of their subsidiaries can allow MNEs to participate in, and benefit from, these aspects of host-country development. In the cases of MS and, especially, ES it is the import of existing MNE group technologies that provide subsidiaries with the capacity to activate undifferentiated local inputs. Development, however, imparts particular skill capacities to local inputs, with wider aspects of an emerging national technological competence increasingly providing the central impetus to growth. Then it becomes the accessing and realisation of such localised knowledge potentials by subsidiaries that can differentiate their status and define a position in their group's strategic progress. Thus a deepening of interdependence with sources of local development, through the emergence of a commitment to KS, seems a necessary attribute of subsidiary evolution.

In the previous section we indicated two forms through which the KS imperative might emerge in MNEs' CEE operations, both being manifested through subsidiary-level product development processes. The first, KS1, was defined as 'to use specific local creative assets (e.g. local market knowledge, original local technology) available to the subsidiary to develop new products for the host-country and other CEE markets'. As already observed this represents a deepening of the MS motivation. The CEE market area remains one that is considered to need particularised treatment within MNEs' strategic growth. However, the approach to this evolves from routine adaptation of existing group technologies and goods towards the greater individualisation that can be secured around more substantive product development that reflects local knowledge and skills in a more radical fashion. The already observed pervasiveness of MS in MNEs' CEE operations clearly provides a substantial foundation for the emergence of KS1 behaviour. In fact 8.8 per cent of respondents considered that KS1 was now one of the main concerns of their CEE operations, and 38.3 per cent more felt that it occupied a secondary status.

KS2 was defined as 'to use important creative assets and talents available to the subsidiary to help develop new products for wider markets (e.g. Western Europe) of the MNE group'. As observed in the previous section KS2 can be perceived as another means through which the wider competitive environment of the MNE can allow for CEE economies to secure an effective internationalisation. The basis for this, however, moves from sources of static comparative advantage (cost-effective inputs in ES) to aspects of dynamic or created comparative advantage (knowledge and creative expertise). Though we hypothesised two alternative routes through which KS2 activity might emerge in MNEs' CEE operations, we have now seen that both of the potential foundations for such evolution (ES and KS1) are themselves currently of only moderate importance. It is, therefore, not surprising that KS2 behaviour is so far relatively sparse. Thus 64.7 per cent of respondents did not perceive any KS2 activity in their CEE operations and 32.4 per cent considered it played only a secondary role.

To obtain some more direct evaluation of the evolutionary potentials that we perceive as conditioning the ability of MNEs to support sustained progress in transition economies, responding HQs were asked to indicate whether they felt each of the four motivations would become more important in the future, less important or of unchanged importance. Table 9.3 summarises the replies for the same respondents as covered by Table 9.2.

Two broad perceptions emerge from the replies to this question. Firstly, it is clear that MS remains overwhelmingly at the core of the ways in which the responding MNEs expect their CEE operations to expand and evolve. Thus 79.4 per cent of the replies indicated the expectation that MS would become more important in the future and only 5.9 per cent anticipated that it would become less important.

Nevertheless the second indication of these results is of a quite strong tendency towards a widening of the strategic scope of these MNEs' CEE operations. Thus each of the remaining three motivations were provided with net evaluations as likely to become more important in the future (that is, values of above 2.00 in Table 9.3).

Here ES was expected to become more important by 44.1 per cent of respondents, with only 14.7 per cent anticipating a decline in its status. It thus seems that, alongside a continuation of the drive to build effective market positioning within the CEE economies themselves, there is an emerging propensity for familiarity with the local production environment to lead to implementation of cost-effective supply of wider markets (those outside the CEE region) as a complementary objective.

Another evolutionary potential we have discerned would be for a deepening of the MS role, with a localised product development gradually replacing adaptation

Table 9.3 Anticipated changes in importance of motivations of MNEs' subsidiaries in CEE economies

	Evaluation of change in importance of motivations (average response)[*]			
	MS	ES	KS1	KS2
By industry				
Chemicals	2.57	1.86	2.43	1.86
Electronics	2.78	2.33	2.22	2.33
Mechanical engineering	2.67	2.50	2.00	2.17
Motor vehicles	3.00	2.67	1.67	1.67
Miscellaneous	2.86	2.29	2.14	2.00
By home region				
Asia	3.00	3.00	1.33	1.33
North America	2.67	2.00	2.20	2.27
Western Europe	2.75	2.44	2.38	2.06
Total	2.74	2.29	2.21	2.07

Notes:
Investment motivations: for definitions see Table 9.2.
[*] respondents were asked to evaluate each role as likely to be (i) more important in the future, (ii) less important in the future, (iii) of unchanged importance. The average response was calculated by allocating 'less' important the value of 1, 'unchanged' the value of 2, 'more' important the value of 3.

of existing products as the subsidiaries are increasingly able to implement a KS1-oriented enhancement of their functional scope. This is indeed reflected in a quite strong net movement towards KS1 activity, with 32.3 per cent of respondents considering this as likely to become more important and only 11.8 per cent less so. Earlier we indicated that of the two product development roles KS2 would be likely to be the slower to emerge. Thus, though there is a net expected movement towards KS2, it is rather more marginal than for KS1, with 20.6 per cent of respondents expecting more importance for it but 11.8 per cent anticipating decline.

A further potentially rewarding dimension in the analysis of anticipated changes in the strategic status of MNEs' CEE activity is to relate the future perceptions to the current prevalence of the corresponding set of motivations. This could, hopefully, indicate some of the particular routes of strategic evolution that may be expected to occur as these companies develop their approach to the potentials of the industrial transformation and economic development of the CEE region. One immediate constraint on this mode of investigation is, however, the massive pervasiveness (both in terms of current status and expected development) of MS. Nevertheless some tentative patterns can be discerned in terms of the positioning of the other three roles, with these most notably differentiated by the present status of ES.

Firstly, it emerges that those respondents that already recognise the presence of ES activity in their CEE operations seem to respond positively to its performance, and therefore to anticipate its future reinforcement. Thus those respondents that rate ES as currently a main objective provide the strongest evaluation of its future growth, with an AR of 2.75 (Table 9.4) and none predicting a decline in its importance. Furthermore, the remainder that consider ES to be a part of the present scope of their CEE activity (albeit with only a secondary status) also provide a positive evaluation of its growth, with an AR of 2.29 (though 28.6 per cent of them did indicate an expectation of decline). However, those respondents that so far have not activated ES operations have not assimilated the positive perception of its potential, recording an absolutely neutral AR of 2.00. Thus the ES motivation does appear to be generating a self-reinforcing impulse in MNEs' CEE operations, but does not seem to communicate its virtues to those groups that are not yet applying it.

Secondly, the degree of commitment to ES also seems to have an influence on the predicted growth of the two KS-oriented product development roles. Thus we find (Table 9.4) a quite clear indication of a negative relationship between the current prevalence of ES and anticipated movement towards KS1 (that is, product development for CEE markets). Here those respondents that see ES as currently a main objective predict a decline in KS1, with an AR of 1.62. However, where ES is now only a secondary role the prediction is for a modest rise in KS1 (an AR of 2.21), whilst its absence allows for the strongest prediction for a rise in KS1 (an AR of 2.58). Two facets of the ES motivation seem likely to contribute to this negative relationship. Firstly, the powerful cost consciousness at the centre of ES behaviour is likely to mitigate against the commitment of those types of overhead expenditures involved in generating the in-house capabilities needed for product development at the subsidiary level. ES pursues precisely measurable short-run objectives, whilst KS1 involves more speculative investments that seek more

Table 9.4 Anticipated changes in importance of motivations of MNEs' subsidiaries in CEE economies by current strength of efficiency seeking

	Evaluation of change in importance of motivations (average response)[*]			
	MS	*ES*	*KS1*	*KS2*
Current strength of ES				
Main objective	2.88	2.75	1.62	1.88
Secondary objective	2.71	2.29	2.21	2.07
Not part of objective	2.67	2.00	2.58	2.25

Notes:
Investment motivations: for definitions see Table 9.2.
* see note to Table 9.3.

medium-term returns. Secondly, fulfilment of ES aims at supply of non-CEE whilst KS1 is oriented towards the deepening of strategic commitment to the CEE region. Overall, therefore, the less prevalent is the ES motivation the more decisively the operations target the CEE markets and the more flexibility there is likely to be in the cost structure to allow for investment in creative resources.

The two factors just discerned can be expected to provide contradictory influences on the relationship between ES and KS2 (that is, product development for markets outside the CEE). Once again the cost consciousness of ES will mitigate against the overhead expenditures involved in the capacity for product development. On the other hand KS2 aims to develop products for the same markets as are the targets of ES. So the greater the current prevalence of ES, the more information on, and better access to, the appropriate markets is likely to be available.

The respondents for which ES is currently rated a main objective provided an AR of 1.88 for the future status of KS2. This still represents a decline in the future positioning of this type of product development (reflecting the strong cost influence in ES), but nevertheless provides a higher AR than for KS1 (1.62), which does suggest some positive influence from the more appropriate market orientation. Where ES is perceived as currently only a secondary motivation the reduction of the cost imperative again (as for KS1) allows for a modest rise in the expected future status of KS2 (to an AR of 2.07). However, the simultaneous lessening of the influence of non-CEE markets (when ES is only of secondary status) means that the anticipation for KS2 is now less than for KS1 (2.07 compared to 2.21). Once again the growth of KS2 is predicted most strongly (AR of 2.25) where ES is absent, but these respondents also anticipated a much stronger growth for KS1 (AR of 2.58). This reflects the decisive CEE-market-orientation of these non-ES operations. Thus it seems that of the two routes through which we indicated that KS2 might originate it is the second (i.e. building on KS1 and, therefore, ultimately deriving from MS rather than ES activity) that emerges as the more plausible.

SOURCES OF TECHNOLOGY APPLIED IN MNEs' CEE OPERATIONS

We have argued that it is a process of creative transition at the subsidiary level that allows MNEs' operations in CEE transition economies to retain a positive participation when these countries' developmental priorities metamorphose from those of phase one transformation to the more orderly growth of phase two. This creative transition involves a widening of the technological bases of a subsidiaries' competences. The crucial factor in this becomes the interjection of locally derived knowledge inputs that serve to differentiate and individualise the subsidiary's status within its group's strategic profile. In essence the change is from a mainly static dependence on a MNE's currently mature competitive technology, to a more dynamically interdependent contribution to the regeneration of the parent group's overall creative capacity. The survey asked respondents to evaluate the relevance to their CEE operations of seven sources of technology that encompass these potentials.[6]

The first source of technology offered for assessment was defined as 'existing technology of the MNE group that is already embodied in established products that the subsidiaries undertake to produce' (ESTPRODTECH). These technologies provide the basis of the current commercial success of MNEs, through their embodiment in the most competitive of their mature goods. Thus they are likely to be at the core of MNEs' initial penetration of the CEE economies, whether this is to attract an enhanced consumer base there (MS) or secure a competitive new supply source (ES). In playing this role ESTPRODTECH is an essential part of the 'inward investment' package that helps activate the phase one restructuring possibilities of the transition economies. Since the results reported earlier indicate that these phase one priorities still seem the more prevalent in MNEs' CEE activity it is not surprising that ESTPRODTECH dominates, with 87.9 per cent of respondents considering it a 'main' source and 9.1 per cent more rating it a 'secondary' one.

However, movement into phase two is likely to reduce dependence on ESTPRODTECH as MNE subsidiaries reflect the new needs and capabilities of CEE host countries. As these economies become more prosperous their consumers will become more discriminating and ambitious, with an emerging demand for goods that are not only of generally higher quality but also more responsive to idiosyncratic facets of local taste. Though part of this could be met by superior goods from the MNE's extant range (involving the import of new ESTPRODTECH) the more thorough response, pursued by ambitious MS-subsidiary management, would be the localised product development of KS1. Similarly the upgraded quality, but higher cost, of local inputs could be absorbed through ES supply of more demanding goods (again mainly dependent on import of new elements of EST-PRODTECH). But the interests of subsidiaries are once more likely to point towards the more positive activation of local creative attributes in pursuit of KS2 possibilities.

One of the sources of technology that might allow MNEs' CEE operations to escape from dependency on ESTPRODTECH, as they seek to extend the scope and individuality of their activity, can still derive from the knowledge capabilities of their parent MNE group. This was defined as 'MNE group technology from which the subsidiaries develop new products for their markets' (GROUPTECH). The new group-originated technologies envisaged here have not yet been definitively embodied in products, but are available in sufficiently precisely defined forms as to be accessible to different subsidiaries for possible operationalisation. CEE subsidiaries could pick up such potentials in GROUPTECH for distinctive activation. This could aim to respond strongly to local-market needs in KS1 activity, or use complementary local technology to secure a particularly radical development of the potentials of GROUPTECH in the form of new goods that are competitive in the MNE's Western European (and other) markets (KS2). Though we can distinguish the relevance of GROUPTECH as mainly an input to evolutionary process in

CEE subsidiaries it was, in fact, evaluated as already a main source by 22.6 per cent of respondents as well as a secondary one by 51.6 per cent more. This rates it as the second most important of the seven sources of technology (Table 9.5).

The first of the local sources of technology evaluated was 'established host-country technology' (LOCALTECH). Where MNEs enter CEE through acquisition of indigenous enterprises this provides them with the option of continuing the use of the existing technologies of these firms (often, but not inevitably, as already embodied in established products). However, greenfield entrants may also discern a potential in licensing technology from independent local enterprises where they can distinguish scope for better, or alternative, formats for its commercial development. LOCALTECH may, in fact, play some role in MNEs' phase one achievements by providing aspects of any product adaptation needed to better secure the MS bridgehead that is expected to be built around the MNEs' established goods (mainly embodying ESTPRODTECH). The more important potentials, however, do reside in the possibility for LOCALTECH to provide a significant input into the more substantial product individualisation of the KS

Table 9.5 Evaluation of technologies used in MNE subsidiaries in CEE economies

	Sources of technology (average response)[*]						
	ESTPROD TECH	GROUP TECH	LOCAL TECH	OWNLAB	ENGUNIT	UNIRAD	COLLABRAD
By industry							
Chemicals	2.67	1.83	1.83	1.17	1.50	1.00	1.00
Electronics	2.78	2.13	1.38	1.25	1.50	1.25	1.38
Mechanical engineering	2.83	1.80	1.60	1.00	1.80	1.00	1.00
Motor vehicles	3.00	1.67	1.33	1.00	1.00	1.00	1.33
Petroleum	3.00	1.67	2.00	1.33	1.33	1.33	1.33
Miscellaneous	3.00	2.33	1.17	1.17	1.33	1.00	1.00
By home region							
Asia	3.00	2.33	1.33	1.00	2.00	1.00	1.33
North America	2.79	2.14	1.50	1.14	1.29	1.14	1.14
Western Europe	2.88	1.71	1.57	1.21	1.50	1.07	1.14
Total	2.85	1.97	1.52	1.16	1.45	1.10	1.16

Notes:
Sources of technology: ESTPRODTECH – existing technology of our MNE group that is already embodied in established products that the subsidiaries undertake to produce; GROUPTECH – MNE group technology from which the subsidiaries develop new products for their markets; LOCALTECH – established host-country technology; OWNLAB – results of R&D carried out in the CEE subsidiaries; ENGUNIT – development and adaptation carried out less formally by members of subsidiaries' engineering units and production personnel; UNIRAD – R&D carried out for the subsidiary by local scientific institutions (e.g. universities, independent laboratories, industry laboratories); COLLABRAD – R&D carried out in collaboration with local firms.
* respondents were asked to grade each source of technology as (i) a 'main' source, (ii) a 'secondary' source, (iii) 'not' a source. The average response was calculated by allocating 'main' the value of 3, 'secondary' the value of 2 and 'not' the value of 1.

imperative through which MNEs involve themselves in phase two progress. LOCALTECH was reported as a main source of technology by 6.5 per cent of respondents and as a secondary source for only 38.7 per cent more.

A means of bringing wider aspects of host-country scientific capability into MNEs' CEE operations is through the setting up by their subsidiaries of in-house R&D laboratories. Thus 'results of R&D carried out in the CEE subsidiaries' (OWNLAB) was evaluated as a source of technology. This will probably not be significantly relevant to MNEs' activity within phase one, where the local adaptation in MS is unlikely to need this degree of scientific commitment whilst the cost-consciousness of pure-ES behaviour will usually preclude the costs of a laboratory. By contrast in-house R&D facilities are a very plausible means through which MNEs can seek to harness the emerging local technological potentials of phase two in support of their own KS motivations.

Here the capabilities of the subsidiaries' labs may generate key new technologies themselves and/or provide the capacity to assimilate, for commercial use, other knowledge sources (GROUPTECH, LOCALTECH or results from other collaborative R&D arrangements). In fact OWNLAB was never rated as a main source of technology and only considered to be a secondary one by 16.1 per cent of respondents. This may, however, understate the potential of in-house R&D in supporting the sustained evolution of MNEs' CEE activity. Thus OWNLAB (output of laboratories) is defined as an activated technological input into ongoing operations. Bearing in mind the prolonged nature of the process of implementing labs in a new situation and operationalising research results commercially, it may be thus too early for MNEs' commitment to this aspect of their development in CEE economies to be bearing substantial fruit.

Another means by which MNEs' CEE operations might encompass distinctive local sources of creative scope is in the form of 'development and adaptation carried out less formally by members of our subsidiaries' engineering units and production personnel' (ENGUNIT). Though adequate skill quality in local engineering units would be necessary to secure the effective assimilation of ESTPRODTECH in phase one, the emphasis here is on the possibility that the more talented of their personnel will embody explicit forms of expertise (tacit knowledge) that can support the creative transition into the sustained development of phase two. Whether ENGUNIT can be more than a valuable facilitating agent (i.e. can be effective in the absence of other innovation-oriented sources of technology) must be open to doubt, however. In fact 6.5 per cent of respondents did consider ENGUNIT to be a main source of technology, but only a further 32.3 per cent rated it as even of secondary relevance.

Finally, two externalised means of tapping into local technological potentials were investigated in the forms of 'R&D carried out for the subsidiary by local scientific institutions (e.g. universities, independent laboratories, industry laboratories)' (UNIRAD) and 'R&D carried out in collaboration with local firms' (COLLABRAD). Such arrangements are likely to be relatively inexpensive (and perhaps inconspicuous, from the point of view of intra-group supervision) means of attempting to secure subsidiary-level access to new technological perspectives. In this way they may be seen as predominantly means of building a basis towards the achievement of KS objectives. Though collaborations with extant local research facilities could speed up the operationalisation process, neither of these are more prevalent than OWNLAB as research-based sources of technology (Table 9.5). Thus only 9.7 per cent of respondents rated UNIRAD as even a secondary source of technology, whilst the comparable figure for COLLABRAD was 16.2 per cent.

REGRESSION TESTS

Regression tests were run with the four motivations for investment as the dependent variables. Along with dummy variables for industry (miscellaneous serving as the omitted industry group) and home-country origins of the MNE (Europe as the omitted source region) the seven sources of technology were included as independent variables. With a relatively small number of observations, and the inherently evolutionary nature of many of the relationships, it is not surprising that the overall explanatory power of the regressions, reported in Table 9.6, is quite weak. Nevertheless some interesting patterns, worthy of at least speculative interpretation, do emerge.

Though positive, as would clearly be predicted, the relationships between ESTPRODTECH and both MS and ES were relatively weak.[7] However, EST-PRODTECH is significantly negatively related to KS1. This indicates that those cases where the presence of ESTPRODTECH is relatively weak tend to be those where the KS1 role is emerging into MNEs' CEE operations. Thus product development for the CEE region does seem to be asserting itself in a manner that is quite strongly independent of those technologies (ESTPRODTECH) through which the initial MS penetration was achieved. The comparable relationship for KS2 is only weakly negative.

In view of its quite extensive presence as a technology source (Table 9.5), the results for GROUPTECH are quite enigmatic. Against our expectation for its likely status as a supporting input into CEE product development operations, GROUPTECH in fact produces negative signs for its relationship with both KS1 and KS2 (approaching significance in the former case). This suggests that the CEE subsidiaries generating KS capabilities seek to do so independently of new MNE-group technology and to substantially derive their knowledge impetus locally. Though the role of GROUPTECH may, therefore, seem to be more oriented to support differentiation needs in initiating MS or ES the regression results here are very weak (and negatively signed).

LOCALTECH is significantly positively related to KS1 and its relationship with MS is also clearly positively signed (though short of significance). By contrast the results for both KS2 and ES are very weak. This suggests that the main contribution of LOCALTECH is in localised activity, helping with the adaptation of ESTPRODTECH in securing effective MS entry to the CEE and, especially,

Table 9.6   Regressions with strategic roles of subsidiaries as dependent variable

	Dependent variable (motivation of subsidiaries)[1]			
	MS	ES	KS1	KS2
Constant	2.800**	0.575	1.891**	0.163
	(2.811)	(0.385)	(2.349)	(0.167)
Asia	0.324	0.706	0.433	0.557
	(0.740)	(1.074)	(1.224)	(1.292)
North America	0.165	0.043	0.040	0.244
	(0.632)	(0.109)	(0.189)	(0.954)
Electronics	0.051	−0.185	0.129	0.007
	(0.204)	(−0.296)	(0.384)	(0.015)
Chemicals	−0.311	−0.272	−0.057	0.491
	(−0.826)	(−0.481)	(−0.188)	(1.329)
Mechanical eng.	−0.358	0.193	−0.379	0.115
	(−1.016)	(0.365)	(−1.332)	(0.331)
Motor vehicles	−0.240	−0.529	−0.541	−0.297
	(−0.496)	(−0.730)	(−1.387)	(−0.625)
Petroleum	−0.321	−1.630	0.704	−1.070
	(−0.319)	(−1.077)	(0.864)	(−1.079)
ESTPRODTECH[2]	0.183	0.243	−0.441*	−0.137
	(0.672)	(0.594)	(−2.003)	(−0.511)
GROUPTECH	−0.086	−0.042	−0.262	−0.255
	(−0.433)	(−0.139)	(−1.627)	(−1.300)
LOCALTECH	0.291	0.083	0.618***	0.024
	(1.321)	(0.251)	(3.469)	(0.112)
OWNLAB	−0.559	−0.906*	0.048	−0.038
	(−1.636)	(−1.765)	(0.172)	(−0.114)
ENGUNIT	−0.188	0.037	−0.153	−0.150
	(−0.935)	(0.123)	(−0.938)	(−0.759)
UNIRAD	−0.024	0.654	−0.133	1.172**
	(−0.050)	(0.875)	(−0.329)	(2.393)
COLLABRAD	0.191	0.862	0.749*	0.765
	(0.415)	(1.246)	(2.009)	(1.686)
R^2	0.412	0.457	0.819	0.620
F	0.701	0.843	4.530***	1.629
n	28	28	28	28

Notes:
[1] For definition of investment motivations see Table 9.2.
[2] For definition of sources of technology see Table 9.5.
*** significant at 1%; ** significant at 5%; * significant at 10%; n = number of observations.

providing key inputs into distinctive product development for the region. Notably it does not seem to be a source of ideas for those product developments that might secure entry to markets outside the transition economies.

OWNLAB is significantly negatively related to ES, whilst the similar relationship with MS only just misses significance. For ES this confirms that the cost-consciousness of the role, and its lack of need for local adaptation, systematically works against in-house R&D. Whilst MS could require local adaptation it seems that this is again unlikely to justify the expenditures of in-house R&D, with other inputs (notably LOCALTECH) adequately facilitating the process. The relationships between OWNLAB and KS1 and KS2 are both very weak. This does indicate escape from the active alienation of in-house R&D implied by the results for MS and ES, but does not yet show KS operations as systematically using the results of subsidiaries' own R&D units.

The regression results for ENGUNIT are all rather weak. This suggests that, so far, the types of tacit knowledge and engineering expertise possessed by these personnel are found to be useful in rather *ad hoc* circumstances that do not relate predominantly to any specific motivation.

The significant result for UNIRAD is a positive relationship with KS2. This may indicate that KS2-style pursuit of quite radical product development for markets outside CEE is more science-driven than market-driven. This may be because CEE subsidiaries have less direct familiarity with market needs in, for example, Western Europe, than rival subsidiaries that are already located in those areas. Whilst often denied access to in-house labs (for cost reasons) subsidiaries developing KS2 ambitions may try to get new ideas from joint research with universities. This may be cheaper and also less open to central-group surveillance or suppression.

COLLABRAD is significantly positively related to KS1, whilst the positive sign for KS2 also approaches significance. In the case of KS1 COLLABRAD may complement the use of LOCALTECH in this form of product development, and also provide more generalised knowledge of local needs that can help the MNE to activate research towards development of new local-market goods. In KS2 COLLABRAD may provide inputs to the same research programmes that involve local universities (UNIRAD). An alternative possibility, however, is that research collaborations between MNE operations and local firms may aim at the improved development of technological potentials already present in the CEE enterprise. Success in this may be activated by both partners, with MNE experience helping, in particular, to secure entry of new goods into markets outside the region (i.e. KS2 product development). The various sources of technology are summarised in Table 9.7.

CONCLUSIONS

The most pervasive motivation for MNEs' early entry into the CEE transition economies has been to ensure the successful and responsive penetration of these new market areas for their most competitive established goods (market seeking (MS) behaviour). This degree of commitment is also seen as providing valuable knowledge of distinctive local tastes and productive capabilities. Responding to these may not only be valuable within immediate MS operations but also provide pointers towards longer-term developmental possibilities. However, the local-market

Table 9.7 Summary of positioning of sources of technology in MNEs' CEE operations[1]

Source of technology	Positive	Negative	Comment
ESTPRODTECH	MS ES	KS1	At the core of initial entry of CEE operations, but systematically avoided in developing goods for local markets
GROUPTECH	None	KS1 KS2	Systematically avoided in product development by CEE subsidiaries
LOCALTECH	MS KS1	None	Utilised in both adaptation of existing goods and development of new goods for CEE markets
OWNLAB	None	MS ES	Costs of R&D rule out in-house research early in subsidiaries' operations in CEE
ENGUNIT	None	None	Quite extensive applications of these skills and tacit knowledge, but in a rather *ad hoc* fashion
UNIRAD	KS2	None	Provides distinctive local knowledge for science-driven product development for new CEE markets
COLLABRAD	ES KS1 KS2	None	Helps local enterprises to better utilise technological potentials for non-CEE markets (ES KS2) or new product development for CEE (KS1)

Notes:
[1] Authors' interpretation of results in Tables 9.5 and 9.6.
[2] For definitions of sources of technology see Table 9.5.
[3] For definitions of investment motivations see Table 9.2.

focus of MS may have constrained relevance to the achievement of what we termed the phase one objective of industrial transformation. The industries that are most supported by MS investment of MNEs may not be the ones with the greatest competitive potential in international markets. Furthermore, the somewhat isolated situation may not generate international levels of efficiency in those operations that do flourish (in the short-run at least). Ultimately it would be desirable to discern evolutionary potentials within the MS operations.

The use of cost-efficient operations in CEE to supply MNEs' existing markets outside the region (efficiency seeking (ES) behaviour) has emerged to quite a significant degree, though much less pervasively than MS. We also noted, as the first of the evolutionary possibilities in MS, that rationalisation of MNEs' original portfolio of CEE subsidiaries may lead to some of these claiming wider supply responsibility for the transition economy region on the basis of more efficient production. Generally the ES-oriented facilities are more likely to help to secure the phase one objective of an internationally competitive industrial sector. Other parts of our evidence, however, appear to confirm that the dominating short-term cost consciousness of ES activity mitigates against investment in those knowledge-generating expenditures that can provide such subsidiaries with alternative potentials into the medium term. If this leaves ES facilities mainly dependent on standardised cost-based local production inputs it certainly opens up the possibility that changes in these (most immediately in their price) may cause the footloose exit of such subsidiaries. This would hollow out any development processes the ES subsidiaries were initially contributing to. Emphatically, therefore, pure ES does not generate MNE capabilities that can complement and support CEE economies' movement into phase two.

However, we also suggest that the wider needs of MNEs' strategic evolution can benefit from creative potentials (scientific results, research capacity, tacit knowledge) available in transition economies. As manifest through local product development we see the knowledge seeking (KS) imperative of MNEs supporting CEE economies' phase two progress. Development of products for the CEE region (KS1) is a second evolutionary potential for MS facilities as they appear to build on local technological possibilities and to actively reject dependence on established technology of their MNE group. But it would be KS2-type product development, for other markets (notably Western Europe), that is likely to provide the most valuable potential. Again for cost reasons, there seems limited scope to achieve this as a deepening of the ES imperative. But, given adequate access to, and experience in, intra-group-network bargaining procedures, the more successful and distinctive KS1 innovations (originally targeting CEE markets) may extend their market scope into the more profitable non-CEE markets. Indeed the more these are built on idiosyncratic CEE knowledge and tastes the more different they may be from existing MNE product lines and, therefore, the less resistance they may be subjected to from established suppliers outside the transition region.

Generally it is to be hoped that, over time, MNEs will pursue the more systematic integration of their CEE operations with their wider strategic priorities.

Meanwhile it may be that the apparently isolationist emphasis on MS as the initial motivation for activity in this region does, in fact, provide more possibilities for generating the bases for a more sustainable outward-looking status than might at first appear to be the case.

Notes

1. Bellak (1997) has explicitly related the restructuring processes of leading MNEs to the catching up of small Eastern countries.
2. The activation of MNEs' operations in transition economies through differentiated roles and motivations has been discussed and analysed by Lankes and Venables (1996), Mutinelli and Piscitello (1997), Meyer (1998), Rojec (1994), Rojec and Svetlicic (1993), Estrin, Hughes and Todd (1997) and Donges and Wieners (1994).
3. The starting point was the *Fortune* listing of leading global corporations, published in August 1996. Since this, for the first time, covered all areas of business, only 207 relevant manufacturing and extractive enterprises were found. To increase the relevant population the last listing of 500 industrial companies (*Fortune*, July 1994) was consulted and 201 firms not already derived from the 1996 listing were added to the 207.
4. The remainder either exported to the CEE countries (three cases), or currently had no active commitment to the region (eight). These eleven only replied to questions on attitudes to the investment environment of transition economies and to possible future involvement.
5. Thirty-four respondents provided the information reported in Tables 9.2, 9.3 and 9.4. These covered 27 of those with manufacturing operations in CEE and seven of those with a substantial commitment to other significant parts of the value-added chain.
6. Thirty-one respondents offered evaluation of the technologies used in their CEE operations. In the case of those that did not have producing subsidiaries in the region the reported technology sources are those relevant to the activities carried out and/or the technologies embodied in products distributed there.
7. This may reflect the generalised pervasiveness of ESTPRODTECH and its expected role at the centre of initiating both MS and ES. Thus where, for example, MS is only a secondary role or is absent, then ES is most likely to be the superior motive and will also provide a strong status for ESTPRODTECH. The reasoning can be applied similarly to ES.

10 Modes of Integration and the Diffusion of Best Practice in the Multinational Enterprise

Martyn Wright and Paul Edwards

In research into the diffusion of 'best practice' within MNEs, two points stand out as requiring further development. First, an increasing body of work suggests that best practice is difficult to transfer and reproduce internally due to a range of cultural, organisational and motivational barriers (for example, Kostova 1999; Szulanski, 1996). Until recently, there has been little discussion of systems for distributing information within MNEs – what have variously been termed 'transmission mechanisms' (Gupta and Govindarajan, 2000), 'modes of integration' (Kim *et al.*, 1999) or 'delivery systems'. Yet these channels may be critically important in regulating the volume and nature of data to which users have access. Second, prior research into knowledge transfer has concentrated upon discrete items of product and technology (Hansen, 1999; Kogut and Zander, 1992; Zander and Kogut, 1995) to the neglect of organisation systems. Yet innovative work systems have been correlated with superior labour productivity and process quality outcomes (Huselid, 1995). And, as complex configurations of human, organisational and technological assets, work systems may be difficult for rivals to imitate and may therefore constitute a valuable competitive resource. Recent research, notably the study of ABB by Bélanger *et al.* (1999) is beginning to address these issues. It identifies, for example, cultural and social factors in the development of organisational learning. But it gives relatively little attention to the precise operation of these factors.

The present chapter compares two primary modes for communicating information about best practice in work organisation in a pair of global, integrated MNEs – Alcan aluminium, the Canadian corporation, and 'EUROIL', a pseudonym for a European oil major. At Alcan, dense networks of interaction among senior management facilitated the diffusion of teamworking to plants in several countries. At EUROIL, by contrast, electronic communication networks produced a large but unstructured volume of material, which recipients had difficulty in assimilating, and which effected a discontinuous pattern of change at the workplace. The chapter is set out in the following sections: previous research literature; research design and methods; best practice networks at Alcan and EUROIL; discussion.

DEBATES ON BEST PRACTICE TRANSFERS IN MULTINATIONALS

The internal transfer of 'best practice' refers to a demonstrably superior organisational routine which is replicated in another part of an enterprise. A growing body of research suggests that best practice is 'sticky' (Szulanski, 1996) or 'inert' (Kogut and Zander, 1992) and that transferring such practices across organisational boundaries is problematic. This immobility of knowledge has been attributed to a wide range of cultural, organisational and relational barriers (Kostova 1999; Szulanski, 1996), and to the complexity and degree of ambiguity of the practices themselves (Simonin, 1999; Zander and Kogut, 1995; Reed and DeFillippi, 1990). By contrast, systems for delivering information about best practice have only recently begun to be examined. Although the studies are few in number and often preliminary in nature, they indicate that information delivery systems may be a critical determinant of the degree to which recipients internalise knowledge, and of the subsequent speed with which organisational 'best practice' is adopted by MNE subsidiaries.

Two primary modes of integration within MNEs have been identified. In the first method, information is exchanged through direct personal interaction (DPI) among senior managers, in forums such as international conferences, visits to overseas sites, training and induction programs and service on international project teams. The second mode of communication is via electronic communications technology (ECT), which encompasses e-mail networks, electronic bulletin boards, video-conferencing, on-line databases and groupware programmes.

The literature relating to these two integrating modes has developed largely separately, and with competing and somewhat contradictory claims made for each. Institutional economists, in particular, have argued that ECT has a profound effect upon communication patterns within MNEs (Malone *et al.*, 1994; Crowston and Malone, 1994). Cohendet *et al.* (1999: 234) go so far so to claim that ECT is 'the key factor' in the organisational integration of global firms. Several reasons for these claims may be adduced. First, through such media as e-mail and groupware systems, ECT massively reduces the marginal costs of internal messaging, while greatly accelerating the speed of communication. The cultural and geographical barriers which impede information flows across national boundaries are therefore reduced and data circulates more with greater fluidity. Second, and related, ECT raises the frequency of contact between parties and increases the opportunity for collective dialogue. In nurturing a common corporate experience and creating new contexts for social interaction, ECT may increase organisational competences in the articulation of 'tacit', or intuitive, knowledge.

Empirical support comes from Kim *et al.* (1999) who surveyed 182 MNEs and found that the only integrating mode consistently associated with the development of core competences was communication through information technology. Case study research is more equivocal as to the effects of ECT. Much appears to depend upon the organisational culture into which the technology is introduced, and upon the existence of appropriate training and incentive payment systems. Orlikowski (1996) found that groupware technology did little to promote information-sharing among consultants in a large consultancy, because it ran counter to the prevailing competitive and individualistic ethos. At Unilever, insufficient training and a lack of time hindered the practical exploitation of groupware technology (Ciborra, 1996; Ciborra and Patriotta, 1996). At Arthur Andersen, the introduction of an integrated system for electronic data interchange was initially 'disappointing', and improved only when usage was factored into consultants' compensation and promotion reviews (Quinn *et al.*, 1996; see Hansen *et al.*, 1999 for similar findings).

If the evidence that ECT promotes MNE integration is mixed, that for DPI appears rather more persuasive. In a survey of 66 MNEs, Nohria and Ghoshal (1997) find that dense networks of inter-personal contact were associated with a more rapid rate of diffusion of innovations. In the R&D literature, engineers' productivity appears to depend greatly upon their direct interaction with colleagues, while ECT was used for coordination but not for the more complex innovation work (de Meyer, 1994). Coller *et al.* (1998) show for four British MNEs that work practices were diffused by headquarters subjecting plant-level managers to subtle pressures to conform, through such means as frequent meetings of managers.

DPI may have some important advantages over ECT as a medium for communication. First, face-to-face contact may assist in forming bonds of trust and common language – what Weick (1995) terms a 'mutually validated grammar' – which may be a prerequisite to the exchange of information. The successful exchange of ideas may depend upon the existence of a shared set of meanings, language and assumptions. There are strong parallels here with the literature on trust within and between organisations, which stresses the development of inter-personal relations as a means of building up confidence that obligations will be honoured (Lane and Bachmann, 1998). Second, DPI allows for a fine-grained description of practices, which may be refined and clarified through questioning and dialogue. Nahapiet and Ghoshal (1998) refer to the ethnography by Orr (1996) of photocopier repair workers. This study shows that technical knowledge could not be codified and that it was contained in a rich oral tradition; this tradition was also the means through which knowledge was diffused. Third, face-to-face contact may have a socialising influence, and assist in building a common culture and a shared sense of purpose among managers from diverse cultural backgrounds (Bartlett and Ghoshal, 1998: 80). Fourth, DPI may increase the possibility of communication by telephone and other means at a later date (Hedlund, 1986; Prahalad and Doz, 1987).

Drawing upon these observations, earlier research argued that DPI is a more efficient mode of information exchange than ECT and that use of the latter may require more, rather than less, face-to-face contact (Nohria and Eccles, 1992). More recent work suggests a contingency perspective, whereby selection between the two modes depends upon the degree to which the products or service is standardised (Hansen *et al.*, 1999). ECT is deemed more appropriate to firms producing uniform goods, where knowledge may be more readily codified, while direct interaction is considered best suited to more customised products. Contrary to the contingency perspective of Hansen *et al.*, we will show that both firms under study produced a highly standardised product but employed quite different integrating mechanisms, for a variety of reasons which the case study will explore.

RESEARCH DESIGN AND METHODS

A comparative case study method was employed. The two companies under examination, Alcan aluminium and EUROIL, are similar in several respects. First, they are highly globalised; in terms of the proportion of employees located outside the home company, Alcan and EUROIL are the most globalised firms in their sectors (Alcan Facts 1996: 1, *Financial Times*, 23 March 1995). Second, the two companies are large and, when measured by production output in the 1997 calendar year, ranked second in their respective sectors (Annual Reports, cited above). Third, they produce a standardised product in a product market with a single world price. Fourth, the workforce of both companies is similar, composed predominantly of highly unionised, male, manual and semi-skilled workers, with smaller numbers of skilled craft workers and technologists/ engineers educated to university degree level or above. Manual workers are paid in the upper quartile for their local labour market. Finally, both oil refining and aluminium smelting require capital-intensive, continuous process production technology.

Data were collected mainly through semi-structured interviews, undertaken at several levels and multiple sites in both organisations. Colleagues from Université Laval, Quebec, Canada and the present writers collaborated closely and followed a common methodology. Managers were interviewed at headquarters and national head offices, while detailed case studies were undertaken at plant level. To date, three Alcan aluminium smelters (two Canadian, one British) and a single British EUROIL refinery, called here NORTH, have been examined. Each case featured interviews with managers in a range of functions, and also with supervisors, trade union representatives and operatives. Where possible, these methods were supplemented by follow-up interviews, by the distribution of a questionnaire to employees, and by observation of work practices.

In addition, we have made use of FT Profile, an on-line database of press reports from the *Financial Times* since 1990, and of internal company documentation. We do not cite these sources except where quoting directly.

BEST PRACTICE TRANSFERS AT
ALCAN ALUMINIUM AND EUROIL

The key features of the information distribution systems in each corporation are reviewed in turn. Both firms operate extensive, standardised systems of performance monitoring, whereby each plant sends large amounts of data to the corporate centre at monthly intervals. The crucial differences arise in the interpretation of these data, and in particular, the degree to which corporate management reply upon in them as an indicator of plant performance. A summary is provided in Table 10.1.

Alcan

Each Alcan plants records over one hundred separate measures of production efficiency. These measures encompass efficient use of raw materials, output per person, total staff hours worked and the number of lost time accidents. Because smelters differ in their production technology, most notably between the older

Table 10.1   Summary of developments at case study companies

	Alcan	Euroil
Performance benchmarking systems	100+ measures of all aspects of smelter performance recorded monthly at each plant Differences in refinery technology limit comparison Senior corporate executives gather 'impressionistic' data through personal visits to sites	Biannual industrywide benchmarking; internal company-wide league tables of refinery performance Benchmarks form performance targets for refinery in 5-year plan Staffing levels kept constantly under review in line with output/person benchmarks
Information exchange system	Regular plant visits by executives from headquarters Technical audits by HQ engineers. Annual meetings of technical personnel at HQ Annual conferences for 70 most senior managers Global management development programme	Desk studies of maintenance organisation distributed to refineries worldwide Electronic media – newsgroups, e-mail networks – confined to technical issues. Electronic newsletter on general management issues. Ad hoc personal interaction
Corporate policy on workplace management	Preference for human relations style employee management; emphasis upon employee involvement and consultation	Statement of group 'general business principles'; no espoused policy on operational matters
Workplace change	Diffusion of sociotechnical systems model of teamworking to Alcan smelters: Isle Maligne, Latterriere (Quebec), Lynemouth (UK), Kurri Kurri, Granville (Australia)	No coherent model for workplace change. Large no. piecemeal initiatives launched and abandoned. Employee complaints of 'information overload'. Reliance on external consultancies to devise and drive workplace change programmes

Söderberg systems and the more modern 'pre-bake' methods, corporate management do not depend exclusively upon the benchmark data in assessing plant performance. Even within specific generations of technology, there are important differences in system configuration, physical environment and in the availability of ancillary equipment. It is therefore considered difficult to draw meaningful comparisons, even across 'families' of technologically similar plants. Recognising this, corporate management spend a great deal of their time personally visiting plants, with the aim of collecting qualitative data on performance. During these inspections, senior management are exposed, through conversation and observation, to examples of innovative work practices, which they then pass on to other sites. In addition to these visits from corporate executives, personnel with specific technical expertise make bi-annual visits to all plants. These meetings take place in a cooperative spirit – they are not 'inquisitions', in the words of one interviewee – but offer a medium through which plant technicians may take advantage of corporate advice and know-how. Plant technicians also gather annually in Montreal for improvement workshops, convened by a Vice President with dedicated responsibility for technology transfer.

Two-to-three day conferences of the 70 most senior Alcan executives take place annually to discuss prevailing issues and improvement initiatives. Through these meetings, held since 1979, senior management become personally acquainted with one another to the extent, according to one member, that executives feel comfortable in 'picking up the telephone to talk to each other'. A similar forum exists for managers at senior vice-president level or below, which is a week in duration and runs one or two times per year. Finally, Alcan operates a global management development programme, in which managers in their late twenties and early thirties are seconded to headquarters for a period, and are detailed to serve on international project committees. In this way, younger managers have the opportunity to establish a network of personal contacts.

There is, therefore, a stable network of dense personal relationships among Alcan senior management, similar to the direct personal interaction mode outlined in the Introduction. Through a combination of regular meetings of senior management and technicians, frequent visits to overseas plants, an established management development programme and participation in project teams, executives establish bonds of mutual acquaintance and affiliation. In this way an elaborate transmission mechanism is formed through which information flows both vertically, between headquarters and subsidiaries, and laterally, between subsidiaries. Alcan also expresses a normative preference for the management of work relations based in the socio-technical systems tradition of encouraging the integration of job tasks and the relaxation of direct control of the primary workgroup. This value system evolved from experiments with quality of work life initiatives and employee involvement which date back to the early 1970s. As such, there is no central template for teamworking, unlike the food MNE studied by Coller (1996). Instead, there is a process of conditioning, what we have elsewhere termed an 'elective affinity' (Bélanger *et al.*, 1999), whereby plant-level managers are systematically exposed to the norms and values of teamworking. This takes place mainly through repeated contact with colleagues at headquarters and at other plants. There is no obligation upon plant managers to abide by these principles, and the decision of how to organise production rests squarely with them. But in an environment in which production efficiency is closely scrutinised, and where access to capital investment is competitive, the decision to adopt teamworking may have symbolic properties in signalling to headquarters that appropriate actions are being taken to improve performance (Ahlstrand, 1990).

The outcome of this process, evident at several smelters although not all of them, was a trend away from direct production control, towards teamworking. But important differences were apparent in the structure of teams and in the timing of their introduction. At the UK Lynemouth smelter, for example, the level of supervision was eliminated. Control over work scheduling, attendance, training and minor budgeting was devolved to work teams. Team members are trained in, and rotate through, all tasks typically performed by the group. More recently, team members have also been granted control over the selection of new recruits and the authorisation of internal transfers. This configuration mirrors that at the Latterière plant in Quebec, a new smelter which commenced production in 1990, where team members are also polyvalent and rotate fully across all tasks (Bélanger and St Laurant, 1998: 12). Teams have taken responsibility for a variety of regulating, monitoring and coordinating tasks. By contrast, at the Isle Maligne smelter, also in Quebec, teams had less autonomy than in the above cases. The number of supervisors was reduced by half, rather than completely removed, and team members rotated through two or three job tasks rather than the full range undertaken by the group (Bélanger and Dumas, 1998). A similar pattern was evident at the Kurri Kurri smelter in Australia (which Alcan has since disposed of; see Burgess *et al.*, 1994). At the Rogerstone rolling mill in South Wales, direct control of production and a more traditional pattern of supervision had been retained.

In summary, Alcan corporate management espouse a set of principles consistent with a socio-technical model of teamworking at plant level; these principles are diffused through a structured and integrated network of personal interaction between headquarters and plant-level management. The need for senior managers to visit plants on a regular basis arises from the perceived limitations of performance benchmarking, which it is felt must be supplemented by additional 'impressionistic' data. The outcome has been the diffusion of the teamworking principle to many although not all Alcan smelters, with important differences in the adaptation of the principle and in the structuring of teams at plant level.

EUROIL

Comparisons of plant performance are arguably even more extensive at EUROIL than at Alcan. Benchmarking is undertaken internally and on an industrywide basis. With the latter, an external consultancy measures the production efficiency of each refinery for all participating companies every two years. There is widespread involvement in these studies among the major oil companies. Several indicators of production efficiency are collected – output of barrels of oil per employee is a key one – and the performance of each refinery is expressed in relation to the median and quartile levels for the industry as whole. EUROIL also engages in detailed internal benchmarking. As with Alcan, each refinery compiles data on a multiplicity of issues, including output per person, frequency of lost time accidents, and number of employees. Headquarters collates the data, making adjustments for differences in capital, technology and other idiosyncrasies, and produces a performance league table which is then distributed to each refinery in the company.

Unlike Alcan, where it was considered impossible to control adequately for plant heterogeneity in the benchmarking data, EUROIL was much more confident in the reliability of the procedure. Although the methodological issues were similar in the two companies, in EUROIL the validity of the data as an indicator of efficiency were largely unquestioned. Consequently, their relative performance in the studies was of greater importance to EUROIL plant managers and more directly shaped their policies and actions. On the basis of a poor benchmark ranking alone, plants could be 'red-flagged' and investment withheld until improvements occurred. Plant management therefore explicitly incorporated benchmark standards into their performance targets. The NORTH plant, for example, aimed to achieve efficiency levels in the upper quartile for the industry as a whole, and set its goals accordingly. Because the critical measure was output of oil per person, staffing levels were kept constantly under review. In the year before the present study, none of the twenty-five apprentices trained at NORTH was retained because the number of employees at the site had drifted above the benchmark level.

Given the uncritical acceptance of benchmarking in EUROIL, staff responsible for compiling the data see no need personally to visit plants. In the eighteen months prior to the present study, a member of the benchmarking staff had only once visited NORTH. Corporate staff are willing to pass on examples of best practice where they are aware of it. But such information is not volunteered – it has to be requested by the recipient – and no protocol exists for ensuring that the information is systematically disseminated to all interested parties.

EUROIL had no equivalent to the 'dominant logic' of sociotechnical systems witnessed at Alcan. The corporate centre does not espouse a set of preferred norms or values which might inform the design of work organisation, remuneration or communication systems. Guidance from the centre is confined to a number of general business principles, such as a commitment not to bribe government officials, but there are no specifics on matters of organisation structure. Only on group-wide issues, such as pension entitlements, does the centre lay down binding regulations, although it is prepared to intervene where the actions of one plant, awarding a large pay increase for example, might have implications for other plants.

EUROIL has several mechanisms intended to promote information sharing and the dissemination of best practice (Table 10.1). A series of desk studies are produced by head office, which relate primary to the organisation of maintenance. They are illustrated by examples drawn from EUROIL plants and are distributed to all sites worldwide. In addition, there are electronic media, such as newsgroups, e-mail networks and electronic bulletin boards. EUROIL has an integrated IT system with standard software and a common portal, so that theoretically there is great scope for cross-border dialogue. In practice, however, electronic communications technology (ECT) is considered a poor means of disseminating information, for reasons which reflect those set out in the Introduction. First, e-mail networks and intranet discussion groups tend to hold rather generic discussions at a level removed from the unique systems and historical features of individual plants. As a result, recipients often cannot see the relevance of much of the material that is circulated and how it might be operationalised in their own contexts. Second, material sent through ECT suffers from a low level of readership particularly among those senior managers with the power to initiate change at plant level. Third, for many e-mail groups, postings are collated and distributed on a daily basis, and the resulting volume of information can be too great for managers to absorb. Fourth, forms of ECT such as newsgroups require users to actively search out the information by logging into the system, often without knowing in advance whether any new postings have been made. Inevitably, given the required investment of time and the uncertain returns, many managers do not access this source of information regularly. Fifth, the large majority of networks exist to discuss technical and engineering issues, and membership is restricted to those with specialist training and qualifications. Very few groups include as part of their remit broader managerial and organisational concerns, which limits the scope for discussion of the sort of socio-technical practices observed at Alcan.

The corporate centre does publish a bimonthly newsletter, available worldwide through the intranet, which contains short articles on business matters. These often summarise material covered in practitioner-oriented outlets, such as *The McKinsey Quarterly* or *Harvard Business Review*. The newsletter has great potential to raise awareness of novel ideas or topical issues pertaining to business. The October 1998 edition, for example, includes articles on 'organisational clusters', strategy under uncertainty and leadership styles. But the magazine is not widely read because much of its content cannot be immediately applied and there is limited time available to devote to background materials.

The earlier 'best practice' set out several reasons why face-to-face interaction may be a more efficient means for diffusing organisational practices, compared with ECT. These included the ability through direct personal contact to establish a relationship based on trust and to develop a common framework for analysis. Crucially, EUROIL managers themselves argued that that inter-personal contact through meetings, project groups etc. was the most effective medium for exchanging ideas about organisation structure and design. The opportunities for learning through these channels were few. Refinery managers do meet collectively but at irregular intervals. Technical personnel convene more frequently but their agenda is restricted to engineering and technology issues.

Plant managers are therefore forced to rely heavily upon their own networks of personal contacts when searching for information about innovations in management and organisational issues. Individual managers do converse with their couterparts at overseas plants and visit them but these arrangements are on an ad hoc basis and are contingent upon whether the parties happen to know each other. As a result, personal characteristics such as career histories frame the information to which individuals have access. Whether a manager learns of the best practice, or the most optimal solution to be found in the corporation, depends to a large extent upon chance. As one EUROIL manager commented, ideas of best practice are 'not very alive at the moment' and the results obtained are 'more on an incidental than a structural basis'.

In summary, under the EUROIL benchmarking system, plant performance is continually compared and site managers are subject to great pressure to increase production efficiency. But in the absence of a set of corporate norms and values which might inform change and without a systematic means of promoting face-to-face contact with their overseas counterparts, plant managers have to be self-reliant in devising programmes for reform. At NORTH, the resulting pattern was that a large number of reforms were launched, many of which were designed and delivered by outside consultants. During the 1990s alone, twelve distinct, major change initiatives could be discerned. These varied widely in their orientation, from teamworking, to the redesign of operations procedures, to changes to plant level union recognition. Unlike Alcan, where plant-level reforms were incremental and drew upon a socio-technical systems tradition, those at NORTH were commonly piecemeal in nature and lacked cohesion. Workers responded negatively, complaining of 'initiative overload'. The outcome, it may be argued, was that workplace change initiatives lacked the mutually re-enforcing quality of those at Alcan, and were consequently more liable to failure.

DISCUSSION

This chapter has examined the effect of 'modes of integration' upon the transfer of innovative forms of work organisation in two MNEs. The Introduction described two currents of literature. In the first, institutional economists have argued that ECT reduces the cost and increases the speed of communication, thereby reducing geographical and cultural barriers to learning and advancing integration within MNEs. Others (for example, Nohria and Ghoshal, 1997; De Meyer, 1994; Nohria and Eccles, 1992) offer an alternative perspective, positing that DPI is a more efficient method for disseminating information and transferring best practice. DPI, it is maintained, assists in building trust and mutual understanding between the parties, while also enhancing discussion through dialogue, along with questions and feedback. Organisations in effect practise the 'thick description' advocated by anthropologists as a means of understanding what they do.

In practice, in both organisations, extensive systems of benchmarking framed the pattern of information flows, and the degree to which DPI was seen to be necessary or desirable. Although the volume and form of data collected was similar, the firms differed markedly in extent to which they were prepared to rely upon it as a gauge of efficiency. At Alcan, corporate management were more suspicious of quantitative data and spent a great deal of time visiting plants, talking to plant managers and examining operations. These networks of structured interaction in effect created a transmission mechanism through corporate personnel learned of innovations which they then relayed to other sites as appropriate. This process was underwritten by an approved ethos based in the human relations/ job redesign tradition, a 'dominant logic' or common cognitive framework shared by many of the firm's senior management (Prahalad and Bettis, 1986). Prior exposure to these core notions may have raised managers' 'absorptive capacity' (Cohen and Levinthal, 1990): their ability to rapidly assimilate and apply complex new ideas, such as the notion of 'advanced' forms of teamworking. The combination of a developed network of personal interaction among the senior management cadre and a long-established set of corporate norms and values, ensured that information pertaining to teamwork rapidly filtered through the Alcan system. The adoption of teamworking was rapid and widespread but not universal, as certain plants choose to retain a Taylorist system of tight supervision and fragmented job tasks. Given the relative autonomy of plants in operational affairs and the absence of any corporate blueprint for work organisation, the structure of teams and the rights and responsibilities of team members differed from plant to plant.

At EUROIL, the validity of the performance benchmarking data was generally not disputed, so there was little perceived need for corporate managers to make personal inspections of plants. As a result, there was little opportunity available to corporate personnel to act as conduits for the dissemination of innovative practice. Instead, ECT was relied upon to a much greater extent to radiate ideas, many of which were confined to narrow issues of engineering and technology. Time constraints, especially upon senior managers, unmanageably large volumes of information and accounts of 'best practice' denuded of context, meant that managers had difficulty digesting much of the material circulated through ECT and applying it in their own environments.

These questions have considerable relevance for management practice. There are now several case studies which suggest that software designed to facilitate information-sharing is rarely exploited to its full degree and is hampered by individualistic cultures (Orlikowski, 1999) and by a lack of training and resources (Ciborra and Patriotta, 1996). Only where the use of ECT is encouraged with rewards such as pay and promotion do such systems appear to have been used extensively. Even then the available case studies are confined to particular organisations such as management consultancies (Quinn *et al.*, 1996; Hansen *et al.*, 1999). Whether ECT is viable as a primary form of communication in other, more conventional industries must remain a moot point. It may be that Nohria and Eccles' (1992) observation that the successful introduction of ECT requires more, rather than less, face-to-face contact between actors will prove to have been a pre-scient one.

Although the two study companies share many characteristics, they differ in three important respects. First, as touched upon above, they have rather different cultures. EUROIL has traditionally concentrated upon engineering and technical, rather than general management and organisational matters. Other than the present incumbent, its CEOs have all been engineers. Alcan has historically been an outwardly focused organisation, for example in founding the International Management Development (IMD) business school in Lausanne, Switzerland. The 'dominant managerial logic', or the lack of one at EUROIL, are thus rooted in long histories during which the two organisations have been exposed to quite different sets of influences. Second, the two companies differ in size, with EUROIL appreciably greater in terms of market capitalisation and numbers employed. Greater size may impede the formation of dense personal networks among the dominant elite, as it restricts the ease with which individuals can become personally acquainted. Third, the organisational structures of the two companies produced quite different patterns of communication. Alcan had a more integrated hierarchy in which plant managers reported directly to head office, while EUROIL was fragmented into distinct and competing national subsidiaries which obstructed cross-border information flows. As managers at NORTH repeatedly stressed, until very recently the firm had been a collection of national companies rather than an integrated MNE. At the level of the site there was, as we aim to demonstrate elsewhere, a substantial effort to develop best practice. But this was not connected to inter-personal systems across the company.

These results suggest some important developments in research on MNEs. As noted above, some companies seem to stress benchmarking and coercive comparisons between plants, while others stress social and cultural values. ABB is one company which blends the two approaches (Bélanger *et al.*, 1999). The case of Alcan illustrates how DPI can be a central mechanism in such a balance, while EUROIL points to the remaining difficulties. A future research task is to explore the conditions under which DPI or ECT is a preferred route, the connections between them and the diffusion of best practice, and the ways in which MNEs combine different sorts of mechanism for the coordination and control of their operations.

Acknowledgements

For their comments on an earlier version of this chapter, the authors thank participants at the Academy of International Business, UK Chapter meeting at the University of Strathclyde, April 2000, particularly Rebecca Marschan-Piekkari and Alan Rugman, and the editor and anonymous reviewers of this collection. The usual disclaimers apply. The chapter arises from joint research with Professor Jacques Bélanger, Université Laval, Quebec. The UK research was supported by the Economic and Social Research Council.

11 Global Operations Managed by Japanese and in Japanese

Hideki Yoshihara

DRASTIC CHANGE IN STRATEGY OF MANUFACTURING MULTINATIONALS

Export-centred International Business

Export occupied a central position in the international business strategy of Japanese companies until 1985. The export ratio (rate of exports to sales) of Japanese manufacturing companies listed on the first section of Tokyo Stock Exchange Market consistently increased, with 8 per cent in 1970 to peak at 15 per cent in 1985.[1] In September 1985 the Plaza Accord was reached, and the sharp appreciation of Japanese yen started. From 1986 the export ratio decreased for several years, and has not shown any substantial change since then.

The export ratio of Japanese manufacturing multinationals (the definition will be shown later) has been higher than that of manufacturing companies, but the shape of the trend has been quite similar. The export ratio consistently increased from 12 per cent in 1970 to 24 per cent in 1985, which was the peak year. After 1985 the export ratio decreased and then levelled off.

Overseas Production

Even in the 1960s and 1970s when exporting was the central strategy of international business, there was some overseas production. The overseas production in those days had the following characteristics:[2]

- concentration in the less developed countries and areas like Asia and Latin America,
- small-scale investment,
- transplant of labour intensive production,
- mature technology,
- production for local markets rather than for export markets,
- joint ventures,
- green field investment.

The overseas production of Japanese enterprises in those days attracted attention as Japanese style multinationalisation. Compared with American multinational enterprises that had such characteristics as investment in advanced countries, large scale investment, advanced technology, complete ownership, and M&A of local companies, Japanese multinationals showed a distinct difference.[3]

Japanese overseas production gradually changed its characteristics from the mid-1970s. Local production of color television sets in the United States by Matsushita, Honda's production of passenger cars in the United States and local production of plate glass in Belgium by Asahi Glass are important examples of overseas production at that time. They had the following new characteristics: local production in USA and Europe, 100 per cent ownership, M&A of local companies, large-scale investment and advanced technology.

When exporting occupied the central position in the international business strategy, overseas production was rather reluctantly pursued. Manufacturing companies actually wanted to export, but they were not able to do so because of import restrictions and protectionism of the countries of exporting markets. They did not want to lose market position that they acquired by exporting. Overseas production was pursued not for economic but for political reasons.

As overseas production has become the major part of the international business strategy after 1986, the motive has changed and benefits of overseas production are now emphasised more. Where are the most suitable places of production, in Japan, or USA, or Malaysia, or China? Japanese multinationals have come to make decisions about the location based on the global optimal criterion.[4]

Overseas R&D

An important factor in the recent development of the international business strategy is the overseas R&D. According to our questionnaire survey, nearly half (47 per cent) of overseas manufacturing subsidiaries are conducting R&D.[5] Most of the overseas R&D started within the last ten years. The questionnaire survey data show that 82 per cent of the overseas R&D began after 1985. Nearly two-thirds (62 per cent) of the overseas R&D started after 1990. Recently large-scale overseas plants increased and many of them have a research and development function.

Geographical Change of Investment

Until the first half of the 1970s, we observed a distinctive geographical distribution of the two types of investment, that is, marketing investment concentrated in advanced areas like North America and Europe, and manufacturing investment concentrated in Asia and other developing countries. In 1971, as regards manufacturing investment, developing countries occupied 78 per cent (in terms of the amount of investment) and 89 per cent (in terms of the number of investment projects) of the total investment. By contrast, in the case of marketing investment, advanced countries accounted for 91 per cent (in terms of the amount of investment) and 73 per cent (in terms of the number of investment projects) of the total investment.

During the last quarter of the 20th century a substantial change took place. Manufacturing investment is now centred in advanced regions like North America and Europe. In 1996, advanced countries occupied 37 per cent of the total manufacturing investment in terms of the number of investment projects, and 62 per cent in terms of the amount of investment. As for marketing investment, the change is not so big. The share of the advanced countries changed from 91 per cent to 80 per cent in terms of the amount of investment, and from 73 per cent to 72 per cent in terms of the number of investment projects.

As a matter of fact, the USA has received the largest portion of Japanese foreign direct investment. The share of the investment made in the USA amounts to 41 per cent of total manufacturing investment and 48 per cent of total marketing investment (both in terms of amount of investment).

Increase of Multinational Enterprises

The above-mentioned development of international business strategy has produced many Japanese multinational enterprises, which we define as the companies meeting two conditions.[6] The first is company size. They are among the 500 largest (in terms of sales) companies. The second condition is commitment to overseas production. They have overseas manufacturing subsidiaries (their ownership is equal to 25 per cent or more) in at least five countries. In 1994, 149 companies met these two conditions. The Japanese multinationals totalled 67 in 1982 and 37 in 1974. Thus the Japanese multinationals roughly doubled every ten years.[7]

LITTLE CHANGE IN INTERNATIONAL MANAGEMENT

Management by Japanese Persons

The above examination tells us that international business strategy of Japanese multinationals has changed drastically over the last nearly fifty years. In short, Japanese multinationals have largely abandoned their Japanese-style strategy and gained commonality with strategy of American multinationals. However, when we pay attention to the management of international business, we see that changes have been subtle. Japanese multinationals have long sustained their Japanese-style international management, the first characteristic of which is the management by Japanese persons.

On conducting field research in Bangkok in 1974 on personnel problems of Japanese companies, one of my findings was that Japanese companies had more expatriates than America and European firms. In other words, localisation of the management of Japanese firms was lagging behind Western companies.[8]

Localisation of management gradually progressed in Japanese foreign subsidiaries. At the present time nearly all lower management posts are occupied by local persons; also, middle managers are mostly local persons. Japanese overseas subsidiaries are now trying to localise top management.

As far as the department head (*bucho* in Japanese) level is concerned, localisation has been substantially realised. According to my questionnaire survey, in 1994, local persons were heads of the personnel department at 80 per cent of the overseas subsidiaries.[9] In the case of the marketing departments, local managers were heads of 63 per cent of the overseas subsidiaries. Localisation has progressed least in the department of accounting, where Japanese expatriates are still department heads in more than half (52 per cent) of the foreign subsidiaries.

The localisation of CEOs of overseas subsidiaries lags far behind that of department heads. In 1994, the number of foreign subsidiaries which have locals as CEOs was only 22 per cent. Japanese are still CEOs at the majority (78 per cent) of overseas subsidiaries. It should be pointed that localisation of CEOs at foreign subsidiaries has not progressed in the past twenty years or so. The percentage of CEOs who are local nationals (non-Japanese) was 38 per cent in 1972, 47 per cent in 1981, 35 per cent in 1990 and 22 per cent in 1994.[10]

In discussing the management by Japanese persons, we also need to pay attention to Japanese who work at overseas subsidiaries for a short while. The number of these Japanese people varies depending on such factors as history of the company, operational conditions and the location of foreign subsidiaries. Generally speaking, more Japanese persons work at subsidiaries at the start-up stage than at subsidiaries with a long history. When foreign subsidiaries introduce new products and/or build new plants, they need more Japanese persons than in usual operational conditions.

The number of Japanese who stay for a short period is generally between 20 and 30 per cent of all Japanese expatriates. But there are exceptions. Matsushita Electric Industrial has 34 subsidiaries in China (not including subsidiaries in Hong Kong). The total employees number approximately 23 500 and Japanese expatriates about 250. In addition to these Japanese expatriates, from 350 to 450 Japanese persons work at subsidiaries for a short period on business trips. The number of short stay Japanese staff exceeds the number of Japanese expatriates. The Matsushita's subsidiaries in China generally have a short history and most of them are in a start-up period of unstable conditions, thus needing involvement of many Japanese persons.[11]

Ajinomoto is a representative multinational enterprise in the food industry and has 48 foreign subsidiaries in 20 countries. Its Japanese expatriates number about 185. Except for unusual situations such as new product introduction and plant expansion, Japanese who work at foreign subsidiaries for a short time number between 20 and 30.[12]

Here, let us consider the localisation of the management of foreign companies in Japan, that is, Japanese subsidiaries of American and European multinationals, and compare it with the case of Japanese multinationals.[13] Nearly two-thirds

(63 per cent) of foreign companies in Japan have Japanese CEOs, that is, CEOs are local persons. This is in sharp contrast to the case of foreign subsidiaries of Japanese multinationals. Local persons are CEOs only at 22 per cent of the subsidiaries. Localisation at the department head level is also more advanced at the foreign companies in Japan than at the foreign subsidiaries of Japanese companies. The ratio of the subsidiaries whose department heads are local persons is 80 : 92 for the personnel department (the former ratio refers to foreign subsidiaries of Japanese companies and the latter refers to Japanese subsidiaries of American and European companies), 63 : 83 for the marketing department, 61 : 83 for the production department and 48 : 84 for the accounting department.

American and European multinationals have promoted more localisation of management than Japanese multinationals in other countries, too. According to research that compared the localisation of the management of American, European and Japanese multinationals, the percentage of foreign subsidiaries that have local persons as CEO is highest at American companies (69 per cent), followed by European firms (52 per cent), and the lowest at Japanese companies (26 per cent).[14]

Other research that compares the localisation of marketing managers in China also shows that Japanese companies lag behind Western companies. In the case of Japanese companies, sixteen marketing managers are Japanese expatriates and only two are Chinese. In the Western companies expatriates managers number only three and Chinese managers thirteen.[15]

Now let us turn our attention from foreign subsidiaries to Japanese parent companies. Do foreigners work and participate in the decision-making process at the headquarters of the Japanese parent companies? Seventeen per cent of all Japanese parent companies accept local employees from their foreign subsidiaries. On average, eleven foreigners from overseas subsidiaries work at each Japanese parent company. Foreigners who are hired in Japan work at two-thirds (66 per cent) of Japanese parent companies. The two kinds of foreigners that we examined above are not top management or even middle management. Eighteen Japanese parent companies have foreigners among their board members, but most of them do not stay in Japan.[16]

In short, at the Japanese parent companies, managers who participate in the decision-making process are all Japanese.

Management in the Japanese Language

The second characteristic of Japanese-style international management is management in the Japanese language. At foreign subsidiaries the Japanese language is not often used, except for communication among Japanese staff. In communication among local staff, the local language is used. Communication between local and Japanese staff is usually done in English.

According to the data of my questionnaire survey, at meetings which both Americans and Japanese attend, English is used at 87 per cent of all foreign subsidiaries in the United States. The Japanese language is used only at 1 per cent of the subsidiaries. There are some subsidiaries (12 per cent) that use both Japanese and English.[17]

However, Japanese parent companies often send information to their foreign subsidiaries in the Japanese language. For example, when Japanese staff at the Japanese parent companies make telephone calls to their American subsidiaries, they communicate in the Japanese language to 76 per cent of all subsidiaries. They call in English to only 12 per cent of the subsidiaries. A mixture of half Japanese and half English is observed at 12 per cent of the subsidiaries. Communication by FAX is similar. When Japanese staff at Japanese parent companies send information by FAX to their overseas subsidiaries in the USA, they use the Japanese language to 56 per cent of all subsidiaries. FAX messages in English are sent to only 17 per cent of the subsidiaries.

As a characteristic of language usage in the international business communications of Japanese companies, I would like to point out that important information is usually exchanged in the Japanese language. In exchanging information on routine operations between Japanese parent companies and their foreign subsidiaries, English is usually used. But, when Japanese managers at the Japanese parent companies talk, write or FAX to foreign subsidiaries on rather important business matters such as personnel problems of top management, large-scale investment, introduction of new products or change of marketing strategy, they usually communicate in the Japanese language. As their English language ability is limited, they have difficulties in communicating in English for these important matters.

The above examination reveals two points concerning language in the international business communications of Japanese companies. First, Japanese parent companies send information to their foreign subsidiaries more often in the Japanese language than in English or other foreign languages. Second, important information is usually exchanged in the Japanese language between the Japanese parent companies and their foreign subsidiaries.

NON-MANUFACTURING MULTINATIONALS

Travel Companies

In the above we have focused our attention on manufacturing companies. Let us now turn our attention to non-manufacturing companies and see if their global operations are also managed by Japanese-style international management.

Japanese overseas tourists numbered 127 000 in 1964, when overseas travel was liberalised. The figure increased to 168 million by 1997. With this huge increase of Japanese overseas tourists, Japanese travel companies have made foreign direct investment and established overseas subsidiaries, branches and representative offices, big travel companies have many overseas subsidiaries, branches and representative offices, as follows: Japan Travel Bureau 135, Kinki Nippon Tourist 26, Tokyu Tourist Corporation 16, Nippon Travel Agency 34.[18]

These travelling companies are doing business globally with their networks of many foreign subsidiaries and branches. Do they manage their global operations the Japanese style, like manufacturing multinationals?

CEOs of almost all of their foreign subsidiaries are Japanese expatriates. Except for a few small foreign branches, top branch managers are also Japanese expatriates. And the heads of all representative offices are Japanese expatriates. I identified only one foreign subsidiary that has a non-Japanese CEO and two branches headed by non-Japanese staff. Regarding management by Japanese persons, travel companies have an additional characteristic. They employ many Japanese and Nisei for jobs such as guiding tours and over-the-counter services.

Local employees working at foreign organisations communicate among themselves in their local language and use English when they communicate with Japanese staff. However, in the communication among Japanese staff and communication between Japanese parent companies and their foreign organisations, the Japanese language is usually used. This is similar to manufacturing firms.

Thus Japanese travel companies manage their global operations by Japanese persons and in the Japanese language.

Sogo Shosha

It is widely known that Japanese *sogo shosha*, that is, general trading companies, are doing business globally. As early as in the prewar period Mitsui Bussan and Mitsubishi Shoji developed global network of foreign subsidiaries and branches, and conducted business globally.

Here, I want to point out that sogo shosha manage their global operations by the Japanese style of international management. Sogo shosha have both characteristics identified above of the Japanese-style international management.

Nine sogo shosha have 1248 overseas subsidiaries and branches in 1999.[19] Except for a few of these, Japanese expatriates occupy the post of the CEO or the branch head. I identified only one case with a non-Japanese CEO, Mr Jay W. Chai, who is the CEO at Itochu International in the United States and also CEO at Itochu Europe in UK. In addition, he is the senior vice president at the Japanese parent company. He was born in Korea and graduated from a Korean university. He once worked at a Japanese company and speaks Japanese.

Sogo shosha's overseas subsidiaries and branches have many Japanese expatriates. The number of Japanese expatriates of the nine sogo shosha is 4625. The ratio of the Japanese expatriates to the total employees is 19 per cent. This ratio is much higher than that of overseas subsidiaries of manufacturing companies that were examined earlier in this chapter.

Japanese expatriates at the overseas subsidiaries and branches of sogo shosha are usually top and middle management. Non-Japanese top management rarely exists and non-Japanese middle managers are few. Most local employees are non-managerial ordinary office workers and sales staff, many of whom work as assistants to Japanese expatriates.

Sogo shosha have a long history of international business and have long played the role of a vanguard in the internationalisation of Japanese economy and business. They have many employees who speak English well. Considering these points, we may well think that sogo shosha may be exempted from the characteristic of the management in the Japanese language.

As a matter of fact, language usage in sogo shosha resembles that in manufacturing companies.[20] At overseas subsidiaries and branches the Japanese language is not so often used. Local employees communicate in their local language among themselves. In the communication between local staff and Japanese expatriates English is usually used. Also, in the regular communication on routine daily operations between Japanese parent companies and overseas organisations, English is a common language. However, the Japanese language plays an important role in sogo shosha in the following ways.

First, even at overseas subsidiaries and branches the Japanese language is used in communications dealing with important matters. Most managers in high-ranking posts are Japanese expatriates and they exchange information and make decisions in the Japanese language. The American subsidiary of Mitsui Bussan changed the language used at the department managers' meeting from English to Japanese.[21] Nearly forty managers attended the meeting, and three of them were Americans who did not understand the Japanese language. Why did the company change the language?

The Japanese expatriates at Mitsui America were able to communicate in English. Probably their English aptitude was much higher than that of average Japanese businessmen. Despite that, when they discussed and made decisions in English, they had problems. They were not active in their discussions. The quantity of information exchanged at meetings decreased and the quality of discussion and decision making gradually deteriorated.

Here is another example. An Indian subsidiary of a sogo shosha had two kinds of managers meeting.[22] The first was a formal meeting which both local and Japanese staff attended. The language of this formal meeting was English. The second meeting was rather informal in nature and only Japanese expatriates attended. They discussed and made decisions using the Japanese language. Important issues were discussed at this meeting beforehand, and decisions made at this meeting were presented at the formal meeting to be formally agreed upon.

Banks and Shipping Companies

Bank A, which is one of the city banks in Japan, has eight overseas subsidiaries and seventeen overseas branches. The CEOs of these overseas subsidiaries are all Japanese expatriates and the branch heads of the overseas branches are also all Japanese expatriates. Bank B, also a Japanese city bank, has eighteen overseas branches and all of them have Japanese heads. It has fourteen overseas subsidiaries, two of which have non-Japanese CEOs, one subsidiary engaged in leasing and the other engaged in the securities business. Thus all overseas subsidiaries that are engaged in banking business have Japanese CEOs.[23]

Do the Japanese banks manage their global banking business in the Japanese language? The answer to this question is 'Yes', in the same sense as at other Japanese manufacturing companies and non-manufacturing companies. At overseas subsidiaries and branches local staff communicate in their local languages among themselves. In communications involving Japanese staff, English is usually used. But, when Japanese managers discuss important matters, they often use the Japanese language. And in communications between Japanese parent companies and overseas organisations the Japanese language is usually used.

Shipping company C, which is one of the major Japanese shipping companies, has twenty overseas subsidiaries, seventeen of which have Japanese CEOs. The three overseas subsidiaries that have non-Japanese CEOs are either 50 : 50 joint ventures or joint ventures with less than 50 per cent ownership by the Japanese parent company. All of the completely owned overseas subsidiaries have Japanese CEOs who are dispatched from the Japanese parent company.[24]

The language usage of this shipping company is the same as at other Japanese manufacturing and non-manufacturing companies that we have already observed.

REASONS FOR JAPANESE-STYLE INTERNATIONAL MANAGEMENT

Customer Suitability

As we have noted in this chapter, international business strategy has greatly changed. But management of international business has changed little. Even now, global operations are managed by Japanese persons and in the Japanese language. There must be reasons why Japanese-style international management has continued for so long. One reason is that Japanese-style international management suits Japanese customers.

Practically all customers of Japanese travel companies are Japanese tourists. Japanese customers want to be served by tour guides who speak Japanese. They want to visit sightseeing spots that are well known in Japan. They like to stay at hotels with bath tubs rather than hotels with only shower equipment. They want to have Japanese meals periodically. To meet these needs of Japanese customers, Japanese-style international management is most suitable.[25]

This kind of customer suitability also exists in sogo shosha. Operations of sogo shosha are brokerage business between sellers and buyers. And the majority of these sellers and buyers are Japanese companies. The total sales of the nine sogo shosha were 71 billion yen in 1998. Domestic sales are 32 billion yen and account for 45 per cent of total sales. Exports and imports are almost equal and account for 18 per cent and 17 per cent, respectively. These three kinds of trades involve Japanese companies as sellers and/or buyers, and account for 80 per cent of all trades of sogo shosha.[26] Since the majority of the customers are Japanese companies, Japanese-style international management suits sogo shosha just as it does travel companies. Japanese customers prefer be served by Japanese persons than foreigners and to be communicated with in the Japanese language rather than in foreign languages. Main customers of international business of Japanese banks and shipping companies are also Japanese companies. Thus Japanese-style international management is preferred.

Technology Transfer

Do we see the same kind of customer suitability in manufacturing companies? The majority of customers of manufacturing companies are foreign. In the case of consumer products such as consumer electronics and passenger cars, almost all customers are foreign individuals. Customers for capital goods such as machines, parts and materials are mostly foreign companies. Thus we cannot rationalise Japanese-style international management from the standpoint of customer suitability. We may say that in responding to the needs of foreign customers Japanese persons and the Japanese language do not fit well.

A different reason exists in manufacturing companies. It is regarding technology transfer. Foreign subsidiaries manufacture products that are developed at their Japanese parent companies. Manufacturing equipment that is used at foreign subsidiaries is often transferred from Japanese headquarters. Manufacturing know-how is also transferred from Japan. Managers, technicians and skilled workers who are sent from Japanese parent companies control production operations at overseas subsidiaries. In order to realise smooth and efficient production at overseas subsidiaries, Japanese-style international management is well suited.

Japanese-Style Management at Parent Companies

Needless to say, Japanese-style management is practised at parent companies in Japan. Employees are practically all Japanese. They use the Japanese language in doing their work within their companies and business transactions with other companies.

There are Japanese employees with competency in English, but the number of these is limited and most of the employees do not have sufficient ability in English. It is primarily because companies only have a handful of employees with sufficient English competency that the Japanese language is used in most of the information sent from parent companies in Japan to overseas subsidiaries and in communication with overseas subsidiaries. This being the case, communications between Japan and overseas is primarily done in the Japanese language between Japanese employees in parent companies and those in overseas subsidiaries. This is particularly evident when complicated communication is required to deal with important matters directly related to management.

In addition to the language problem, we may point out some features of Japanese-style management as reasons for the Japanese-style international management being used over such a long period of time. These features include the following :

- non-verbal communication is as important as verbal communication;
- the management control system is not fully developed;
- companies have job descriptions, but when actual work is being carried out they are not abided by;
- responsibilities and authorities are sometimes unclear or duplicated;
- work flow is not systematised, and there is a lot of off-line communication;
- there are more generalists than specialists;
- management philosophy and organisational culture are shared by the members of the organisations as a result of long-time employment. Also the integration and the coordination by management philosophy and organisational culture are important;
- the management is characterised as that of high-context.

The Japanese-style management with the above features is transferred to overseas subsidiaries. Its implementation in overseas subsidiaries requires the involvement of Japanese staff. Management by Japanese people comes from such a need.

LIMITS OF JAPANESE-STYLE INTERNATIONAL MANAGEMENT

Japanese-style international management has weaknesses. Here I would like to point out two problems. The first problem is that global operations of Japanese multinationals are costly and inefficient because of their Japanese-style international management, under which many Japanese expatriates work at overseas subsidiaries. Their salaries and other costs are much higher than those of local staff and thus raise costs of operations of foreign subsidiaries. Also Japanese expatriates play leading roles and local staff assist Japanese expatriates. Under this kind of division of work, local employees do not have opportunities to display their abilities and skills. Furthermore, since Japanese expatriates are leading actors at overseas subsidiaries, and the Japanese language is used, such Japanese-style management does not appear attractive to capable local persons. This makes it difficult to recruit these people and keep them.

For example, sogo shosha have attempted many times to increase the use of English in their international businesses. If the Japanese language is used, it is difficult for local employees to participate in the decision-making process. They are forced to play supporting roles to Japanese persons who are leading actors. But, as we have pointed out earlier, the Japanese language is still a basic common language at sogo shosha. And the similar language situations also exist at other Japanese companies.

The second problem of the Japanese-style international management is that it depresses initiatives and innovation of overseas subsidiaries. There are sectors of industries and technologies where foreign countries are in more advanced positions than Japan. For these kinds of industries and technologies overseas subsidiaries that are located in the most advanced countries are in the position to develop new technology and products, and transfer them to Japanese parent companies. Those overseas subsidiaries are innovation centres in the sense that they provide sources of new technology and products.[27] At these types of overseas subsidiaries that function as innovation centres, local CEOs fulfil entrepreneurship roles, and capable local technical staff play leading roles in the R&D. Under the Japanese-style international management, this kind of local entrepreneurship and local innovation will not take place.

WILL MANAGEMENT FOLLOW STRATEGY?

Over the last half-century the international business strategy of Japanese companies has changed drastically. Now we have many Japanese multinational enterprises that do their business globally. However, management of their international business has changed little. Global operations are managed by Japanese people and managed in the Japanese language.

This combination of global operations and Japanese-style international management has some good points. It is well suited to respond to Japanese customers and to transfer technology from Japanese parent companies to their overseas subsidiaries. As internationalisation at Japanese parent companies is not well developed, Japanese-style international management may suit Japanese multinationals.

However, we must now pay attention to the problematic side of the Japanese-style international management. The number of Japanese people directly involved in the international business is so great that it is costly. And this style of management does not provide opportunities to local employees to display their abilities and initiatives. Under the Japanese management we cannot expect overseas subsidiaries to become innovation centres in the global business network.

Here, I would like to point out the impact of the Internet on Japanese-style international management. The Internet has been having a significant influence on business activities in many countries such as the United States. It has been bringing about many new types of business. We cannot discuss international business without considering the importance of the Internet.

Japanese companies have to pay attention to the fact that the English language is used in the Internet; it can only be appreciated by those who have competency in English. The development of international business and the growth of the use of the Internet are challenging the conventional style of the management of Japanese multinationals which is based on the use of the Japanese language.

These two trends put together are now demanding that Japanese companies change their management style based on the Japanese language to the one based on the English language.

Japanese multinationals are now facing a challenge of innovation in their international management. Japanese-style international management has continued for a long time. It is based on Japanese management at Japanese parent companies. It is also based on cultural factors such as the Japanese language and interpersonal relationships. Thus it will be not an easy task to innovate in Japanese-style international management.

Notes

1. Yoshihara (1997, pp. 73–6).
2. Yoshihara *et al.* (1988, p. 4).
3. Kojima (1985).
4. Yoshihara (1997, pp. 114–17).
5. Yoshihara *et al.* (1999, pp. 17–20). We sent questionnaires to 2159 overseas manufacturing subsidiaries and received responses from 809 foreign subsidiaries (response rate 38 per cent) in 1998.
6. This definition is basically the same as the definition of the Multinational Enterprise Research Project of Harvard Business School (Vernon, 1971, pp. 4–11).
7. Yoshihara (1997, pp. 17–22).
8. Yoshihara (1975).
9. Yoshihara (1997, pp. 208–10). I sent questionnaires to 1221 foreign subsidiaries in five countries (USA, UK, Germany, Singapore and Taiwan) and received 634 responses (response rate 52 per cent) in 1994.
10. Yoshihara (1995, p. 227).
11. Yoshihara (1998, p. 24).
12. Yoshihara (1998, p. 24).
13. Khan and Yoshihara (1994, pp. 115–17).
14. Kopp (1994, p. 586).
15. Yachi (1999, p. 11).
16. Yoshihara (1996, pp. 121–7).
17. Yoshihara (1996, ch. 4). As for the questionnaire, see note 9 above.
18. The data are provided by Tamami Imanishi, who is a Professor at the University of Marketing and Distribution Sciences, Kobe, Japan.
19. The data are provided by Etsuo Takahashi, who is a Professor of the Graduate School of Business, Kobe University. The data are originally from *Yuka Shoken Hokokusho Soran* (annual financial statement).
20. Based on my interviewing businessmen of *sogo shosha*.
21. 'Beikoku Mitui Bussan' (American Subsidiary of Mitui Bussan),' *Nikkei Business*, 31 January 1994, p. 43.
22. Based on my interviewing a businessman who once worked at an Indian branch of a *sogo shosha*.
23. The data are provided by the companies.
24. The data are provided by the company.
25. Imanishi (1999).
26. As for the data, see note 19 above.
27. As for the foreign subsidiaries of the innovation centre, see Yoshihara (1997, pp. 260 and 286) and Yoshihara (1992). See also Bartlett and Ghoshal (1986).

Part Three

Implementing International Strategy

12 A New View of the Advantage of Multinationality

Mo Yamin

INTRODUCTION

Do multinational enterprises (MNEs) enjoy an advantage over national firms? Clearly, the fact that national and multinational firms do coexist indicates that MNEs do not necessarily enjoy an absolute advantage over national firms. Nevertheless it may be still be true that particular attributes of multinationality create value for MNEs which national firms cannot enjoy. Such value must be set against possible costs of multinationality. Whether MNEs do enjoy a net advantage over national firms in a particular sector or activity is dependent on the relative magnitudes of the cost and benefits of multinationality in the particular case. In this chapter we are interested in organisational attributes that may, *ceteris paribus,* generate advantages for MNEs.

Currently, operational flexibility is seen as a potential source of MNE advantage (see, for example, Kogut, 1990). It requires a high degree of control by the parent over subsidiaries Kogut and Kulatilaka (1994) note, the existence of managerial discretion is the critical requirement for operational flexibility. One possible drawback of operational flexibility is that the exercise (or even the mere possibility) of cross-border production shifting introduces an additional dimension of uncertainty for MNE subsidiaries compared to national firms. The subsidiary has less freedom in determining its future capacity or output levels. This is true of *all* subsidiaries since, *ex ante*, none of them can anticipate whether they are likely to be losers or gainers as a result of the exercise of operational flexibility by the parent. To the extent that subsidiaries have an influence over local investment decisions, it is likely that they will exercise it in a conservative and risk-reducing direction. For example, subsidiaries may well forgo opportunities for deepening their commitment to the local market or for forging strong links with local networks. This can damage the long-term development of the MNE as an integrated network, as the existence of subsidiary capabilities is a prerequisite for cross-fertilisation and network-wide learning (Bartlett and Ghoshall, 1990).

This chapter departs from the usual emphasis on operational flexibility and proposes a different organisational attribute as a possible source of the advantage of multinationality. The attribute we highlight may be labelled 'organisational

169

isolation' (see later). Our basic proposition is simply that MNEs are subject to a greater degree of organisational isolation compared to multi-unit national firms. Organisational isolation is likely to be greater in multinational compared to multi-unit national firms because two key mechanisms that help to provide cross-unit organisational integration, namely, replication of routines and (formal and informal) control instruments, work less effectively across national boundaries than within the same country. We argue that organisational isolation is beneficial to the MNE as a whole. Thus, because organisational isolation enhances the potential for entrepreneurial action by subsidiaries, it increases the likelihood of a *differentiated* set of competencies within the MNE. The existence of these can counteract strategic inertia at the HQ and improve adaptive capabilities in the MNE.

We state three assumptions at the outset. First, we assume that all subsidiaries are established through green field entry. Expansion through mergers and acquisition does not invalidate MNE advantage though it may weaken it somewhat. Second, we assume that all subsidiaries are in 'important' markets. The advantages of multinationality are likely to arise from performance in important rather than in peripheral markets. And, finally, and most important, we assume that MNE subsidiaries and sub-units of national firms have equal support in terms of provision of key assets by the organisation of which they are a part. It is also important to stress that the comparison is specifically with multi-unit or multi business national firms rather than with national firms more generally.

The remainder of the chapter is organised as follows. The second section explains the conceptual basis of the argument presented in this chapter. This relates to the organisational consequences of 'autonomous' action within complex organisations. The third section provides an explanation of the basic proposition advanced in this chapter, namely that, *ceteris paribus*, MNEs are subject to a greater degree of organisational isolation compared to multi-unit national firms. The fourth and fifth sections draw out the implications of organisational isolation for subsidiaries and for the MNE as a whole, while the sixth section concludes.

CONCEPTUAL BACKGROUND: ORGANISATIONAL CONSEQUENCES OF AUTONOMOUS ACTION

A number of management scholars have highlighted the relevance of exploration in the strategic activities of firms (for example, Hedlund and Rolander, 1990; March, 1991; March and Levinthal, 1993). Thus, whereas exploitation is the utilisation, refinement and extension of existing capabilities, exploration is the search for alternative capabilities that may underpin future exploitative potential. The value of exploratory activities is therefore that they help to create *adaptive* capabilities for the organisation. Of course, it is true that organisations cannot focus exclusively on either exploitation or exploration and that 'maintaining an appropriate balance between exploration and exploitation is a primary factor in system survival and prosperity' (March, 1991, p. 71). However it is generally agreed that 'exploitation drives out exploration' (March, 1991; Levinthal and March, 1993; Birkinshaw and Ridderstrale, 1999). Whilst in most organisations exploratory/ adaptive capabilities could be beneficially enhanced, the question of interest to this chapter is what factors may determine the exploratory potential of companies.

We suggest that the ability of 'subsidiary' units within an organisation to undertake initiatives independently of the centre is an indication of that organisation's exploratory capabilities, since, exploratory capability is at least partly a consequence of the 'weakness' of the centre to control behaviour of sub-units. In tightly controlled multi-unit organisations, the ability of sub-units to detect new ideas, develop initiatives around these ideas and hence generate new 'local' competencies is severely curtailed. In such corporations exploratory capability is likely to be low.

Linking an organisation's exploratory potential with its sub-units' ability to undertake initiative reflects the premise that exploratory initiatives are unlikely to stem from the centre. The reason for this is that top decision makers are likely to have a strong commitment to the firm's current concept of strategy and thus a preference for activities that are 'consistent' with it. Typically, top executives display a high degree of attachment to the *status quo* (Hambrick *et al.*, 1993). In addition, as Burgelmen (1983, p. 67) suggests, because top managers have an inflexible stance in relation to current strategy, their 'capacity to deal with substantial issues pertaining to new technological and market developments can be expected to be low'. Thus even in apparently dynamic and progressively managed companies, there is a remarkable degree of inertia in official corporate strategy. Top-level commitment to current strategy remains strong even when environmental changes have eroded the value of the competencies that underlined the strategy (Burgelman, 1994).

By comparison, operational and middle-level managers are naturally sensitised or exposed to exploratory stimuli because, to a large extent, the operational locus *is* where the opportunities and pressures for change are most keenly felt (Seely-Brown and Duguid, 1991; Dutton *et al.*, 1997). Top managers are deprived of this important source of exploratory stimuli, because by the very nature of their position in the organisation, they are too distant or removed both spatially and cognitively, from the operational locus.

Furthermore, top management's inflexible adherence to the current concept of corporate strategy inevitably implies that it overlooks or even suppresses noncanonical knowledge at the 'periphery' or at the operational domain. In Burgelman's words, top managers rely 'on the structural context to bring autonomous behaviour under control' (1983, p. 67). As Birkinshaw and Ridderstrale (1999) convincingly argue, corporations develop a strong 'immune system' the function of which is to repel or resist initiatives even though they may promise an improvement in performance.

Consequently, exploratory activities are often manifested as 'autonomous behaviour' – that is, strategic activities by operational and middle-level managers that are not authorised or even encouraged by top level decision makers in the firm (Burgelman, 1983; Birkinshaw and Hood, 1998b). Given the multi-layered structure of large organisations, some leeway or opportunity is likely to exist for these managers to undertake autonomous activities unnoticed by top decision makers. Thus some autonomous behaviour is inevitable in complex organisations.

The importance of autonomous behaviour is that new strategic directions are often charted through initiatives by the operational and middle level mangers. In fact, as Burgelman (1991, 1994) suggests, in companies where autonomous activities are strong, strategy making should not be considered purely as a pre-rogative of the top decision makers. Rather, strategy making should be viewed in terms of an 'intra-organisational ecology' or internal selection environment in which autonomous initiatives *offer strategic choices to top management.* An immediate advantage of this is that considering simultaneous alternatives may reduce excessive commitment to any one strategic option. The danger that core competencies become core rigidities may be somewhat reduced (Dutton *et al.*, 1997, p. 408; Leonard-Barton, 1992). Furthermore, given that environmental changes will inevitably undermine the value of competencies that underpin any current strategy, the existence of alternative capabilities within the firm enhances adaptive capabilities.

THE ADVANTAGE OF MULTINATIONALITY:
THE RELEVANCE OF ORGANISATIONAL ISOLATION

A stream of recent literature has focused on the development of MNE subsidiary capabilities for strategic actions. Different authors have focused on different man-ifestations of this, such as competence for product development (for example, Andersson and Forsgren, 1996; Andersson and Pahlberg, 1997; Fratocchi and Holm, 1998; Forsgren *et al.*, 1999a); subsidiary mandate development (Birkinshaw, 1996; Birkinshaw and Hood, 1998b) subsidiary initiatives and entrepreneurship (Birkinshaw, 1997; Birkinshaw and Ridderstrale, 1999) and subsidiary contribu-tion to the development of firm-specific assets in MNEs (Birkinshaw *et al.*, 1998). The question of interest to this chapter is whether the propensity for initiative and autonomous competence development is greater for MNE subsidiaries compared to sub-units of national firms? We believe that the answer to this question is in the affirmative.

The reason for this is rooted in the fact that subsidiaries are a part of an organ-isation that is dispersed internationally. Note that, by assumption, the advantage envisaged does not derive from *access* to the resources (such as R&D output from the centre or other units) of the MNE organisation. On the contrary, the emphasis is on the fact that, compared to a sub-unit of a national firm, the subsidiary oper-ates in an organisational context characterised by international dispersal and, con-sequently, by a greater degree of organisational separation between different units.

Units of the MNE are not only separated by geographical distance (which may be equally the case for national firms) but also by the fact they operate within distinct legal, political, cultural and economic domains. Any organisation whose sub-units operate in a fragmented environment may be characterised by some degree of organisational 'isolation'. We define organisational 'isolation' as a condition, brought about by environmental fragmentation, in which the *constraints* forcing sub-unit fidelity to organisational norms and strategies are weak.

Note that the emphasis is on weak constraints. The sub-unit may choose to conform to organisational norms or strategies but the constraints are relatively ineffective. More generally, it is important to stress that we envisage 'isolation' as a *structural* condition or attribute of a multi-unit organisation the impact of which, *ceteris paribus*, is to weaken the constraints on sub-units. We do not consider managerial policies or strategies, either at the level of the firm or at the subsidiary (with regard to the latter see, for example Taggart, 1997). Clearly such strategies may counter (or, of course, reinforce) the impact of isolation. In particular it is always possible for the centre to create monitoring structures and control devices to enforce a high degree of conformity by sub-units. This can extend to limiting the degree and scope of subsidiary initiatives. However whilst it is clearly feasible for the centre to impose a tight control regime, the *logic* of organisation isolation suggests that this can only be achieved at great costs in terms of the amount of time and effort that headquarter managers would need to devote to the control function. In particular, we suggest the costs of achieving any given level of control may be higher within an MNE compared to that within a national firm (see below). Thus our basic proposition is that, *ceteris paribus*, MNEs are subject to a greater degree of 'organisational isolation' than multi-unit national firms. The logic underlying this proposition is that, compared to national firms, MNEs are characterised to a greater extent by the following interdependent phenomena: imperfect organisational replication and incomplete control and coordination from the centre.

Imperfect Organisational Replication and the Development of Subsidiary Capabilities

Kogut and Zander (1993) note that the 'cornerstone' of their evolutionary approach to the theory of the MNE is the 'treatment of the firm as a *social community* whose productive knowledge defines a comparative advantage' (pp. 625–6, emphasis added). However, precisely because a firm is a social community, its extension across national boundaries must be problematic as national boundaries demarcate different societal arrangements. Organisational principles (Kogut, 1991) and strategic transitional practices (Kostova, 1999) are deeply embedded both locationally and organisationally and hence are relatively immobile compared to well packaged or embodied technologies (Badaracco, 1991; Szulanski, 1996; Sölvell and Zander, 1998). More generally, as Nelson and Winter (1982) have pointed out, the feasibility of close (let alone perfect) organisational replication is quite problematic. Replication is practically always partial. Organisational routines, it may be said, do not 'travel' well. Knowledge, and more generally routines that are transferred to the subsidiary by the parent lose some of their value and effectiveness simply because they are largely context dependent (Madhok, 1997). Significantly, Nelson and Winter (1982) note that routines 'have their clearest relevance at the establishment level' and that 'the memory of an organisation that comprises many *widely separated establishments* exists mainly in the establishments' (p. 97, emphasis added). If 'widely separated establishments' are located in different countries, then it is only reasonable to assume that the original, replicated routines provide a rather weak 'glue' for coupling or binding the different establishments (see also Kilduff, 1992, 1993).

Furthermore, it is important to consider the possibility that subsidiaries cannot be merely *passive* recipients of routines. In fact, precisely because initial organisational replication from the parent to the subsidiary is imperfect and incomplete, a process may be triggered that propels the long-term development of the subsidiary. Because subsidiaries inevitably inherit an incomplete 'template', they are forced to engage in a process of searching for markets and other knowledge about the local environment. This knowledge, due to its often tacit, localised and experiential nature, will not be transparent to the parent and could not thus have been given to the subsidiary 'at birth'. Incomplete replication makes it imperative that the subsidiary establishes external (to the MNE) avenues for attracting additional resources, particularly from its host environment. Consequently it may well develop linkages with various information, finance, technology and production oriented networks in the host country. As a number of studies have recently emphasised, particularly in relation to production and technology networks, membership in such networks can boost a subsidiary's technological and innovative capabilities (Andersson and Forsgren, 1996; Andersson and Pahlberg, 1997; Forsgren *et al.*, 1999a).

Thus we suggest that embeddedness in external networks should be viewed as a deliberate compensation strategy by the subsidiary to 'anchor' itself on to a significant resource base. Overall, this process of development, triggered in part by its initial handicap, enables the subsidiary to compete in the host environment. Clearly, membership in local networks also gives the subsidiary a degree of independence from the rest of the corporate system. Furthermore, such independence may become a source of (resource-based) power or, at least, influence for the subsidiary. Thus, if access to the local networks is valued by the parent or other units in the MNE and if such access can only be obtained through the resident subsidiary, then this gives the latter a leverage with which to influence MNE strategy (Andersson and Pahlberg, 1997).

Incomplete Control and Coordination from the Centre

There is a large literature addressing control and coordination issues in MNEs (for example, Ghoshal and Nohira, 1989; Martinez and Jarillio, 1989; Hennart, 1993;

Nohira and Ghoshal, 1994; Ghoshal *et al.*, 1994; Birkinshaw and Morrison, 1995; Roth and O'Donnell, 1996; Johanson *et al.*, 1996). The starting point of this literature is the recognition that in MNEs 'the control problem is particularly acute' (Hennart, 1993, p. 157). However no study explicitly compares MNEs and national firms from the control perspective. Nevertheless, it is self-evident that the control environment facing MNEs is significantly more demanding. As the previous section has indicated, each subsidiary will operate in an environment that is increasingly 'enacted' by itself in terms of more extensive and intensive linkages in the host market. As Holm *et al.* (1995) have suggested, a subsidiary's 'network context' is not necessary transparent. Hence the headquarter's ability to effectively control the subsidiary is progressively compromised.

Furthermore, the MNE's control environment is significantly more variegated than that faced by national firms. Each subsidiary presents the MNE with a somewhat differentiated control task depending on the characteristics of the environment in which it is operating and the organisational capabilities that the subsidiary possesses (Ghoshal and Nohira, 1989; Nohira and Ghoshal, 1994). Sub-units within a national firm, by comparison, operate in a relatively more homogenous environment. Greater differentiation at the subsidiary level translates to significant control-task complexity at the headquarter level. The complexity is intensified as control is often multi-dimensional, involving not only elements of centralisation and formalisation but also 'more subtle' informal methods including normative integration (Martinez and Jarillio, 1989). Recent empirical analysis by Birkinshaw and Morrison (1995) indicates a high reliance on normative integration for all categories of subsidiaries. This is an interesting finding.

Traditional control mechanisms – centralisation and formalisation may be relatively ineffective. As Sundram and Black (1992) note, an MNE is affected by multiple sources of external authority while sub-units of a national firm reside within a single (legal and political) external authority domain. Consequently, the parent in a multi-unit national firm would be less constrained in imposing conformity to organisational goals by sub-units, as long as imposition is allowed by the rules of external authority. On the other hand, the ability of the MNE parent to demand or impose conformity to organisational goals is constrained by the fact that the sub-unit resides in different legal and political domains. This has an important implication for control mechanisms in MNEs. In particular, 'it may be *impossible* for the parent firm to force all subsidiaries to implement centrally made decisions that run counter to pressures in the host country. Thus socialisation 'may substitute for the void in the superstructure to mediate conflicts' (Sundram and Black, 1992, p. 743).

Broadly speaking, the control literature has been concerned with determining the 'right' or 'optimal' degree of control and the appropriate mix of instruments to achieve it. The relevant point, from the perspective of this paper, is that the MNE will inevitably experience a residual degree of control 'gap'. Whilst in any complex system the 'optimal' degree of control falls short of complete control (due to rising marginal control costs), it is likely that this residual is greater in an

MNE than in a comparable national firm. Furthermore, it is reasonable to suggest that a subsidiary of an MNE has more opportunity for utilising a given level of 'control gap' than a sub-unit of a national company. The MNE subsidiary can, more easily than a sub-unit of a national firm, engage in an 'unauthorised' initiative that is oriented towards the local market and external networks. The process of developing such initiatives is more likely to remain 'hidden' from the centre until it is a *fait accompli* (Birkinshaw, 1996; Birkinshaw and Ridderstrale, 1999).

IMPLICATIONS OF ORGANISATIONAL ISOLATION FOR SUBSIDIARIES

The discussion in the preceding sub-sections suggests that, compared to sub-units of a national company, MNE subsidiaries are more likely to develop an 'entrepreneurial' orientation. One consequence of weak organisational ties (Hansen, 1999) is that sub-units have greater search opportunities and tend to be more adaptive than sub-units in tightly coupled organisations.

More specifically, Birkinshaw (1997) identifies three aspects of an entrepreneurial orientation: 'a predisposition to proactive or risk-taking behaviour', 'use of resources beyond the individual's direct control' and 'departure from existing practices' (1997, p. 208). We have argued that the subsidiary's 'isolation' from the rest of the MNE forces it to behave in ways similar to the above descriptions. For example, seeking linkages with local networks is essentially proactive and risk-taking behaviour for a foreign subsidiary, and it is in part motivated by gaining access to or benefiting from resources at present outside its control. Finally, 'departure from existing practices' is, at least initially, what a subsidiary has to do to survive. This is simply the logical implication or consequence of imperfect organisational replication. It is also relevant that compared to sub-units of a national firm, a foreign subsidiary has (or, more accurately, gradually gains) greater independence to do what it has to.

Moreover, because, compared to its national competitors, a subsidiary's development is inevitably shaped by dual influences from the host environment and the MNE organisation (Rosenweig and Singh, 1991; Westney, 1993), it may gain an advantage over its national rivals. A degree of diversity is 'built-in' into the perspective of the subsidiary. It is therefore less at risk of becoming too 'acculturated' or socialised into the host environment or to the MNE system and hence losing the entrepreneurial edge (March 1991; Levinthal and March, 1993).

In summary, compared to a sub-unit of a national firm, an MNE subsidiary (a) has a higher degree of organisational freedom to undertake initiatives, (b) by virtue of its *foreignness* it faces greater pressure to develop capabilities appropriate to its local market and to the various networks in which it needs to operate effectively and (c) by virtue of its membership of an *internationally dispersed organisation* it has a more diverse perspective (in terms of markets, technologies and networks) that may enhance its ability to define and develop initiatives. Thus, tentatively, we can put forward the following hypothesis:

Hypothesis 1: Compared to sub-units of a national firm the MNE subsidiaries will display a greater degree of entrepreneurial orientation.

Will a foreign subsidiary also have an innovative advantage over its national competitors? To a certain degree, of course, entrepreneurial and the innovative processes overlap. To the extent that entrepreneurship is a precursor of innovation, the foreign subsidiary will perceive greater opportunities for innovation in a given environment compared to sub-units of national firms. Furthermore the subsidiary's linkages with exchange partners in production and technology networks tend to boost its innovative capabilities (production and technology) (Andersson and Forsgren, 1996; Andersson and Pahlberg, 1997; Forsgren *et al.*, 1999a). Clearly, membership in local networks also gives the subsidiary a degree of independence from the rest of the corporate system (Andersson and Pahlberg, 1997). Such independence also reinforces the subsidiary's ability to devote resources to its innovative projects. There are clearly a number of other factors that will effect innovative success. For example, the importance attached to customer or user needs, and the effective coordination of R&D activities with marketing and production are widely recognised as important to innovative success. However there is no analytical reason to expect that multinationality as such will affect these factors very strongly one way or another. Thus, given the aforementioned advantages that may be enjoyed by foreign subsidiaries, we put forward the following hypothesis:

Hypothesis 2: Compared to sub-units of a national firm, MNE subsidiaries will have a greater ability to undertake innovation successfully.

IMPLICATIONS OF ORGANISATIONAL ISOLATION FOR THE DEVELOPMENT OF THE MNE AS A WHOLE

The concept of organisation isolation suggests that the MNE is likely to develop into a differentiated system, and that the degree of sub-unit diversity within MNEs is, *ceteris paribus*, greater than in national firms. Initially, of course, subsidiary capabilities are limited and rely on technological and other skills transferred from the parent. In a 'young' MNE therefore there may be little differentiation. However, the evolution of each subsidiary reflects a unique combination of market, technological and institutional influences (Birkinshaw and Hood, 1998b; Luostarinen and Marschan-Piekkari, 2000) that may give the subsidiaries distinctive market and technological competencies. By comparison sub-units of a national firm will have capabilities more closely *tied* to that of the parent unit. Thus the national firm will display a lower degree of differentiation in terms of competencies. The existence of differentiated competencies within the MNE suggests that it should be viewed as a federation rather than as a unitary system (Ghoshal and Bartlett, 1993) in which the possibilities for inter-unit transfers are relatively limited. Limited intra-MNE transferability results from exactly the same considerations that make subsidiary competencies differentiated in the first place. Thus even though the subsidiary's capabilities may be based on technological and market skills inherited from the parent, subsequent development will be progressively shaped by the subsidiary's attempt to meet the market and competitive challenges in the host country or in its regional/global mandate areas. From the point of view of the subsidiary, it becomes more important to nurture local/regional relationships by tailoring innovation to customer needs than to produce less customised, or more standardised products that may also be of interest to other units within the MNE as a whole.

Low transferability within the MNE network could be interpreted as implying that subsidiary competencies have only a limited value for the MNE as a whole (Forsgren, 1977). We suggest that this may be a valid inference but only in the context of the MNE's *current* strategy and in relation to the set of competencies that underpin this strategy. From this perspective, subsidiary competencies will tend to be highly valued by the centre only if they can be utilised to support company-wide products and technologies. Subsidiary competencies that do not easily fit into the MNE's current strategy may impose extra control and coordination costs on the MNE.[2]

However, from the point of view of the MNE's adaptive capabilities – its ability to replace current competencies – low transferability may be an advantage. For the MNE as a whole, low transferability does imply that (some) subsidiary competencies are currently partially 'redundant' as they are utilised only locally, with limited intra-MNE transfers. However such redundancy can be a dynamic advantage in a rapidly changing environment. The deliberate creation of spare capacity has long been recognised as an important competitive instrument in oligopolistic markets (for example, Steindl, 1976; Spence, 1977). In an MNE, 'spare capacity' in the form of differentiated but under-utilised competencies within subsidiaries is an unintended consequence of organisational isolation. Low network transferability is a necessary condition for the maintenance of differentiation and diversity within the MNEs. If it were the case that knowledge transfers across national boundaries were totally smooth and 'un-sticky', the organisational differentiation that is characteristic of MNE would itself be gradually eroded. Thus organisational isolation helps both to generate and maintain differentiation within the MNE. In terms of Burgelman's (1991) analysis, this means that the MNE possesses a richer internal selection environment. The existence of differentiated competencies potentially provides the MNE with a wide range of strategic choices. If major technological or market changes undermine the value of the MNE's currently dominant strategy, then alternative proven competencies, which can become the basis of a new strategic direction for the MNE may well exist within the network. In particular, subsidiaries that have successfully gained global mandates through their own initiatives will have broadly-based competencies that can underpin a new strategic direction for the MNE as a whole (Birkinshaw *et al.*, 1998). Such transformation is by no means an easy process, a fact confirmed by recent case studies (Burgelman, 1994; Macnamara and Baden Fuller, 1999). But the prior existence of a wider range alternative competency within an MNE compared to a national firm gives the former a potential advantage. A major obstacle facing organisational renewal is the risk associated with abandoning current competencies when new competencies are not fully operational (Macnamara and Baden Fuller, 1999; Kogut and Zander, 1992). This risk is clearly attenuated in an MNC to the extent that it may avoid the need to generate wholly new competencies. In this sense, it can be said that organisational isolation may enhance the survival prospects of an MNE.

CONCLUSION

This chapter has argued that a key advantage of multinationality is that its dispersed structure inadvertently creates conditions conducive to entrepreneurial and innovative activities by the subsidiaries. This is a valued characteristic of the MNE as a generic organisational form if one accepts (a) the view that the organisational structure of most large firms tends to frustrate entrepreneurial and innovative activities at the 'periphery' and (b) that this is an undesirable outcome. The notion that in most organisations, 'exploitation drives out exploration holds that both these statements are true. From this perspective, the advantage of multinationality can be captured in the following statement: multinationality evens out the odds between exploitative and exploratory aspects of firm activities.

Notes

1. I am grateful to an anonymous reviewer for a number of useful comments and suggestions. I have also benefited from comments by Fred Burton, Mats Forsgren, James Taggart and Torben Pedersen. The usual caveat applies.
2. However we should consider the possibility that organisational isolation may also enhance network integration skills and capabilities at the centre. Thus because organisational isolation is an *inescapable* feature of the MNE, it is a continuing source of pressure on the centre to achieve a degree of cross-unit integration. Much in the same way that 'selective factor disadvantage' stimulates innovation and competitive advantage at country level (Porter, 1990), organisational isolation can be viewed as a structural condition that 'prods and stimulates' MNE headquarters towards organisational innovation that to a degree negates its centrifugal consequences. The literature on 'loosely-coupled' organisation has a similar implication for the management of MNEs. Thus, as Orton and Weick (1990) observe, there is a 'voice of compensation' within this literature. Because loose coupling is perceived as an unsatisfactory condition, compensating mechanisms such as 'enhanced leadership' or 'shared value' may be necessary. This has an echo, to say the least, in conceptualisation of the MNE as a heterarchy or a transnational form.

13 Strategic Evolution of Foreign-owned Subsidiaries in a Host Country: a Conceptual Framework

Reijo Luostarinen and
Rebecca Marschan-Piekkari

INTRODUCTION

During the last few years, researchers have become increasingly interested in better understanding changes in subsidiary roles over time (Holm and Pedersen, 2000; Papanastassiou and Pearce, 1998; Pearce and Papanastassiou, 1999; Taggart, 1996, 1998a; see Birkinshaw and Hood, 1998a for a review). It is commonly accepted that the management relationship between the headquarters and subsidiaries evolves, as the internationalisation process unfolds (Brooke and Remmers, 1978; Forsgren *et al.*, 1992; Fratocchi and Holm, 1998). In some cases, subsidiaries start to adjust products received from the parent firm, and adapt them to local market needs. Eventually, they may become less dependent on headquarters for competence and able to carry out their activities on the basis of local competence. In this way, the parent firm and the home country of the corporation become less vital for the subsidiary, while the host country starts playing an important role for subsidiary evolution. Yamin (chapter 12) argues that because of environmental fragmentation foreign subsidiaries are organisationally 'isolated' from other parts of the multinational corporation (MNC). To compensate, they tend to develop close linkages with the host country and become embedded in local and regional environments. One may argue that subsidiary evolution is driven by the dynamism of the host country, and by the subsidiary's ability to access resources from the multinational corporation and the parent company (Birkinshaw and Hood, 1998b).

However, much of the earlier research in the area tends to explain changes in subsidiary evolution in a specific host country solely through performance indicators. Following the principles of portfolio management, the primary function of headquarters is to run an internal capital market and re-distribute resources within the firm (Mudambi, 1999; Stein, 1997). Building on prior research in the internationalisation process approach, strategic management and subsidiary management literature, we propose a broad conceptual framework to explain subsidiaries' strategic evolution. Based on Birkinshaw's and Hood's (1998b) work, we define subsidiary evolution as the process through which the value of a subsidiary unit to the multinational company is increased or decreased. It is important to note that subsidiary evolution may involve both rise and decline of resources in the subsidiary over time. We argue that parent and/or subsidiary based drivers, which incorporate the dynamic role played by the host country, initiate subsidiary evolution. In this context, we are concerned with strategic – rather than operative – changes in subsidiary evolution. The unit of analysis is the foreign subsidiary, but the perspective we adopt is that of a strategist at corporate headquarters or subsidiary top management. We focus primarily on wholly or dominantly owned subsidiaries in a host country.

In prior research, the macro level effects of MNCs on host countries have been examined (see, for example, Hood and Young, 1979). Moving down to subsidiary level, scholars have, for the most part, not explicitly considered the foreign-owned sector and its dynamic relationship with the host country (Birkinshaw, 1998a; Hurdley and Hood, 1999). The few investigations dealing with foreign-owned subsidiaries have focused on Canada, Scotland and Sweden (Birkinshaw, 1998a; Birkinshaw *et al*. 1998; Birkinshaw and Hood, 1997; Taggart, 1996; White and Poynter, 1984; Young *et al.*, 1988), the UK (Hood and Young, 1988; Hood *et al*. 1994; Pearce, 1999; Taggart, 1998b), Denmark (Forsgren *et al.*, 1999) and Finland (Baldauf, 1970; Baldauf *et al.*, 1984; Kautovaara, 1999; Luostarinen, 1981, 1999; Paasonen, 1994). An important conclusion of this work is that the process of subsidiary evolution varies significantly from country to country, justifying the focus on a single host country in our study.

To support our argumentation, we draw on illustrative examples of foreign-owned units in Finland and prior studies conducted within the FIBO (Finnish International Business Operations) Programme, Centre for International Business Research established by Reijo Luostarinen at the Helsinki School of Economics and Business Administration. Within FIBO, data on foreign subsidiaries in Finland have been collected since 1974. In 1999, this data bank included altogether 1143 foreign subsidiary units. The selection of Finland is based on the following considerations. Traditionally, Finland has been characterised by heavy outward flows of foreign direct investment. Finnish internationalising companies have engaged in large cross-border acquisitions and transferred to an increasing extent value-added activities outside Finland. During the last few years, however, the country has also experienced considerable inward investment flows, as Finnish policy makers have adopted a favourable attitude towards such investments. Recently, Finland's entry into the European Union and the European Monetary Union, and the transition of former socialist countries in eastern and central Europe towards market economy have positively changed Finland's strategic position on the world map, and increased its attractiveness as a location of foreign direct investment. For many MNCs, though, the Finnish units have traditionally been peripheral, with narrow power bases. These subsidiaries are often situated far away from the centre of the corporation, hierarchically, geographically and linguistically. Interestingly, we do see a number of foreign-owned units in Finland, which have – despite this – developed into regional or global centres of knowledge and expertise within multinationals. Others, at the same time, may have ceased to exist. Given the above, understanding the strategic evolution of foreign-owned subsidiaries in Finland offers a particularly interesting ground for scientific inquiry.

The remainder of this chapter is organised into four sections. First, we discuss subsidiary evolution initiated by parent or subsidiary based drivers and incorporate both internal and external factors. Second, we explain and classify two major strategic evolution paths of foreign subsidiaries – host country-based internationalisation and de-internationalisation – with eight relevant sub-paths. In the third section, we develop a conceptual framework and discuss a number of implications for headquarter and subsidiary managers, policy makers, and avenues for further research.

DRIVERS OF SUBSIDIARY EVOLUTION

Much of the earlier work in multinational management has focused on the entire firm as the unit of analysis. Since the late 1970s and 1980s, however, a new approach has emerged with an explicit emphasis on the foreign subsidiary. In their literature review of subsidiary management in large and geographically dispersed multinationals, Birkinshaw and Hood (1998a, p. 5) identify three main streams of research: (1) headquarters-subsidiary relationships, (2) subsidiary roles and (3) subsidiary development. The third stream of research differs from the first two in that it is aimed at a dynamic question, not a static one, namely: 'How and why do the activities of the subsidiary change over time?' (Birkinshaw and Hood, 1998a, p. 7). These authors argue that such a research question has been given little explicit attention, as most prior research has been cross-sectional by nature (cf. Papanastassiou and Pearce, 1998; Pearce and Papanastassiou, 1999; Taggart, 1996, 1998b).

Whatever the nature of subsidiary evolution, it is clear that after the initial foreign direct investment decision – which necessarily is a headquarter decision – subsequent activities in subsidiaries are open to other influences (Egelhoff *et al.*, 1998). Birkinshaw and Hood (1998b, p. 774) propose an organising framework for understanding the various determinants and drivers of subsidiary evolution. They divide them into three groups:

1. Parent-based drivers: decisions made by headquarter managers to assign a specific role to the subsidiary by allocating certain activities to the subsidiary (top-down approach);
2. Subsidiary-based drivers: decisions made by subsidiary managers regarding the activities undertaken by the subsidiary (bottom-up, entrepreneurial approach);

3. Host country based drivers: influence of environmental factors on decisions made by head office and/or subsidiary managers regarding the activities undertaken by the subsidiary.

The three drivers above interact to determine the subsidiary's role at a given point in time. The interplay between them creates a cyclical process through which the subsidiary's role changes over time. Particularly the parent and subsidiary based drivers should be seen as complementary rather than interdependent. Based on a study of foreign-owned subsidiaries in Canada and Scotland, Birkinshaw and Hood (1997, p. 344) state that 'our expectation is that the relative emphasis of the drivers of development will shift over time as the subsidiary matures.' They argue that in the early stages of development, parent and host country drivers (for example, through incentive programmes) may be the primary triggers of evolution, while other issues are likely to be more prevalent as the subsidiary matures. Given the overlap between the drivers, we simplify and modify Birkinshaw's and Hood's (1998b) framework by dividing strategic evolution into two groups of drivers, namely parent based and subsidiary based. The influence of the host country is incorporated into these drivers. Each of them will be examined in the following.

Parent-based Drivers

The parent company can play a critical role in shaping subsidiary evolution. The internationalisation process approach provides an explanation of subsidiary evolution at the company level (Luostarinen, 1979) and at the host country level (Luostarinen, 1970; Johansson and Vahlne, 1977). While foreign subsidiaries increase their responsibilities from sales activities to manufacturing, they remain instruments of the parent company to increase its commitment to a specific host country, and to transfer experiences and knowledge back to the parent. Traditionally, the internationalisation process approach has limited the subsidiary definition to sales/marketing and manufacturing functions, without considering the transfer of other functions to the host country and the subsequent broadening of subsidiaries' functional responsibilities (cf. Hentola and Luostarinen, 1995).

From a strategic management perspective, corporate decision-makers may manage foreign subsidiaries as a portfolio of assets, which should continuously be reviewed in terms of financial and strategic considerations (Mudambi, 1999; Stein, 1997). The opportunities for subsidiary evolution may arise internally from within the corporation, or they may be based on possibilities identified in the external marketplace (at local, regional or global levels). For example, an important network partner in a strategic alliance or supplier-buyer relationship may trigger further investments in subsidiary operations. Some subsidiaries will develop into centres of excellence with R&D, strong exports and interdependencies with the rest of the multinational network (Forsgren and Pedersen, 1998; Holm and Pedersen, 2000), while others may become targets of downsizing, out-sourcing, or divestments. Traditionally, divestment cases have been explained very narrowly by focusing on indicators of poor subsidiary performance (such as low profitability, losses, bankruptcies) in a given host country, thus neglecting the broader strategic considerations of the entire corporation. Particularly large and geographically dispersed corporations such as Electrolux and Philips, which have expanded through foreign acquisitions, have restructured and strategically re-positioned their global operations at some stage.

Such a move from various country-based strategies to one coordinated global strategy at corporate level is likely to change the evolution paths of subsidiaries, which have historically enjoyed fairly autonomous positions. A good example of an internally oriented evolution process is the Philips case in Finland in the early 1980s. Many communes and cities made competing offers to Philips subsidiary management in Finland in order to influence favourably the location decision of the fourth manufacturing unit. However, corporate headquarters in the Netherlands cancelled the investment plan. Moreover, a radical decision was implemented to divest the three existing subsidiaries in Finland on the grounds that the Finnish units did not fit with the new, global strategy of the corporation. This suggests complete miscommunication between headquarters and Finnish subsidiary units.

Subsidiary-based Drivers

Moving from a top-down approach to a bottom-up perspective, the subsidiary-driven evolution process offers different explanations. In a survey of 229 manufacturing subsidiaries of large MNCs in Canada, Scotland and Sweden, Birkinshaw *et al.* (1998) conclude that subsidiaries should not only be seen as contributors to firm-specific advantages but also as driving the process through their own initiative. By focusing on subsidiary initiative as the unit of analysis, Birkinshaw and his fellow researchers have been able to move below the level of parent-subsidiary relationships. This has allowed us to gain a better understanding of the processes behind subsidiary evolution, which often take place within the units themselves. Subsidiary initiative is defined 'as the entrepreneurial pursuit of international market opportunities to which the subsidiary can apply its specialized resources' (Birkinshaw *et al.*, 1998, p. 226). From a dynamic perspective, subsidiary initiative is seen to result in resource growth and visibility within the MNC, forming a virtuous circle of development.

The study by Birkinshaw and Ridderstrale (1999) of 44 initiatives undertaken by Canadian subsidiaries of US-owned MNCs shows that these initiatives take two different forms. Internal initiatives are based on opportunities identified within the corporation, and are pursued through a traditional bottom-up process. For example, Egelhoff *et al.* (1998) examined the role of technology transfer in subsidiary evolution. They argue that in leading-edge technology companies, subsidiaries engage in the transfer process jointly with the parent company and other units, and become specialised technology centres. Their findings of sixteen Irish

MNC subsidiaries show the importance of internal technology-based initiatives by subsidiaries for continuous development.

In contrast, external initiatives are based on opportunities in the external marketplace (local, regional or global). For example, a foreign joint venture partner, particularly if it is a private company, may be the driver of the unit's development. However, the evidence for subsidiary-driven evolution, which would be triggered from outside, is rather limited (Birkinshaw, 1998a; Birkinshaw and Hood, 1998b). It seems that subsidiary evolution is influenced by several aspects of the environment: the dynamism and attractiveness of the host country, the specific incentive programs offered by local development agencies, and the broader trends in regional and global business contexts. Birkinshaw (1998a) considers the relationship between the MNC subsidiary and the host country as an ongoing process, whereby the subsidiary draws resources from the host country, while simultaneously reacting and contributing to the host country economy as a whole, and to specific business partners. Pearce (1999) and Papanastassiou and Pearce (1997) have investigated how creative subsidiaries access and apply local technological knowledge from the host country and share it with the rest of the group. Set against this background, the subsidiary has the potential to drive not only its own evolution but also that of the MNC. Here the Swiss Fotolab in Finland is a case in point. The Finnish members of the subsidiary board had good knowledge of the emerging Russian and Baltic markets. They strongly advised the parent company to pay considerable attention to these increasingly important external possibilities. Based on trust between the parent company and the Finnish subsidiary, the unit in Finland was nominated regional headquarters for Russia and the Baltic States. After successful entry into these new regions, the Finnish subsidiary was also given the status of regional headquarters for other Nordic markets.

However, subsidiary initiatives, which may drive the evolution process, tend to face obstacles: firstly, the usual resistance to anything new or unproven and secondly, additional resistance because the initiating unit is 'foreign' (Birkinshaw, 1998b). Similar findings have been generated in studies of decision making in internationalisation processes, suggesting that decision-makers are 'laterally rigid' towards new, unorthodox product, operation or market strategies (Luostarinen, 1979). Many multinational corporations are still ethnocentric in their world-view, which results in additional scepticism being attached to any proposal coming from outside the home country. In this context, Birkinshaw and Ridderstrale (1999, p. 150) use the term 'corporate immune system' to denote forces that resist subsidiary initiatives. They describe this system as fundamentally conservative, where individuals prefer to work within existing routines, throw their support behind low-risk projects, and resist ideas that challenge their own power base. Because of this immune system, corporate top management often view subsidiary initiatives with suspicion or hostility. Obviously, the entrepreneurial challenge facing a subsidiary manager is considerable (Birkinshaw, 1998b). This applies particularly to initiatives coming from peripheral subsidiaries situated far away from the centre, both hierarchically and geographically. Moreover, such initiatives originating from subsidiaries located in non-English speaking countries such as Finland may not penetrate the corporate immune system because of the dominance of English in MNCs (Marschan-Piekkari *et al.*, 1999). For many foreign MNCs, Finnish subsidiaries represent peripheral units whose evolution paths may be very time-consuming and complex.

STRATEGIC EVOLUTION PATHS OF FOREIGN-OWNED SUBSIDIARIES IN A HOST COUNTRY

We shall now classify strategic evolution paths of foreign-owned subsidiaries into two major categories. On the one hand, we have host country based internationalisation. After the initial market entry, subsidiaries may gain broader functional and geographical responsibilities. This means penetration within the host country or even escalation to other markets (Luostarinen, 1979). On the other hand, we see the opposite evolution path occurring when the base of subsidiary resources and capabilities becomes narrower as a result of host country based de-internationalisation. This evolution path may, however, encompass re-internationalisation in a later stage. Hence, our starting point here is that the MNC has already entered the host country and established foreign subsidiaries, whose strategic evolution we are concerned with.

Host Country-based Internationalisation

Much of the earlier work in this area has typically focused on the process where the subsidiary gains value-added and greater decision-making autonomy (see, for example, Egelhoff *et al.*, 1998; Birkinshaw *et al.*, 1998; Birkinshaw and Hood, 1997; Forsgren *et al.*, 1999). In this context, we examine host country-based internationalisation through four relevant sub-paths.

Local Penetration Process
Luostarinen (1970) defines the subsidiary penetration process within a host country as additional investments in existing units, establishment of new units with similar functional responsibilities, or establishment of new units with different functional responsibilities from those of existing units. Based on the FIBO data bank covering 5894 Finnish subsidiaries abroad, Hentola and Luostarinen (1995) examined changes in subsidiaries' functional scope. We apply their findings to foreign-owned units in a host country and classify them into six broad functional categories with 26 specific types (see Table 13.1). Obviously, some changes in subsidiaries' functional scope are operative by nature (i.e. changes within each category). We are primarily concerned with strategic changes such as transforming a sales unit into a production unit, or a production unit into an R&D unit (i.e. shifts between functional categories). The fifth category, R&D units, demonstrates the increasing decentralisation of technological capabilities from the home

Table 13.1 Functional classification of foreign-owned units in a host country

Functional responsibility	Type of unit
1. Units related to sales and marketing	• sales promotion unit • sales unit • marketing unit • maintenance unit • installation unit • planning and consulting unit • trading unit
2. Units related to purchasing and logistics	• purchasing unit • transport unit • warehousing unit • materials management unit
3. Units related to accounting, financial and fiscal issues	• finance unit • insurance unit • reinsurance unit • holding unit • real estate unit • invoicing unit • name protection unit • investment unit
4. Units related to production	• production unit • assembly unit
5. Units related to research and development (R&D)	• product R&D unit • production R&D unit
6. Units related to management and administration	• regional headquarters • divisional headquarters • corporate headquarters

Source: Adapted from Hentola and Luostarinen (1995, p. 12).

country of the MNC to various subsidiary locations (Papanastassiou, 1999; Pearce, 1999).

From a host country perspective, the value-added content and benefit of each functional unit is likely to vary (White and Poynter, 1984). For example, ABB announced recently that it will strengthen its R&D activities by establishing a new research unit in Finland as part of ABB Corporate Research. Like previous R&D units of ABB in Finland, this will also be situated within a local technical university. The new unit will develop variable speed drives and power electronic products, and in this way support ABB's strong drives business as a whole. Through the creation of this unit ABB will further improve its position as a leading company in applying new technologies to power electronics (Taloussanomat, 16 September, 1999).

Regional Escalation Process
In terms of geographical scope, subsidiaries' responsibilities may develop from being purely local to being regional. In this context, White and Poynter (1984) use the term 'market scope', while Luostarinen (1979) defines such a process as regional escalation. When subsidiaries develop such roles that are deployed beyond the host country borders, this is termed 'internationalisation of the second degree' (Forsgren *et al.*, 1992, p. 237; Taggart and Berry, 1997). As stated previously, this evolution may be driven by the parent company (top-down process), or initiated by the subsidiary (bottom-up), where subsidiaries are seen to earn or capture new roles and responsibilities within a company.

Like the Swiss Fotolab in Finland, a subsidiary may also be granted the status of regional headquarters; a sort of 'super-subsidiary' that faces many of the same evolution patterns as 'ordinary' foreign units (Birkinshaw and Hood, 1998a; Schutte, 1998). In his survey of 128 foreign manufacturing subsidiaries in Finland, Luostarinen (1981) found that 65 of them (51 per cent) were primarily used for serving the local market, 30 had exports to the parent company, 22 had regional and 11 global export operations. At that time, only six (five per cent) subsidiaries had the status of regional headquarters. An on-going study by Luostarinen (2000) shows interesting comparative results. Out of 1143 foreign-owned subsidiaries in Finland included in the study, 375 (33 per cent) had been promoted to regional headquarters. Regional headquarters were primarily established to develop and coordinate operations in the Baltic and Russian markets; in addition, a minority of them served other markets in central and eastern Europe, and/or the Nordic countries. The increasing share of regional units can mainly be explained by the positive changes in Finland's strategic position during the 1990s markets (Luostarinen, 2000).

Global Escalation Process
In some cases, the local unit may even gain global responsibilities as a product unit, for example within a particular division. Furthermore, a unit may be promoted to divisional headquarters transferred by the parent company to the host country or established by the parent as a new division of the corporation. A good example of this is ABB's acquisition of Stromberg in Finland in the late 1980s. In certain business areas such as drives, the Finnish company was stronger than the parent company. Its stage of technological development was advanced and the global sales figures were promising. Consequently, in the post-acquisition integration process, the Finnish business and product units were granted global responsibilities and grouped partly under the business area called ABB Drives. During the 1990s, the Finnish units have further strengthened their position as important contributors to ABB's global performance (Maattanen, 1999).

Reverse Internationalisation
The last path of deeper internationalisation in the host country is reverse internationalisation, which we define as the process of switching home countries. In

other words, the host country becomes the home country of the MNC. Today, this previously exceptional phenomenon is getting more common, as corporate head-quarters are increasingly being relocated, particularly as a consequence of cross-border mergers and acquisitions (see Table 13.1, sixth category). For example, Swedish companies have transferred new corporate headquarters to Finland after merging with Finnish firms (for example, Merita-Nordbanken, Stora-Enso). This type of development is mainly due to taxation and other country specific advan-tages. Since the economic advantages of relocating corporate headquarters are obvious, countries start competing for the position as the most favourable loca-tion for foreign MNCs.

Host Country-based De-internationalisation

In contrast to the first major strategic evolution path – host country based inter-nationalisation – research on de-internationalisation or withdrawals from a host country is far less common because of its sensitivity as a research object (see, for example, McDermott, 1989). The concept of de-internationalisation introduced by Luostarinen (1979, p. 201) has subsequently been elaborated and applied by other scholars (see, for example, Benito and Welch, 1997; Hakkinen, 1994). Benito and Welch (1997, p. 9) define de-internationalisation as 'any voluntary or forced actions that reduce a company's engagement in or exposure to current cross-border activities'. Hence, subsidiary decline in any form gets essentially no consideration in either the theoretical or the empirical literature (Birkinshaw and Hood, 1997). Here we identify and discuss four relevant sub-paths.

Complete De-internationalisation
In a subsidiary setting, complete de-internationalisation means shutdown of a unit in a given host country. This may be due to, for example parent company's need for cash flow, low profitability of subsidiary operations, or bankruptcy of the par-ent company or subsidiary (Mudambi, 1999). The parent company may even decide to fully withdraw from successful subsidiary operations, if the activities in the host country are not considered part of the company's core competencies, and/or focused business portfolio. This is often justified by a new growth strat-egy, globalisation and focusing, which particularly Finnish and Nordic firms have been following (Luostarinen, 1994). More generally, it reflects the global restruc-turing development within international companies.

Partial De-internationalisation
The strategic evolution of foreign-owned subsidiaries may also involve partial de-internationalisation. A foreign subsidiary may have been established too early, and is thus closed down, while an agent will continue to operate locally in the hope of future market potential. This is a typical example of partial de-interna-tionalisation encompassing a simultaneous change from higher to lower level operations modes. It may also mean terminating subsidiaries in one business area,

while continuing subsidiary operations within another. From a functional perspective, this type of de-internationalisation may involve transferring certain activities from one country to another. For example, GM, the world's largest car manufacturer, will establish the new regional headquarters for northern Europe in Sweden. This will involve transferring marketing resources from Finland and other Nordic countries to Sweden. The resultant cost savings are estimated to amount to about 5 per cent. The FIBO data provide another example. Out of 375 regional headquarters in Finland, which were primarily established in the 1990s, already 50 (13 per cent) have been closed down. After losing the regional status, sales and/or production units have continued their operations as local units. This would indicate that the primary reason behind such partial internationalisation stems from global restructuring at corporate level rather than from unfavourable business conditions in Finland (Luostarinen, 2000).

Nominal De-internationalisation
The last de-internationalisation path is termed nominal, because of its 'neutral' impact on the host country. This path involves the sales of the subsidiary or the parent company to another foreign firm in the host country. For example, a Dutch company, NKF Holding, was the owner of NK Cables in Finland until its competitor, another Dutch firm Draka Holding, bought the unit. In 2000, the Italian company, Pirelli Cable and Systems, which is the world's largest power cable producer, is planning to buy one of the three Finnish cable factories owned by Draka, and the power cable production of Draka in the Netherlands.

Temporary De-internationalisation
De-internationalisation can be described as temporary, if it is later followed by re-internationalisation. In this context, the original operation mode may be inappropriate. The parent company may first decide to withdraw from the host country, but establish a new subsidiary at a later stage with higher or lower value-added. For example, the initial manufacturing subsidiary may be closed down and later substituted with a sales unit. To illustrate, ABB has been advocated as the most important Western investor in Eastern Europe (Hofheinz, 1994). However, during recent years ABB has faced significant difficulties in these markets, which have led, at least for the time being, to divestment decisions and withdrawals. Thus, the last evolution path demonstrates that an MNC may engage in re-internationalisation within a specific host country as the business circumstances or foundation for corporate strategy change.

Overall, de-internationalisation decisions tend to involve major upheaval and conflicts between corporate and subsidiary interests. From the perspective of the corporate strategy, however, de-internationalisation moves may be well justified and have positive long term effects. Benito and Welch (1997) argue that multinational corporations with a large number of subsidiaries in different locations have a broader range of options, when faced by problems in one particular subsidiary, than companies with only few foreign units. In a sense, the multinational becomes

less committed to any one particular subsidiary even though its overall commitment to international operations is high (Benito and Welch, 1997).

CONCEPTUAL FRAMEWORK AND CONCLUDING REMARKS

The purpose of this chapter was to classify the forces behind strategic evolution
of foreign subsidiaries and explain the evolution paths in a host country. In
order to summarise the previous discussion and guide our empirical work in the
Finnish context, we propose a conceptual framework in the form of a matrix
(see Table 13.2).

Based on the literature review, we divide the drivers of subsidiary evolution
into two broad categories: (1) parent based, and (2) subsidiary based and further
into two sub-categories, internal and external (see vertical dimension of the
matrix). Internal drivers such as corporate strategy, subsidiary performance or
local management's entrepreneurial activity may trigger subsidiary evolution.
alternatively, it may be initiated by external drivers from a single country such as
the home, host or third country, or from a group of countries in regional or global
markets. Inter-subsidiary influences come into play through these external drivers
but they may also be reflected through parent company decisions. The evolution
paths, in turn, indicate two major directions of change, namely host country based
internationalisation and de-internationalisation (see horizontal dimension of the
matrix).

This framework is suitable for examining the nature of subsidiary evolution and
its underlying forces. It bridges earlier research findings on foreign subsidiary
management, strategic management and internationalisation processes of the firm
in a dynamic, longitudinal way. In early stages of subsidiary evolution and host
country based internationalisation, parent company drivers together with local
incentives are likely to shape the evolutionary path of the new unit. In later stages,
subsidiary based drivers may dominate. On the other hand, in host country based
de-internationalisation, the parent company is likely to play an important role.

What are the managerial and policy implications of this study? At this stage of
conceptual development, it is inappropriate to be too specific, but a few issues can
be highlighted. Corporate managers should be well aware of the need to consider
multiple perspectives when attempting to assess the performance and especially
the future potential of individual subsidiary units. This framework offers a tool
for such strategic reasoning. For subsidiary managers, the primary message is that
attention should be paid to the various forces that influence subsidiary evolution,
and the possibility of harnessing them to sharpen and upgrade subsidiary capabilities. Particularly in the context of restructuring, as the Philips case in Finland
shows, corporate and subsidiary managers should jointly ensure smooth communication and open information exchanges. In this way, de-motivation among subsidiary managers may at least be reduced. Turning to the purely Finnish aspects
of this research, there are some interesting implications for inward investing

Table 13.2 Conceptual framework

Drivers / Strategic evolution paths	Host country-based internationalisation				Host country-based de-internationalisation			
	local/ functional	regional/ functional	global/ functional	reverse/ functional	complete funct./ geog.	partial funct./ geog.	nominal funct./ geog.	temporary funct./ geog.
Parent-based drivers								
• internal								
– corporate strategy								
• external								
– home country								
– host country								
– third country								
– regional								
– global								
Subsidiary-based drivers								
• internal								
– initiative								
– performance								
• external								
– home country								
– host country								
– third country								
– regional								
– global								

MNCs and for policy makers. Corporate management should be encouraged to view the Finnish business environment as an attractive location for establishing strategically important foreign subsidiaries such as regional headquarters for central and eastern Europe (Luostarinen, 2000). Policy makers should fully utilise the newly accepted concept of the northern dimension in the European Union and promote Finland as an important business centre and gateway to this area.

In conclusion, there is a need for case studies of subsidiary evolution and more detailed examination of the interplay between parent company and subsidiary drivers, and the impact of host country policies. Future research could investigate stages of decline and reduced subsidiary activities as part of this evolution process. Our hope is that this discussion outlines some of interesting research avenues which can be followed in the future.

14 Multinational Enterprises in Ireland: The Dynamics of Subsidiary Strategy

Ana Teresa Tavares

INTRODUCTION

Ireland was a precursor of a pro-FDI approach in the 1950s. Since then, and mainly under the auspices of the Industrial Development Authority (IDA), Ireland has adopted a remarkably proactive stance towards attracting multinational enterprises (MNEs). Irish industrial strategy is usually seen as a successful case of forging a strategic partnership between local institutions and foreign investors, in particular in comparison to other 'peripheral' EU economies.

This chapter aims to contribute to the increasingly topical literature on subsidiary strategy and evolution by focusing on a new survey of MNEs' subsidiaries in Ireland. The first section will provide the background to the Irish case, discussing the importance of MNEs in the Irish manufacturing sector and elaborating on certain aspects of the evolution of the Irish policy stance towards MNEs. The second section will focus mainly on the strategies of foreign-owned subsidiaries operating in Ireland. After preliminary considerations on the relevance of adopting a subsidiary-level perspective and issues such as subsidiary development and its role on the firm's competitiveness, empirical evidence will be provided, based on the results from this survey of the main foreign subsidiaries in Ireland. Their strategic roles will receive particular attention, as well as related aspects regarding their market scope, product scope and functional scope. The motivations underlying investment in Ireland will be also discussed. Finally, the main findings will be highlighted and implications for theory and practice outlined.

BACKGROUND TO THE IRISH CASE

The Relevance of MNEs' Activities in the Irish Manufacturing Sector

Irish industry is considerably dependent on the activities of multinational firms. Foreign subsidiaries are responsible for about half of the manufacturing employment and two-thirds of gross manufacturing output (Delany, 1998). MNEs from three home countries control about 70 per cent of foreign subsidiaries (ibid.). The US is unequivocally the main investor (40 per cent of foreign plants), followed by the UK (16 per cent) and Germany (15 per cent). Greenfield operations have been the preferred entry mode.

Foreign MNEs in Ireland exhibit an extremely high export propensity (87.7 per cent of total production), *vis-à-vis* 35.2 per cent exported by their Irish counterparts (Ruane and Gorg, 1999). In terms of export markets, the EU has gained importance at the expense of Ireland's traditional trading partner, the UK (Irish exports for the UK decreased from 90 per cent in 1960 to about 30 per cent now). Indeed, as Barry and Bradley (1997) note, Ireland constitutes a 'textbook case study of the effects on an EU host economy of export oriented FDI'.

It is thought that foreign investment brought about a long term boost to the Irish growth rate. Moreover, FDI motivated a sectoral and regional shift in the Irish industry (Ruane and Gorg, 1999). FDI was not attracted to sectors where Ireland traditionally had a comparative advantage (Barry and Bradley, 1997). It tended to happen in relatively high-tech sectors. Given this high tech bias, the skill levels in the foreign sector tend to be superior to those of domestic firms, and the main share in R&D in Irish manufacturing is accounted for by MNEs' subsidiaries (Ruane and Gorg, 1999).

Generally, foreign firms are larger, more productive, and more profitable than their indigenous counterparts (Barry and Bradley, 1997). They are also characterised by a low level of backward linkages. However, these linkages increased over time, while domestic sector linkages declined (McAleese and McDonald, 1978; Barry and Bradley, 1997).

Ireland's success in attracting FDI may be attributed to a combination of factors at the economic and institutional levels. Certain location advantages (Dunning, 1977), notably institutional credibility (well-organised and competent development agencies providing expertise and resources), and various fiscal and financial incentives were paramount in justifying its performance in attracting foreign MNEs. Relatively favourable costs (for example, comparatively cheap and qualified labour), and other non-financial attributes (for example, an indigenous knowledge base, universities, high quality pool of suppliers, technically skilled, English-speaking labour force, entrepreneurial local managers) have acted as a location pull. Far from being a demand-side phenomenon, this success was a result of Irish supply-side conditions. In fact, the Irish domestic market is insignificant for most MNEs, and this explains why the majority uses Ireland mainly as a production platform.

The most relevant negative location factors have been probably Ireland's geographic peripherality and modest level of physical infrastructure (although it is improving). Due to its peripheral location, Ireland is seen as a good base for activities with low transport costs.

Another critical factor that deserves credit for the success in FDI attraction is Ireland's commitment to free trade. The first tariff reductions occurred in 1966 with the Anglo-Irish Free Trade Area Agreement, and Ireland's accession to the (then) EC in 1973 represented a turning point. Dismantling of tariffs continued actively until 1978, after a five year adjustment following EC accession (Ruane and Gorg, 1999). It is no surprise that, for a small economy like Ireland, the importance of belonging to trade agreements is fundamental to enhance its attractiveness to foreign investors. Nevertheless, as the case of Greece proves by the negative side, trade liberalisation is not enough *per se* (Barry and Bradley, 1997). However, Irish institutions have taken proactive measures to secure Ireland's position as a host country in a free trade environment. It is expected that closer European integration will impact on all aspects of the Irish economy (McAleese and Hayes, 1995). Ireland is a net recipient of EU funds, geared, among other aims, to upgrade its industrial fabric, infrastructure and human capital. Particularly with the scenario of EU enlargement, it is likely that these Funds will be drastically reduced, and that prospective members from Central and Eastern Europe will be regarded as serious contenders for new FDI projects or relocation of existing activities.

Evolutionary Aspects of the Irish Policy Stance towards FDI

Since Ireland became an independent State in 1922, two fundamental phases in policy orientation towards multinationals and FDI can be clearly discerned. An anti-FDI approach characterised the period 1930s to late 1950s. Foreign ownership of firms was prohibited by law (Control of Manufactures Act), invoking the protection of incipient Irish industries. This prohibition also purported to impede UK firms from setting up companies in the Irish market (Ruane and Gorg, 1999), capturing market share from local manufacturers. In the late 1950s, a total *volte-face* occurred, and an approach emphasising FDI attraction became the cornerstone of Irish industrial policy (Ó'Gráda and O'Rourke, 1995). This drastic shift was justified by the failure of protectionist policies in promoting a viable manufacturing sector (Ruane and Gorg, 1999), and by the recession affecting the Irish economy in the mid-1950s. FDI attraction was thought to boost economic growth and employment.

The focus on FDI, fundamentally materialised in a zero corporate profits tax on manufactured exports, was hence the mainstay of industrial policy since the 1950s. This automatic tax holiday (ibid.) originated a striking boom of export-oriented manufacturing FDI. In addition to these fiscal incentives, financial support was provided through cash grants. The zero corporate profit tax for exporters was deemed incompatible with the principles of the Treaty of Rome in 1982, being replaced by an automatic preferential flat rate of 10 per cent on all manufacturing, complemented by considerable investment grants and also accompanied by the commitment of dismantling most tariff barriers in less than a decade.

Emphasis has always been on greenfield investments and on exporters (thus protecting somehow indigenous industry from 'disloyal' competition from MNEs in the Irish market). The parameters for grant elegibility were altered in 1982 (ibid.). A discretionary basis replaced the former automatic procedure, and grants were not any more attached to exporting behaviour.

The IDA adopted a proactive 'hands-on' industrial policy ('micro-dirigisme'), designed to upgrade the performance of Irish industry, including that of overseas subsidiaries (Amin *et al.*, 1994). Due to its initiatives, the IDA gained considerable international credibility, especially for emphasising independence (from the annual budget, thus being unaffected by political volatility), policy certainty and continuity (ibid.). Payment of grants occured up-front, requiring repayment (linked to fixed assets) if the MNE failed to meet pre-established targets, notably concerning employment. Therefore, both government and firms had a stable framework on which to take decisions, and an important bargaining process between policy makers and prospective investors ensured transparency to the public domain.

Another important aspect of policy, beyond its type and content, is its practical implementation, since the same policy may have a quite distinct impact depending on the way it is put into practice (ibid.). Over the last four decades, Irish industrial policy implementation has always been on a project basis. The levels of selectivity and proactivity have markedly increased, especially since the 1970s (ibid.). Fine-grained sectoral selectivity has been a defining feature of Irish industrial policy. High tech sectors were explicitly favoured, aiming to stimulate positive spillovers to indigenous industry (for instance through demonstration effects and learning opportunities). There was a tentative of creating industrial clusters to facilitate spillovers. In the 1970s the electronics and pharmaceuticals sectors were identified by the IDA as the most promising, hence heavily targeted. The US was the home country most favoured by this choice. Investments with incorporated R&D were privileged, and a close interaction IDA-EOLAS (the Irish Science and Technology Agency) was important to manage these projects.

As already mentioned, Irish industrial policy since the 1960s emphasised the attraction of new (greenfield) investments. Apart from certain initiatives to prevent closures, policies aiming to strengthen the subsidiaries' scope have been limited. However, with tighter competition from alternative locations, the survival and development of existing operations is gaining momentum (Delany, 1998). Moreover, since foreign ownership is already at a very high level, it is not expected to rise much further. The present strategy is realistically trying to stimulate an increase in the functional/value-added scope of existing operations, placing a greater emphasis on after-care (Young and Hood, 1994) and 'deepening', rather than expanding the foreign sector commitment to the Irish manufacturing base. The location of high profile HQ and R&D activities in the Irish subsidiary is a priority of recent policy initiatives.

This shift towards greater value-added and complexity is accompanied by the establishment of a more synergistic relationship with an increasingly sophisticated local industrial fabric (favouring the consolidation of existing clusters and the promotion of outsourcing linkages). The National Linkage Programme (established in 1985 by the IDA) constitutes a recent important effort to promote linkages with the local industrial environment.

Hence, even if it has been an important investment location since the 1960s, and especially after EC accession in 1973, Ireland is an example of a location whose attributes are changing over time (Amin *et al.*, 1994). Ireland seems to attract now higher quality MNE operations. In evolutionary terms, there is also evidence that existing subsidiaries are gaining a wider range of functions and levels of management autonomy (to be developed later in the chapter).

STRATEGIES OF MNEs' SUBSIDIARIES IN IRELAND: A DYNAMIC PERSPECTIVE

A Subsidiary-level Approach

The rapidly expanding body of literature on subsidiary strategy is providing important insights on the nature of the contemporary MNE, emphasising the usefulness of considering a subfirm level of analysis (White and Poynter, 1984; D'Cruz, 1986; Young *et al.*, 1989; Pearce, 1992; Pearce and Papanastassiou, 1997; Birkinshaw, 1997; Birkinshaw and Hood, 1997; Taggart, 1996, 1998). Often, the subsidiary is like a 'quasi-firm' (Andersson and Forsgren, 1998) and the MNE can be considered as an 'interorganisational network' (Ghoshal and Bartlett, 1991).

This chapter adopts the subsidiary as the unit of analysis and uses a tripartite typology of subsidiary roles (for greater detail see Tavares and Pearce, 1998), based on the 'scope' typology originally suggested by White and Poynter (1984), and from which many variants have been developed (D'Cruz, 1986; Pearce, 1992; Taggart, 1996, 1998). The three roles/strategies considered are the truncated miniature replica (TMR), the rationalised product subsidiary (RPS) and the product mandate (PM), as explained in Table 14.1 for the Irish case.

The idea of a variety of subsidiary types is consistent with the fact that there are pluralistic motivations for investment (Dunning, 1993), and with the conceptualisation of the MNE as a portfolio of heterogeneous subsidiaries that act as embedded subsystems (Tavares, 1999), forming a 'differentiated network' (Forsgren and Johanson, 1992).

Subsidiary Development and the Corporation's Competitiveness

Certain subsidiaries play a critical role in their firm's ability to compete (Hedlund, 1986; Bartlett and Ghoshal, 1989; Birkinshaw and Hood, 1998b; Birkinshaw *et al.*, 1998; Taggart, 1998). The subsidiary may even act as a 'centre of excellence' within the MNE (Andersson and Forsgren, 1998).

Subsidiaries' roles/strategies are neither static nor merely assigned by headquarters (HQ). An important process of intra-MNE competition for upgraded roles may exist, by which subsidiaries compete for resources and higher profile responsibilities in the MNE network. These internal competitive forces are no less relevant than their external counterparts, and they have often been overlooked (Birkinshaw, 1997; Luostarinen and Marshan-Piekkari, 2000). Therefore, the internal and external embeddedness of subsidiaries (Andersson and Forsgren, 1998) is crucial in the analysis of their activities and potential for development.

For the purposes of understanding the evolutionary aspects of MNEs' activities in Ireland, the concept of subsidiary development (which contrasts with a static consideration of roles) is crucial. Subsidiary development, an inherently dynamic idea, may be defined as 'the growth and enhancement of subsidiary's resources that add increasing levels of value to the MNC as a whole' (Birkinshaw and Hood, 1997). However, development may or may not occur, and deterioration in the subsidiary's resources is a possible scenario (Birkinshaw and Hood, 1998b). Hence any sustainable position requires continued effort on the part of the subsidiary and its staff. However, there is more to the process than merely subsidiary initiative. In this vein, Birkinshaw and Hood (1997) identify three main drivers of subsidiary development:

- parent-driven development (linked to the concept of 'structural context' – Bower, 1970)
- internal development (related to the entrepreneurial efforts of subsidiary management/staff);
- host country-driven development (that can operate both in the early stages in the investment or at the level of 'after-care' measures)

The relative importance of these three distinct drivers tends to change over time (as the subsidiary matures, probably host country and parent drivers will lose importance in favour of subsidiary initiative). Luostarinen and Marshan-Piekkari (2000) also stress the importance of studying 'longitudinal changes in subsidiaries' roles and responsibilities over time', and suggest a division of the drivers of subsidiary evolution into two categories, parent-based and subsidiary-based (each divided into internal and external factors). In their interpretation, the host country role is incorporated in both parent and subsidiary drivers.

This dynamic perspective contemplating the possibility of subsidiary upgrading (in the context of the corporate value chain) and the existence of many possible evolutionary paths in their transition process is a core concept underlying the analysis. It helps to understand the subsidiary, the MNE, and to design appropriate policies in order to maximise subsidiary value-added and to revitalise or even reverse (if needed) this process of subsidiary life cycle.

Crucial for subsidiary development is the nature of local inputs subsidiaries can access (Pearce, 1999c). Subsidiaries may have (unique) specialised capabilities embodied in the technology they develop or in the skills of their human resources. It is particularly opportune to study the issue of subsidiary development in the Irish case (see previous work by Hood and Taggart, 1997; Taggart and Hood, 1999). Given its precocity in attracting MNEs, and the vast changes that occurred in the last decades in the world economy and in the geography of international production, traditional advantages (low taxes and relatively lower labour costs) are becoming more volatile and weaker (Egelhoff *et al.*, 1998). Wage convergence intra-EU and the increasingly head-to-head, stronger competition from non-EU, low wage countries, reinforce the idea that probably the importance of technology MNEs can access in Ireland tends to be greater. The in-house development of unique technological capabilities that can be leveraged throughout the MNE appears as a solid basis for furthering subsidiary development (Taggart, 1996). Such a 'technology-driven' strategy contrasts for instance with a 'market-driven' strategy of subsidiary development (that, given the exiguity of the local market, would never be realistic in the Irish case).

A supportive institutional environment has also assisted this process, in which the creation of 'centres of excellence' and product mandates were stimulated. Evidence supports that first class technology has been transferred to Ireland in the last decade (Egelhoff *et al.*, 1998).

Evidence for the Irish Case: Survey Results

Preliminary Considerations
This section is based on a questionnaire survey, in which 200 of the biggest manufacturing operations in Ireland were asked about several aspects of their operations and strategy. A total of 49 replies were received at the time of this analysis (25 per cent response rate). Of these, three replies were not used because they were incomplete. This response rate is quite usual in international business surveys, although ideally the survey would contemplate a larger number of firms. However, the firms which replied are all major MNE subsidiaries in the Irish context and their prominence enables a consistent, mainly qualitative, analysis of the data.

A section of the survey focused on aspects related to the impact of economic integration on FDI and MNEs strategies in Ireland. It is interesting to note that 77.8 per cent of the firms surveyed were established after integration in the EU (1973). 95.6 per cent of the respondents were established after 1959. This may indicate their sensitivity to the change in Irish industrial policy and the considerable incentives they were offered since the late 1950s.

Concerning ownership, 47.8 of respondents were US companies. Greenfield investments were the most common entry mode (78.3 per cent of the companies surveyed). In general, each parent MNE had only one subsidiary in Ireland. The industries more heavily represented in the current sample were pharmaceuticals (twelve firms, 26.1 per cent of sample) and electronics (six firms or 13.1 per cent of all subsidiaries surveyed).

Motivations for Establishing a Subsidiary in Ireland
Most respondents considered the incentives they were given by Irish authorities to set up a subsidiary in Ireland as the primary motivation underlying their investment. The second major motivation for this sample of firms was the level

of qualification and distinctiveness of skills of the Irish workforce in their sector of activity. This shows that FDI in Ireland has occurred in sectors where a qualified workforce was required. The third main motivation was the improvement of the firm's competitiveness in the EU market, just reinforcing the relevance of free trade for a small open European economy like Ireland. The next motivation was the improvement of their competitiveness in other (non-EU) countries. All non-European subsidiaries perceived this motive as quite relevant. Comparative low input costs were mentioned by several respondents, even though rather behind the more qualitative aspect of the workforce's qualification (which contrasts with for instance the Portuguese case, studied by Tavares and Pearce, 2000). The unimportance of the local market was obvious in the results.

Roles/Strategies of MNEs' Subsidiaries in Ireland
The particular roles or strategies developed by subsidiaries of foreign MNEs in Ireland constituted the core aspect of this investigation (see Table 14.1). Three moments in time were considered in the survey, aiming to capture some dynamics in subsidiary activity and eventual subsidiary development processes.

The year 1986 is a benchmark concerning EU integration as it was found that 1973 (year of Irish accession) was too remote to ask the respondents. It coincides with the period in which adjustments towards the Single Market started to be seriously implemented, with the concomitant emphasis on free trade intra-EU. Furthermore, it is the year of accession of other peripheral EU economies (Portugal and Spain). 'Now' refers to the period April–July 1999, and '10 years' time' corresponds to 2009. Projections for the next 10 years should be interpreted with caution.

In dynamic terms, the rationalised product subsidiary (RPS) has been consistently the main role, without significant change throughout the three periods. It is the only role for the two firms of 'Other' countries and it also has particular relevance for EU-owned firms. Automotive, pharmaceuticals and healthcare were the sectors in which rationalised operations are most paramount.

The second most important role, the product mandate (PM), is clearly the one that shows more tendency to increase, in particular in the cases of US and Japanese firms. Electronics, chemicals and plastics and the residual category 'other manufacturing' are the sectors showing more pronounced product mandating responsibilities. The PM role in the pharmaceutical industry is negligible, as most operations are clearly of the rationalised type.

This increase in the relevance of PMs appears consistent with the sustained effort of the IDA and EOLAS in attracting 'quality' projects, especially in high tech sectors.

Given the already emphasised exiguity of the local market, the truncated miniature replica (TMR) represents the least relevant role, and its importance tended to decline substantially between the period prior to 1986 and now. Most (77.8 per cent) of the subsidiaries in the sample were actually set up after EU integration in 1973, so in a free trade environment the TMR role loses its *raison d'être*.

Table 14.1 Evaluation of the relative importance of distinct subsidiary roles/strategies, by home country and industry

	Roles of subsidiaries[1] (average response[2])								
	A			B			C		
	Before 1986	Now	10 years' time	Before 1986	Now	10 years' time	Before 1986	Now	10 years' time
By home country									
EU	2.13	1.31	1.31	2.60	3.20	3.20	1.40	1.65	1.94
USA	1.06	1.04	1.05	3.06	2.78	2.55	1.72	2.22	2.45
Japan	1.00	1.00	1.00	4.00	2.33	2.33	1.00	3.00	3.33
Other	n.a.*	1.00	1.00	n.a.	4.00	4.00	n.a.	1.00	1.00
Total	1.51	1.14	1.14	2.91	2.95	2.83	1.54	2.00	2.25
By industry									
Automotive	1.00	1.00	1.00	4.00	4.00	4.00	2.50	1.50	2.00
Chemicals and plastics	1.75	1.00	1.00	1.75	2.50	2.25	1.75	2.25	2.50
Electronics	1.00	1.00	1.00	2.83	2.89	2.25	1.67	2.33	3.13
Food and beverages	2.00	1.00	1.00	3.00	3.00	3.50	1.50	2.00	2.00
Healthcare and related products	1.57	1.14	1.14	3.14	3.17	3.17	1.00	2.14	2.14
Pharmaceuticals	1.43	1.20	1.20	3.43	3.60	3.60	1.43	1.27	1.45
Other manufacturing	1.86	1.30	1.30	2.57	2.20	2.20	1.71	2.40	2.50
Total	1.51	1.14	1.14	2.91	2.95	2.83	1.54	2.00	2.25

Notes:
Roles (or strategies) of subsidiaries: A – truncated miniature replica, the Irish subsidiary produces some of the parent's already existing product lines (or related product lines) for the Irish market; B – rationalised product subsidiary, the Irish subsidiary produces a certain set of component parts or existing final products for a multi-country or global market; C – product mandate, the Irish subsidiary has autonomy and creative resources to *develop*, produce and market a restricted product range (totally innovative products) for multi-country (regional or global) markets.
[1] Respondents were asked to evaluate each role/strategy as (i) our only role/strategy, (ii) our main role/strategy, (iii) a secondary role/strategy, and (iv) not a part of our role/strategy.
[2] The average response (AR) was calculated by allocating 'only role' a value of 4, 'main role' a value of 3, 'secondary role' a value of 2 and finally 'not a part of our role' a coefficient of 1.
* n.a.: not available (there are just two firms in this category).

Source: survey conducted by author.

The only firms that had a reasonably important TMR role were EU firms, which confirms the impression that the local market was slightly more important for them (corroborating previous research by Pearce and Papanastassiou, 1997; and Hood and Young, 1988). It is also due to the fact that UK firms were precursors in FDI in Ireland, and some of them developed TMR operations. In industry terms, food and beverages was the sector that had a more marked TMR role before 1986, which is not surprising concerning that, due to the characteristics of the goods involved, this is usually one of the industries with stronger local market focus.

Aspects Related to the 'Scope' Typology Used

Markets Supplied by Foreign Subsidiaries Operating in Ireland
Market scope is one of the main defining characteristics of the scope typology used in this chapter. As can be inferred from Table 14.2, the main market for this sample of firms is the EU (excluding Ireland and the UK). The UK and the rest of the world are also very relevant as export markets. Again, the lack of importance of the local market is evident from the data.

Moreover, 84.8 per cent of respondents exported between 90.1 and 100 per cent, which just confirms the extremely pronounced export propensity of foreign subsidiaries in Ireland. It also confirms that these subsidiaries act primarily as production platforms, hardly selling in the local market, which reinforces the results presented above.

Product Scope
The majority of the firms were final products manufacturers. Most of the respondents considered that they had strong manufacturing and product development capabilities. The width of the product range increased slightly throughout the three periods (Table 14.3).

Functional Scope
In this case, functional/value-added scope was evaluated with reference to two indicators: decision-making autonomy and technology used by the subsidiary.

A specific part of the survey aimed at evaluating the extent of decision-making autonomy of these subsidiaries. Table 14.4 shows the results for four criteria: market area, product range, broad strategic direction and technology used. Most decisions (overall mean values) are taken by HQ, consulting the subsidiary. As a general trend, decision-making autonomy tends to increase and the subsidiary seems to be moving towards more ability to decide (in all four selected aspects). A key finding that seems consistent with previously expounded ideas is that subsidiaries are developing increased autonomy with respect to technology.

Developing this aspect, when asked about the *technology* they used, most firms mentioned that it was usually that from the MNE parent, or that they developed products based on core group technology. A significant number of respondents used their own R&D output. A positive trend in technological activities is perceptible. This trend includes activities such as adaptation of manufacturing technology or manufacturing processes and development of new/improved products for EU and world markets. Generation of new technology for the parent had commenced in only few subsidiaries but tended to expand over the time period considered.

Table 14.2 Markets supplied by foreign MNEs' subsidiaries operating in Ireland

Importance of markets
(average response*)

	A			B			C			D			E		
	Before 1986	Now	10 years' time	Before 1986	Now	10 years' time	Before 1986	Now	10 years' time	Before 1986	Now	10 years' time	Before 1986	Now	10 years' time
	1.70	1.74	1.82	2.22	2.12	2.17	2.61	2.67	2.71	1.78	1.88	2.09	1.42	2.20	2.37

Notes:

Markets supplied by MNEs' subsidiaries: A – Ireland; B – UK; C – rest of EU (excluding Ireland and the UK); D – other non-EU Europe (including Central and Eastern European countries); E – rest of the world (i.e. all countries excluding Europe).

[1] Respondents were asked to evaluate each market area as (i) our only market, (ii) our main market, (iii) a secondary market and (iv) a market area not supplied.

[2] The average response (AR) was calculated by allocating 'only market' a value of 4, 'main market' a value of 3 'secondary market' a value of 2 and finally 'a market area not supplied' a coefficient of 1.

Source: as for Table 14.1.

Table 14.3 Width of the subsidiary's product range *vis-à-vis* parent company

	Before 1986	Now	10 years' time
Mean value for all firms in sample*	1.81	3.05	3.50

Note:
* 1 = much narrower, to 5 = much wider.

Table 14.4 Degree of decision-making autonomy (mean values for firms in sample)

	Before 1986	Now	10 years' time
Market area supplied by Irish subsidiary	1.59	2.11	2.36
Product range supplied by Irish subsidiary	1.7	2.24	2.38
Broad strategic direction of Irish subsidiary	1.62	2.29	2.49
Technology used by Irish subsidiary	1.82	2.60	2.76

Notes:
In order to calculate the respective means, the following values apply: (1) decisions taken mainly by parent/regional HQ *without* consulting/seeking advice from Irish subsidiary; (2) decisions taken mainly by parent/regional HQ *after* consulting/seeking advice from Irish subsidiary; (3) decisions taken mainly by Irish subsidiary *after* consulting/seeking advice from parent/regional HQ; (4) decisions taken mainly by Irish subsidiary *without* consulting/seeking advice from parent/regional HQ.

CONCLUSION

Summary of Main Findings

Ireland pioneered a welcoming stance towards MNEs, and succeeded in creating a credible institutional matrix to manage FDI attraction. Irish industrial policy has played a decisive role in influencing both the quantity and quality of FDI attracted to Ireland. A coordinated and proactive approach was adopted that avoided short-term concerns. It aimed at deepening the MNE's commitment and forging a positive dialectic with local stakeholders.

The chapter analysed evidence from a new database on MNEs' subsidiaries in Ireland, and the main results are as follows. The principal motivation for FDI was the provision of incentives, followed by the qualification of the workforce, the provision of the EU market and relatively attractive costs. With regard to their strategic roles, Irish subsidiaries are mainly production platforms (although product mandates are becoming more common). Their main markets are the EU and the rest of the world, the local market being insignificant. Irish subsidiaries are also characterised by an overwhelming export propensity and level of intra-group trade. These features point to a modest level of local linkages, although there is a positive trend concerning their evolution. The survey also points to increased decision-making autonomy and functional scope in these subsidiaries. These results seem to provide an optimistic view of the Irish situation, and should serve as an example to other 'peripheral' EU economies.

Implications for Theory and Practice

The evolution of the Irish subsidiaries illustrates the importance of entrepreneurial and proactive local management. It should motivate subsidiary managers to try to sustain and, if possible, improve their position in the MNE system (subject to a constant benchmarking in which subsidiary charters are contestable: Birkinshaw and Hood, 1997). Nonetheless, this process of upgrading and developing the subsidiary's capabilities should be coherent with the broad strategic direction of the MNE, otherwise it may have an entropic effect.

For HQ managers, the 'custodians' of the MNE system (Pearce, 1999b), the implication is that they ought to observe closely these evolutionary processes occurring at the subsidiary level in order to evaluate whether or not they are positively contributing to the group, in a 'freedom *ma non troppo*' basis, demotivating 'empire-building' tendencies (Birkinshaw and Hood, 1998) and negative principal–agent behaviours (Mudambi, 1998). However, positive development of resources by the subsidiary and synergistic interaction with the host environment should be encouraged (Pearce, 1999b). Indeed, as Yamin (2000) notes, 'organisational isolation is an inescapable structural feature of the MNE'. This does not mean that subsidiaries should act autarkically but instead that they should enrich the incomplete template that they inherit with the addition of new resources, in particular from the environment in which they are embedded.

The Irish focus on the quality of operations and deepening/embedding the local subsidiary should serve as an example to policy-makers in other countries, particularly in small open (thus more vulnerable) economies. The aspects of discretionarity and selectivity in the evaluation of projects, as well as attention to implementation of policies rather than to their content only also tends to be a winning strategy. Furthermore, policy makers have to understand the necessary evolution in locational factors over time and over the subsidiaries' life cycles. They must also appreciate that the advantages that attracted MNEs in the first instance tend to self-obsolesce and not serve as a long-term basis for survival and development. For this reason, the recent Irish focus on fostering linkages and after-care seems a sensible strategy.

In terms of future research, it is intended to increase the formality of the analysis by testing econometrically the survey results and comparing the Irish case with that of other 'peripheral' economies (e.g. Portugal and Spain). Important contrasts can emerge from these comparisons, which will contribute to and enrich the already blossoming literature on subsidiary dynamics.

15 From Globalisation to Internationalisation to Americanisation: the Example of 'Little Americas' in the Hotel Sector

Dennis Nickson and Chris Warhurst

INTRODUCTION

There is currently much debate and discussion about the globalisation of the world's economy. Much of this rhetoric, however, has little empirical purchase. A range of studies have questioned both the ontology and epistemology of globalisation (for a review of this literature, see Warhurst *et al.*, 1998). These authors conclude that the epistemology of globalisation is erroneously applied to the ontology of an international economy. At the same time, despite claims for its demise, some commentators are suggesting that Americanisation best characterises the world's economy (see for example, Friedman, 1999; Hutton, in Giddens and Hutton, 2000). This chapter enjoins these debates by critiquing the globalisation thesis and asserting the internationalness of the world's economy, providing an empirical illustration of Americanisation with the development of the international hotel sector.

The chapter thus examines Americanisation by reference to the American model of production within the international organisation of economy activity coupled with a sectoral analysis. Specifically, with a review and critique of secondary literature concerning the globalisation, internationalisation and Americanisation of economic activity, the chapter firstly examines the diffusion of ideology, ideas and techniques associated with the American model. The chapter then develops these themes with an examination of the role of American organisations in the genesis, development and consolidation of the international hotel sector. This section draws on original empirical material from three multinational hotel companies, and in doing so is doubly important because analysis of the American model to date has tended to focus on the manufacturing sector. This material clearly indicates the continuing influence of the American model of hotel internationalisation in terms of both the 'hardware' and 'software', that is for the former, the physical product, for example the rooms and operating systems; and with the latter, the utilisation of human resources and style of service delivery. Through this analysis we aim to reiterate the residual importance of Americanisation and the American model within the international economy.

LEST WE FORGET ... BRINGING BACK AMERICA/NA INTO THE ANALYSIS

In this section we provide a critique of the globalisation thesis, presenting and augmenting some of the arguments made by Warhurst *et al.* (1998). As these authors point out, from the 1970s, it is argued that a number of 'global shifts' have occurred in the organisation of the world's economy with regard to transport and telecommunications technology; increased and increasingly diffused flows of foreign direct investment (FDI); and the emergence of stateless, footloose transnational corporations (TNCs), supranational institutions and regional proto-states (Dicken, 1992) and a single world market (Levitt, 1983). The global economy then is more than an *inter*national economy in which trade and investment flows across national borders directed by essentially national companies engaging national markets. Together, it is argued that these developments have rendered the national state dead and national state economic management ineffective at best and superfluous at worst (Ohmae, 1995). Three dimensions of globalisation – economic, political and cultural – have been identified by Sklair (1991) which encapsulate these shifts, manifest firstly in TNCs; secondly in the emergence of a transnational capitalist class (TCC); and, finally, in the diffusion of a cultural ideology of consumerism.

The Importance of the (US) Firm

Any critique of globalisation must begin with an analysis of TNCs for it is these organisations that are 'the single most important force creating global shifts' according to Dicken (1992, p. 47) and, as the putative 'stateless' company, have become the exemplar and leitmotiv of the newly 'globalised' world economy. Despite the rhetoric, however, many remain sceptical of the extent to which such companies have emerged. Using four key measures – geographical spread and scope, ownership and control, people in the organisation and legal nationality and taxation – Hu (1992) has been at the forefront of those refuting the notion of the 'stateless' TNC, arguing that there are no global enterprises, but rather national firms with international operations. Consequently, it comes as no surprise to learn that genuinely 'stateless', global organisations are rare, perhaps 4–5 per cent of all ascribed TNCs (Dicken, 1992, p. 49).

Moreover, the geographical origin and diversity of these TNCs can be exaggerated. Ninety per cent of all TNCs are registered to just ten developed countries and most of these are from the US, Germany, Japan and Britain (Waters, 1995). Moreover, the largest of these TNCs are from the US. The *FT 500 Annual Review* (1999) demonstrates that nine out of ten of the world's top firms are American. Outside the top ten, US firms comprise 15 of the top 20 and 18 of the top 25 in the ranking. This ranking is based on market capitalisation and is not without limitations (Dickson, 1999). However, it does highlight two points: first, the pre-eminence of US companies and, secondly, the sharp decline of Japanese and emerging market country companies. In the top 500 as a whole, 244 companies are now from the US, up from 222 in 1998. Japan's number declined from 71 to 46, Hong Kong's from eleven to seven, Singapore four to one, Taiwan eight to two, while Malaysia has lost all representation. From South America, Brazil's contingent has dropped from five to two. A third point worth noting is that investors believe that US companies are at the technological 'leading edge' rather than the 'trailing edge' in comparison with companies from other countries – especially Japan.

It is more than presence that contributes to Americanisation. The hegemonic national economy will often provide 'methods of organising production and work organisation which establish standards of "best practice" argues Ferner (1994, p. 94). The 'American model' was once regarded as one such best practice. By the early twentieth century US firms were becoming more important players in the international economy, beginning to eclipse their established European competitors. As early as 1902, *The American Invaders* was signalling the US challenge with increased and increasingly successful FDI in Europe (cited in Dicken, 1986). By 1913 the US contributed 36 per cent of world industrial output compared to the UK's 14 per cent (Dicken, 1998). This rise to dominance can be attributed to US firms use of (then) leading edge manufacturing techniques or Fordism. This system involved the extensive use of machinery, the interchangablity of manufacturing machinery and parts, and the standardisation of products. The critical addition was the moving assembly line which facilitated mass production and a drastic lowering of labour costs. This American model emerged when it did as a consequence of social and institutional considerations (the public education system, less rigid craft manufacture and labour mobility) and economic factors in the US (huge national resources, and labour shortages requiring labour saving production techniques). General Motors further enhanced this system with more stringent cost accounting methods in which US accountants became 'partners in production', not merely noting outcomes but part-determining inputs – with an emphasis on 'higher output for less costs' (Williams, n.d., p. 16). During the Second World War and into the postwar period, US firms were thus in a position to exploit, by trade and with foreign direct investment, firstly the inadequacies and then the decline in European manufacturing capacity, aided of course by Marshall Aid and US government desires to create bulwarks against communism in Europe and Asia – *Pax Americana*. During this time American management methods were vigorously exported through FDI, and education and training institutions in Europe (Locke, 1996). The outcomes were European economic subordination to the US and exposure of Europe to the American model of production as best practice. In the words of Dunning (1993, pp. 10–11):

> The argument in the 1950s and early 1960s seemed to run something like this. US industry in the US is efficient; its technology, management and marketing skills are the best in the world. Therefore when a US industry goes abroad, US products, skills and production methods should follow ... From the perspective of a hegemonic power any reaction of other firms or governments to what US firms or the US government did or did not do was assumed to be of negligible significance.

US economic hegemony began to slip in the postwar period due to a number of factors, both macro and micro-economic and political: the ending of the convertibility of gold into dollars, so dismantling the 'gold standard'; the financial burden of the war in Vietnam; the 1973 oil crisis; the increased competitiveness of European firms utilising cheaper labour with relocated production in Asia; and, finally the rise of corporate Japan (Ruigrok and van Tulder, 1995). The latter has been prominent because of Japanese FDI in Europe and the US underpinned by a supposedly superior technique of production – the Japanese model of lean production or Toyotism. The American model's weaknesses were now exposed: the over-emphasis on both the financial costs of production which was subject to manipulation by organisational politics and short-term financial considerations at the expense of long-term investment (Williams, n.d). With its just-in-time rather than just-in-case stock inventory system and emphasis on flexibility and quality, for example, suddenly all countries and firms were exhorted to 'learn from Japan' and 'Japanisation' became the management buzzword of the 1980s and 1990s (see, in this respect, Womack *et al.*, 1990). The end of US economic hegemony seemed imminent. With the 'shock' of Japan, even Locke (1996) announced the death of American management as best practice.

Nevertheless, as the FT 500 indicates, US firms have bounced back and continue to dominate. Part of the reason is that US firms such as Ford have learnt from Japan and partly reconfigured their organisational structures and practices (see, for example, Starkey and McKinlay, 1994). Part of the reason is that Japanese superiority *vis-à-vis* US firms has been exaggerated by the proponents of lean production, as Williams *et al.* (1994) point out. Those proponents also failed to appreciate that the Japanese model of production incorporated and developed rather than simply obviated elements of the American model (see, for example, Warner, 1994). Another reason is that US firms appear to have rediscovered the importance of production techniques, as Fernandez with Barr (1993), demonstrate. The most obvious new such technique is business process re-engineering (BPR). Significantly, BPR is 'Made in the USA' exploiting 'the same characteristics that made Americans such great business innovators: individualism, self-reliance, a willingness to accept risk and a propensity for change.' (Hammer and Champey, 1993, p. 2) BPR seems to be the latest best practice for adoption around the world, as Peppard and Fitzgerald

(1997) demonstrate with the case of Germany (and for a more general discussion of the Americanisation of German management see also, Schlie and Warner, 2000).

World and US Economic Governance

The unfettered mobility of capital, in the form of footloose TNCs integrated by technology, leads many writers to also assert that national states are usurped by a 'borderless economy' (Omhae, 1994). Dicken (1992) has also suggested that the national state is further eroded by the development of supranational governance institutions such as the European Union (EU), United Nations, World Bank and International Monetary Fund (IMF). The TCC claimed by Sklair (1993) to now govern the world's economy comprises senior TNC management, globalising politicians and state bureaucrats as well as consumerist elites, for example individuals working in the media. With its 'global capitalist project' (ibid., p. 9) this class intends to transform the world and 'is growing stronger and is more united.' (Sklair, 1991, p. 62) Owning and controlling the means of production and ideas through its TNCs, economic governance is now no longer national or even international but a transnational process.

And yet national economic management is still both existent and desired, as Henderson (1993), Tomlinson (1993), Hutton (1995) and Porter (1990) respectively illustrate. Barnevik, the CEO of ABB, one of the oft-cited global companies, has noted the role that national governments play in his company's production location decisions: production in Germany or Italy for example, depends on the direct and indirect support received by the company from Bonn and Rome (Taylor, 1991). By noting that 'there are very few countries anywhere in the world that do not have some incentives to attract FDI', Sklair (1991, p. 62) too acknowledges residual state economic management. This management even occurs in the US and UK – the champions of the 'free market'. 'It is far from the case,' Hirst and Thompson (1995, p. 408) thus rightly conclude, 'that national economies are being subsumed in and dominated by a global economy driven by volatile and ungovernable market forces.'

If the governments of national states both desire and engage economic management, then the extent and capacity of such management by supra-national institutions must be questioned. Indeed, the usurping of national sovereignty by supra-national institutions seems more apparent than real. In reality, the national state remains a 'pivotal institution of governance within the international economy' (ibid., p. 409). Supranational institutions are not detached from national states but, instead, heavily reliant upon them. With political and financial support as well as personnel deployment, national states create, maintain and offer legitimacy for these supra-national institutions. Moreover, it is not unusual for the attitudes and actions of these institutions to be extensions of particular national government attitudes and actions.

Importantly, it is the US particularly and to a lesser extent the industrialised countries of the EU which drive the operations and policies of institutions such as the World Bank, IMF and the World Trade Organisation (WTO), as even Jeffrey Sachs (1998) acknowledges. Historically, this situation arose with the post-war desire for US internationalisation and the 'One World' concept which in reality was an attempt to create a 'US-led liberal world economic order.' (Ruigrok and van Tulder, 1995, p. 123.) This new order was formalised at Bretton Woods with the creation of the IMF and what would become the World Bank, both of which were and continue to be bank-rolled by the US. As Hoekman and Kostecki (1995) note, world trade is characterised by horse trading between national governments. Each government has its own agenda and constituents, and each differs in its level of economic power. This latter point is important because the countries of the EU, and the US more particularly, shape the policies and rules of the WTO. Japan is often regarded by these others as a country with which they must contend. It is in this light that the drive for the liberalisation of world trade should be seen: an ideology that creates a particular form of economic organisation which serves particular interests. A good example is the changes impressed upon the patent system in the Indian pharmaceutical industry by the US. Even the loopholes in multinational agreements are best exploited and even created by the more power-ful Members. The recently failed Multilateral Agreement on Investment would have bound all national states to accept investment indiscriminately but which contained exception clauses for US states. Such clauses exist, we would argue because an ambiguous agenda exists on the part of the US government to promote the free market idea with its necessary deregulation for other countries but which is to be implemented by regulation by the US government through these three pillars of world economic governance. In other words, the World Bank, WTO and IMF operate to the benefit of the US whilst claiming to be beneficial to all. As Wade (1998–99, p. 47) states:

> It is the US interest to have the rest of the world play by American rules for both international finance and multinational corporations. The goal is to make the rest of the world adopt the same arrangement of shareholder control, free labor markets, low taxes, and minimal welfare state that US corporations enjoy at home. US firms could then move more easily from place to place and com-pete against national of regional firms on a more equal basis.

This situation exists for a number of reasons; the need for the US to access the rest of the world's savings (which are larger than domestic US savings) and emerging markets (which are growing faster than the domestic US market). A very good example of the way in which the US government is prepared to flout international agreements occurred with the 'banana war' between the US and the EU, despite majority support within the WTO for the EU position (Watson, 1999). This war was effectively about the US government leveraging US firms' competitive advantage against European firms in the same sectors, and being willing and able to circumvent international agreements to do so. This incident is not isolated. The US has broken a myriad of internationally brokered trade policies (see for example the Japanese claims reported by Thompson, 1992). Although not specifically referring to the 'banana war' or any other particular incident, Ruigrok and van Tulder (1995, p. 124) seem right to argue then that even the European states are integrated into the 'game of international competition according to US rules' – as are the newer emerging national markets, such as China. As that country attempts to join the WTO and normalises its trade relations with the US to do so, the deal agreed between the two countries is 'so one-sided in favour of the US you have to pinch yourself', Hutton (2000, p. 18) wryly commented.

Undoubtedly, those people identified by Sklair (1991, 1993) as comprising a TCC do have formal and informal occasion to meet, but to suggest that they have a specified collective project is to exaggerate their coherence. National economic interests still prevail. Moreover, it must be recognised that a particular national state – the US – dominates world economic governance. As Hutton (2000, p. 18) commented succinctly recently, 'The US runs the world for its own advantage, just as any other hegemonic power would do.'

Culture, Consumerism and Americana

Sklair (1991, 1993) claims that an ideology or culture of consumerism now exists across the world's economy. Necessarily, therefore, that economy is governed by market transactions. This culture has emerged as one consequence of TNCs' ownership and control of worldwide media vehicles.

There does seem to be some evidence to support Sklair's basic premise, as consumerism becomes more pervasive. It is no secret that the General Agreement on Tariffs and Trade (GATT) and its recent transmutation, the WTO, along with the World Bank and IMF are intended to promote and implement the market system. These supra-national organisations are thus the instruments through which one ideology – capitalism and its expression in the market – is imposed on all by the more economically powerful countries. Indeed, starting at Bretton Woods, the task of the GATT and now the WTO appears to be the opening up the world's national economies to trade from the US and, to a lesser extent, industrialised Europe. It is for this reason that the management of trade between the US and EU on the one hand and the emergent economies of South East Asia on the other is likely to be the future central issue for the WTO as identified by Hoekman and Kostecki (1995).

Through trade liberalisation, privatisation and deregulation the market now pervades the economic organisation of countries in Europe, the Americas, most of Asia and increasingly Africa and the Middle East. However, the market is not abstract. Instead, 'the market' is an institution. Comprising social rules that provide for an organised pattern of action for economic actors, the market is the mechanism of co-ordination and allocation within capitalism. To date, the rules which affirm these social relations are determined by national states, either directly or indirectly through their client supra-national organisations. China's acceptance and assuming of this task has been a key condition of its membership application to the WTO.

This last point also serves to illustrate the weakness of those who move from accepting the existence of a global culture of consumerism – which has some validity – to asserting that a homogenised global market has emerged for goods and services. Even within a global culture of consumerism, consumer needs, wants and demands across the globe may continue to vary by country. In short, it is one thing to argue that the world's economic activity is becoming dominated by consumerism and market transactions and quite another to then insist that this market and its consumers are homogenised. The two phenomena should not be conflated: a domineering ideology of consumerism does not equate with a single world market. Even Ford has failed so far to produce an acceptable 'world car' and its latest attempt will still be 'tailored to local tastes' (Flint, 1994, p. 41).

Nevertheless, there are some products which are undoubtedly consumed around the world. Disney and McDonald's for example, are available to consumers in most countries and, likewise, demand for IBM laptops and Microsoft software is shared by industrial markets across the globe. However even these products, while ubiquitous, are, as with the companies which produce them, often reflective of their country of origin, either by design or default. Two points are worth raising here in relation to country of origin. Firstly, companies often draw upon the identity of their country of origin to create brand identity; Nestle and Switzerland, and Marlboro and the US offer good examples. Secondly, although there are such products from firms of countries other than the US, the most iconic are from the US. The roll-call of putatively global products, such as Coca-Cola, Pepsi-Cola, McDonald's, Levi's and GM, is dominated by the US as country-of-origin. With retail outlets sited in almost every continent, McDonald's is instructive here. Although Ritzer (1993, p. 1) maintains that McDonaldisation is 'an inexorable process … coming to dominate more and more sectors of American society as well as the rest of the world', he has also more recently acknowledged that this global reach cannot be equated with 'globalisation'; for McDonald's, in terms of product and production process, is distinctly American. In this respect, although it is ubiquitous, McDonald's offers an example not of globalisation but *Americanisation*. 'There appears to be a growing passion around the world for things American and few things reflect American culture better than McDonald's' Ritzer (1996, p. 299) suggests, citing others' statements that the company is 'a piece of America'. This argument is not new, being first aired in 1901 in Blunt's *The Americanisation of the World* (cited in Spybey, 1996) but its force is more convincing in the postwar period of US hegemony.

The domination of US products in so-called 'global markets' should surprise no-one. The *Pax Americana* of the postwar period was, and continues to be underpinned by US military and economic hegemony, as argued by Hirst and Thompson (1995). Of course there is a more nuanced argument here and one which is articulated by Waters (1995). He suggests that the so-called 'global' markets that are being created are merely those responding primarily to European culture (with its subsequent, derivative manufactured artefacts) as it expands across the world 'via settlement, colonisation and cultural mimesis' (ibid., p. 3). Thus the culture of consumerism with its emphasis on individual choice is the particular masquerading as the universal or, in marketing jargon, the local repackaged as the global. The hegemony of European culture, transmuted in North America is now being promoted by TNCs as a global culture. The storylines of Disney movies are an obvious illustration. The classic *Snow White*, adapted from the fairytales of the brothers Grimm, is one example.

These products, therefore, cannot properly or accurately be described as 'global products'. It is more fitting to describe them as 'universalised products' to indicate that they have particular locales of origin – typically Western products at least filtered through the US, if not US in origin – that are then marketed on a huge scale. As Friedman states (1999, p. 309):

> the distinction between what is globalisation and what is Americanisation may be clear to most Americans, it is not to many others around the world. In most societies people cannot distinguish anymore between American power, American exports, American cultural assaults, American cultural exports and plain vanilla globalisation. They are now all wrapped into one.

Despite pronouncements to the contrary, the US is still hegemonic in the world's economy. It is in this context that the influence of the American model in the hotel industry, to be now presented, should be perceived. Discussions of Americanisation have tended to focus on the cultural imperialism outlined above or, with reference to the diffusion and the adoption of American best practice, the manufacturing sector. The following section offers a brief history of hotel internationalisation and the emergence of the American model before going on to examine evidence of the continuing dominance of American-type practices current in the industry.

SETTING THE STANDARDS: THE INTERNATIONAL HOTEL SECTOR

Conrad Hilton is often talked of in venerable terms as the 'founder' of internationalisation in the hotel industry. Strand (1996, p. 83) suggests that Hilton 'had the vision of what we now call globalisation back in 1947, but he did not have the means to achieve such a vision because the board of directors wanted no part of it'. Nonetheless due to Hilton's pioneering spirit and his ability to persuade the board of the company to give him greater latitude (see Comfort, 1964; Hilton, 1957), the company did internationalise and Strand (1996, p. 84) further argues that 'The genesis of Hilton's – and the industry's – globalisation was a confluence of three factors, almost historic accident.' These factors being: demand and particularly the fact that the only tourists travelling in any numbers in the immediate post war period were American; the entrepreneurial spirit of Hilton; and, the availability of financing through relationships established between Hilton and host governments. Allied to these factors Nickson (1997) notes a further reason for Hilton's internationalisation, the role of his hotels as a bulwark against communism. Indeed, such an overt political rationale for internationalisation is not unusual given the contemporary prevailing political circumstances engendered by the Cold War and the need for American business to be seen as championing free enterprise against the perceived evils of communism (for a general review of this issue see Mills and Hatfield, 1999).

Hilton is, then, perhaps the best example of the American model of hotel internationalisation which Nickson (1998, 1999) argues continues to dominate the sector and provide notions of best practice. What, then, was the American model exported by Hilton, and others such as Holiday Inn, Intercontinental and Sheraton? Nickson (1998, p. 56) believes that 'companies like Hilton, Holiday Inn, Intercontinental and Sheraton were concerned with creating a, usually upmarket, home-away-from-home for American travellers, particularly business travellers'. Thus they sought to offer, in Hilton's own words, 'little Americas' which drew heavily on the certainties offered by the chains in the US (Hilton, 1957). Consequently Hilton and his fellow entrepreneurs, such as Kemmons Wilson (the founder of Holiday Inn) sought to develop for export a product based on concept standardisation to ensure operational control and guest consistency, allowing chains to make their reputation on the basis of universality, quality and consistency. This seemingly, though, was what the majority of American travellers were comfortable with in their search for the 'pseudo-event', where they could disregard the 'real' world outside (Boorstin, 1963). Urry (1990, p. 7) describes this in terms of the familiar American-style hotels providing an 'environmental bubble' which 'insulates the tourist from the strangeness of the host environment', or more prosaically '*instant America*' (Comfort, 1964, p. 231, emphasis in original).

As Nickson (1998) notes this model was one that endured in the international hotel sector for the period from the late 1940s until the mid-1980s. However changes in ownership – most obviously and iconically the acquisition of Hilton International and Holiday Inn by, respectively, the British-owned companies Ladbrokes and Bass – and a recognition of the potential limitations of standardisation as a source of competitive advantage led to much speculation on the decline of the American model. Nevertheless as Nickson (1999) argues standardisation and the creation of a home-away-from-home remains an integral part of the competitive strategies of major international hotel companies, whatever their country of origin. Thus this aspect of the American model remains alive and well. Furthermore in a more concrete sense, despite the aforementioned acquisition of several well known American companies the dominance of American chains is still apparent. Again, nine of the top ten hotel chains in the world are American (*Hotels*, 1999). (See Table 15.1.)

Moreover the shift from a concentration on the hardware of the physical product to the software and the role of people as a source of competitive advantage

Table 15.1 Top 10 hotel chains in the world

Rank	Firm	Country
1.	Cendant Corporation	US
2.	Bass Hotels	UK
3.	Best Western	US
4.	Choice Hotels International	US
5.	Marriott International	US
6.	Accor	France
7.	Starwood Hotels and Resorts	US
8.	Promus Hotel Corporation	US
9.	Hilton Hotels Corporation	US
10.	Carlson Hospitality	US

Source: HOTELS *Magazine* Corporate 300 ranking (1999). HOTELS is a Cahners Business Information Publication, a division of Reed Elsevier. (Reprinted with permission.)

could equally be seen to be still indirectly dominated by an American influence. There is still much support for the notion that the US continues to be the predominant supplier of what is considered good practice approaches to both general business practices and particularly human resource management (HRM). For example, Brewster (1995, p. 207) asserts that, 'the analyses and prescriptions laid out in the standard management textbooks are, fundamentally, drawn from one particular culture: that of the USA'. The contention is that American dominance of the international hotel sector is well established and this view is now discussed in relation to empirical material drawn from three case study organisations. It should be noted here that all of the companies are represented pseudonymously to allow for anonymity amongst interviewees.

Case Study Evidence

This section develops an analysis based on over 80 semi-structured interviews undertaken in three international hotel groups with managerial personnel, including representatives from corporate headquarters and unit-level managers throughout the world (for further details of this research, see Nickson, 1999). The first case study company is Americo which is regarded as exemplifying the established organisational form in the international hotel sector. Their approach, although more recently overlaid with a recognition of the need to customise the service encounter in response to the demands of local markets, continues to be characterised by high levels of standardisation, certainty and consistency, particularly for the American business traveller abroad. Second, evidence is drawn from interviews within the hotel operation of the French travel and tourism group Frenco, a major player across the globe with a presence in over 70 countries. The final case study organisation is Swedco, a relatively small regional player whose major strength lies within the Nordic region, with only limited coverage in other parts of Europe.

Given that Americo's interest in internationalisation is relatively recent their overall approach could be characterised as ethnocentric or even Amerocentric, reflecting the fact that a large part of their overseas hotels customer base was Americans travelling abroad. In the Americo export product the importance of brand identity continued to be significant, and consistency and certainty in the hardware, in terms of catering for the American customer, were perceived to over-ride local considerations: 'obviously in places like Jedda there are separate rules there, but the product itself, the rooms, the size of the rooms, they are designed here because our customers, 50 per cent of them are Americans, so we want them to feel at home' (general manager, American). Americo managers saw little prob-lem with attempting to disseminate the archetypal home away from home which characterised the American model of hotel internationalisation: 'respective of whether you are in Warsaw, London or downtown Washington, or whatever, it is very American, Holiday Inn were, but [Americo] are more so' (front of house manager, British). Although the company were seeking to move away from a prescriptive approach, based solely on the application of standard operating pro-cedures (SOPs), in individual units Americo still insisted that each hotel con-tained the 'core deliverables', which included a copy of *USA Today* and an American flag.

While Frenco managers were keen to differentiate the Frenco product and approach from the model established by the pioneering American chains it is clear that, in fact, the benefits of standardisation and standard operating systems were well understood within, and were a central organising principle for, Frenco. This underpinning is perhaps most apparent within the company's budget and mid-market brands:

> The fundamental characteristic of [Frenco's mid-market brand] is of interna-tional standardization of the offering. What is therefore required is consistency of the offering in every location in which it is available ... Standardization of the offering means putting into place a service delivery system that is robust enough to survive transferability across borders and generate consistent service standards to satisfy customer expectations, irrespective of local conditions or infrastructure. (Segal-Horn, 1995, p. 16)

Certainly this was a point recognised by a British front of house manager who, in response to the question of what attracted people to the mid-market brand, replied, 'standardisation, yes the concept is simplicity, the bedroom is very basic but it has got in there everything that you need' consequently 'whichever hotel you go to, people expect the same, that is the attraction.' Any minor concessions to local markets tended to be in terms of things such as regional variations in the menu in the hotel restaurant.

As with Frenco, within Swedco there was strong evidence to suggest that the physical product developed by the company drew heavily upon an approach established by the American chains, particularly in the use of concept manuals and SOPs. Thus although some managers (reflecting a similar view as Frenco managers) liked to see the company as qualitatively different from the American model-type approach, evidence suggested that this manuals driven approach was still very apparent in Swedco. Manuals had been produced to cover operational aspects of front of house, food and beverage and conference facilities. The manuals were supposed to be operative both as an overall approach and specifically applicable in departmental areas, with checklists being used for ensuring adherence to correct standards:

> Of course there are concepts for how the rooms are to look, the number of opening hours, the marketing programmes that we have to follow, there are a number of facilities in the room of course, what kind of bar, restaurant, brasserie, you should have, the lay out of the conference room, all these things. (General manager, Swedish)

In summary, in relation to the hardware, it is clear that many aspects of the standardisation, certainty and consistency which characterise the American model are still apparent within the case study organisations. Equally interesting is the extent to which a number of managers in the non-American case study organisations sought to deny the debt owed to the American model. In many respects this ambiguity illustrates the janus nature of Americanisation, as noted by authors such as McKay (1997) and Ritzer (1998, p. 71), the latter citing Kuisel's (1993, p. 3) view that 'America appeared [to the French and Europeans in general] as both a model and a menace.' Thus Americanisation becomes something to either be decried or embraced, or in the case of the case study companies, seemingly both. Indeed, this ambiguity was also apparent in terms of the software of the management style.

In relation to management style Americo were still concerned with exporting an 'American way of life' (head of the works council, Austrian) and managers had some awareness of the likelihood of this being seen as imperialistic or in pejorative terms by host countries. More recent debates about the character of the successful global company have arguably intensified the belief that the most successful companies are those who are able to, in the oft-repeated prescription, 'think globally and act locally'. This is most clearly expressed in the notion of the transnational as a company with the ability to manage across national boundaries, whilst retaining local flexibility (see, for example, Scullion, 1993). Within Americo though it is interesting to note that the espousal of transnationalism was tempered by the view that the US was perceived to be the benchmark for other countries in terms of providing an internationally acceptable management and operating style:

> What is right? What are the standards? What are the systems that are appropriate internationally and in the United States? When you are a US company you make an assumption that expectations are fairly uniform ... Now the interesting thing is, and we're still studying this, is that if a person travels to an

[Americo] in Munich, are they expecting a German hotel or a [Americo] American hotel. We still do have quite a few US travellers going abroad, because they're the ones who know the name. Now what happens when an Arab or a Chinaman or an American goes there, do they have different expectations and perceptions? Right now we seem to think that our standards are pretty good, they're fairly uniform, there are some challenges, with it, but there doesn't seem to be an overriding issue right now with other people accepting the US standard in a foreign country. (Director of service development, American)

The ethnocentrism implicit in this statement was further exemplified by the recognition by the same interviewee that in the early phase of internationalisation, host country managers were likely to be sent to the US as 'it's in their best interests, they can come over and learn our standards and take them back'. The company also used specialist 'task forces' to train within the country of operation, although the underlying rationale was still to train 'the local people in our way of doing things'. This highlights the assumption that American companies perceive their practices and systems to be 'natural' rather than constructed in or contingent upon a particular institutional framework – that of the US.

There was also evidence of Frenco utilising several HRM techniques in a similar way to Americo, and in many respects these could be considered anathema to traditional conceptions of a French management style, as described by Barsoux and Lawrence (1997) and Poirson (1993). Most obviously this was in relation to the ideas of autonomy, openness and responsibility which were held to characterise the Frenco management style and the Frenco concept of intrapreneur or in-house entrepreneur in which managers were expected to identify improvements themselves. In relation to autonomy it was though noteworthy that managers within Frenco again liked to consider the company as qualitatively different from the American chains who exemplified the American model:

It's two worlds, it's completely different. American chains are structured, fully centralised, everything comes from the top and this makes a whole difference. If you take Sheraton, Hilton, Marriott we have nothing in common, nothing. We are fully de-centralised, maximum power at the lowest level, we don't have books, they have books and they have a lot of things, if you don't know something open page 250 and find the answer. This is the American way. (Managing director of hospitality studies and training, Swiss)

An American chief concierge also suggested that Frenco's approach could be compared favourably to the more rigid American approach, which was concerned with creating 'robots' who were supposed to do as they were told. In contrast, in Frenco, 'you are completely free ... and that is one of the main ingredients that make employees loyal and productive ... they don't change your personality like some other companies.' Although this was somewhat contradictory with his later recognition that at times employees were told to say things in specific ways in interacting with the customer. Thus Frenco were perceived to have 'standards and philosophies' which provided 'guidelines' as opposed to 'rules'.

With the shift in emphasis towards the softer aspects of the product, it is noteworthy that, initially, Frenco continued to base some aspects of their operations around established business systems. An example of the continuing use of American-type practices was seen within their mid-market brand where attempts to base quality in both the hardware and the software were on the basis of what were known as the 'Frenco Bolts'. This system to monitor standard procedures was introduced into the company in 1987 and was centrally designed and centrally driven and emphasised structural elements of service. As the then managing director of the brand wrote in the introduction to the booklet outlining the 'bolts':

> In our language a 'bolt' signifies a quality requirement which contributes towards our client's loyalty to the brand. There are some 'bolts' that define your attitude to the different clients and to the service you provide, while others are more technical and concern investment. By respecting all the 'bolts' mentioned in this booklet, we will obtain the total satisfaction of our clientele.

The 'bolts' covered thirteen areas within the hotel, including elements of staff-customer interaction, these areas being: reservation, arrival/access, parking, check-in, the lobby area, bedrooms, bathroom and WC, restaurant evening, breakfast, boutique, bar, playground/swimming pool and check-out. In effect, the 'bolts' were a series of compulsory directives to staff in terms of how to set out a bedroom, lay a plate setting, welcome a guest and so on. Moreover the 'bolts' became an integral part of the induction and socialisation of all new recruits as they received the booklet as part of their orientation procedure.

Despite the view of the managing director of the company of the efficacy of this approach, within interviews, there was some disquiet amongst some managers at the attempt to codify a 'zero defects' quality approach via the 'bolts', as, in reality, it was very much like the old SOPs, as developed by the Americans, a point not lost on one French general manager:

> Yes, I don't give a damn about 'bolts', why are they there? The company has them, you just make sure you do it, but I don't think they make a big issue out of it. There is also an inspection when people come twice a year, and when I lose a point because we didn't say 'thank you for choosing [Frenco]', I don't give a damn ... that is very American, and the American way of doing things.

DISCUSSION AND IMPLICATIONS FOR PRACTICE

The earlier discussion of the importance of, in particular, the American firm and the contention for the inextricable link between culture, consumerism and Americana would seem to be supported by the sectoral overview and case study evidence.

In relation to the sector context generally, Mather and Todd (1995) recognise that a consequence of American hegemony of the early years of the international hotel industry is that even though there may have been a shift in ownership, there is, it seems, a residual and somewhat amorphous notion of American influence within such hotels:

> While some of the larger chains are no longer American in ownership – to take Holiday Inn and Intercontinental as two significant examples – many nevertheless have their roots and culture based in North America and can be regarded as American in spirit if not in fact. (Ibid., p. 54)

Indeed, they go on to suggest that, in the general public's eyes, it is unlikely there is any real awareness of who owns what, and as an example, most people would still perceive Holiday Inn and Hilton International as American. Moreover the lack of awareness of ownership of these famous names extends to academia, as Kumar (1995) exemplifies. Discussing globalisation, and particularly how it is synonymous with standardisation and homogeneity and the 'global product', he suggests we should look to the 'global marketing of McDonald's, Mickey Mouse, Dallas and Disneyland, Hilton and Holiday Inn' and just to make his point clear adds in parenthesis, 'the American provenance is of course significant' (ibid., p. 189).

More specifically the case study evidence supports the contention that much of what is considered to be good practice in the international business arena would seem to stem from American influences, as Brewster (1995), cited earlier, noted in his comments on the contents of standard management textbooks. In the 1950s, British and Scottish manufacturing were exhorted to learn from America and US FDI was encouraged to the UK in that respect. The same exhortations are still being made today. In 1999 the Institute of Directors Scotland launched a programme to 'enable Scottish firms to learn from the best American practice' (Fraser, 1999, p. 16). Now, however, the service sector and not just the manufacturing sector can learn from America. The Scottish tourist industry, for example, might learn from Disney it is suggested. The durability of the American model is certainly apparent within the international hotel sector, both in relation to the hardware and software. Therefore, despite claims as to a lessening of the competitive advantage to be derived from high levels of standardisation, it is clear from the evidence that standardisation, for example, remains an integral part of the competitive strategies of major international hotel companies, whatever their country of origin.

The interesting aspect of this finding is not so much that standardisation remains a major part of the companies' approach, rather, it lies in the perception of managers as to its desirability. In those terms the evidence did produce something of a dichotomy between Americo, and Frenco and Swedco managers. For example, Americo managers saw little problem with attempting to disseminate the archetypal home away from home that characterised the American model of hotel internationalisation. Likewise within Frenco and Swedco there was strong evidence to suggest that the physical product developed by these companies drew heavily upon an approach established by the American chains. They continued to rely to a great degree upon the business and financial systems developed by chains in the US, particularly in the use of concept manuals and SOPs. Nonetheless some managers within Frenco and Swedco liked to see their companies as qualitatively different from the American model-type approach. In a limited sense this may of course be true in the way that Frenco and Swedco also utilised obvious national signifiers to infuse their products with elements of 'Frenchness' and 'Swedishness', reflecting Mathe and Perass' (1994) view of international service organisations seeking to strive for 'exotic' or 'foreign' appeal in their product. Overall though it is clear that the underpinning approach of standardisation remains unchanging.

As was noted in the review of the importance of the US firm a key theme which would offer some explanation for the durability of American hegemony is the ability of American business to develop new techniques, such as BPR. Reflecting Schuler *et al.*'s (1993) view that the 'competitive strategy imperative' is likely to depend on the existence of a common set of needed employee role characteristics for quality improvement and a common set of human resource practices for those characteristics, the case study organisations evidenced a high degree of similarity in their approaches. Most obviously this convergence can be seen in relation to empowerment-type mechanisms, which were an integral part of the competitive strategies of all of the companies. Thus it could be suggested that the organisations exemplify Waters (1995) view that increasingly there is a recognition of a burgeoning idealisation of organisational behaviour premised on a strong corporate culture which, in turn, envisions a key role for the new cultural paradigm's symbols and tools, such as BPR, total quality management, empowerment, functional flexibility/multi-skilling, and high levels of staff training and development. In short, much of what is considered best practice traces its lineage to America.

The recognition of prevailing American dominance in business life is also likely to have significant implications for the likes of headquarters managers, subsidiary managers, policy makers and academics. As prime minister of the UK, Tony Blair has repeatedly exhorted other European political leaders to adopt American business culture arguing that its free market emphasis is superior to the of the European 'social model'. This superiority arises because, as Madeleine Albright, US Secretary of State, put it, 'Americans "see farther" because they "stand taller" (Pfaff, 2000, p. 8). Some worry however, that the Wilsonian 'benevolent hegemony' that would be said to result from American ideology, ideas and techniques dominating the world's economy is a mask for a more self-serving purpose. As Hutton (2000, p. 18) states boldly in reference to the US leverage of other countries' economies:

> it gives the lie to those who would argue that globalisation is somehow driven by the invisible hands of markets and technology. This is a self-conscious political programme with one major author who is a self-declared beneficiary – the US.

We have all become pawns in the great game of designing the world so that it befits Wall Street and Main Street ...

While Hutton is sceptical, even cynical, he is accepting of US hegemony for its Schumpterian creative and destructive tendencies, and because alternatives to it are 'retreating as globalisation spreads' (in Giddens and Hutton, 2000, p. 12). His plea however is for non-US policy makers to be able to conceptually distinguish the practical conflation of Americanisation and globalisation so that European states do not passively accept or eulogise the latter but instead make conscious choices about the appropriateness of their own models of economic organisation.

Paradoxically, this point is likely to be particularly true for American TNCs, especially those seeking to become more 'global' in their outlook. A certain reflexivity on the part of both headquarters and subsidiary managers is likely to be crucial in any attempts by TNCs to become 'global' and less tied to a national outlook. Continuing belief in the synonymity of American and 'global' standards may in reality sustain a world view which remains Amerocentric. A further issue which has been implicit throughout this analysis is the extent to which organisations' business practices, and particularly their human resource practices are becoming similar or remain distinctive. The recent collections by *The International Journal of Human Resource Management* (vol. 9, no. 4) and Rowley (1998) illustrate that the issue of convergence and divergence remains a source of interest and debate to both academics and practitioners. Generally a case for convergence can be made on the basis of several trends which are likely to drive converging tendencies, most notably: patterns of globalisation; economic integration; opening of markets; and the transference by TNCs of what is considered best practice. To date, much of this analysis has been dominated by debates within the manufacturing sector and the re-emergence of what Martin and Beaumont (1998) term 'one-best-wayism' – perhaps best illustrated by the lean production literature. However, within the service sector this literature remains relatively sparse. Consequently, there is scope for further research to consider two key questions. First, to what extent can converging tendencies still be considered American? Secondly, is the American dominance of the hotel sector described in this chapter apparent in other industries within the service sector and, indeed, more generally across the whole range of the manufacturing sector?

CONCLUSION

This chapter had two aims; firstly, through critique of the global economy, to affirm the residual importance of the US and Americanisation within the international economy and, secondly, to illustrate this residual importance by reference to the hotel sector. We have examined claims that a global economy has now emerged and sought to evaluate such claims by reference to the empirical evidence, drawn from secondary and then primary sources. Such evidence strongly indicates that an international, rather than a global economy still exists. National states continue to matter, as does the relationship between states and firms. US firms still dominate this international economy, as do their products and practices. Likewise, US national economic management is central to the governance of the world's economy. Of course, presence alone does not establish dominance. The American model and US government influence is underpinned by a pervasive ideology, diffused by the US through the main institutions of world economic governance. Similarly, the ideas and techniques of the American model are again dominating the organisational structures and practices of other firms. Those who prosecute the globalisation thesis therefore lack both an understanding of the developments and an appreciation of the empirical data. The international economy remains strongly shaped by America – firms and government – and Americanness in terms of ideology, ideas and techniques, so that it is still premature to talk of the end of US economic hegemony.

Despite its dominance, that American ideology, ideas and techniques are diffused and adopted elsewhere within the international economy is an issue to be tested empirically. We have gone some way to address this issue with the research presented here on the international hotel sector which, it was argued, exemplifies continuing American dominance in terms, again, of ideas and techniques. The high level of standardisation of the physical product has long been recognised as an essential part of the success of the American-driven internationalisation process in the hotel sector in the period to the early 1980s and it is clear from the evidence that international hotel companies will continue to see standardisation of the physical product as a central feature of their internationalisation strategies. Thus, in relation to the hardware, the American model of internationalisation established by the early international chains continues to provide many of the key organising principles and the decline and demise of the model is exaggerated. In relation to the software, the key finding is that the self-perception of Americo managers of the company becoming more transnational is within the framework of American standards being seen as synonymous with global standards. Equally, claims as to the distinctiveness of management style in Frenco and Swedco seem spurious when much of their approach could be considered as drawing on notions of good practice HRM, which in turn traces its origins to the US (see for example, Guest, 1990). As with BPR, this latter author suggests that HRM arose in the US as a response to the changing political and economic climate of the 1980s, and became popular because it reinforced existing American managerial values.

The description of American hegemony should not be surprising given the economic strength, and political and cultural influence of America. No doubt there will be continuing debate as to whether the influence represents a menace or a model, but to deny American dominance of the international economy, and business ideology, ideas and techniques is premature.

16 A Survey-based Investigation of the Determinants of FDI in Portugal

Peter J. Buckley and Francisco B. Castro[1]

INTRODUCTION

A long established recipient of FDI, Portugal has all the characteristics of a small open economy of recent industrialisation. In 1960 Portugal became a member of EFTA and industrialisation was finally made a policy objective putting an end to several decades of restrictions to foreign and domestic investment. EFTA membership represented a radical change in the country's geopolitical orientation. For the first time in its 850 years as an independent nation, Portugal was engaged in a process of integration in Europe. The collapse of economic relations with Africa after the independence of the colonies, in 1975, only consolidated this trend.

FDI flows can also be said to be characteristic of a recently industrialised nation, albeit one fast approaching a stage of development close to that of the most developed countries (Buckley and Castro, 1998a). During the 1960s and early 1970s, FDI inflows averaged 0.5/0.6 per cent of GDP, but were reduced to about half that value in the years that followed the 1974 democratic revolution. They picked up again after 1980, to reach the highest values ever in the late 1980s and early 1990s (Figure 16.1). Membership of the European Union, in 1986, certainly helps to explain this evolution.

In recent years, however, the flows decreased sharply and in 1999 registered the lowest level since the 1950s. The average flows of the 1990s were much lower than those in other countries of similar or smaller size, such as The Netherlands, Belgium, Ireland or Sweden (OECD, 1997). Buckley and Castro (1998b, c) suggested that the end of the cold war was part of the explanation. Portugal lost much of its attractiveness as a low cost location, which may have been amplified by its small domestic market if compared with some of the emerging markets in Central and Eastern Europe.

Given that this chapter is centred on manufacturing and commercial firms, it is important to add a brief note on the industry distribution of FDI. According to Banco de Portugal (1998b, p. 28), the manufacturing industries represented in 1996 about one third of the stock of inward FDI in Portugal, while commerce was

226

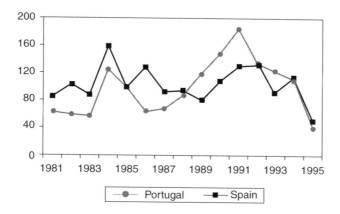

Figure 16.1   Inward FDI flows, 1965–99 (% of GDP)

Source: Own calculations based on Banco de Portugal (1997a, b, 2000a various).

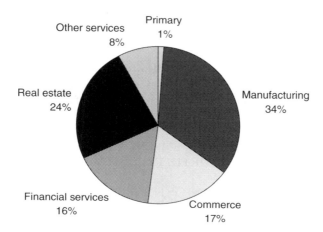

Figure 16.2   Stock of inward FDI in Portugal, 1996

Source: Banco de Portugal (1998b).

responsible for a further 17 per cent. The primary sector represented no more than 1 per cent (Figure 16.2).

In terms of the distribution of the stock of manufacturing FDI (Figure 16.3), transport equipment and electric machinery concentrated, in 1996, respectively, 19 per cent and 17 per cent of the stock of manufacturing FDI in Portugal. Forest products, chemicals, and food and beverages were the other industries with a share above 10 per cent. This distribution confirms that inward FDI is in Portugal essentially concentrated in capital intensive industries. Gonçalves and Guimarães

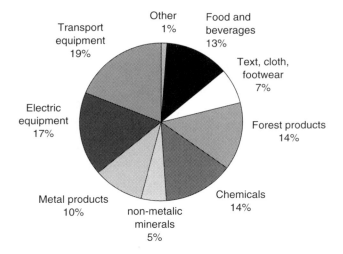

Figure 16.3   Stock of manufacturing FDI in Portugal, 1996

Source: Banco de Portugal (1998b).

(1996, p. 10) compared this with the distribution of domestic investment (more concentrated in labour intensive industries) to conclude that FDI has been an important contributor to the diversification of the local industrial structure.

BRIEF SURVEY OF PREVIOUS EMPIRICAL RESEARCH
ON THE DETERMINANTS OF FDI IN PORTUGAL

In the first study ever published of FDI in Portugal, Matos (1973) identified several reasons why foreign firms chose to invest in Portugal. Access to the local market was considered the most relevant. The size of the market did not make it very attractive, but after investing in more promising markets, expansion to Portugal and other small markets could be considered a logical step for any MNE. Access to the markets of Angola and Mozambique, then Portuguese colonies, was also a motivation for some industries.

   Low wages and access to natural resources were other determinants of FDI. Portugal was at the time (and to a certain extent remains today) in an intermediary position in terms of production costs. Wages were in the early 1970s five to seven times lower than in the most developed countries (Matos, 1973). But the quality of the labour force and infrastructure were superior to those of developing countries. Natural resources, mining, tourism, and forest products were examples of sectors where Portugal seemed to have a comparative advantage. Other determinants of FDI listed by Matos (1973) were the access to the market of other EFTA members, low interest rates, and low corporate and personal income taxes. The last two vanished in the crises that marked the 1970s.

Taveira (1984) used regression analysis to test the determinants of FDI in Portugal. She also concluded that market related variables were more important than those associated with production costs or natural resources. Other significant determinants were the level of concentration of the industry, government intervention (a negative influence), and quantitative barriers to trade. When only the export-oriented industries were being analysed, however, production costs were a relevant determinant. Nevertheless, market related variables remained highly significant. This suggests that access to the local market played a role even in the case of FDI that was apparently export-oriented.

Fontoura (1995) also found little relevance of labour costs with an econometric model that used aggregate FDI flows in 1991/1992. She claimed that Morais (1993) obtained similar results with a different methodology. Labour skills, however, were found by Fontoura (1995) to be significant in that period. With a survey of 37 firms, Santos (1997) found both labour costs and access to the local market critical determinants of FDI in Portugal. Other relevant variables were the international image of Portugal, labour skills, stability and proximity.

Finally, Buckley and Castro (1998b) found market related variables to be the most strongly associated with inward FDI in Portugal between 1980 and 1995. But labour costs were also significant, as was a dummy variable for the aftermath fall of the Berlin Wall.

METHOD, POPULATION AND SAMPLE

A major limitation of existing studies of the determinants of FDI in Portugal was the data used. Not only it was of poor quality as it was limiting in terms of the disaggregation available. The use of alternative methods of data collection was, therefore, highly advisable. In order to obtain the information at the firm level a questionnaire was devised and distributed to the subsidiaries of foreign firms operating in Portugal. Appendix A presents the section of the questionnaire relevant for this paper.[2]

The population for this study was defined as comprising the subsidiaries of foreign firms operating in Portugal in manufacturing (including the agro-industries) and commercial activities. A number of sources were used to identify the population: the National Institute of Statistics (INE), the Institute for Foreign Trade and Investment (ICEP), national chambers of industry and commerce operating in Portugal, and assorted publications by leading business newspapers and magazines.

Due to the poor quality of some of the databases obtained, firms were selected if: (a) they were not known to have less than 50 per cent of foreign capital; and (b) they were not known to have less than 10 employees. The latter was a pragmatic criteria: it generated a sample of 1517 firms, which was considered viable on the face of the resources available. As a result of the way the sample was selected, as many as 253 firms were excluded during the field work period. They should have not been included in the population.[3] The field work was conducted between June and October 1998. It produced 237 valid questionnaires,[4] which represented 18.8 per cent of the adjusted sample.

BRIEF DESCRIPTION OF THE SAMPLE

The sample distribution per industry is presented in Figure 16. 4. Given the way the sample was obtained, it can be expected to reflect the distribution of the stock of inward FDI in Portugal. But the representativeness of the sample is difficult to assert. Bank of Portugal's data (see the first section of this chapter) is not directly comparable because the average size of firms in different industries can be expected to vary substantially.

Most firms in the sample were very recent (Figure 16.5). Over two-thirds were created or acquired after Portugal joined the (then) EEC, in 1986. This largely translates the evolution of FDI in Portugal (see the section). However, the most recent years may be expected to be over-represented in the sample. Older firms still operating in Portugal are the ones that survived the changes in the Portuguese and international markets, the evolution of relative costs across the world, and the transformations in the structure, competitiveness and strategy of the parent companies. The most recent firms, on the hand, were not yet submitted to the sieve of time.

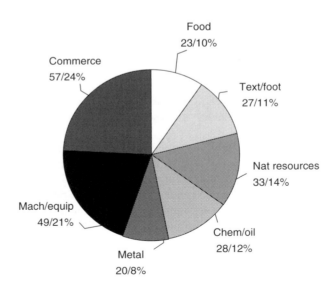

Figure 16.4   Distribution of the sample per industry

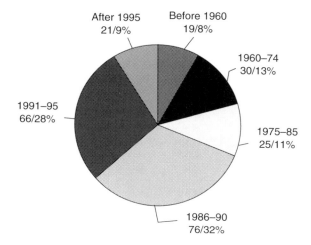

Figure 16.5   Distribution of the sample per year of investment

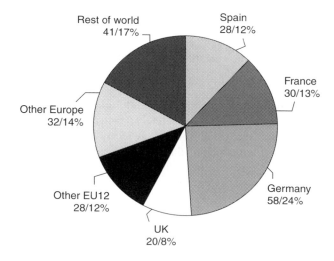

Figure 16.6   Distribution of the sample per country of origin

In terms of country of origin (Figure 16.6), Germany alone accounted for 24 per cent of all firms in the sample. Overall, Germany is only the fifth foreign investor in Portugal, but German investment is largely concentrated on manufacturing industries (Simões, 1989; Câmara de Comércio e Indústria Luso-Alemã, 1996). Henceforth, the importance of German investors in the sample was likely to represent the country's true weight in the Portuguese economy when services

Determinants of FDI in Portugal

Table 16.1   Country of origin versus year of investment

Country		Before 1975	1975–85	1986–90	1991–98	Total	Mean
Spain	no.	3	2	10	13	28	1987
	%	10.7	7.1	35.7	46.4	100.0	
France	no.	8	3	9	10	30	1981
	%	26.7	10.0	30.0	33.3	100.0	
Germany	no.	13	5	18	22	58	1984
	%	22.4	8.6	31.0	37.9	100.0	
UK	no.	6	2	4	8	20	1963
	%	30.0	10.0	20.0	40.0	100.0	
Other EU12	no.	8	4	8	8	28	1980
	%	28.6	14.3	28.6	28.6	100.0	
Other Europe	no.	4	3	9	16	32	1987
	%	12.5	9.4	28.1	50.0	100.0	
Rest of the world	no.	7	6	18	10	41	1984
	%	17.1	14.6	43.9	24.4	100.0	
Total	no.	49	25	76	87	237	1982
	%	20.7	10.5	32.1	36.7	100.0	

are excluded. France, Spain, the UK and the US were the other countries with a significant representation in the sample. With the exception of Spain, the only country with a border with Portugal, these are the main foreign investors worldwide. Only Japanese firms, with a negligible presence in Portugal, were absent from this list.

The confrontation between the country of origin and the year of investment (Table 16.1) revealed a more or less predictable pattern. Spanish subsidiaries were younger than the average, which shows how recent the phenomenon of economic integration in the Iberian peninsula is. Other recent investors in Portugal were the non-EU12 European countries (which included the three most recent EU members), who seem to have 'discovered' Portugal in 1986. The older firms in the sample were those from the UK, Portugal's main economic partner until 1974. But even in this case two in five investments took place in the 1990s.

Table 16.2 presents the industry distribution for different countries of origin. One immediate observation was the weight of machinery and equipment manufacturing in the investment by non-European, German, and French firms. This translated those countries' worldwide position in the sector. However, the inability of Portugal to attract Japanese investors was here particularly apparent. Despite being Japanese many of the biggest machinery and equipment producers in the world, few of the non-European investors in the sample were from Japan (most were from the US). The fact that all the other dominant powers in those industries were well represented in the sample only made the absence more noticeable.

Among the remaining industries, textiles, clothing and footwear were particularly important for German and non-EU12 European investors (of which Switzerland

Table 16.2 Country of origin per industry

Country		Food and beverage	Text, cloth, footwear	Natural resources	Chemicals and oil	Metal industries	Machinery + equip.	Commerce	Total
Spain	no.	4		6	1	4	4	9	28
	%	14.3		21.4	3.6	14.3	14.3	32.1	100.0
France	no.	5	3	5	3	3	7	4	30
	%	16.7	10.0	16.7	10.0	10.0	23.3	13.3	100.0
Germany	no.	1	11	4	8	4	16	14	58
	%	1.7	19.0	6.9	13.8	6.9	27.6	24.1	100.0
UK	no.	2	3	6	2	1	1	5	20
	%	10.0	15.0	30.0	10.0	5.0	5.0	25.0	100.0
Other EU12	no.	8	2	3	4	3	4	4	28
	%	28.6	7.1	10.7	14.3	10.7	14.3	14.3	100.0
Other Europe	no.	1	6	8	4	3	3	7	32
	%	3.1	18.8	25.0	12.5	9.4	9.4	21.9	100.0
Rest of the world	no.	2	2	1	6	2	15	13	41
	%	4.9	4.9	2.4	14.6	4.9	36.6	31.7	100.0
Total	no.	23	27	33	28	20	50	56	237
	%	9.7	11.4	13.9	11.8	8.4	21.1	23.6	100.0

Table 16.3   Turnover and employment: descriptive statistics

Descriptive Statistics		Turnover 1997 (million PTE)	Labour Force 1997
Mean		7 918	304
Std deviation		19 403	795
Minimum		0	2
Maximum		160 000	7 455
Percentiles	25%	560	30
	50%	1 678	98
	75%	6 901	267

represented a substantial proportion). The percentage assumed by the food industries in the investment by 'other EU12 countries' was to a big extent due to Dutch
firms. Finally, the high percentage of commercial subsidiaries among Spanish firms
probably reflects geographic proximity. In many industries it is perfectly possible
to supply efficiently the whole Iberian market from one single productive location
(Buckley and Castro, 1999). However, non-European firms also included a big
percentage of purely commercial subsidiaries, which seems contradictory.

In terms of turnover and number of employees the sample was quite diversified
(Table 16.3). Turnover ranged from nil, corresponding to five firms that only
started operations in 1998, to 160 billion PTE. Over half the firms in the sample
had a turnover above 1.6 billion PTE, and one quarter above 6.9 billion PTE. As
for the number of employees, the sample reflects the small scale of firms operating in Portugal. The median was 98 employees, and one quarter of the firms in
the sample had a labour force of no more than 30.

THE DETERMINANTS OF INWARD FDI IN PORTUGAL

Introduction

Regarding the determinants of foreign direct investment in Portugal, the participants in the survey were confronted with two different but inter-related questions.
First, they were asked to classify 32 potential determinants using a 5-point Likert
scale, where 1 corresponded to irrelevant and 5 to very important. Next, the
participants were required to, out of the same 32 determinants, single out the one
they considered the most important reason for their firm to have invested in
Portugal (see Appendix A). Table 16.4 summarises the results. Because the differences between manufacturing and commercial firms were substantial, two separate lists were produced.

In the case of manufacturing firms (Table 16.4a), five determinants were
rated well above all the others. However, the reduction of labour costs was unques-
tionably the top answer – it presented the highest mean in the Likert scale and was

Table 16. 4 Why invest in Portugal

Rank	Reason	Mean[1]	Main reason[2]	
			N	%
(a) Manufacturing firms				
1	Reduction of labour costs	3.49	41	25.8
2	Increase group's turnover	3.10	11	6.9
3	Economic stability	3.08	1	0.6
4	Political stability	3.07	1	0.6
5	Quality of labour force	3.02	5	3.1
6	Reaction to competitors	2.59	1	0.6
7	Market expected growth	2.55	8	5.0
8	Competition home market	2.51	2	1.3
9	Transport costs	2.50	2	1.3
10	Portugal's image	2.43	0	0.0
11	Public incentives	2.42	8	5.0
12	Follow customers	2.33	13	8.2
13	Local firm for sale	2.32	15	9.4
14	Establish sales network	2.32	11	6.9
15	Market diversification	2.23	0	0.0
16	European Single Market	2.19	0	0.0
17	Local infrastructure	2.11	1	0.6
18	EU market	2.10	4	2.5
19	Quality of local cluster	2.10	3	1.9
20	Market size	2.01	2	1.3
21	Cultural proximity	1.97	0	0.0
22	Invitation	1.96	6	3.8
23	Geographic proximity	1.95	3	1.9
24	Complementarity locals	1.87	1	0.6
25	Reduce depend. agents	1.84	0	0.0
26	Access natural resources	1.82	8	5.0
27	International experience	1.68	1	0.6
28	Acquire technology	1.66	1	0.6
29	Avoid barriers	1.65	2	1.3
30	Reduce depend. suppliers	1.61	1	0.6
31	Inefficiency of agents	1.55	1	0.6
32	Inefficiency of suppliers	1.29	0	0.0
(b) Commercial firms				
1	Establish sales network	3.71	14	29.8
2	Increase group's turnover	3.38	10	21.3
3	Follow customers	3.31	3	6.4
4	Market expected growth	3.24	2	4.3
5	Economic stability	3.11	1	2.1
6	Political stability	3.07	0	0.0
7	Market diversification	2.82	2	4.3
8	Reaction to competitors	2.81	1	2.1
9	Reduce depend. agents	2.76	1	2.1
10	Market size	2.59	2	4.3

Table 16.4   (Continued)

Rank	Reason	Mean[1]	Main reason[2]	
			N	%
11	Portugal's image	2.58	1	2.1
12	Competition home market	2.33	0	0.0
13	Inefficiency local agents	2.26	0	0.0
14	International experience	2.24	0	0.0
15	Quality of labour force	2.08	0	0.0
16	Geographic proximity	2.06	1	2.1
17	European Single Market	2.04	0	0.0
18	Reduction of labour costs	1.98	1	2.1
19	Quality of local cluster	1.93	0	0.0
20	Local firm on sale	1.91	4	8.5
21	Complementarity locals	1.91	1	2.1
22	Invitation	1.85	1	2.1
23	Cultural proximity	1.83	1	2.1
24	Local infrastructure	1.82	0	0.0
25	EU market	1.74	0	0.0
26	Reduce depend. suppliers	1.72	0	0.0
27	Inefficiency of suppliers	1.63	0	0.0
28	Acquire technology	1.57	0	0.0
29	Transport costs	1.53	0	0.0
30	Public incentives	1.53	0	0.0
31	Avoid barriers	1.47	0	0.0
32	Access natural resources	1.24	0	0.0

Notes:
[1] Mean of a scale that ranged from 1 (irrelevant) to 5 (very important).
[2] Number of respondents that chose it as the 'most important reason to have invested in Portugal'.

chosen as the most important reason by over one quarter of the respondents. The quality of the labour force was also among the top five determinants, but it was chosen as the main reason by only three per cent of the participants. It seems that the location decision was mainly a response to labour costs, the quality of the labour being relevant but secondary.

The second most important determinant in terms of the overall mean was to increase the group's turnover. It was considered the top reason by 7 per cent of the respondents. This should be no surprise. It simply translates the notion that internationalisation is a special case of the growth of the firm (Buckley, 1993).

Economic and political stability were the other top determinants. Although econometric tests normally fail to find any association between stability and FDI inflows, survey-based studies tend to show political and economic stability to be at the top of managers' concerns (see Chase *et al.*, 1988, for a survey). Tu and

Schive (1995) and Akhtar (1999) used both approaches and found that political and economic stability were ranked highly by the surveyed managers *despite* not being significant determinants in parallel econometric models.

The explanation for this contradiction when different methodologies are adopted has to do with what is exactly being tested in each case. Econometric tests investigate the relationship between the magnitude of the variables. However, as we argued before (Buckley and Castro, 1998c, 1999), only when risk is very high political and economic stability can be expected to affect foreign investment. Once a certain level of stability is attained, the impact on FDI will be minimal. That is, stability is a precondition for FDI, but has little relationship with the volume of investment (Tu and Schive, 1995).

This is precisely what is suggested in Table 16.4. Despite the high mean of political and economic stability in terms of the Likert-scale, very few managers considered these determinants the main reason to have invested in the Portugal. For most managers, these were highly valued characteristics of the country, probably a precondition for their decision. But other determinants were more decisive to the location choice. Interestingly, there was a group of variables in the opposite situation: their overall rating was low but they were pointed out as the main reason by a substantial number of firms. These included the existence of a local firm on sale (10 per cent), to follow customers (8 per cent), to establish a distribution network (7 per cent), and access to natural resources (5 per cent).

As for purely commercial subsidiaries (Table 16.4b), the establishment of a distribution network was, not surprisingly, the main reason to invest in Portugal. Not only its mean was well above all the others, as it was singled out as the main reason by 32 per cent of the participants. It was followed by the need to increase the group's turnover (chosen as the main reason in 23 per cent of the responses), to follow customers, and market growth. As above, economic and political stability were among the top reasons but were rarely chosen as the main reason to invest in Portugal. Another similarity with manufacturing firms was that the existence of a local firm on sale was the main determinant of investment for 9 per cent of the commercial subsidiaries. But in overall terms its influence was mild.

The Determinants of Inward FDI in Portugal

Despite these preliminary conclusions, the analysis of the determinants of FDI was seriously hampered by the high number of variables involved. This called for the use of data reduction techniques, such as factor analysis (Hair *et al.*, 1998, p. 90). Factor analysis permits to reduce the number of dimensions to be used in further tests, simplifying the investigation. Normally, it implies the loss of some information, since the new factors do not fully represent the original variables. In this case, however, the aim was not to create new variables based on the factor loadings. Factor analysis was simply a tool to investigate the way the variables were grouped by the respondents.

The number of factors to extract was a difficult choice. Two common criteria are to select the factors with an eigenvalue above unity or to base the decision on the observation of the scree plot (Hair *et al.*, 1998). This suggested nine and eight factors, respectively However, factor cohesion was particularly critical for this study. If they were to represent the determinants of FDI in Portugal, the factors needed to be consistent with existing theory. The representativeness of the factors extracted (total variance explained) was of secondary importance but not irrelevant. Taking all these elements into account, the decision was to extract 10 factors, which accounted for more than two thirds of total variance. With fewer factors some individually relevant determinants were combined, making the analysis confusing. With more factors the theoretical interpretation of some of the determinants was difficult.

It turned out, however, that the behaviour of 'transport costs' had little in common with any of the factors in the analysis. It presented a low communality and dispersed factor loadings irrespectively of the number of factors extracted. This does not necessarily mean that transport costs were irrelevant. Table 16.4 showed they were important for some firms, in particular in manufacturing. Nonetheless, the association with any of the factors (factor 2 in this case) was spurious and an alternative model, without transportation costs, was adopted.

Interestingly enough, this new model differed very little from the original one. The ten factors extracted were exactly the same that were obtained before, with the obvious absence of transportation costs. These factors constitute a theoretically consistent list of the determinants of foreign direct investment in Portugal (Table 16.5). They include location determinants (stability, local market, labour conditions, proximity), internalisation determinants (upstream and downstream integration, market diversification) and strategy determinants (home conditions, passive expansion). However, before they could be used in a more detailed the analysis, some adjustments were needed.

It was particularly interesting that public incentives were consistently associated with labour costs and skills. This suggests that public incentives have attracted to Portugal essentially efficiency seeking FDI and will be further exploited in a later section. However, if the aim is to investigate the relevance of labour conditions as a determinant of FDI the variable public incentives cannot be associated with labour quality and costs. A similar reasoning applies to the variable 'to increase the group's turnover'. Its association with the local market is easy to understand. It is only reasonable to admit that the host country's market size and growth are important variables when (market) growth is a major motivation for internationalisation. But the variable cannot be part of a proxy for the importance of the local market in attracting inward FDI. Henceforth, both 'public incentives' and 'to increase the group turnover' were excluded from the analysis that follows (the tables associated with this new model can be found in Appendix B).

The importance of the new determinants was assessed by computing the mean of the respective variables (cf. Table 16.4). Like the original ones, these new variables had a minimum of 1 (when all the variables of the determinant had received

Table 16.5   Factors (determinants) associated with investment in Portugal

Factor	Variables included	Factor	Variables included
Political and economic stability	Political stability Economic stability International image	EU market	Access to the EU market Reaction to European Single Market Need to avoid barriers
Upstream Integration	Acquisition of technology Reaction to suppliers' inefficiency Access to natural resources	Labour conditions	Reduction of labour costs Quality of labour force
	Reduce dependency on suppliers Local cluster Local infrastructure	Geographic and cultural proximity	Geographic proximity Cultural proximity Invitation
Downstream Integration	Reduce dependency on agents Reaction to agents' inefficiency Establishment distribution network Following customers	Passive expansion Market diversification	Local firm for sale Search complementarity with locals Market diversification Acquisition international experience
Local market	Market growth Market size	Home conditions	Increased competition at home Reaction to competitors' move

the lowest rating in the Likert-scale) and a maximum of 5 (when all received the top rating). Table 16.6 presents the ranking of the ten determinants. The respective means can be found inside brackets in the first line.

As was already mentioned in the preliminary analysis, there were marked differences between commercial and manufacturing firms. For the former, downstream integration – the internalisation of the sales function (Buckley and Casson, 1976) – was the main motivation. It was followed by access to the local market, economic and political stability, and the competitive conditions at home. Market diversification was also relatively important for purely commercial subsidiaries.

As for manufacturing FDI, labour conditions and economic and political stability were clearly the dominant determinants. Competition in the home country, access to the local market, and downstream integration were next in importance. This combination of determinants confirms the duality of motivations (efficiency seeking and market seeking) suggested in the previous chapter. The differences between industries, however, were more important than it is apparent in Table 16.6. The analysis of the determinants' mean for each industry presents a more clear picture. Table 16.7 shows that labour conditions and stability were

Table 16.6 Rank of the determinants of investment in Portugal: all firms and per industry

Determinants of FDI Industry	Labour condit.	Stability	Compe- tition	Local market	Down- stream	Market divers.	Passive expan.	EU market	Proxi- mity	Up- stream
All firms	1 (2.87)*	2 (2.81)	3 (2.54)	4 (2.39)	5 (2.25)	6 (2.05)	7 (1.95)	8 (1.90)	9 (1.88)	10 (1.72)
Food, beverages (20)	1	4	7	2	3	6	5	10	9	8
Text, cloth, foot. (20)	1	2	3	5	10	9	8	4	7	6
Natural resources (19)	3	2	1	4	5	6	8	10	7	9
Chemicals and oil (23)	4	1	2	3	5	7	6	8	10	9
Metal industries (17)	1	3	2	4	7	9	5	8	6	10
Machinery/equip. (42)	1	2	3	5	9	6	8	4	7	10
All manufact. (141)	1	2	3	4	5	7	6	8	9	10
Commerce (39)	7	3	4	2	1	5	8	9	6	10

Notes: *Figures in parentheses are the mean of a scale that ranged from 1 (irrelevant) to 5 (very important).

even more important for textiles, clothing and footwear, and for machinery and equipment (the most export-oriented industries) than for the other industries in the sample. Access to the EU market was also above the average in these industries, being in both cases the fourth most important determinant. The local market, on the other hand, was much less important in these industries than in any other group of firms, and downstream integration was completely irrelevant.

There was, nevertheless, an important difference between the two groups of firms. In the case of machinery and equipment, labour and stability can almost be considered the only relevant determinants. There was a very big difference for the next two determinants (competition and EU market). In textiles, clothing and footwear, however, competition was only slightly less important than stability, well above the EU market. In both cases we are in the presence of efficiency seeking FDI. But the 'push' factors seemed to be very different. The competitive conditions in the home country were critical in the decision of textiles, clothing and footwear producers to invest in Portugal, a politically and economically stable low cost location that is part of the European Union. Machinery and equipment manufacturing are more global industries in which the competitive conditions are at a different level.

Naturally, this analysis at the industry level hides differences in terms of the strategies of individual firms. These differences are due to firm specific characteristics, but also to the fact that the industries are not completely homogeneous. Figure 16.7 shows very clearly that most firms in textiles, clothing and footwear and in machinery and equipment fell in the fourth quadrant. This corresponds to an above average rating of the labour conditions and a below average rating of the importance of local market. In other words, their investment can be classified as efficiency seeking.

When local market was replaced with downstream integration (Figure 16.8), however, almost all firms in these export oriented industries fell in quadrant 4. This suggests that the location determinants were more important than internalisation. Even when the local market was an important determinant of FDI, to internalise the sales function was not a priority. As for the presence of firms from other industries in quadrant 4 of Figure 16.7, it conveys that there are export oriented segments (or individual strategies) in all industries. As an example, all firms in the oil and chemicals group in these conditions were manufacturers of plastic products.

The differences between textiles, clothing and footwear, and machinery and equipment were mentioned above and are illustrated in Figure 16.9. Almost all textiles, clothing and footwear producers appear in quadrant 2. Most machinery and equipment manufacturers are represented in quadrant 4. The difference corresponds to the role of the home country competitive conditions in the decision to invest in Portugal. Figure 16.9 also shows that textiles, clothing and footwear represent a much more homogeneous group than machinery and equipment.

The comparison of the determinants of investment in Portugal according to the country of origin is presented in Table 16.8. As could be expected, the biggest differences were found in the assessment of cultural and geographic proximity. This was the second most important determinant for Spanish firms, only behind

Table 16.7 The determinants of investment in Portugal per industry: mean values

Determinants of FDI	Labour condit.	Stability	Compe- tition	Local market	Down- stream	Market divers.	Passive expan.	EU market	Proxi- mity	Up- stream
Food, beverages	3.1	2.3	2.2	2.5	2.4	2.3	2.3	2.0	2.0	2.1
Text, cloth, footwear	3.9	3.0	2.9	1.9	1.5	1.6	1.6	2.1	1.7	1.8
Natural resources	2.4	2.7	2.8	2.3	2.3	2.3	2.1	1.7	2.2	1.8
Chemicals and oil	2.8	2.9	2.8	2.8	2.5	2.2	2.2	1.9	1.7	1.8
Metal industries	3.0	2.5	2.6	2.4	1.9	1.4	2.2	1.7	2.0	1.3
Machinery/equip.	3.5	3.0	2.2	1.9	1.7	1.9	1.8	2.1	1.8	1.7
All manufacturing	3.2	2.8	2.5	2.3	2.0	1.9	2.0	1.9	1.9	1.8
Commerce	1.8	2.9	2.5	2.9	3.1	2.4	1.8	1.8	1.8	1.6

Note: Mean of a scale that ranged from 1 (irrelevant) to 5 (very important).

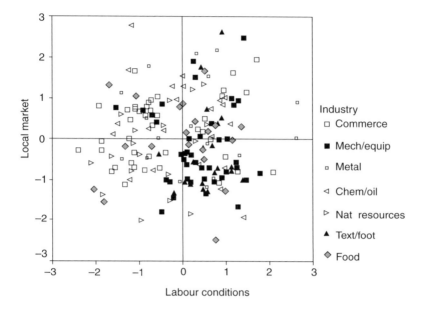

Figure 16.7   Labour conditions versus local market

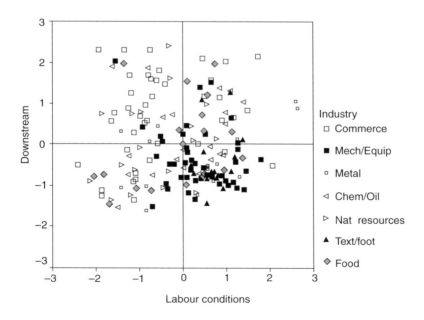

Figure 16.8   Labour conditions versus downstream

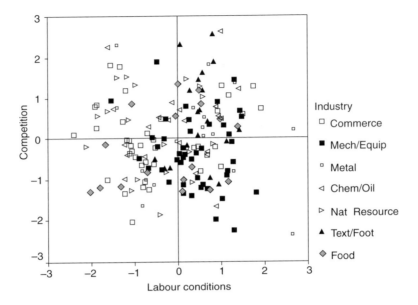

Figure 16.9   Labour conditions versus competition

the conditions in the local market. It was also relevant for French and Italian firms (included in 'other EU12'), but irrelevant for all the others.[5] Also very much predictable was that access to the EU market was more important for firms from outside the Union.

According to Table 16.8, Spanish firms were essentially market seekers. This was the only source country for which local market was the main determinant. Labour conditions, on the other hand, were of relatively little importance. As for UK investors, they differed from the rest of the sample in the role of downstream integration. The UK was until 1974 the main trading partner of Portugal. This position is now less relevant, but the results obtained seem to translate a deeper involvement of British firms in Portugal, which over the years may have internalised their operations, replacing exports with FDI.

It should be noted, however, that the groups obtained using the firms' country of origin were very heterogeneous in terms of their motivations. Much more so than in the case of industries. That probably explains why so few differences were found in Table 16.8. The only determinants that seem to be country specific are those with geopolitical connections: proximity and access to the EU market.

Not many differences in the determinants of FDI can be attributed to the size of the subsidiaries (Table 16.9). In fact, the differences found reflect no more than different market orientations (Figure 16.10). Smaller firms (fewer than 50 employees) were particularly concerned with the conditions in the local market and with the sales function (downstream integration). For bigger firms the main determinant of FDI in Portugal was labour conditions. Rather interestingly, the

Table 16.8 Rank of the determinants of investment in Portugal per country of origin

Determinants of FDI country	Labour condit.	Stability	Compe-tition	Local market	Down-stream	Market divers.	Passive expan.	EU market	Proxi-mity	Up-stream
All firms	1	2	3	4	5	6	7	8	9	10
Spain (21)	6	4	3	1	5	7	8	10	2	9
France (24)	3	1	2	5	6	8	7	10	4	9
Germany (48)	1	2	3	5	4	6	8	7	10	9
UK (16)	2=	2=	5	4	1	6	8	10	9	8
Other EU12 (19)	1	2	6	5	9	7	4	8	3	10
Other Europe (21)	1	3	2	4	7	8	5	6	10	9
Rest of the world (31)	2	1	3	4	6	8	8	5	10	9

Table 16.9 Rank of the determinants of investment in Portugal for firms of different sizes

Determinants of FDI labour force	Labour condit.	Stability	Competition	Local market	Down-stream	Market divers.	Passive expan.	EU market	Proximity	Up-stream
All firms	1	2	3	4	5	6	7	8	9	10
Less than 20 (31)	9	3	4	2	1	5	8	7	6	10
21 to 50 (28)	5	2	1	3	4	6	7	9	10	8
51 to 100 (30)	1	2	3	4	7	10	6	5	9	8
101 to 200 (34)	1	2	3	4	6	5	7	9	8	10
201 to 500 (32)	1	2	3	4	7	5	6	9	8	10
More than 500 (25)	1	2	3	5	10	6	7	4	8	9

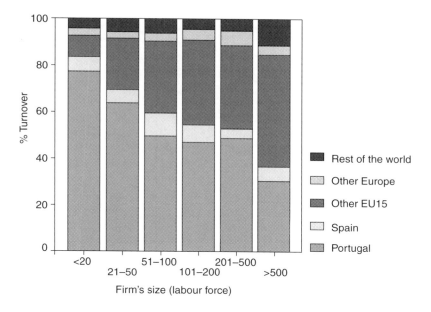

Figure 16.10   Market distribution versus firm's size

importance of the local market and downstream integration decreased linearly with the size of the firm, while labour conditions registered a linear increase with size (all statistically significant at 10 per cent).

The differences in the determinants of FDI that could be associated with the year of investment were particularly interesting. Table 16.10 suggests that two periods in Portugal's recent history saw efficiency seeking being replaced by market seeking as the main motivation of inward FDI in Portugal. The first was the decade that followed the 1974 revolution, which also corresponds to a major economic crisis worldwide. The second was the period after 1995, which somehow seems to consolidate the trend of the first half of the 1990s. The latter is particularly worrying. It confirms that the recent decrease of inward FDI in Portugal (see section 1) affected in particular efficiency seeking FDI. This is further confirmed by the decreasing importance of competition as a determinant of FDI. Foreign investors seem to be searching in other locations the solution for stronger competition in the domestic market.

At face value, this trend is not necessarily negative for the Portuguese economy. Economic development and the resulting higher production costs tend to reduce countries' ability to attract these footloose investments. However, this evolution should translate into a growing importance of internalisation variables over localisation (Dunning, 1981). In terms of the determinants identified here, that would mean a growing importance of downstream and upstream integration, which was not the case.

Table 16.10 Rank of the determinants of investment in Portugal per year of first investment

Determinants of FDI year of investment	Labour condit.	Stability	Compe-tition	Local market	Down-stream	Market divers.	Passive expan.	EU market	Proxi-mity	Up-stream
All firms	1	2	3	4	5	6	7	8	9	10
Before 1960 (11)	3	1	2	5	4	9	7	10	6	8
1960 to 1974 (25)	1	2	3	4	6	5	7	8	9	10
1975 to 1985 (15)	4	1	3	2	5	6	10	8	7	9
1986 to 1990 (58)	1	2	3	4	5=	7	5=	8	9	10
1991 to 1995 (51)	2	1	4	3	5	6	7	8	9	10
After 1995 (20)	4	1	5	2	3	7	10	8	6	9

ALTERNATIVE LOCATIONS

The decision to invest in a foreign country should normally involve the consideration of alternative locations. In the sample, however, only 42 per cent of the respondents (88 firms) claimed to have analysed other locations before investing in Portugal. Most of these, however, considered more than one alternative. Eastern Europe and Spain were the most common alternatives considered (46 and 44 firms, respectively), followed by the most developed EU members (considered by 40 of the respondents). Ireland and Greece were an hypothesis for a much smaller number firms (Table 16.11).

In general, the European locations were positively correlated, which suggests they were frequently considered simultaneously. The exception was the correlation coefficient (Spearmans's rho) between Spain and Eastern Europe, which was negative and statistically significant at 10 per cent. That is, Spain and Eastern Europe did not seem to be, in general, alternatives to each other. Finally, non European locations were positively correlated with Eastern Europe and negatively with Spain. But the level of statistical significance of these relationships was rather low, impeding further speculation.

The differences in the ranking of the determinants of FDI between firms that considered alternative locations and those that only considered Portugal for their investment were less marked than anticipated (Table 16.12). Nevertheless, labour conditions and EU market were much more important for firms that considered alternative locations than for those that did not. The opposite was true for local market and downstream integration. This suggests that efficiency seeking investment was more common among firms that considered alternative locations, and market-seeking among those that did not. But the two types of investment coexisted in both groups.

Table 16.11 Alternative locations

		Strong alternative	Considered	Total
Eastern Europe	no.	33	13	46
	%	72	28	100
Spain	no.	35	9	44
	%	80	20	100
Ireland	no.	10	8	18
	%	56	44	100
Greece	no.	6	9	15
	%	40	60	100
Other EU	no.	24	15	39
	%	62	38	100
Other locations	no.	13	12	25
	%	52	48	100

250

Table 16.12 Rank of the determinants of investment in Portugal

Determinants of FDI	Labour condit.	Stability	Competition	Local market	Down-stream	Market divers.	Passive expan.	EU market	Proxi-mity	Up-stream
No alternative location considered	2 (2.58)	1 (2.76)	4 (2.51)	3 (2.54)	9 (1.74)	6 (2.14)	5 (2.50)	7 (2.00)	8 (1.96)	10 (1.71)
Alternative location considered	1 (3.36)	2 (2.93)	3 (2.61)	4= (2.21)	4= (2.21)	6 (1.99)	7 (1.96)	8 (1.92)	9 (1.76)	10 (1.75)
Spain considered	1 (3.04)	2 (3.02)	4 (2.51)	3 (2.53)	5 (2.21)	7 (2.14)	6 (2.19)	8 (2.06)	9 (1.74)	10 (1.72)
Eastern Europe considered	1 (3.61)	2 (3.16)	3 (2.83)	5 (2.29)	4 (2.39)	6 (2.22)	9 (1.84)	7 (2.11)	10 (1.69)	8 (1.92)

Note: Figures in parentheses are the mean of a scale that ranged from 1 (irrelevant) to 5 (very important).

Equally surprising was that only small differences were found in the determinants associated with firms that considered Spain as the alternative location and those that considered Eastern Europe (Table 16.12). The suspicion was that efficiency-seeking investment should be more common when Eastern Europe was the main alternative, and market-seeking investment dominant when the main alternative was Spain. However, the evidence to support this was weak. Firms that considered Eastern Europe the main alternative location did rate labour conditions higher and local market and downstream integration lower than those that considered Spain. But this is far from conclusive evidence.

PUBLIC INCENTIVES AND THE ROLE OF THE GOVERNMENT

It was seen above that, as a determinant of FDI, public incentives were consistently associated with labour costs and skills. This was interpreted as evidence that they have attracted essentially efficiency seeking FDI – projects that exploited the Portuguese relatively low labour costs but reasonable labour skills. This idea was reinforced by the fact that public incentives were especially valued as a determinant of investment by the export-oriented industries: textiles, clothing and footwear, and machinery and equipment. In the sectors most oriented towards the local market, on the other hand, (commerce and chemicals and oil), public incentives were completely irrelevant. Furthermore, there was a linear positive relationship (statistically significant at 1 per cent) between the importance of public incentives and firm size (no statistically significant differences were found when the firms were grouped by country of origin or year of investment).

These characteristics reflect very much the public policies towards FDI, particularly concerned with attracting big industrial projects with a stronger impact on employment and on the public opinion. The official website of ICEP, the institution responsible for promoting Portugal as a location of FDI, is very clear about what Portugal can offer to foreign investors. 'Imagine a country with the lowest labour costs in Europe (...). Add to this a stable political environment (...) and low criminality' (ICEP, 2000).

As many as 38 per cent of the manufacturing firms in the sample that accepted examining this topic in more detail reported having received public incentives in their investment in Portugal. The figure was especially high in machinery and equipment, where 55 per cent of the subsidiaries received some sort of public support. On the other hand, in the natural resources-based industries only one in five firms were supported by the local authorities (Figure 16.11). Since foreign investment qualifies for support of the European Union's structural funds, the especial incidence of public support in the most recently created firms should be expected (Figure 16.12).

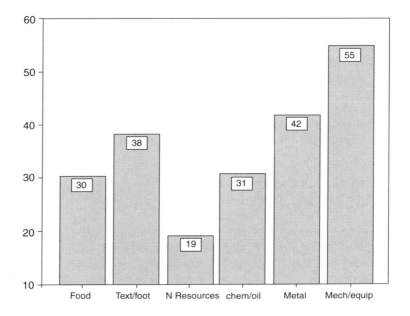

Figure 16.11   Percentage of firms that received public incentives, per industry

Despite the number of projects that received public support, only 11 per cent of the respondents claimed that without public incentives they would have not invested in Portugal. 54 per cent would have invested less than they did, but in 35 per cent of the cases public support was no more than a bonus for the investors: they claimed that the investment would have been exactly the same even without public incentives. Government intervention was, however, more important than these figures suggest. At least that is the inference that can be made of the opinion of the biggest firms (with more than 500 employees). One third would not have invested in Portugal without incentives, and a further half would have invested but on a smaller scale.

The need for government intervention was, nevertheless, felt much more strongly at a different level. When inquired about the main problems faced in Portugal, the managers that participated in the survey gave especial emphasis to bureaucracy and the legal system and to a shortage of skilled workers.[6] Both problems correspond to institutional failures. The failure to promote and efficient legal environment, and the failure to create advanced assets that may compensate rising production costs. Successive governments seemed to have been aware of these difficulties. Investment on education and vocational training increased substantially in the last two decades, supported by the European Union structural funds. However, the dramatic fall of inward FDI in recent years suggests that not enough has been done yet.

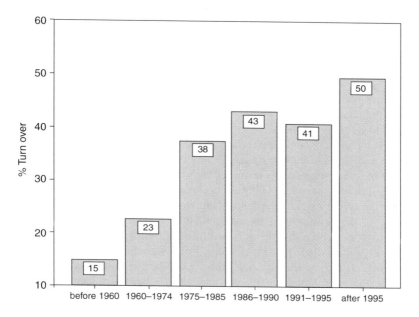

Figure 16.12   Percentage of firms that received public incentives, per year of investment

CONCLUSION

Previous work on the determinants of FDI in Portugal (Matos, 1973; Taveira, 1984; Simões, 1985; Buckley and Castro, 1998b) suggested a dichotomy of motivations. Investment in export oriented industries aimed to exploit Portugal's low labour costs and privileged access to some of the most developed markets in Europe. However, the dominant motivation seemed to be access to the local market; when aggregated data was analysed the relevance of labour costs was eclipsed by market related variables.

Past research has, however, been limited by the poor quality of the data available and the deficient disaggregation in terms of industries and countries of origin. This firm level study overcomes that problem by using a questionnaire survey of 237 manufacturing and commercial foreign subsidiaries established in Portugal. The respondents' evaluation of a number of potential reasons to invest in Portugal permitted to identify ten determinants of FDI, a list that is a combination of location variables with internalisation determinants and push factors.

The dominant motivations were, for the manufacturing industries, labour costs and skills, political end economic stability, competition in the home country, and access to the local market. However, the determinants associated with the most export oriented industries (textiles, clothing and footwear, and machinery and equipment) were substantially distinct from the others. Firms in these industries saw Portugal as a stable low cost location with easy access to the EU markets. Nonetheless, it was possible to confirm Simões (1985) distinction between 'traditional' and 'modern' labour intensive industries. The former were especially sensitive to the competitive conditions in the home country, while the latter were more responsive to the global competitive conditions.

In the remaining manufacturing industries and in commerce market access was the dominant motivation. However, in all the manufacturing industries there seemed to be export oriented segments (e.g. fabricated plastic goods in the chemicals and oil industries) or at least strategies of individual firms. An attempt to aggregate the subjects using cluster analysis produced fairly poor results. The clusters showed little homogeneity in terms of the industries represented in each cluster, which certainly constitutes an interesting element to be exploited in future research.

The country of origin of the investing firm was much less relevant than the industry in the definition of the determinants of FDI. Geographic and cultural proximity was, expectedly, the only determinant clearly country-related. The surprise was probably that proximity seemed to induce market seeking investment, rather than efficiency seeking FDI. However, the explanation may lay simply on the fact that the countries more engaged in the latter, notably Germany, Switzerland, the Nordic countries, are all rather 'distant' from Portugal.

Eastern Europe and Spain were, according to the participants in the study, the locations more likely to compete for foreign investments with Portugal. The two seemed to compete for different projects, but the evidence was not clear in terms of the expected differences despite hints that Spain was more commonly a competing location when market access was the main motivation, while Eastern Europe was more often considered in the case of efficiency seeking FDI. The fact that the investigation did not cover firms that did not choose Portugal restricted the analysis.

Finally, the bigger firms in the sample considered that public incentives were of uttermost importance for their decision to invest in Portugal. Among smaller firms, however, the opinion was that incentives had little impact upon the investment decision. There was, nevertheless, a generalised concern with the difficulties created by bureaucracy and the unavailability of skilled workers. The sharp fall of inward FDI in Portugal in the past decade suggests that not enough has been done to overcome these problems.

Notes

1. This research was partially financed by Programa Parxis XXI, Fundação para a Ciência e Tecnologia.
2. The full questionnaire is available from the authors on request. For their suggestions in the elaboration of the questionnaire, we are indebted to a number of people: Vitor Corado Simões (ISEG, Universidade Técnica de Lisboa), Vasco Rodrigues and Leonor Sopas (Universidade Católica do Porto) and Ana Teresa Tavares (University of Reading and Faculdade de Economia do Porto). The formats were supplied by Madalena Araújo (Universidade Católica do Porto).

3. Many of these firms had ceased operations in Portugal. Others had merged or changed their name, and had been contacted twice. In others the foreign participation had been sold to Portuguese investors.
4. Of the 257 questionnaires received, 19 could not be used, either for not being correctly filled in or because they corresponded to firms that, contrary to the information previously available, did not meet all the criteria for sample selection. One questionnaire was excluded during the data analysis because several of the answers were strongly inconsistent.
5. Brazilian companies also ranked this determinant very high, but they were too few to exert a significant influence over their group's mean.
6. This is particularly ironic since ICEP (2000) publicises Portugal as 'a flexible economy with little bureaucracy and low taxes'.

Appendix A   Foreign firms' questionnaire

Table 16A.1   Sample of the questionnaire (page 3)

1. REASONS TO INVEST IN PORTUGAL: What was the influence of each of the following elements in the decision to invest in Portugal [1 – *irrelevant* ... 5 – *very important*]?

1. Size of the Portuguese market	1	2	3	4	5
2. Expected growth of the Portuguese market	1	2	3	4	5
3. To increase the Group's turnover	1	2	3	4	5
4. To establish/acquire your own distribution network	1	2	3	4	5
5. Follow-up of customers in their entry into the Portuguese market	1	2	3	4	5
6. Reaction to competitors' move	1	2	3	4	5
7. Increased competition in the home market	1	2	3	4	5
8. Need to reduce dependency from sales agents	1	2	3	4	5
9. Need to reduce dependency from suppliers	1	2	3	4	5
10. Reaction to the inefficiency of sales agents	1	2	3	4	5
11. Reaction to suppliers' inefficiency	1	2	3	4	5
12. Need to reduce risk through market diversification	1	2	3	4	5
13. Reduction of labour costs	1	2	3	4	5
14. Quality of labour force	1	2	3	4	5
15. Transportation costs	1	2	3	4	5
16. Access to natural resources	1	2	3	4	5

17. Need to avoid tariff or non-tariff barriers	1	2	3	4	5
18. Quality of local infrastructure	1	2	3	4	5
19. Quality/density of the Portuguese *cluster* relevant to the firm	1	2	3	4	5
20. Acquisition of technology/catch up with technological developments	1	2	3	4	5
21. Search for complementarity with local partners	1	2	3	4	5
22. Acquisition of international experience	1	2	3	4	5
23. Good opportunity to buy local firm	1	2	3	4	5
24. Invitation/suggestion of Portuguese individual or firm	1	2	3	4	5
25. Easier access to the European Union market	1	2	3	4	5
26. Reaction to the new conditions set by the European Single Market	1	2	3	4	5
27. Public incentives to foreign investment in Portugal	1	2	3	4	5
28. Cultural proximity between Portugal and the home country	1	2	3	4	5
29. Geographical proximity between Portugal and the home country	1	2	3	4	5
30. Economic stability in Portugal	1	2	3	4	5
31. Political stability in Portugal	1	2	3	4	5
32. International image of Portugal	1	2	3	4	5
33. Other	1	2	3	4	5

- Which of the previous elements would you single out as the most important?

2. DID THE FIRM CONSIDER ALTERNATIVE LOCATIONS BEFORE INVESTING IN PORTUGAL?

No [ ]   Yes [ ]

1.	Spain	1	2	3
2.	Ireland	1	2	3
3.	Greece	1	2	3
4.	Other European Union countries	1	2	3
5.	Eastern European countries	1	2	3
6.	Other	1	2	3

[1 – *not considered*; 2 – *considered*; 3 – *strong alternative*]

Appendix B   The Determinants of FDI

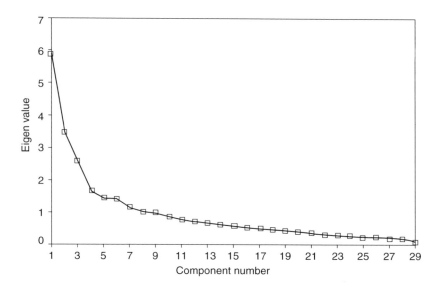

Figure 16B.1   Scree plot

258

Table 16B.1 Factors' loadings, rotated component matrix

	Component									
	1	*2*	*3*	*4*	*5*	*6*	*7*	*8*	*9*	*10*
Political stability	**.904**	−.014	.001	.084	.071	.052	.160	.083	.075	.044
Economic stability	**.885**	−.015	−.007	.103	.079	.163	.159	.080	.065	.043
International image	**.791**	.119	.127	−.014	.073	.203	−.063	.153	−.040	.128
Acquiring technology	.050	**.722**	.036	.159	.013	.071	.081	.132	.086	.227
Access natural resources	−.117	**.662**	.052	−.204	.099	.225	.128	−.091	.155	−.085
Inefficiency suppliers	−.003	**.652**	.261	.010	.076	−.082	.331	.200	.155	−.037
Local cluster	.326	**.633**	.011	.252	.183	−.073	−.231	−.129	.063	.056
Local infrastructure	.461	**.553**	−.111	.057	.196	.008	−.122	.153	.027	.175
Reduce depend. suppliers	−.126	**.546**	.314	−.044	.080	−.094	.398	.344	.046	.116
Reduce depend. agents	.015	.176	**.841**	.015	.078	−.073	.066	−.100	−.039	.127
Inefficiency agents	−.005	.178	**.779**	.056	.049	.023	.039	−.055	.096	.095
Establish network	.056	−.047	**.698**	.301	−.020	.162	.093	−.180	−.032	.035
Follow customers	.058	−.180	**.594**	.466	−.067	−.048	.144	.000	.083	−.046
Market growth	.122	.067	.166	**.831**	−.007	.110	.055	−.128	.042	.043
Market size	.027	.099	.170	**.825**	.039	−.004	.055	−.143	.036	.122
EU market	.043	.089	−.032	.015	**.822**	.061	.128	.106	−.001	.028
ESM	.209	.128	.168	.041	**.703**	.270	−.126	.202	.166	.047
Avoid barriers	.111	.178	.010	−.067	**.612**	−.205	.376	−.060	.192	.059
Geographic proximity	.187	.042	.109	.018	−.006	**.874**	−.013	.002	.005	.075
Cultural proximity	.168	.049	−.088	.076	.121	**.786**	.207	.018	.092	.037
Market diversification	.282	.094	.216	.098	.031	.089	**.673**	−.108	−.067	.095
International experience	.010	.116	.045	.104	.248	.210	**.630**	.028	.178	.233
Reduction labour costs	.113	.064	−.235	−.229	.064	.016	−.059	**.835**	−.056	.073
Quality of labour	.347	.170	−.128	−.108	.198	.025	.016	**.727**	.016	.121
Invitation	.088	.011	.062	.089	.337	−.024	.122	−.044	**.754**	.121
Local firm on sale	.024	.200	−.030	−.073	−.111	.064	−.132	−.050	**.701**	−.040
Complementarity locals	−.010	.331	.091	.211	.139	.152	.325	.119	**.588**	.246
Competition at home	.091	.095	.038	.014	.110	.153	.137	.087	−.060	**.818**
Reaction to competitors	.146	.088	.223	.162	−.024	−.054	.099	.077	.200	**.694**

Note: Rotation Method: Varimax with Kaiser Normalisation. Rotation converged in 14 iterations.

Bibliography

Aaby, N. and S.F. Slater (1989) 'Management influences on export performance: a review of the empirical literature 1978–1988', *International Marketing Review*, 6(4), 7–23.

Ahlstrand, B. (1988) *The Quest for Productivity* (Cambridge: Cambridge University Press).

Akhtar, M. Hanif (1999) 'Foreign direct investment in Pakistan,' unpublished PhD thesis, University of Leeds.

Aldrich, H. and C. Zimmer (1986) 'Entrepreneurship through Social Networks', in D. Sexton and R. Smilor (eds), *The Art and Science of Entrepreneurship* (Cambridge, Mass.: Ballinger).

Amin, A., D. Bradley, J. Howells, J. Tomaney and C. Gentle (1994) 'Regional Incentives and the Quality of Mobile Investments in the Less Favoured Regions of the EC', *Progress in Planning*, 41(1).

Andersen, O. (1993) 'On the internationalisation process of firms: a critical analysis', *Journal of International Business Studies*, 24(2), 209–31.

Anderson, P. (1999) 'Local external influence on SME export marketing activity in Marshallian districts: an investigation of the Danish Furniture Industry', paper presented at the EIBA Meeting, Manchester.

Andersson, U. and C. Pahlberg (1997) 'Subsidiary influence and strategic behaviour in MNCs: an empirical study', *International Business Review*, 6(3), 319–34.

Andersson, U. and M. Forsgren (1996) 'Subsidiary embeddedness and control in the multinational corporation', *International Business Review*, 5(5), 425–46.

Andersson, U. and M. Forsgren (1998) 'In search of the centre of excellence: network embeddedness and subsidiary roles in MNCs', paper presented at the Academy of International Business (AIB) Conference, Vienna.

Angelides, M.C. (1997) 'Implementing the internet for business: a global marketing opportunity', *International Journal of Information Management*, 17(6), 405–19.

Arthur, W.B. (1990) 'Silicon valley locational clusters: do increasing returns imply monopoly?', *Mathematical Social Sciences*, 19, 235–51.

Axelsson, B. and G. Easton (1992) *Industrial Networks – A New View of Reality* (London: Routledge).

Badaracco, J. (1991) *The Knowledge Link: How Firms Compete Through Strategic Alliances* (Boston: Harvard Business School Press).

Baker, W.E. (1994) *Networking Smart: How to Build Relationships for Personal and Organizational Success* (New York: McGraw-Hill).

Baker, W.E. (1999) 'Building social capital as an organisational competence', *Financial Times*, 22 November.

Baldauf, S. (1970) *Ulkomaisten ja Monikansallisten Yritysten Innovaatiovaikutukset Suomessa* (Innovative Impact of Foreign and Multinational Firms in Finland), FIBO publications no. 14 (Helsinki: Helsinki School of Economics Press).

Baldauf, S., S. Kulkki and L. Ranta (1984) *Ulkomaisten Teollisten Tytaryritysten Divestoinnit* (Divestments of Foreign Industrial Subsidiaries). FIBO publications no. 25 (Helsinki: Helsinki School of Economics Press).

Banco de Portugal (1997a) *Séries Longas para a Economia Portuguesa – Pós II Guerra Mundial*, Volume I – Séries Estatísticas (Lisbon: Banco de Portugal).

Banco de Portugal (1997b), *Boletim Estatístico*, March (Lisbon: Banco de Portugal).

Banco de Portugal (2000a), *Boletim Estatístico*, January (Lisbon: Banco de Portugal).

Banco de Portugal (various years) *Relatório e Contas* (Lisbon: Banco de Portugal).
Baptista, R. (1996) 'Industrial Clusters and Technological Innovation', *Business Strategy Review*, 7(2), 59–64.
Baptista, R. (1998) 'Clusters, Innovation, and Growth: A survey of the literature', in G.M. Peter Swann, Martha Prevezer, and David Stout (eds), *The Dynamics of Industrial Clustering – International Comparisons in Computing and Biotechnology* (Oxford: Oxford University Press).
Barbosa de Melo, J.P. (1995) 'Identificação de um Distrito Industrial na Marinha Grande', *Cadernos Regionais do INE*, 2.
Barheim, K. and C. Heimer (1998) *ABB The Dancing Giant* (London: Pitman).
Barry, F. and J. Bradley (1997) 'FDI and Trade: The Irish Host-Country Experience', *Economic Journal*, 107, November, 1798–1811.
Barsoux, J. and P. Lawrence (1997) *French Management: Elitism in Action* (London: Cassell).
Bartlett, C.A. and S. Ghoshal (1986) 'Tap your subsidiaries for global reach', *Harvard Business Review*, November–December, 87–94.
Bartlett, C. and S. Ghoshal (1989) *Managing Across Borders: The Transnational Solution* (Boston: Harvard Business School Press).
Bartlett, C. and S. Ghoshal (1990) 'Managing innovations in the transnational corporation', in C. Bartlett, Y. Doz, and G. Hedlund (eds), *Managing the Global Firm* (London: Routledge).
Bartlett, C.A. and S. Ghoshal (1995) *Transnational Management,* 2nd edition (Chicago: Irwin).
Bartlett, C.A. and S. Ghoshal (1993) 'Beyond the M-form: toward a managerial theory of the firm', *Strategic Management Journal*, 14, 23–46.
Behrman, J.N. (1984) *Industrial Policies: International Restructuring and Transnationals* (Lexington, Mass: Lexington Books).
Bélanger J. and Y.-P. St. Laurent (1998) *Équipes de Travail et Activités de Gestion: Étude Empirique à L'Usine Laterrière* (Québec: Université Laval).
Bélanger, J. and M. Dumas (1998) 'Teamworking and internal labor markets: observation in a Canadian aluminium smelter', *Economic and Industrial Democracy*, 13, 3.
Bélanger, J., C. Berggren, T. Björkman and C. Köhler (eds) (1999) *Being Local Worldwide*: *ABB and the Challenge of Global Management* (Ithaca: ILR Press).
Bell, J. (1995) 'The internationalisation of small computer software firms – a further challenge to 'stage' theories', *European Journal of Marketing*, 29(8), 60–75.
Bell, J. and S. Young (1998) 'Towards an integrative framework of the internationalisation of the firm', in G. Hooley, R. Loveridge and D. Wilson (eds), *Internationalisation: Process, Context and Markets* (London: Macmillan).
Bell, J.D. Crick and S. Young (1998) 'A holistic perspective on small firm growth and internationalisation', in C.C.J.M. Millar and C.J. Choi (eds), *25th Annual Conference – Academy of International Business Volume 1* (London: City University Business School).
Bellak, C. (1997) 'The contribution of the restructuring of (large Western) MNCs to the catching up of (small Eastern) countries', *Development and International Cooperation*, 13, 181–216.
Benito, G. and L. Welch (1997) 'De-internationalization', *Management International Review,* 37(2), 7–25.
Bennett, R. (1997) 'Export marketing and the internet – experiences of web site use and perceptions of export barriers among UK businesses', *International Marketing Review*, 14(5), 324–44.
Bilkey, W. and G. Tesar (1977) 'The export behaviour of smaller Wisconsin manufacturing firms,' *Journal of International Business Studies*, 8, 93–8.

Bilkey, W.J. and G. Tesar (1977) 'Attempting integration of the literature; the export behavior of firms', *Journal of International Business Studies*, Spring/Summer, 33–46.

Birkinshaw, J. (1988a) 'Foreign-owned subsidiaries and regional development: The case of Sweden', in J. Birkinshaw and N. Hood (eds), *Multinational Corporate Evolution and Subsidiary Development* (London: Macmillan).

Birkinshaw, J. (1996) 'How multinational subsidiary mandates are gained and lost', *Journal of International Business Studies*, 27(3), 467–495.

Birkinshaw, J. (1997) 'Entrepreneurship in Multinational Corporations: The Characteristics of Subsidiary Initiatives', *Strategic Management Journal*, 18(3), 207–29.

Birkinshaw, J. (1998b) 'Corporate entrepreneurship in network organizations: How subsidiary initiative drives internal market efficiency', *European Management Journal*, 16(3), 355–64.

Birkinshaw, J. and A. Morrison (1995) 'Configurations of strategy and structure in subsidiaries of multinational corporations', *Journal of International Business Studies*, 26(4), 769–94.

Birkinshaw, J. and J. Ridderstrale (1999) 'Fighting the corporate immune system: a process study of subsidiary initiatives in multinational corporations', *International Business Review*, 8(2), 1149–80.

Birkinshaw, J. and N. Hood (1997) 'An empirical study of development processes in foreign-owned subsidiaries in Canada and Scotland', *Management International Review*, 37(4), 339–64.

Birkinshaw, J. and N. Hood (1998a) 'Introduction and overview', in J. Birkinshaw and N. Hood (eds), *Multinational Corporate Evolution and Subsidiary Development* (London: Macmillan).

Birkinshaw, J. and N. Hood (1998b) 'Multinational subsidiary evolution: capability and charter change in foreign-owned subsidiary companies', *Academy of Management Review*, 23(4), 773–95.

Birkinshaw, J. and N. Hood (eds) (1998c) *Multinational Corporate Evolution and Subsidiary Development* (London: Macmillan).

Birkinshaw, J., N. Hood and S. Johnsson (1998) 'Building firm-specific advantages in multinational corporations: the role of subsidiary initiative', *Strategic Management Journal*, 19(3), 221–41.

Birkinshaw, J., N. Hood and S. Jonsson (1998) 'Subsidiary initiative in multinational corporations', *Strategic Management Journal*, 19(3), 221–41.

Blankenburg, D. and J. Johanson (1992) 'Managing Network Connections in International Business' *Scandinavian International Business Review*, 1(1), 5–19.

Bloodgood, J.M., H.J. Sapienza and J.G. Almeida (1996) 'The internationalization of new high-potential U.S. ventures: antecedents and outcomes', *Entrepreneurship: Theory & Practice*, 20, 61–76.

Bonaccorsi, A. (1992) 'On the relationship between firm size and export intensity', *Journal of International Business Studies*, 23(4), 605–35.

Boorstin, D. (1963) *The Image or What Happened to the American Dream* (London: Penguin).

Bower, J. (1970) *Managing the Resource Allocation Process* (Homewood: Richard D. Irwin).

Brewster, C. (1995) 'National culture and international management', in S. Tyson (ed.), *Strategic Prospects for Human Resource Management* (London: IPD).

Brewster, C. and A. Hegewisch (1994) 'Human resource management in Europe: issues and opportunities', in C. Brewster and A. Hegewisch (eds), *Policy and Practice in European Human Resource Management* (London: Routledge).

Brock, J.K.-U. (2000) 'ICS and the Small Firm', in S. Carter and D. Jones-Evans (eds), *Enterprise and Small Business: Principles, Practice and Policy* (London: Addison-Wesley Longman).

Brooke, M. and L. Remmers (1978) *The Strategy of Multinational Entreprise* (London: Pitman).
Brooks, M.R. and P.J. Rosson (1982) 'A Study of export behaviour of small and medium sized manufacturing firms in three Canadian provinces', in M.R. Czinkota and G. Tesar (eds), *Export Management: an International Context* (New York: Praeger Publishers).
Brown, S. (1989) 'Retail Location Theory: The legacy of Harold Hotelling', *Journal of Retailing*, 65(4), Winter, 450–70.
Buckley, P.J. and M. Casson (1976) *The Future of the Multinational Enterprise* (London: Macmillan).
Buckley, J. Peter and Francisco B. Castro (1998a) 'The investment development path: the case of Portugal', *Transnational Corporations*, 7(1), 1–15.
Buckley, J. Peter and Francisco B. Castro (1998b) 'A time-series analysis of the locational determinants of FDI in Portugal', paper presented at the 25th Annual Conference of the Academy of International Business, Vienna, October.
Buckley, J. Peter and Francisco B. Castro (1998c) 'The locational determinants of FDI in the European periphery', paper presented at the 24th Annual Conference of the European International Business Academy, Jerusalem, December.
Buckley, J. Peter and Francisco B. Castro (1999) 'Outward FDI in Manufacturing from Portugal: internationalisation strategies from a new foreign investor', paper presented at the 25th Annual Conference of the European International Business Academy, Manchester, UK, December.
Buckley, P.J. (1996) 'The role of management in international business theory: a meta-analysis and integration of the literature on international business and international management', *Management International Review*, 36 (Special Issue I), 7–53.
Buckley, P.J. and M. Casson (1998) 'Models of the multinational enterprise', *Journal of International Business Studies*, 29(1), 21–44.
Buckley, Peter J. (1993) 'Barriers to Internationalization', in L. Zan, S. Zambon and A. Pettigrew (eds), *Perspectives on Strategic Change* (Dordrecht Kluwer Academic Publishers); reprinted in Peter J. Buckley, *Foreign Direct Investment and Multinational Enterprises* (London: Macmillan, 1995), pp. 17–37.
Burgel, O. and G.C. Murray (1998) 'The International Activities of British Start-Up companies in High-Technology Industries: differences between Internationalisers and Non-Internationalisers', *Frontiers of Entrepreneurship Research*, 449–64.
Burgelman, R. (1983) 'A Model of the Interaction of Strategic Behaviour, Corporate Context, and the Concept of Strategy', *Academy of Management Review*, 8(1), 61–70.
Burgelman, R. (1991) 'Intraorganisational ecology of strategy making and organisational adaptation: theory and field research', *Organisational Science*, 2(3), 239–62.
Burgelman, R. (1994) 'Fading memories: A process theory of strategic business exit in dynamic environments', *Administrative Science Quarterly*, 39(1), 24–55
Burgess, J., R. Green, D. MacDonald and S. Ryan (1994) *Workplace Bargaining in a Regional Context: Hunter Region Case Studies* (University of Newcastle: Employment Studies Research Centre).
Burt, R.S. (1992) 'The Social Structure of Competition', in N. Nohria and R.G. Eccles (eds), *Networks and Organizations: structure, form and action* (Boston: Harvard Business School Press).
Butler, P., T.W. Hall, A.M. Hanna, L. Mendonca, B. Auguste, J. Manyika and A. Sahay (1997) 'A revolution in interaction', *McKinsey Quarterly*, 1, 4–23.
Calof, J.L. (1994) 'The relationship between firm size and export behaviour revisited', *Journal of International Business Studies*, 25(2), 367–87.
Câmara de Comércio e Indústria Luso-Alemã (1996) *Empresas Alemãs em Portugal*, Lisbon, 16 Mass.

Carlson, J.R. and R.W. Zmud (1999) 'Channel expansion theory and the experiential nature of media richness perceptions', *Academy of Management Journal*, 42(2), 153–70.

Carson, D., S. Cromie, P. McGowan and J. Hill (1995) *Marketing Entrepreneurship in SMEs: An Innovative Approach* (London: Prentice-Hall).

Casson, M. (1993/94) 'Internationalisation as a learning process, a model of corporate growth and geographical diversification', *Discussion Papers in International Investment and Business Studies*, Series B, VI (173), University of Reading, Department of Economics.

Casson, M. (1996) 'The nature of the firm reconsidered: information synthesis and entrepreneurial organisation', *Management International Review*, 36 (Special Issue I), 55–94.

Casson, M. (1997) *Information and Organization. A New Perspective of the Theory of the Firm* (Oxford: Clarendon Press).

Cateora, P.R. (1993) *International Marketing*, 8th edn (Homewood: Irwin).

Cavusgil, S., S. Tamer and J. Naor (1987) 'Firm and management characteristics as discriminators for export behavior', *Journal of Business Research*, 15(3), 221–35.

Cavusgil, S., W. Bilkey and G. Tesar (1979) 'A note on the export behavior of firms', *Journal of International Business Studies,* 10(1), 91–7.

Cavusgil, S.T. (1980) 'On the internationalization process of firms', *European Research*, November, 273–81.

Cefamol, *O Molde*, numbers 0–41 (Cefamol, 1988–99).

Chandler, A.D. (1962) *Strategy and Structure* (Cambridge, MA: MIT Press).

Chandler, A.D. (1986) 'Technological and organizational underpinnings of modern industrial multinational enterprises: the dynamics of competitive advantage', in A. Teichova, M. Levy-Leboyer and H. Nussbaum (eds), *Multinational Enterprise in Historical Perspective*, Chapter 2 (Cambridge: Cambridge University Press), pp. 30–54.

Chandler, A.D. (1994) 'The functions of the HQ unit in the multibusiness firm', in R.P. Rumelt *et al.*, *Fundamental Issues in Strategy. A Research Agenda* (Boston: Harvard Business School Press).

Chase, D. Carmen, L. James Kuhle and Carl H. Walther (1988) 'The relevance of political risk in direct foreign investment', *Management International Review*, 28(3), 31–8.

Ciborra, C.U. 'Introduction: what does groupware mean for the organisations hosting it?', in C.U. Ciborra (ed.), *Groupware and Teamwork: Invisible Aid or Technical Hindrance* (Chichester: Wiley).

Ciborra, C.U. and G. Patriotta (1996) 'Groupware and teamwork in new product development: the case of a consumer goods multinational', in Ciborra (ed.), *Groupware and Teamwork* (Chichester: Wiley).

Clark, T., D.S. Pugh and G. Mallory (1997) 'The process of internationalization in the operating firm', *International Business Review*, 6(6), 605–23.

Cohen, W.M. and D.A. Levinthal (1990) 'Absorptive capacity: a new perspective on learning and innovation', *Administrative Science Quarterly*, 35, 128–52.

Cohendet, P., F. Kern, B. Mehmanpazir and F. Munier (1990) 'Knowledge Coordination, competence creation and integrated networks in globalised firms', *Cambridge Journal of Economics*, 23, 225–41.

Coller, X. (1996) 'Managing flexibility in the food industry: a cross-national comparative study in European multinational companies', *European Journal of Industrial Relations*, 2, 153–72.

Coller, X., T. Edwards and C. Rees (1998) 'Structure and Internal Politics in MNCs: The Diffusion of Employment Practices', paper presented at Kingston University 23 March.

Comfort, M. (1964) *Conrad N. Hilton – Hotelier* (Minneapolis: T.S. Dennison and Company).

Contractor, N.S. and E.M. Eisenberg (1990) 'Communication networks and new media in organizations', in J. Fulk and C. Steinfield (eds), *Organizations and Communication Technology* (Newbury Park: Sage).

Coviello, N. and A. McAuley (1999) 'Internationalisation and the smaller firm: a review of contemporary empirical research', *Management International Review*, 39(3), 223–56.

Coviello, N. and H. Munro (1997) 'Network relationships and the internationalisation process of small software firms', *International Business Review*, 6(4), 361–86.

Coviello, N.E. and H.J. Munro (1995) 'Growing the entrepreneurial firm: networking for international market development', *European Journal of Marketing*, 29(7), 49–61

Crawston, K. and T.W. Malone (1994) 'Information technology and work organisation', in T.J. Allen and M.S. Scott Morton (eds), Information technology and the corporation of the 1990s (New York: Oxford University Press), pp. 249–75.

Crick, D. and M.R. Czinkota (1995) 'Export assistance: another look at whether we are supporting the best programmes', *International Marketing Review*, 12(3), 61–72.

Crick, D. and S. Chaudhry (1995) 'Export practices of Asian SMEs: some preliminary findings', *Marketing Intelligence and Planning*, 13(11), 13–21.

Culnan, M.J. and M.L. Markus (1987) 'Information Technologies', in F.M. Jablin, L.L. Putnam, K.H. Roberts and L.W. Porter (eds), *Handbook of Organizational Communication* (Newbury Park: Sage), pp. 420–23.

Czinkota, M.R. (1982) *Export Development Strategies: US Promotion Policies* (New York: Praeger Publishers).

Czinkota, M.R. and G. Tesar (eds) (1982) *Export Management: an International Context* (New York: Praeger Publishers).

D'Cruz, J. (1996) 'Strategic Management of Subsidiaries', in Hamid Étemad and Louise Séguin-Dulude (eds), *Managing the Multinational Subsidiary: Response to Environmental Changes and to the Host Nation R&D Policies* (London: Croom Helm).

Daft, R.L. and R.H. Lengel (1986) 'Organizational Information Requirement, Media Richness and Structural Design', *Management Science*, 32(5), 554–71.

de Meyer, A. (1994) 'Tech Talk: How Managers are Stimulating Global R&D Communication', *Sloan Management Review*, 32(2), 49–58, reprinted in R. Drew (ed.) (1995) *Readings in International Enterprise* (London: Thompson International Press).

Delany, E. (1998) 'Strategic Development of Multinational Subsidiaries in Ireland', in Birkinshaw and N. Hood (eds), *Multinational Corporate Evolution and Subsidiary Development* (London: Macmillan).

Depperu, D. (1993) *L'internazionalizzazione delle piccole e medie imprese* (Milan: EGEA).

Dicken, P. (1986) *Global Shift*, 1st edn (London: Paul Chapman).

Dicken, P. (1988) *Global Shift*, 2nd edn (London: Paul Chapman).

Dicken, P. (1992) *Global Shift*, 3rd edn (London: Paul Chapman).

Dickson, M. (1999) 'How to find your way around the tables', *FT 500 Annual Review Financial Times*, 28 January, p. 3.

Dominquez, L.V. and G.G. Sequeira (1993) 'Determinants of LDC exporters' performance: a cross-national study', *Journal of International Business Studies*, 24(1), 19–40.

Donges, J.B. and J. Wieners (1994) 'Foreign investment in the transformation process of Eastern Europe', *The International Trade Journal*, VII (2), 163–91.

Dubini, P. and H. Aldrich (1991) 'Personal and extended networks are central to the entrepreneurial process: executive forum', *Journal of Business Venturing*, 6, 305–13.

Dunning, H. John (1981) 'Explaining the international direct investment position of countries: towards a dynamic and development approach', *Weltwirtschaftliches Archiv*, 117, 30–64.

Dunning, J. (1993) *The Globalisation of Business* (London: Routledge).

Dunning, J. (1997) 'The Economic theory of the firm as the basis for a 'Core' theory of international production', in I. Islam and W.F. Shepherd (eds), *Current Issues in International Business* (Cheltenham: Edward Elgar).

Dunning, J.H. (1977) 'Trade, location and economic activity and the multinational enterprise: The search for an eclectic approach', in Ohlin, Bertil, Hesselborn, P. and Wijkman (eds), *The International Allocation of Economic Activity* (London: Macmillan), pp. 395–419.

Dunning, J.H. (1993) *Multinational Enterprises and the Global Economy* (Wokingham: Addison Wesley).

Dunning, J.H. (1993b) *The Globalization of Business* (London and New York: Routledge).

Dutton, J., S. Ashford, R. O'Neill, E. Hays and E. Wierba (1997) 'Reading the wind: how middle managers assess the context for selling issues to top managers', *Strategic Management Journal*, 18(5), 407–25.

Egelhoff, W., L. Gorman and S. McCormick (1998) 'Using technology as a path to subsidiary development', in J. Birkinshaw and N. Hood (eds), *Multinational Corporate Evolution and Subsidiary Development* (London: Macmillan).

Egelhoff, W.G. (1991) 'Information processing theory and the multinational enterprise', *Journal of International Business Studies*, 22(3), 341–68.

Eisenhardt, K.M. (1989) 'Building theories from case study research', *Academy of Management Review*, 14(4), 532–50.

Enright, M. (1998) 'Regional clusters and firms strategy', in A.D. Chandler, P. Hagstrom and O. Solvell (eds), *The Dynamic Firm: the role of Technology, Strategy, Organizations and Regions* (New York: University Press).

Enright, M. (1998) 'The globalisation of competition and the localisation of competitive Advantage: Policies toward regional clustering', paper presented at the Workshop on Globalisation of Multinational Enterprise Activity and Economic Development, University of Strathclyde, May.

Estrin, S., K. Hughes, and S. Todd (1997) *Foreign Direct Investment in Central and Eastern Europe* (London: Pinter).

Feldman, M.P. (1994) *The Geography of Innovation* (Dordrecht: Kluwer Academic Publishers).

Fernandez, J.P. with M. Barr (1993) *The Diversity Challenge* (New York: Lexington).

Ferner, A. (1994) 'Multinational companies and human resource management: an overview of research issues', *Human Resource Management Journal*, 4(2), 79–102.

Ffowcs Williams, I. (1997a) 'Local clusters and local export growth', *New Zealand Strategic Management*, Summer, 24–9.

Ffowcs Williams, I. (1997b) 'Stimulating local clusters', paper presented at the World Bank Workshop for Practitioners in Cluster Formation, Chihuahua, Mexico.

Flint, J. (1994) 'One world, one Ford', *Forbes*, 20 June, pp. 40–1.

Fontoura, Maria Paula (1995) 'O Efeito do IDE na Composição das Exportações da Indústria Transformadora Portuguesa', *Estudos de Economia*, 15(2), 123–41.

Ford, D., H. Håkansson, and J. Johanson (1986) 'How do companies interact?', *Industrial Marketing and Purchasing*, 1(1), 26–41.

Forester, T. (ed.) (1980) *The Microelectronics Revolution* (Oxford: Basil Blackwell).

Forsgren, M. (1997) 'The advantage paradox of the multinational corporation', in I. Bjorkman and M. Forsgren (eds), *The Nature of the International Firm: Nordic Contributions to International Business Research*, pp. 69–85.

Forsgren, M. and J. Johanson (1992) *Managing Networks in International Business* (Philadelphia: Gordon and Breach).

Forsgren, M. and T. Pedersen (1998) 'Centres of excellence in multinational companies: The case of Denmark', in J. Birkinshaw and N. Hood (eds), *Multinational Corporate Evolution and Subsidiary Development* (London: Macmillan).

Forsgren, M., U. Holm and J. Johanson (1992) 'Internationalization of the second degree: the emergence of European-Based centres in Swedish Firms', in S. Young and J. Hamill (eds), *Europe and the Multinationals* (Alderhot: Edward Elgar).

Forsgren, M., T. Pedersen and N. Foss (1999a) 'Accounting for strengths of MNC subsidiaries: The case of foreign-owned firms in Denmark', *International Business Review*, 8(2), 181–96.

Forsgren, M.U. Holm, T. Pedersen and D. Sharma (1999b) The subsidiary role for MNC competence development: information bridgehead or competence distributor', in F. Burton, M. Yamin and M. Bowe (eds), *International Business and the Global Services Economy* – proceedings of 25th Annual Conference of EIBA, Manchester.

Fraser, I. (1999) 'Scots urged to look to the US', *Sunday Herald*, 31 October, p. 16.

Fratocchi, L. and U. Holm (1998) 'Centres of Excellence in the International Firm', in J. Birkinshaw and N. Hood (eds), *Multinational Corporate Evolution and Subsidiary Development* (London: Macmillan).

Friedman, T. (1999) *The Lexus and the Olive Tree* (London: Harper Collins).

FT 500 Annual Review Financial Times, 28 January (1999) pp. 1–55.

Fulk, J., J. Schmitz and C.W. Steinfield (1990) 'A social influence model of technology use', in J. Fulk and C. Steinfield (eds), *Organizations and Communication Technology* (Newbury Park: Sage), pp. 117–40.

Galbraith, J.R. (1973) *Designing Complex Organization* (Reading, Mass: Addison Wesley).

Galbraith, J.R. (1977) *Organization Design* (Reading, Mass: Addison Wesley).

Ghoshal, S. and C. Bartlett (1990) 'The multinational corporation as an interorganisational network', *Academy of Management Review*, 15(4), 603–25.

Ghoshal, S. and C. Bartlett (1993) 'The multinational corporation as an inter-organisational network', in S. Ghoshal and E. Westney (eds), *Organisational Theory and the Multinational Corporation* (New York: St. Martin's Press), pp. 77–104.

Ghoshal, S. and C.A. Bartlett (1997) *The Individualized Corporation* (New York: Harper Business).

Ghoshal, S. and N. Nohira (1989) 'Internal Differentiation within Multinational Companies', *Strategic Management Journal*, 10(4), 323–37.

Ghoshal, S., H. Korine and G. Szulanski (1994) 'Interunit Communication in Multinational Corporations', *Management Science*, 40(1), 96–110.

Giddens, A. and W. Hutton (2000) 'In conversation', in W. Hutton and A. Giddens (eds), *On the Edge: Living with Global Capitalism* (London: Jonathan Cape).

Golinelli, G.M. (1992) 'I problemi strategici dell'impresa minore', *Sinergie*, 27, 36–41.

Gomes-Casseres, B. (1997) 'Alliance strategies of small firms', *Small Business Economics*, 9(1), 33–44.

Gonçalves, F. Octávio, and Paulo F. Guimarães (1996) 'O Investimento Directo Estrangeiro na Indústria Transformadora Portuguesa: Uma abordagem sectorial e regional através do emprego para o período 1982–1992', *Documentos APDR*, 5.

Gooderham, P.N., O. Nordhaug and K. Ringdal (1998) 'When in Rome do they do as the Romans? HRM practices of US subsidiaries in Europe', *Management International Review*, 38 (Special Issue), 47–64.

Gooderham, P.N., O. Nordhaug and K. Ringdal (1999) 'Institutional determinants of organizational practices: Human resource management in European firms', *Administrative Science Quarterly*, 44(3), 507–31.

Goold, M. and A. Campbell (1987) *Strategies and Styles. The Role of the Centre in Managing Diversified Corporation* (Oxford: Basie Blackwell).

Grabher, G. (1993) 'Rediscovering the social in the economics of interfirm relations', in G. Grabher (eds), *The Embedded Firm: On the Socioeconomics of Industrial Networks* (London: Routledge).

Grandinetti, R. and E. Rullani (1992) 'Internazionalizzazione e piccole imprese: elogio della varietà', *Small Business*, 3, 14–25.

Granovetter, M. (1985) 'Economic action and social structure: the problem of embeddedness', *American Journal of Sociology*, 91(3), 481–510.

Granovetter, M.S. (1973) 'The strength of weak ties', *American Journal of Sociology*, 78(6), 1360–380.

Grant, R.M. (1991) 'The resource-based theory of competitive advantage: implication for strategy formulation', *California Management Review*, 33(3), 114–35.

Guest, D.E. (1990) 'Human resource management and the American Dream', *Journal of Management Studies*, 27(4), 378–97.

Gupta, A. and A. Govindarajan (2000) 'Knowledge flows with multinational corporations', *Strategic Management Journal*, 21, 473–96.

Hadjikhani, A. (1997) 'A Note on the criticisms against the internationalization process model', *Management International Review*, 37 (Special Issue II), 43–66.

Hair, F., Joseph Jr. Rolph, E. Anderson, Ronald L. Tatham and William C. Black (1998) *Multivariate Data Analysis*, 5th edn (Englewood Cliff: Prentice-Hall International).

Hakkinen, T. (1994) *Divestments of Foreign Subsidiaries of Finnish Manufacturing Companies,* CIBR, Research reports, X-3 (Helsinki: Helsinki School of Economics Press).

Hambrick, D., M. Geletkanycz and J. Fredrickson (1993) 'Top executive commitment to the *Status Quo:* some tests of its determinants', *Strategic Management Journal*, 14(6), 401–18.

Hamill, J. (1997) 'The internet and international marketing', *International Marketing Review*, 14(5), 300–23.

Hammer, M. and J. Champey (1993) *Re-engineering the Corporation* (London: Brearly).

Hammer, M. and G. Mangurian (1987) 'The changing value of communication technology', *Sloan Management Review*, 28(2), 65–71.

Hansen, M. (1999) 'The Search-Transfer Problem: The role of weak ties in sharing knowledge across organisational subunits', *Administrative Science Quarterly,* 44(1), 82–111.

Hansen, M.T., N. Nohria and T. Tierney (1999) 'What's your strategy for managing knowledge?', *Harvard Business Review*, March–April, 106–16.

Harrison, A., E. Dalkiran and E. Elsey (2000) *International Business* (Oxford: Oxford University Press).

Harrison, B. (1991) 'Industrial districts: old wine in new bottles?', *Regional Studies*, 26(5), 469–83.

Hayek, F.A. (1945) 'The use of knowledge in society', *American Economic Review*, 35(4), 519–30.

Hedlund, G. (1986) 'The Hypermodern MNE: a heterarchy?', *Human Resource Management*, Spring.

Hedlund, G. and D. Rollander (1990) 'Action in heterarchies – new approaches to managing the MNC', in C. Bartlett, Y. Doz and G. Hedlund (eds), *Managing the Global Firm* (London: Routledge).

Hellman, P. (1996) 'The internationalisation of Finnish financial service companies', *International Business Review*, 3(2), 191–207.

Henderson, J. (1993) 'Industrial policy for Britain: lessons from the East', *Renewal*, 1(2), 32–42.

Hennart, J. (1993) 'Control in multinational firms: the role of price and hierarchy', in S. Ghoshal and Westney (eds), *Organisation Theory and the Multinational Corporation* (New York: St. Martin's Press).

Hentola, H. and R. Luostarinen (1995) *'Foreign Subsidiary: The Concept Revisited',* CIBR working paper series Z-4 (Helsinki: Helsinki School of Economics Press).

Hilton, C. (1957) *Be My Guest* (Englewood Cliffs New Jersey: Prentice-Hall).

Hirschman, E.C. (1986) 'Humanistic inquiry in marketing research: philosophy, method and criteria', *Journal of Marketing Research*, 23, 237–49.

Hirst P. and G. Thompson (1995) 'Globalisation and the future of the nation state', *Economy and Society*, 24(3), 408–42.

Hoekman, B. and M. Kostecki (1995) *The Political Economy of the World Trading System* (Oxford: Oxford University Press).

Hofheinz, P. 'ABB's big bet in eastern Europe', *Fortune*, 2 May, 24–30.

Hofstede, G. (1980) *Cultures Consequences: International Differences in Work-related Values* (Beverly Hills: Sage).

Holm, U. and T. Pedersen (2000) *The Emergence and Impact of MNC Centres of Excellence: A Subsidiary Perspective* (London: Macmillan).

Holm, U., J. Johanson and P. Thilenius (1995) 'Headquarters knowledge of subsidiary network contexts in the multinational corporations', *International Studies of Management and Organisation*, 25(1–2), 97–119.

Hood, N. and J.H. Taggart (1997) 'German Foreign Direct Investment in the UK and Ireland: Survey Evidence', *Regional Studies*, 31(2), 139–50.

Hood, N. and S. Young (1979) *The Economics of* multinational enterprise (London: Longman).

Hood, N. and S. Young (1988) 'Inward investment and the EC: UK evidence on corporate integration strategies', in J.H. Dunning and P. Robson (eds), *Multinationals and the European Community* (Oxford: Blackwell).

Hood, N., S. Young and D. Lal (1994) 'Strategic evolution within Japanese manufacturing plants in Europe: UK evidence', *International Business Review*, 3(2), 97–122.

Hoover, E.M. (1937) *Location Theory and the Shoe and Leather Industries* (Cambridge, Mass: Harvard University Press).

Hoover, E.M. (1948) *The Location of Economic Activity* (New York: McGraw-Hill).

Hotels Corporate 300 ranking, July (1999) 36–8.

Hu, Y. (1992) 'Global or stateless corporations are national firms with international operations', *California Management Review*, Winter, 107–26.

Humphrey, J. and H. Schmitz (1996) 'The triple C approach to loocal industrial policy', *World Development*, 24(12), 1859–77.

Hurdley, L.H. and N. Hood (1999) 'Subsidiary strategy and regional economic impact: A conceptual framework', in M. Hughes (ed.), *International Business and Its European Dimensions*, Conference Proceedings of the 26th Annual Conference of AIB UK Chapter, University of Stirling, 16–17 April, pp. 302–20.

Huselid, M. (1995) 'The impact of human resource management practices on turnover, productivity, and corporate financial performance', *Academy of Management Journal*, 38, 635–72.

Hutton, W. (1995) *The State We're In* (London: Vintage).

Hutton, W. (2000) 'Free to trade only on US terms', *Observer*, 27 May, p. 18.

ICEP (2000) 'Investir em Portugal', *Investimento Internacional*, http://www.icep.pt/portugal/investimento.asp [15 March 2000].

Imanishi, Tamami (1999) '*Ryoko* Kigyo no Kokusai Keiei', (International Business of Travelling Companies), unpublished PhD thesis (Kobe University Business School).

ISTA-International Special Tooling Association, *Statistics* (1980–98).

Jackson, G.I. (1981) 'Export from the importer's viewpoint', *European Journal of Marketing*, 15, 3–15.

Jain, S.C. (1989) 'Standardization of international marketing strategy: some research hypotheses', *Journal of Marketing*, 53, 70–79.

Jaworski, B.J. and A.K. Kohli (1993) 'Market orientation: antecedents and consequences,' *Journal of Marketing*, 57(July), 53–70.

Johanson, J. and J.E. Vahlne (1992) 'Management of foreign market entry', *Scandinavian International Business Review*, 1(3), 9–27.

Johanson, J. and F. Wiedersheim-Paul (1975) 'The internationalization of the firm – four Swedish cases', *Journal of Management Studies*, 12, 305–22.

Johanson, J. and J. Vahlne (1977) 'The internationalization process of the firm – a model of knowledge development and increasing foreign market commitment', *Journal of International Business Studies*, 8, 23–32.

Johanson, J. and J.E. Vahlne (1990) 'The mechanism of internationalisation', *International Marketing Review*, 7(4), 11–24.

Johanson, J. and L.G. Mattsson (1988) 'Internationalisation in industrial systems – a network approach', in N. Hood and J.E. Vahlne (eds), *Strategies in Global Competition* (London: Croom Helm).

Johanson, J., C. Pahlberg and P. Thilenius (1996) 'Conflict and control in MNC new product introduction', *Journal of Market Focused Management*, 1, 249–65.

Johnson, J.E. (1999) 'Towards a success factor framework for global start-ups', *Global Focus*, 11(3), 73–84.

Kamath, S., P.J. Rosson, D. Patton and M. Brooks (1987) 'Research on success in exporting: past, present and future', in P.J. Rosson and S.D. Reid (eds), *Managing Export Entry and Expansion* (New York: Praeger).

Katsikeas, C.S. and C.E. Morgan (1994) 'Differences in perceptions of export problems based on firm size and export market experience', *European Journal of Marketing*, 28(5), 17–35.

Kautovaara, A. (1999) *The Relocation of Regional Headquarters: The Case of Moving Regional Headquarters for Central and Eastern Europe away from Finland*, FIBO Programme (Helsinki: Helsinki School of Economics Press).

Khan, Sikander and Hideki Yoshihara (1994) *Strategy and Performance of Foreign Companies in Japan* (Westport, Conn: Quorum Books).

Kilduff, M. (1992) 'Performance and interaction routines in multinational corporations', *Journal of International Business Studies*, 23(2), 133–43.

Kilduff, M. (1993) 'The Reproduction of Inertia in Multinational Corporations', in S. Ghoshal and D. Westney (eds), *Organisation Theory and the Multinational Corporation* (New York: St. Martin's Press).

Kim, K., J.-H. Park and J.E. Prescott (1999) 'The Global Integration of Distinctive Competences: A Study on Multinational Business in Global Industries', *Academy of Management Best Paper Proceedings*.

Knight, G.A. and S.T. Cavusgil (1996) 'The born global firm: a challenge to traditional internationalization theory', *Advances in International Marketing*, 8, 11–26.

Kogut, B. and U. Zander (1992) 'Knowledge of the firm: combinative capabilities and The Replication of technology', *Organisation Science*, 3(3), 338–97.

Kogut, B. (1990) 'International sequential advantages and network flexibility', in C. Bartlett, Y. Doz and G. Hedlund (eds), *Managing the Global Firm* (London: Routledge), 47–68.

Kogut, B. (1991) 'Country capabilities and the permeability of borders', *Strategic Management Journal*, 12(1), 33–47.

Kogut, B. and N. Kulatilaka (1994) 'Operating Flexibility, Global Manufacturing, and the Option Value of a Multinational Network', *Management Science*, 40(1), 123–39.

Kogut, B. and U. Zander (1993) 'Knowledge of the Firm and The Evolutionary Theory of the Multinational Corporation', *Journal of International Business Studies*, 24(4), 625–45.

Kogut, B. and U. Zander (1992) 'Knowledge of the firm, combinative capabilities and the replication of technology', *Organization Science*, 3, 383–97.

Kohn, T.O. (1997) 'Small firms as international players', *Small Business Economics*, 9(1), 45–51.

Kojima, Kiyoshi (1985) *Nihon no Kaigai Chokusetsu Tosi* (Foreign Direct Investment of Japan) (Tokyo: Bunshindo Publishing Company).

Kopp, Rochelle (1994) 'International human resource policies and practices in Japanese, European and United States multinationals', *Human Resource Management*, Winter, 33(4).

Kostova, T. (1999) 'Transnational transfer of strategic organisational practices: a contextual perspective', *Academy of Management Review*, 24(2), 308–24.

Krugman, P. (1991) *Geography and Trade* Massachusetts (Cambridge, Mass: MIT Press).

Kuisel, R. (1993) *Seducing the French: The Dilemma of Americanisation* (Berkley, CA: University of California Press).

Kumar, K. (1995) *From Post-Industrial to Post Modern Society – New Theories of the Contemporary World* (Oxford, Blackwell).

Lane, C. and R. Bachmann (eds) (1998) *Trust within and between Organizations* (Oxford: OUP).

Langley, A. (1999) 'Strategies for theorizing from process data', *Academy of Management Review*, 24(4), 691–710.

Lankes, H.-P. and A.J. Venables (1996) 'Foreign direct investment in economic transition: the changing pattern of investments', *Economics of Transition*, 4(2), 331–47.

Lannon, J. (1988) 'The European Consumer in the Year 2000', *Admap*, November, 20–24.

Lawrence, P.L. and J.W. Lorch (1967) *Organization and Environment* (Homewood, Ill.: Irwin).

Leonard-Barton, D. (1992) 'Core capabilities and core rigidities: a paradox in managing new product development', *Strategic Management Journal*, 13(1), 111–19.

Leonidou, L.C. and C.S. Katsikeas (1996) 'The export development process: an Integrative Review of Empirical Models', *Journal of International Business Studies*, 27(3), 517–51.

Leonidou, L.C. and C.S. Katsikeas (1999) 'Export information sources: the role of organizational and internationalization influences', *Journal of Strategic Marketing*, 5(2), 65–87.

Lessard, D.R. (1986) 'Finance and global competition', in M.E. Porter (ed.), *Competition in Global Industries* (Boston: Harvard Business School Press).

Levinthal, D. and J. March (1993) 'The Myopia of Learning', *Strategic Management Journal*, 14 (Special Issue), 95–112.

Levinthal, D. and J.G. March (1981) 'A model of adaptive organisational search', *Journal of Economic Behaviour and Organisation*, 2, 307–333.

Levitt, T. (1983) 'The globalisation of markets', *Harvard Business Review*, May–June, pp. 92–102.

Liang, Neng (1995) 'Soliciting unsolicited export orders – are recipients chosen at random?', *European Journal of Marketing*, 29(8), 37–59.

Liesch, P.W. and G.A. Knight (1999) 'Information internalization and hurdle rates in small and medium enterprise internationalization', *Journal of International Business Studies*, 30(2), 383–398.

Linder, S.B. (1961) *An Essay on Trade and Transformation* (New York: Wiley).

Lindqvist, M. (1988) 'Internationalisation of small technology-based firms: three illustrative case studies on Swedish firms', *Stockholm School of Economics Research Paper*, 88/15.

Lipparini, A. and M. Sobrero (1997) 'Co-ordinating multi-firm innovative processes: entrepreneur as catalyst in small firm networks', in M. Ebers (ed.), *The Formation of Inter-Organizational Networks* (Oxford: Oxford University Press).

Litvak, I.A. (1990) 'Instant international: strategic reality for small high-technology firms in Canada', *Multinational Business*, 2, 1–12.

Locke, R.R. (1996) *The Collapse of the American Management Mystique* (Oxford: Oxford University Press).

Luostarinen, R. (1979) *Internationalization of the Firm* (Helsinki: Helsinki School of Economics Press).

Luostarinen, R. (1981) *Suomalaisten Yritysten Kansainvalistyminen: Motiivit, Strategiat, Ongelmat ja Vaateet* (Internationalization of Finnish Firms: Motives, Strategies, Difficulties and Challenges), Helsinki: FIBO Research Report 1.

Luostarinen, R. (1994) *Internationalization of Finnish Firms and Their Response to Global Challenges*, WIDER, The United Nations University (Forssa: Forssa Printing House Ltd).

Luostarinen, R. (2000) *Finland as a Business Centre to Central and Eastern European Transitory Economies*, CIBR/FIBO Programme and Centre for Russian and Baltic Studies (Helsinki: Helsinki School of Economics Press).

Lvostarinen, R. and R. Marschan-Piekkari (2000) 'Strategic evolution of foreign-owned subsidiaries in a host country: a conceptual framework', in S. Young and N. Hood (eds), *The Multinational in the Millennium: Companies and Countries, Changes and Choices* (vol. 2), Proceedings of the 27th Annual Conference.

Maattanen, M. (1999) Interview by e-mail. Business development manager, ABB East Ventures, 8 November.

MacNamara, P. and C. Baden-Fuller (1999) 'Lessons from the celltech case: balancing knowledge exploration and exploitation in organisational renewal', *British Journal of Management*, 10(4), 291–307.

Madhok, A. (1997) 'Costs, Value and Foreign Market Entry Mode: The transaction and the firm', *Strategic Management Journal*, 18(1), 39–61.

Madsen, T.K. and P. Servais (1997) 'The internationalization of born globals: an evolutionary process?', *International Business Review*, 6(6), 561–83.

Maleksadeh, A. and A. Nahavandi (1985) 'Small business exporting: misconceptions are abundant', *American Journal of Small Business*, 9(4), 7–14.

Malone, T.W., J. Yates and R.I. Benjamin (1994) 'Electronic markets and electronic Hierarchies', in T.J. Allen and M.S. Scott Morton (eds), *Information Technology and the Corporation of the 1990s* (New York: Oxford University Press).

Manea, J. and R. Pearce (1997) 'The potential role of Romania's technological and scientific capacity in attracting FDI: an exploratory analysis of its national system of innovation', in R. Pearce (ed.), *Global Competition and Technology* (London: Macmillan).

Manea, J. and R. Pearce (1998) 'Technology policies of MNEs and subsidiaries strategies in transition economies: the case of Romania', in E.D. Joffe, I.D. Nebenzahl and D. Teeni (eds), *International Business Strategies and Middle East Regional Cooperation*. Proceedings of the 1998 annual conference, European International Business Academy, Jerusalem.

Manea, J. and R. Pearce (1999) 'Transnational corporation strategies and industrial transition: the case of Romania', University of Reading, Department of Economics, *Discussion Papers in International Investment and Management*, no. 269.

Manea, J. and R. Pearce (2000a) 'Industrial restructuring in European transition economies and MNEs' investment motivations' (mimeo).

Manea, J. and R. Pearce (2000b) 'Market orientation and the strategic development of MNEs in transition economies' (mimeo).

Manufacturers Association of Nigeria, *Nigerian Industrial Directory* (Lagos: MAN, 1994).

March, J. (1991) 'Exploration and exploitation in organisational learning', *Organisation Science*, 2(1), 71–87.

Markus, M.L. (1987) 'Toward a critical mass theory of interactive media – universal access, Interdependence and Diffusion', *Communication Research*, 14, 491–511.

Markus, M.L. (1994) 'Electronic mail as the medium of managerial choice', *Organization Science*, 5(4), 502–27.

Marschan-Piekkari, R., D. Welch and L. Welch (1999) 'In the shadow: The impact of language on structure, power and communication in the multinational', *International Business Review*, 8(4), 421–40.

Marshall, A. (1910) *Principles of Economics,* 6th edn (London: Macmillan).

Marshall, A. (1919) *Industry and Trade* (London: Macmillan).

Marshall, A. (1890/1920) *Principles of Economics*, 8th edn (London: Macmillan).

Martenson, R. (1987) 'Is Standardisation of marketing feasible in culture bound industries?', *International Marketing Review*, Autumn, 7–17.

Martin, G. and P. Beaumont (1998) 'Diffusing 'best practice' in multinational firms: prod-
ucts, practice and contestation', *International Journal of Human Resource
Management*, 9(4), 671–95.
Martinez, J. and J. Jarillio (1989) 'The evolution of research on co-ordination mechanism
in multinational corporations', *Journal of International Business Studies*, Fall, 489–514.
Mathe, H. and C. Perras (1994) 'The challenges of globalisation in the service industry',
in C. Armistead (ed.), *The Future of Services Management* (London: Kogan Page).
Mather, G. and S. Todd (1995) *The International Hotel Industry – Corporate Strategies
and Global Opportunities*, Special Report 463 (London: Economist Intelligence Unit).
Matos, Luís Salgado de (1973) *Investimentos Estrangeiros em Portugal* (Liboa: Seara
Nova).
McAleese, D. and D. McDonald (1978) 'Employment growth and the development of link-
ages in foreign-owned and domestic manufacturing enterprises', *Oxford Bulletin of
Economics and Statistics*, 40, 321–39.
McAleese, D. and F. Hayes (1995) 'European integration, the balance of payments and
inflation', in J. O'Hagan (ed.), *The Economy of Ireland. Policy and Performance of a
Small European Country* (Basingstoke: Macmillan).
McDermott, M. (1989) *Multinationals: Foreign Divestment and Disclosure* (Cambridge:
McGraw-Hill).
McDougall, P.P. and B.M. Oviatt (1991) 'Global start-ups: new ventures without
geographic limits', *The Entrepreneurship Forum*, Winter, 1–5.
McDougall, P.P. and B.M. Oviatt (1996) 'New Venture Internationalization, Strategic
Change, and Performance: a Follow-up Study', *Journal of Business Venturing*, 11, 23–40.
McDougall, P.P. and B.M. Oviatt (1997) 'International entrepreneurship literature in the
1990s and directions for future research', in D.L. Sexton and R.W. Smilor (eds),
Entrepreneurship 2000 (Chicago: Upstart Publishing Company).
McDougall, P.P., S. Shane and B.M. Oviatt *et al.* (1994) 'Explaining the formation of inter-
national new ventures: the limits of theories from international business research',
Journal of Business Venturing, 9, 469–87.
McKay, G. (1997) 'Introduction: Americanisation and popular culture', in G. McKay (ed.),
Yankee Go Home (Take Me With U) (Sheffield: Sheffield Academic Press).
McNaughton, R.B. and J.D. Bell (1999) 'Brokering networks of small firms to generate
social capital for growth and internationalization', *Research in Global Strategic
Management*, 7, 63–82.
Mele, R. (1986) *L'esportazione per la piccola e media impresa* (Padova: CEDAM).
Meyer, K. (1998) *Direct Investment in Economies in Transition* (Cheltenham: Edward
Elgar).
Miesenbock, K.J. (1988) 'Small business and exporting: a literature review', *International
Small Business Journal*, 6(2), 42–61.
Miles, M.B. and A.M. Huberman (1994) *Qualitative Data Analysis: an expanded source-
book* (Thousand Oaks, California: Sage Publications).
Millington, A.I. and B.T. Bayliss (1990) 'The process of internationalisation: UK compa-
nies in the EC', *Management International Review*, 30(2), 151–161.
Mills, A. and J. Hatfield (1999) 'From imperialism to globalisation: internationalisation
and the management text', in S. Clegg, E. Ibarra-Colado and L. Bueno-Rodriquez (eds),
Global Management: Universal Theories and Local Realities (London: Sage).
Mintzberg, H.A. (1979) *The Structuring of Organizations* (Englewood Cliffs: Prentice-
Hall).
Mintzberg, H.A. (1983) *Mintzberg on Management. Inside our Strange World of
Organization* (New York: The Free Press).
Moini, A.H. (1997) 'Barriers inhibiting export performance of small and medium sized
manufacturing firms', *Journal of Global Marketing*, 4, 40–53.

Monitor Company, under the direction of M. Porter, *Construir as Vantagens Competitivas de Portugal* (Lisboa: Forum para a Competitividade, 1994).

Morais, H. (1993), 'Determinantes do investimento Directo Estrangeiro em Portugal: 1987–1992', unpublished Masters dissertation, ISEG.

Morgan, R.M. and S.D. Hunt (1994) 'The commitment-trust theory of relationship marketing', *Journal of Marketing*, 58, 20–39.

Mudambi, R. (1998) 'MNE internal capital markets and subsidiary strategic independence', *University of Reading Discussion Papers in International Investment and Management*, 256, Series B.

Mudambi, R. (1999) 'MNC internal capital markets and subsidiary strategic independence', *International Business Review*, 8(2), 197–211.

Mutinelli, M. and L. Piscitello (1997) 'Differences in the strategic orientation of Italian MNEs in Central and Eastern Europe. The influence of firm-specific factors', *International Business Review*, 6(2), 185–205.

Nahapiet, J. and S. Ghoshal (1998) 'Social capital, intellectual capital and the organisational advantage', *Academy of Management Review*.

Nelson, R. and S. Winter (1982) *An Evolutionary Theory of Economic Change* (Boston: Harvard University Press).

Ngwenyama, O.K. and A.S. Lee (1997) 'Communication richness in electronic mail: critical social theory and the contextuality of meaning', *MIS Quarterly*, 21(2), 145–67.

Nickson, D. (1997) 'Colorful stories' or historical insight? A review of the auto/biographies of Charles Forte, Conrad Hilton, J.W. Marriott and Kemmons Wilson', *Journal of Hospitality and Tourism Research*, 21(1), 179–92.

Nickson, D. (1998) 'A review of hotel internationalisation with a particular focus on the key role played by American organisations', *Progress in Tourism and Hospitality Research*, 4(1), 53–66.

Nickson, D. (1999) *A Study of the Internationalisation Strategies of Three Hotel Companies With A Particular Focus on Human Resource Management*, unpublished PhD Thesis (Glasgow: University of Strathclyde).

Nigerian Export Promotion Council (1995) *Nigerian Exporters Directory* (Abuja: NEPC).

Niss, H. (1996) 'Country of origin marketing over the product life cycle', *European Journal of Marketing*, 30(3), 6–22.

Nohria, N. and S. Ghoshal (1994) 'Differentiated fit and shared values: alternatives for managing headquarter–subsidiary relations', *Strategic Management Journal*, 15, 491–502.

Nohria, N. (1992) 'Introduction: is a network perspective a useful way of studying Organizations?', in N. Nohria and R.G. Eccles (eds), *Networks and Organizations: structure, form and action* (Boston: Harvard Business School Press).

Nohria, N. and R. Eccles (1992) 'Face-to-face: making network organisations work', in N. Nohria and R. Eccles (eds), *Networks and Organisations: Structure, Form and Action* (Cambridge, MA: Harvard Business School Press).

Nohria, N. and S. Ghoshal (1997) *The Differentiated Network. Organising Multinational Companies for Value Creation* (SanFrancisco: JosseyBass).

Ó'Gráda, C. and K. O'Rourke (1995) 'Economic growth: performance and explanations', in O'Hagan (ed.), *The economy of Ireland. Policy Performance of a Small European Country* (Basingstoke: Macmillan).

OECD (1997) *International Direct Investment Statistics Yearbook* (Paris: OECD).

OECD (Organisation for Economic Co-operation and Development) (1997) *Globalisation and Small and Medium Enterprises* (Paris: OECD).

OECD (1998) *The Economic and Social Impact of Electronic Commerce* (Paris: OECD).

Ohmae, K. (1989) 'Managing in a Borderless World', *Harvard Business Review*, May–June, 152–61.

Ohmae, K. (1994) *The Borderless World* (London: Collins).

Ohmae, K. (1995) *The End of the Nation State* (London: Harper Collins).

Olson, H.C. and F. Wiedersheim-Paul (1978) 'Factors effecting the pre-export behaviour of non-exporting firms', in M. Ghertman and J. Leontiades (eds), *European Research in International Business* (Amsterdam: North-Holland).

Orlikowski, W. (1996) 'Learning from notes: organisational issues in groupware implementation', in Rudy L. Ruggles (ed.), *Knowledge Management Tools* (Boston: Butterworth–Heinemann).

Orr, J. (1990) 'Sharing knowledge, celebrating identity: community memory in a service culture', in D. Middleton and D. Edwards (eds), *Collective Remembering* (London: Sage).

Orr, J.E. (1996) *Talking about Machines* (Ithaca: ILR Press).

Orton, D. and K. Weick (1990) 'Loosely coupled systems: a Reconceptualisation', *Academy of Management Review*, 15(2), 203–33.

Ouchi, G.W. (1980) 'Markets, bureaucracies and clans', *Administrative Science Quarterly*, 25, 129–41.

Oviatt, B.M. and P.P. McDougall (1994) 'Toward a theory of international new ventures', *Journal of International Business Studies*, 25(1), 45–64.

Oviatt, B.M. and P.P. McDougall (1997) 'Challenges for internationalization process theory: the case of international new ventures', *Management International Review*, 37 Special Issue (2), 85–99.

Paasonen, V. (1994) *Foreign Direct Investment of Foreign and Multinational Companies in Finland,* FIBO Programme (Helsinki: Helsinki School of Economics Press).

Papanastassiou, M. (1999) 'Technology and production strategies of multinational enterprise (MNC): Subsidiaries in Europe', *International Business Review*, 8(2), 213–32.

Papanastassiou, M. and R. Pearce (1994) 'Host-country determinants of the market strategies of US companies' overseas subsidiaries', *Journal of the Economics of Business*, 1(2), 199–217.

Papanastassiou, M. and R. Pearce (1997) 'Technology sourcing and strategic roles of manufacturing subsidiaries in the UK: local competences and global competitiveness', *Management International Review*, 37(1), 5–25.

Papanastassiou, M. and R. Pearce (1999) *Multinationals, Technology and National Competitiveness* (Cheltenham: Elgar).

Papanastassiou, M. and R. Pearce 'Individualism and interdependence in the technological development of MNEs: The strategic positioning of R&D in overseas subsidiaries', in J. Birkinshaw and N. Hood (eds), *Multinational Corporate Evolution and Subsidiary Development* (London: Macmillan).

Patton, M.Q. (1990) *Qualitative evaluation and research methods*, Sage Publications Inc, California.

Pearce, R. (1992) 'World product mandates and MNE specialisation', *Scandinavian International Business Review*, 1(2), 38–58.

Pearce, R. and M. Papanastassiou (1997) 'European markets and the strategic roles of multinational enterprise subsidiaries in the UK', *Journal of Common Market Studies*, 35(2), 241–66.

Pearce, R. (1999a) 'Decentralised R & D and strategic competitiveness: globalised approaches to generation and use of technology in multinational enterprises', *Research Policy*, 28(2–3), 157–78.

Pearce, R. (1999b) 'The evolution of technology in multinational enterprises: the role of creative subsidiaries', *International Business Review*, 8(2), 125–48.

Pearce, R. (1999c) 'Multinationals and industrialisation: the basis of 'inward investment' policy', *University of Reading Discussion Papers in International Investment and Management*, 279.

Pearce, R. and M. Papanastassiou (1999) 'Overseas R & D and the stategic evolution of MNEs: Evidence from laboratories in the UK', *Research Policy*, 28, 23–41.

Pepe, C. (1984) *Lo sviluppo internazionale della piccola e media impresa* (Milan: Angeli).

Peppard, J. and D. Fitzgerald (1997) 'The transfer of culturally-grounded management techniques: the case of business re-engineering in Germany', *European Management Journal*, 15(4), 446–60.

Petersen, B. and T. Pedersen (1997) 'Twenty years after – support and critique of the Uppsala internationalisation model', in I. Björkman and M. Forsgren (eds), *The Nature of the International Firm* (Copenhagen: Business School Press), pp. 117–134.

Pfaff, W. (2000) Another 'American century'? The Challenge is to do Good', *International Herald Tribune*, 3 January, p. 8.

Philips, L.W. (1981) 'Assessing measurement error in key informant reports: a methodological note on organisational analysis', *Journal of Marketing Research*, 18(4), 395–415.

Poirson, P. (1993) 'Human resource management in France', in S. Tyson *et al.* (eds), *Human Resource Management in Europe* (London: Kogan Page).

Porter, M.E. (1985) *Competitive Advantage* (New York: The Free Press).

Porter, M.E. (1986) *Competition in Global Industries* (Boston: Harvard Business School Press).

Porter, M.E. (1990) *The Competitive Advantage of Nations* (London: Macmillan).

Porter, M.E. (1998) 'Clusters and Competition: New Agendas for Companies, Governments and Institutions', in M.E. Porter (ed.), *On Competition* (Boston: Harvard Business School Press).

Porter, M.E. (1998) 'On Competition', *Harvard Business School Press*, Boston.

Porter, M.E. (1998a) 'Clusters and the new economics of competition', *Harvard Business Review*, 76(6), 77–90.

Porter, M.E. and O. Solvell (1998) 'Regional Clusters and Firms Strategy', in A.D. Chandler, P. Hagstrom and O. Solvell (eds), *The Dynamic Firm: the Role of Technology, Strategy, Organizations and Regions* (New York: University Press).

Portes, A. and P. Landolt (1996) 'The Downside of Social Capital', *The American Prospect*, 26, 18–21.

Pouder, R. and St. C.H. John (1996) 'Hot spots and blind spots: Geographical clusters of firms and innovation', *Academy of Management Review*, 21(4), 1192–225.

Prahalad, C.K. and Y. Doz (1987) *The Multinational Mission* (New York: Free Press).

Prahalad, C.K. and R.A. Bettis (1986) 'The dominant logic: a new link between diversity and performance', *Strategic Management Journal*, 7, 485–501.

Prahalad, C.K. and Y.L. Doz (1987) *The Multinational Mission* (New York: Free Press).

Preece, S.B., G. Miles and M.C. Baetz (1998) 'Explaining the international intensity and global diversity of early-stage technology-based firms', *Journal of Business Venturing*, 14(3), 259–81.

Prevezer, M. (1997) 'The dynamics of industrial clustering in biotechnology', *Small Business Economics*, 9, 255–71.

Putnam, R.D. (1993) *Making Democracy Work – Civic Traditions in Modern Italy* (Princeton: Princeton University Press).

Quinn, J.B., P. Anderson and S. Finkelstein (1996) 'Leveraging Intellect', *Academy of Management Executive* August, 10(3).

Ray, D.M. (1989) 'Entrepreneurial companies born international: four case studies', *Frontiers of Entrepreneurship Research*, 543–4.

Rayport, J.F. and J.J. Sviokla (1994) 'Managing in the Marketspace', *Harvard Business Review*, Nov–Dec, 141–50.

Reed, R. and R.J. DeFillippi (1990) 'Causal ambiguity, barriers to imitation and sustainable competitive advantage', *Academy of Management Review*, 15, 88–102.

Reid, S.D. (1981) 'The decision-maker and export entry and expansion', *Journal of International Business Studies*, 12(2), 101–12.

Reid, S.D. (1983) 'Firm internationalisation: transaction cost and strategic choice', *International Marketing Review*, 1(2), 45–55.

Reid, S.D. (1984) 'Information acquisition and export entry decisions in small firms', *Journal of Business Research*, 12, 141–57.

Rice, R.E. and J.H. Bair (1984) 'New organizational media and productivity', in R.E. Rice (ed.), *The New Media: Communication, Research, and Technology* (Beverly Hills: Sage), pp. 185–215.

Ritzer, G. (1993) *The McDonaldisation of Society* (London: Sage).

Ritzer, G. (1996) 'The McDonaldisation thesis: is expansion inevitable?', *International Sociology*, 11(3), 291–308.

Ritzer, G. (1998) *The McDonaldisation Thesis: Explorations and Extensions* (London: Sage).

Rogers, E.M. (1995) *Diffusion of Innovations* (New York: The Free Press).

Rojec, M. (1994) 'Foreign direct investment in the transformation process', *Development and International Cooperation*, X(18), 5–26.

Rojec, M. and M. Svetlicic (1993) 'Foreign direct investment in Slovenia', *Transnational Corporations*, 2(1), 135–51.

Rosenweig, P. and J. Singh (1991) 'Organisational environments and the multinational enterprise', *Academy of Management Review*, 16(2), 340–61.

Roth, K. and S. O'Donnell (1996) 'Foreign subsidiary compensation strategy', *Academy of Management Review*, 39(3), 678–703.

Rowley, C. (ed.) (1998) *Human Resource Management in the Asia Pacific Region – Convergence Questioned* (London: Frank Cass).

Ruane, F. and H. Gorg (1999) 'Irish FDI Policy and Investment from the EU', in Ray Barrell and Nigel Pain (eds), *Investment, Innovation, and the Diffusion of Technology in Europe* (Cambridge: Cambridge University Press).

Rugman, A. (2000) *The End of Globalization* (London: Random House Business Books).

Rugman, A. and A. Verbecke (1998) 'Multinational enterprises and public policy', *Journal of International Business Studies*, 29(1), 115–36.

Ruigrok, W. and R. van Tulder (1995) *The Logic of International Restructuring* (London: Routledge).

Sachs, J. (1998) 'Out of the frying pan into the IMF fire', *Observer (Business section)*, 8 February, p. 6.

Santos (1997) José de Freitas (1997), 'Localização da Empresa Estrangeira em Portugal (1990/94): Uma abordagem relacional', unpublished PhD thesis, Universidade do Minho.

Saxenian, A. (1990) 'Regional networks and the resurgence of Silicon Valley', *California Management Review*, 33(1), 89–112.

Saxenian, A. (1994) *Regional Advantage: Culture and Competition in Silicon Valley and Route 128* (Cambridge, MA: Harvard University Press).

Schlie, E. and M. Warner (2000) 'The 'Americanisation' of German management', *Journal of General Management*, 25(3), 33–49.

Schuler, R., P. Dowling and H. De Ceiri (1993) 'An integrative framework of strategic international human resource management', *International Journal of Human Resource Management*, 4(4), 717–65.

Schutte, H. (1998) 'Between headquarters and subsidiaries: The RHQ solution', in J. Birkinshaw and N. Hood (eds), *Multinational Corporate Evolution and Subsidiary Development* (London: Macmillan).

Scitovsky, T. (1963) 'Two concepts of external economies', in A.N. Agarwala and S.P. Singh (eds), *The Economics of Underdevelopment* (Oxford: Oxford University Press).

Scott, A.J. (1996) 'Regional motors of the global economy', *Research Policy*, 25, 391–411.

Scott, A.J. (1986) 'Industrial organization and location: division of labor, the firm, and spatial process', *Economic Geography*, 62, 214–231.

Scott, A.J. (1998) *Regions and the world economy: the coming shape of global production, competition and political order* (Oxford: Oxford University Press).

Scullion, H. (1993) 'Strategic recruitment and the development of the 'international manager': some European considerations', *Human Resource Management Journal*, 3(1), 57–69.

Seddon, P.B. (1997) 'A respecification and extension of the DeLone and McLean model of IS Success', *Information Systems Research*, 8(3), 240–53.

Seely-Brown, J. and P. Duguid (1991) 'Organisational learning and communities of practice: towards a unified view of working learning and innovation', *Organisation Science*, 2(1), 41–57.

Segal-Horn, S. (1995) 'Core competence and international strategy in service multinationals', in R. Teare and C. Armistead (eds), *Service Management: New Directions, New Perspectives* (London: Cassell).

Seringhaus, F.H.R. (1987) 'Role of information assistance in small firms' export involvement', *International Small Business Journal*, 5(2), 26–36.

Simmonds, K. and H. Smith (1968) 'The first export order: a marketing innovation', *British Journal of Marketing*, 2, 93–100.

Simões, Vitor Corado (1985) 'Portugal', in John H. Dunning (ed.), *Multinational Enterprises, Economic Structure and International Competitiveness* (New York: Wiley).

Simões, Vitor Corado (1989) *German Direct Investment in Portugal: Report on the empirical study* (Lisboa: Instituto de Estudos para o Desenvolvimento).

Simon, H. (1962) 'The architecture of complexity', *Proceedings of the American Philosophical Society*, 106, December, 467–82.

Simon, H. (1996) *Hidden Champions* (Boston: HBS Press).

Simon, H.A. (1957) 'The compensation of executives', *Sociometry*, 20, 32–5.

Simon, H.A. (1974) *Administrative Behaviour* (New York: The Free Press).

Simonin, B.L. (1999) 'Ambiguity and the process of knowledge transfer in strategic alliances', *Strategic Management Journal*, 20, 595–623.

Sklair, L. (1991) *Sociology of the Global System* (London: Harvester Wheatsheaf).

Sklair, L. (1993) 'Going global – competing models of globalisation', *Sociology Review*, November, 7–10.

Slater, S.F. and J.C. Narver (1994), 'Does competitive environment moderate the market orientation-performance relationship?', *Journal of Marketing*, 58, January, 46–55.

Smilor, R.W. (1997) 'Entrepreneurship – Reflections on a subversive activity: executive forum', *Journal of Business Venturing*, 12, 341–6.

Sölvell, Ö. and I. Zander (1998) 'International diffusion of knowledge: isolating mechanisms and the MNE', in A. Chandler, P. Hagström and Ö. Sölvell (eds), *The Dynamic Firm; The Role of Technology, Strategy, Organisation and Regions* (Oxford: Oxford University Press).

Spence, N. (1977) 'Entry, capacity, investment and oligopolistic pricing', *Bell Journal of Economics*, 3, 535–44.

Spybey, T. (1996) *Globalisation and World Society* (Cambridge: Polity Press).

Starkey, K. and A. McKinlay (1994) 'Managing for Ford', *Sociology*, 28(4), 975–90.

Starr, J.A. and I.C. Macmillan (1990) 'Resource cooptation via social contracting: resource acquisition strategies for new ventures', *Strategic Management Journal*, 11, 79–92.

Stein, J.C. (1997) 'Internal capital markets and the competition for corporate resources', *Journal of Finance*, 52(1), 111–33.

Steindl, J. (1976) *Maturity and Stagnation in American Capitalism* (New York: Monthly Review Press).

Storper, M. (1992) The Limits to Globalization: Technology Districts and International Trade, *Economic Geography*, 68, 60–93.

Storper, M. (1997) *The Regional World* (New York: The Guilford Press).

Storper, M. and R. Salais (1997) *Worlds of Production* (London: Harvard University Press).

Stottinger, B. and B.B. Schlegelmilch (1998) 'Explaining export development through psychic distance: enlightening or elusive?', *International Marketing Review*, 15(5), 357–72.

Strand, C. (1996) 'Lessons of a lifetime', *Cornell Hotel and Restaurant Administration Quarterly*, 37(3), 83–95.

Sullivan, D. and A. Bauerschmidt (1990) 'Incremental internationalization: a test of Johanson and Vahlne's thesis', *Management International Review*, 30(1), 19–30.

Sundram, A. and J. Black (1992) 'The environment and internal organisation of multinational enterprises', *Academy of Management Review*, 17(4), 729–57.

Swann, P. and M. Prevezer (1996) 'A comparison of the dynamics of industrial clustering in computing and biotechnology', *Research Policy*, 25, 1139–57.

Swann, P., M. Prevezer and D. Stout (eds) (1998) *The Dynamics of Industrial Clustering – International Comparisons in Computing and Biotechnology* (Oxford: Oxford University Press).

Szuslanski, G. (1996) 'Exploring internal stickiness: impediments to the transfer of best practice within the firm', *Strategic Management Journal*, 17 (Special Issue), 27–43.

Taggart, J. (1997) 'Autonomy and procedural justice: a framework for evaluating subsidiary strategy', *Journal of International Business Studies*, 28(1), 51–75.

Taggart, J.H. (1996) 'Evolution of multinational strategy: evidence from Scottish manufacturing subsidiaries', *Journal of Marketing Management*, 12, 533–49.

Taggart, J.H. (1998a) 'Identification and development of strategy at subsidiary level', in J. Birkinshaw and N. Hood (eds), *Multinational Corporate Evolution and Subsidiary Development* (London: Macmillan).

Taggart, J.H. (1998b) 'Determinants of increasing R & D complexity in affiliates of manufacturing multinational corporations in the UK', *R & D Management*, 28(2), 101–10.

Taggart, J.H. and M.J. Berry (1997) 'Second stage of internationalisation: evidence form MNC manufacturing subsidiaries in the UK', *Journal of Marketing Management*, 13, 179–93.

Taggart, J.H. (1998) 'Strategy shifts in MNEs' subsidiaries', *Strategic Management Journal*, 19, 663–81.

Taggart, J.H. (1996) 'Multinational manufacturing subsidiaries in Scotland: strategic role and economic impact', *International Business Review*, 5(5), 447–68.

Taggart, J.H. (ed.) (1999) 'Subsidiary strategy', *International Business Review* (Special Issue), 8(2).

Taggart, J.H. and N. Hood (2000) 'Strategy development in German manufacturing subsidiaries in the UK and Ireland', in C. Millar, R. Grant and C. Choi (eds), *International Business: Emerging Issues and Emerging Markets* (London: Macmillan).

Takeuchi, H. and M.E. Porter (1986) 'Three Roles of International Marketing in Global Industries', in M.E. Porter (ed.), *Competition in global industries* (Boston: Harvard Business School Press).

Taloussanomat, 16 September 1999.

Tavares, A.T. (1999) 'Modelling the impact of economic integration on multinationals' strategies', *University of Reading Discussion Papers in International Investment and Management*, 280.

Tavares, A.T. and R.D. Pearce (2000) 'European integration and structural change in the multinational: evidence from foreign subsidiaries operating in Portugal', forthcoming in M. Hughes and J.H. Taggart (eds), *International Business: European Dimensions* (London: Macmillan).

Tavares, A.T. and R.D. Pearce (1998) 'Regional Economic Integration and the Strategic (Re)positioning of Multinationals' Subsidiaries: A Conceptual Investigation', *University of Reading Discussion Papers in International Investment and Management*, 254.

Taveira, Elisa Ferreira (1984) 'Foreign Direct Investment in Portugal', unpublished PhD thesis, University of Reading.

Taylor, W. (1991) 'The logic of global business: an interview with ABB's Percy Barnevik', *Harvard Business Review*, March–April, 91–105.

Teece, D.J. (1977) 'Technology transfer by multinational firms: the resource costs of transferring technological know-how', *Economic Journal*, 87, 242–61.

Teece, D.J. (1980) 'Economies of scope and the scope of the enterprise', *Journal of Economic Behavior and Organization*, 1, 223–47.

Teece, D.J. (1983) 'Technological and organizational factors in the theory of the multinational enterprise', in M. Casson (ed.), *Growth of International Business* (London: Allen and Unwin), pp. 51–62.

Teece, D.J. (1986) 'Transactions cost economics and the multinational enterprise: An assessment', *Journal of Economic Behavior and Organization*, 7, 21–45.

Thompson, R. (1992) 'Japan accuses US and Europe of widespread trade violations', *Financial Times*, 8 June, p. 16.

Thorelli, H.B. (1986) 'Networks: between markets and hierarchies', *Strategic Management Journal*, 7, 37–51.

Tomlinson, J. (1993) 'Full employment and national economic management in the 1990s', *Renewal*, 1(2), 20–31.

Tu, Jenn-Hwa and Chi Schive (1995) 'Determinants of foreign direct investment in Taiwan Province of China: a new approach and findings', *Transnational Corporations*, 4, 93–103.

Turnbull, P.W. (1987) 'A challenge to the stages theory of the internationalization process', in P. Rosson and S.D. Reid (eds), *Managing Export Entry and Expansion* (New York: Praeger).

Urban, S. and S. Vendemini (1992) *European Strategic Alliances. Cooperative Corporate Strategies in the New Europe* (Oxford: Blackwell).

Urry, J. (1990) *The Tourist Gaze* (London: Sage).

Usai, G. (1981) *Le imprese minori ed il loro ambiente* (Padua: CEDAM).

Uzzi, B. (1997) 'Social structure and competition in interfirm networks: the paradox of embeddedness', *Administrative Science Quarterly*, 42, 35–67.

Vandermerve, S. (1989) 'From fragmentation to integration: a conceptual Pan-European marketing formula', *European Management Journal*, 7(3), 267–72.

Velo, D. (1998) 'Nuovi assetti del governo d'impresa nel mutato contesto competitivo', *Sinergie*, 53, 22–34.

Veoka, Kenichi 'Beikoku Mitui Bussan' (1994) (American Subsidiary of Mitui Bussan)', *Nikkei Business*, 31, January.

Vernon, R. (1979) 'The product cycle hypothesis in a new international environment', *Oxford Bulletin of Economics and Statistics*, 41, 255–67.

Vernon, R. (1991) 'Sovereignty at bay: twenty years after', *Millennium Journal of International Studies*, 20(2), 191–95.

Vernon, Raymond (1971) *Sovereignty at Bay: The Multinational Spread of U.S. Enterprises* (New York: Basic Books).

Wade, R. (1998–99) 'The coming fight over capital flows', *Foreign Policy*, Winter pp. 41–54.

Wallis, J.J. and D.C. North (1986) 'Measuring the transaction sector in the American economy, 1870–1970', S.L. Engerman and R.E. Gallman (eds), *Long-Term Factors in American Economic Growth. NBER Studies in Income and Wealth* 51 (Chicago: University of Chicago Press), pp. 95–161.

Walters, P.G. (1986) 'International marketing policy: a discussion of the standardization construct and its relevance for corporate policy', *Journal of International Business Studies*, 17(2), 55–69.

Warhurst, C., D. Nickson and E. Shaw (1998) 'A future for globalisation? International business organisation in the next century', in T. Scandura and M. Serapio (eds), *International Business and International Relations* (Conneticut: JAI Press).

Warner, M. (1994) 'Japanese culture, western management: taylorism and human resources in Japan', *Organisation Studies*, 15(4), 509–33.

Waters, M. (1995) *Globalisation* (London: Routledge).

Watson, R. (1999) 'WTO chief appeals for détente in banana war', *Herald*, 19 February, p. 25.

Weick, K. (1995) *Sensemaking in Organisations* (London: Sage).

Welch, D.E., L.S. Welch, L.C. Young, and I.F. Wilkinson (1998) 'The importance of networks in export promotion: policy issues', *Journal of International Marketing*, 6(4), 66–82.

Welch, L.S. and R. Luostarinen (1993) 'Inward–outward connections in internationalisation', *Journal of International Marketing*, 1(1), 46–58.

Wernerfelt, B. (1984) 'A resource-based view of the firm', *Strategic Management Journal*, 5, 171–80.

Westhead, P.M. Wright and D. Ucbasaran (1998) 'The internationalization of new and small firms', *Frontiers of Entrepreneurship Research*.

Westney, E. (1993) 'Institutional Theory and the Multinational Corporation', in Ghoshal and Westney (eds), *Organisational Theory and the Multinational Corporation* (New York: St. Martin's Press).

Wheeler, C., M. Jones and S. Young (1996) 'Market entry modes and channels of distribution in the machine tool industry in the UK', *European Journal of Marketing*, 30(4), 40–57.

White, R. and T. Poynter (1984) 'Strategies for foreign-owned subsidiaries in Canada', *Business Quarterly*, 48(4), Summer, 59–69.

Whitelock, J.M. (1987) 'Global marketing and the case for international product standardisation', *European Journal of Marketing*, 21(9), 21–37.

Whitelock, J.M. and C. Pimblett (1997) 'The standardisation debate in international marketing', *Journal of Global Marketing*, 3, 45–66.

Williams, K., (n.d) 'The organisation of American production', mimeo, Department of History, University of Wales at Cardiff.

Williams, K., C. Halsam, J. Williams and S. Johal *et al.* (1994) 'Deconstructing car assembly productivity', *International Journal of Production Economics*, 34, 253–65.

Williamson, O. (1985) *The Economic Institutions of Capitalism* (New York: Free Press).

Williamson, O.E. (1971) 'Managerial discretion, organization form and the Multi-division hypothesis', in R. Marris and A. Wood (eds), *The Corporate Economy. Growth, Competition and Innovative Potential* (London: Macmillan).

Williamson, O.E. (1975) *Markets and Hierarchies: Analysis and Antitrust Implications* (New York: Free Press).

Williamson, O.E. (1981) 'The modern corporation: origins, evolution, attributes', *Journal of Economic Literature*, December, 1537–68.

Williamson, O.E. (1986) 'Assessing and classifying the internal structure and control apparatus in the modern corporation', *Economic Organization. Firms, Markets and Policy Control* (Brighton: Wheatsheaf Books); originally published in K. Cowling (ed.), *Market Structure and Corporate Behaviour* (Oxford: Basie Blackwell, 1972).

Williamson, O.E. (1991) 'Comparative economic organization: the analysis of discrete structural alternatives', *Administrative Science Quarterly*, 36, June, 269–96.

Withey, J.J. (1980) 'Differences between exporters and non-exporters: some hypotheses concerning small manufacturing business', *American Journal of Small Business*, 4(3), 29–37.

Womack, J.P., D.T. Jones and D. Roos (1990) *The Machine That Changed The World* (New York: Macmillan).

Yachi, Hiroyasu (1999) *Nihon Kigyo no Eigyo Kanri Taisei* (Marketing Organization of Japanese Companies), Working Paper Series, no. 142, Yokohama National University, Faculty of Business Administration, April.

Yamin, M. (2001) 'A new view of the advantage of multinationality', in J.H. Taggart, M. Berry and M. McDermott (eds), *The Multinational in the New Millennium: Changes and Choices* (London: Macmillan).

Yavas, U. (1987) 'Marketing research in an Arabian Gulf country', *Journal of the Market Research Society*, 29(4), 458–61.

Yin, R.K. (1994) *Case Study Research: Design and Methods* (Thousand Oaks, California: Sage Publications).

Yoshihara, Hideki (1975) *Personnel Practices of Japanese Companies in Thailand* (Thailand: Economic Cooperation Center for the Asian and Pacific Region, Bangkok).

Yoshihara, Hideki (1992) *Fuji Xerox no Kiseki* (Miracle of Fuji Xerox), (Tokyo: Toyo Keizai Publishing Company).

Yoshihara, Hideki (1995) 'Kokusaika to Nihonteki Keiei' (Internationalization and Japanese Management) Hidemasa Morikawa and Seiichiro Yonekura (eds), *Kodo Seicho wo Koete* (Beyond High Economic Growth) (Tokyo: Iwanami Publishing Company).

Yoshihara, Hideki (1996) *Mijuku na Kokusai Keiei* (Immature International Management), (Tokyo: Hakuto Publishing Company).

Yoshihara, Hideki (1997) *Kokusai Keiei* (International Business) (Tokyo: Yuhikaku Publishing Company).

Yoshihara, Hideki (1998) 'Nihon Kigyo no Azia Keiei no Seika to Kadai' (Performance and Problems of Japanese Business in Asia), *Business Insight*, 6(1), Spring.

Yoshihara, Hideki Kichiro Hayashi, and Kenichi Yasumuro (1988) *Nihon Kigyo no Gurobaru Keiei* (Global Business of Japanese Companies) (Tokyo: Toyo Keizai Publishing Company).

Yoshihara, Hideki, David Methe and Satoshi Iwata (1999) 'Kaigai Kenkyukaihatsu no Shinten to Seika' (Overseas R&D and its Performance), *Kokumin Keizai Zassi*, 179(6), June.

Young, S. and N. Hood (1994) 'Designing Developmental After-Care Programmes for Inward Investors in the European Community', *Transnational Corporations*, 3(2).

Young, S., J. Bell and D. Crick (1988) 'The Resource-Based Perspective and Small Firm Internationalisation: An exploratory Approach', *Strathclyde International Business Unit working paper*, 98/3.

Young, S., J. Hamill, C. Wheeler and J.R. Davis (1989) *International Market Entry and Development* (Hertfordshire: Harvester Wheatsheaf).

Young, S., N. Hood and S. Dunlop (1988) 'Global strategies, multinational subsidiary roles and economic impact in Scotland', *Regional Studies*, 22(6), 476–97.

Zafarullah, M., M. Ali and S. Young (1998) 'The internationalisation of the small firm in developing countries – exploratory research from Pakistan', *Journal of Global Marketing*, 11(3), 21–38.

Zander, U. and B. Kogut (1995) 'Knowledge and the Speed of the Transfer and Imitation of Organisational Capabilities: An Empirical Test', *Organisation Science*, 6(1), 76–92.

Index